INDEPENDENT SECTOR

INDEPENDENT SECTOR is a coalition of 830 corporations, foundations, and voluntary organizations with national interests in and impact on philanthropy, voluntary action, and other activities related to the educational, scientific, cultural, and religious life, as well as the health and welfare, of the nation.

INDEPENDENT SECTOR is a meeting ground where diverse elements in and related to the sector can come together and learn how to improve their performance and effectiveness.

INDEPENDENT SECTOR is serving the sector through
- education, to improve the public's understanding of the independent sector
- research, to develop a comprehensive store of knowledge about the sector
- government relations, to coordinate the multitude of interconnections between the sector and the various levels of government
- encouragement of effective sector leadership and management, to maximize service to individuals and society, by promoting educational programs for managers and practitioners
- communication within the sector, to identify shared problems and opportunities

The impact of INDEPENDENT SECTOR's effort can be measured by the growth in support of the sector, as manifested by increased giving and volunteering.

For additional information, please contact

INDEPENDENT
SECTOR
1828 L Street, N.W.
Washington, DC 20036
(202) 223-8100

THE NONPROFIT SECTOR IN THE GLOBAL COMMUNITY

Kathleen D. McCarthy
Virginia A. Hodgkinson
Russy D. Sumariwalla
and Associates

THE NONPROFIT SECTOR IN THE GLOBAL COMMUNITY

Voices from Many Nations

Jossey-Bass Publishers · San Francisco

For sales outside the United States contact Maxwell/Macmillan
International Publishing Group, 866 Third Avenue, New York,
New York 10022

Printed on acid-free paper and manufactured in the
United States of America

 The paper used in this book meets the State of California
requirements for recycled paper (50 percent recycled waste,
including 10 percent postconsumer waste), which are the
strictest guidelines for recycled paper currently in use in
the United States.

Library of Congress Cataloging-in-Publication Data

McCarthy, Kathleen D.
    The nonprofit sector in the global community : voices from many
nations / Kathleen D. McCarthy, Virginia A. Hodgkinson, Russy D.
Sumariwalla and associates. — 1st ed.
        p.   cm. — (The Jossey-Bass nonprofit sector series)
    Includes bibliographcal references and index.
    ISBN 1-55542-397-3 (alk. paper)
    1. Corporations, Nonprofit. I. Hodgkinson, Virginia Ann.
II. Sumariwalla, Russy D. III. Title. IV. Series.
HD2769.15.M33   1992
658.7'4—dc20   91-26280
                                                                   CIP

FIRST EDITION
HB Printing   10 9 8 7 6 5 4 3 2 1   *Code 9202*

The Jossey-Bass
Nonprofit Sector Series

Contents

Contents

12. The Mission, Purposes, and Functions of
    Nonprofit Organizations in France   230
    Dan Ferrand Bechmann

13. The Ties That Bind: The Nonprofit Sector
    and the State in Sweden   240
    John Boli

14. Government and the Nonprofit Sector
    in Australia   254
    Mark Lyons

15. Changing Concepts of Voluntarism in Japan   278
    Anna Maria Thränhardt

16. The Role of Nonprofit Organizations Within
    the Ultra-Orthodox Community in Israel   290
    Eliezer D. Jaffe

**Part Three: Eastern Europe
and the Soviet Union   305**

17. The Revival of the Nonprofit Sector in Hungary   309
    Gábor Hegyesi

18. The Independent Sector in Poland:
    Past and Present   323
    Andrzej Kapiszewski

19. The Emerging Nonprofit Sector in Bulgaria:
    Its Historical Dimensions   333
    Stephan E. Nikolov

20. The Independent Sector in the USSR:
    Formation, Purposes, and Effects   349
    Nina Belyaeva

21. Philanthropy and Charity in the Soviet Union   372
    Deborah A. Brody, Elizabeth T. Boris

Preface

As we approach the twenty-first century, a new paradigm is emerging, one that will change the structure of nations just as the development of the nation-state and the invention of the printing press changed feudalism in medieval Europe. The global community, as many analysts are calling this new paradigm, is coming about through communication technology (which crosses national boundaries) and a worldwide push toward democratic forms of government. The most dramatic evidence of such profound changes occurred in 1989 with the overthrow of communist forms of government in Eastern Europe and, to some extent, in the Soviet Union. These movements were in large part fostered by a form of communication, television, just as the Renaissance and the Reformation were made possible by the printing press. In the global community, national boundaries will not be as important as either international cooperation and collaboration or cross-national public understanding and support. Creation of this international "public" is heralded by growing international movements in nonprofit organizations, most notably the peace movements, environmental movements, and movements to eradicate world hunger. These international movements are developing a "common ground" across nations that focuses on issues of global importance rather than on particular national identities. While great attention is being given to international research relating to government, business, and politics, little attention has been given to the roles and functions of nonprofit organizations and associations in advancing democratic traditions and global concerns in various nations. The authors of *The Nonprofit Sector in the Global Community* describe and analyze the functions and significance of nongovernmental organizations, philanthropy, and voluntarism within their own nations or in comparison with other nations. As a result, this book represents an initial attempt to understand the role of these organizations in a global context.

Several questions need to be addressed in relation to the roles and functions of nonprofit organizations in an international context. Do nonprofit organizations perform similar functions across nations? Does the form of government in a nation determine the roles and strength of nonprofit organizations? Does the type of financial support that nonprofit organizations receive determine their roles and functions in any way; that is, does private philanthropy or government financing affect the functions of services of nonprofit organizations? Do cultural differences affect the nonprofit form? Are nonprofit organizations defined similarly across nations; in other words, are we talking about the same kind of organizations in various nations? Which nations have a tradition of giving and volunteering, and is this tradition necessary in order to have a nonprofit sector? What are the roles of individual philanthropy, private foundations, and corporate contributions in other nations? Historically, have the roles and functions of nonprofit organizations changed? Are certain charitable institutions, such as religious institutions, foundations, or educational institutions, common to nonprofit sectors across nations? What are the legal boundaries or restrictions of nonprofit organizations in various countries?

Addressing these questions may help us develop a conceptual framework for the comparative study of nonprofit organizations. Such a framework could help provide us with an understanding of these organizations, their common functions, and their roles under different forms of government. It may also help illuminate the role of individuals in establishing and supporting such organizations, and the role such organizations play in empowering individuals to influence public policy, to create new public agendas, and, in some cases, to create new governments in various nations. Such research can help us better understand cultural diversity and pluralism in a world community.

Finally, as practitioners, we need to better understand what kind of research is needed to inform and improve practice, what kind of information and skills can be shared across cultures, and what common challenges provide opportunities for nonprofit organizations to work collaboratively across national boundaries. In other words, we need to think about the future of the nonprofit sector in a global community, the form the sector will take, and the roles it will play.

The authors of *The Nonprofit Sector in the Global Community* address these and other issues. After reviewing the chapters of this book, one can only be impressed with the diversity of the research. Some research is grounded in long-standing scholarly traditions. This is particularly true of scholars writing about the nonprofit sector in developed nations in Western Europe and Asia. Chapters written by scholar-activists from Eastern Europe and the Soviet Union are almost running commentaries or history in the making. Chapters by scholars in the developing nations reveal an attempt to define and understand the functions of nongovernmental organizations and private philanthropy in those societies. This book is enriched by the diversity of disciplines represented: economics, sociology, history, political science, policy science, statistics, and the law. There is also a rich blend of perspectives from university professors, voluntary leaders, practicing lawyers, and professionals from foundations.

Such a variety of perspectives is not surprising in an area where little research is available and in countries that are undergoing major change.

Because of the interdisciplinary nature of this book and the number of nations covered, the authors present their topics from a variety of viewpoints and cultural perspectives. This cultural diversity reveals a lack of consensus relating to the roles and functions of the nonprofit sector, its responsibilities, its relationship with government, and even how to define nonprofit organizations. As a result, this book provides a wide terrain for continuing discussion and research. On the other hand, the authors also reveal areas of agreement that can provide a common ground for furthering our understanding of voluntary association across a multiplicity of cultures.

Audience

The Nonprofit Sector in the Global Community is intended for three major audiences. First, because of the book's attempt to explore the roles and functions of the nonprofit sector in many nations and cultures, it should be of interest to scholars concerned with international research, comparative research, and public policy. It offers rich areas for further study to political scientists, historians, economists, sociologists, psychologists, cultural anthropologists, and students of comparative government. Second, it provides an agenda to university administrators, foundation officers, and leaders of voluntary organizations for exploring collaborative international programs in research and training, developing and supporting international projects, and fostering international coalitions. Third, this volume should be of interest to students and members of the general public who are interested in voluntary participation and service in various nations.

Organization of This Book

Following an introductory chapter, which reviews the major themes and issues involved in understanding the roles and functions of nonprofit institutions, voluntary activity, and philanthropy in a comparative international perspective, this volume is structured in four parts. Part One focuses on international trends and issues from a global perspective. The chapters in this section deal with major themes that engage scholars and policymakers when they discuss the nonprofit sector in comparison to government, to business, or to philanthropy as a practice. Chapter Two provides a comparative study of tax policies and their relation to the nonprofit sector in various nations. The issue of the efficiency and equity argument in the provision of major services, such as health and education, and the role that the nonprofit sector may play in the efficient distribution of such services in comparison to government is the topic of Chapter Three, while a discussion of the functions of nonprofit organizations and their role in economic development in Third World countries is the subject of Chapter Four. Chapter Five analyzes the partnership between government and the nonprofit sector in the provision of social services in several European nations struggling with the privatization of social services. The last two chapters of this section deal with the role of philanthropy in foundations and corporations. Chapter Six examines the role of international corporations in South Africa and their effectiveness in helping blacks, and Chapter Seven explores reasons why Japanese corporations must learn a new tradition — philanthropy — in order to participate fully in an interdependent world.

Part Two reviews issues and trends in nonprofit organizations and voluntarism in modern developed democracies. The nations covered in this section are Great Britain, Northern Ireland, the Netherlands, France, Sweden, Australia, Japan, Israel, and what was formerly West Germany. When the research contained in the chapters about Germany was conducted, there were still two Germanys, although the process of unifying East and West Germany was underway. Currently scholars are engaged in a study of the impact of unification on nonprofit organizations in what was formerly East Germany. For the most part, however, nonprofit organizations in East Germany were more similar to their counterparts in other Eastern European nations than to nonprofits in what was formerly West Germany.

Part Three presents a broad sweep of emerging nonprofit organizations, voluntary activities, and philanthropic structures in Eastern Europe and the Soviet Union. The nations covered in this section are Hungary, Poland, Bulgaria, and the USSR.

Part Four focuses on nonprofit activities and voluntarism in developing countries. Argentina, Egypt, Palestinian society, India, Indonesia, Singapore, and the People's Republic of China are reviewed in this section. Finally, the concluding chapter of this volume suggests some practical ways that international collaborative efforts can be fostered by voluntary organizations and foundations.

What characterizes all of the chapters in *The Nonprofit Sector in the Global Community* is the attempt to describe and define what contributions nonprofit institutions, private philanthropy, and voluntary activity bring to various societies and various forms of government. Authors writing about developed democracies are likely to explore nonprofit organizations and their traditional partnership with government in relation to the trend in many nations toward privatization. Authors from formerly communist nations wrestle with the meaning of voluntarism, philanthropy, and the role of government in market economies during the transition from one- to three-sector economies; they question the extent to which voluntary organizations should replace government and what social programs should remain the responsibility of government. In developing nations, the authors are concerned with how voluntarism and nonprofit organizations can strengthen local development and expand individual opportunity and freedom.

The richness of the tapestry of these voices from many nations and cultures—asking similar questions about the balance between government and the nonprofit sector, between individual responsibility to provide time and money voluntarily and government's responsibility to support services—provides new insight into the different ways in which voluntary action, philanthropy, and nonprofit organizations are perceived and defined. The aim of this volume is not only to enrich our understanding of the meaning and extent of voluntary action in other nations but also to reveal how much we still need to know and understand about the traditions of nonprofit organizations, philanthropy, and voluntary service in different cultural contexts.

December 1991   Virginia A. Hodgkinson
                                            Alexandria, Virginia

                                            Kathleen D. McCarthy
                                            New York, New York

                                            Russy D. Sumariwalla
                                            McLean, Virginia

Contributors

Dan Ferrand Bechmann is maître de conférences at the Université de Grenoble II. In 1986 she was adviser to the French secretary of social economy and then from 1988 to 1989 she was adviser to the secretary of humanitarian action during which time she organized the Assises des Nouvelles Solidarités. She has several publications to her credit.

Nina Belyaeva graduated from Moscow University Law School in 1981. She is currently a research fellow at the Institute of State and Law at the Academy of Sciences in Moscow, specializing in the study of independent groups and popular movements and their influence on decision-making processes in local and national government agencies. She is a political observer who covers legal and political reforms for the weekly newspaper *Moscow News*. Belyaeva is president of the Interlegal Research Center of *Moscow News*, which provides a variety of services to Soviet state agencies and to many independent organizations that have become increasingly prevalent in the USSR under democratic and economic reforms introduced since 1985.

Nancy Birdsall is the director of the Country Economics Department of the World Bank. Previously, she has been chief of the Environment Division, Latin America and Caribbean Region; of the Human Resource Operations Division, Brazil Department; and of the Policy and Research Division, Population, Health, and Nutrition Department. She was also staff director of the World Bank's *World Development Report 1984: Population Change and Development*. She has published papers on the economics of population, education, and health in developing countries, on public finances and political economy issues in the social sectors, and more recently on environmental issues in low-income countries.

John Boli is senior research associate in sociology at the University of Lund, Sweden. During the winter quarter of 1990 he taught in the Department of Sociology at Stanford University. He has published many journal articles and chapters in comparative and historical sociology on the state, citizenship, and schooling. His recent work includes *New Citizens for a New Society: The Institutional Origins of Mass Schooling in Sweden*, coauthorship (with G. M. Thomas) of *Institutional Structure: Constituting State, Society, and the Individual*, and "Individual, Polity, and the Voluntary Sector in Sweden," a paper presented at the Conference on Religion and the Independent Sector, Princeton University, June 1988.

Elizabeth T. Boris is director of the Nonprofit Research Fund at the Aspen Institute. Formerly, she was vice president for research for the Council on Foundations. She joined the Council in 1979 to develop a research program. Author of many articles and reports, she is coauthor of a book on foundation careers and a contributor to a new book, *America's Wealthy and the Future of Foundations,* the report of the Foundation, Formation, Growth and Termination Project that she designed and supervised. Boris is currently an associate adjunct professor at the University of Colorado Graduate School of Public Affairs in the nonprofit management program. She is associate editor of the journal *Nonprofit Management and Leadership* and consulting editor for *Nonprofit and Voluntary Sector Quarterly.*

Deborah A. Brody is director of private foundations services at the Council on Foundations. Formerly, she was director of research projects at the Council. Brody has been with the Council since 1986, and she has authored and coauthored several articles and reports on foundation management. Prior to joining the Council, Brody worked for an economic research firm and for a U.S. senator.

Paul P. L. Cheung is senior lecturer in social planning at the National University of Singapore and director of the Population Planning Unit, Ministry of Health. He has written extensively on social and demographic changes in Singapore and Asia. His publications include *Country Report on Aging: Singapore* and *The Demography of Singapore.*

Julie Fisher is an independent consultant on Third World development and author of the forthcoming *The Quiet Revolution: Development Organizations of the Third World.* She recently completed a book for Technoserve on its work with agrarian reform cooperatives in El Salvador and Peru. Fisher has also been a consultant to Save the Children, UNICEF, the International Council for Educational Development, World Vision, and Interaction; and she has written articles about the neighborhood improvement organizations in Latin American squatter settlements. She has taught comparative politics and the politics of Third World development at Connecticut College.

Anil K. Gupta is a professor at the Indian Institute of Management, Centre for Management in Agriculture. Between 1978 and 1981 he worked as a management specialist in rural development at the Indian Institute of Public Administration, New Delhi. His publications include "Why the Poor Do Not Cooperate" in *Research Relationships;* "Design of Resource Delivery Systems: Socio-Ecological Perspective" in *International Studies in Management and Organization; Banking on Non-Bankable Poor: Being Bridges, Brokers and Banias; Banking in Backward Regions;* and *Rural Banking: Learning to Unlearn.*

Gábor Hegyesi is a lecturer in sociology at the Eotvos Lorand University in Budapest, where his teaching focuses on the education of social work students. He is the vice president of LARES, a nonprofit cooperative that provides family and home services to Hungarians of modest means. He was also a founding member and consultant to SZETA, a poverty relief fund established in Hungary in the early 1980s. Hegyesi is the author of more than forty scientific papers that have appeared in professional journals and scholarly collections in the fields of sociology, social work, psychology, and economics. These papers have been on a wide variety of subjects, ranging from marriage counseling to the education of social workers. He has presented papers at eight major international conferences on social work and voluntarism since 1984.

Virginia A. Hodgkinson is currently vice president of research at INDEPENDENT SECTOR and executive director of the National Center of Charitable Statistics. Her most recent publications include *Faith and Philanthropy in America* (with R. Wuthnow and Associates); *Giving and Volunteering in the United States,* findings from a national survey analyzed with Murray S. Weitzman (two editions: 1988 and 1990); *The Future of the Nonprofit Sector* (with R. Lyman and Associates); and *Dimensions of the Independent Sector: A Statistical Profile* (prepared with M. S. Weitzman).

Barbara Lethem Ibrahim is senior representative of the Population Council for West Asia and North Africa. Formerly, she was a program officer and consultant to the Cairo field office of the Ford Foundation. She has contributed chapters to a number of books on women's economic roles, urban research methodologies, and philanthropy. Currently, she is conducting research on the traditional and modern bases of philanthropy in Arab countries.

Eliezer D. Jaffe has been a professor of social welfare at the School of Social Work of the Hebrew University in Jerusalem since 1960. He has served on the social policy advisory committees of three Israeli prime ministers and was a member of the Committee to Determine Israel's Poverty Line and a consultant to departments of the Ministry of Labor and Social Affairs. He was formerly director of the Jerusalem Municipal Department of Welfare. Jaffe is also an editor of Israel's social work journal, *Society and Welfare;* cofounder of Zahavi, the Israel Association of Large Families; first Israel chairman of the New Israel Fund; a board member of the International Sephardi Educational Fund; and a consultant to the Rothschild Foundation, other foundations working in Israel, and to various nonprofit organizations. Jaffe has published many articles on child welfare, social policy, the nonprofit sector, and philanthropy. His books include *Child Welfare in Israel, Givers and Spenders: The Politics of Charity in Israel,* and *A Private Foundation Working in Israel.*

Estelle James is professor of economics at the State University of New York, Stony Brook, where she previously served as provost of social and behavioral sciences. She has written extensively on the economics of nonprofit organizations and education. Most recently, she coauthored (with G. R. Benjamin) *Public Policy and Private Education in Japan* and (with S. Rose-Ackerman) *The Nonprofit Sector in International Perspective: Studies in Comparative Cultures and Policy,* a volume in the Yale Studies on Nonprofit Organizations series.

Ralph M. Kramer is a professor emeritus in the School of Social Welfare at the University of California, Berkeley. Prior to joining the Berkeley faculty in 1964, Kramer was employed for seventeen years as a psychiatric social worker, family service agency executive, and executive director of a social planning council. He is the author of numerous articles on citizen participation, social planning, and the voluntary sector. His books include *Voluntary Agencies in the Welfare State, Participation of the Poor,* and

Community Development in Israel and the Netherlands. His recent research on government–voluntary agency relations focuses on the consequences of purchase-of-service contracting.

Mark Lyons is a senior lecturer and head of the Department of Administrative, Social, and Political Studies at the Kuring-gai campus of the University of Technology, Sydney. He has conducted research and written extensively on the history of welfare services in Australia and on relations between governments and nongovernment organizations. In the early 1980s, he led a team that developed a series of training packages for managers of community organizations and received approval for the first program in Australian higher education aimed at preparing people to occupy management positions in nonprofit organizations. Between 1986 and 1989, he took leave from his academic post and served as director of the Australian Council of Social Service, the national council for the nongovernment welfare sector in Australia.

Kathleen D. McCarthy is the director of the Center for the Study of Philanthropy at the Graduate School of the City University of New York, where she is also an associate professor of history. After receiving her doctorate from the University of Chicago in 1980, she held positions at the Rockefeller Foundation, the National Endowment for the Humanities, and the Metropolitan Life Foundation before returning to academia in 1986. She is the author of *Noblesse Oblige* and many articles on local, national, and international philanthropy.

Stephan E. Nikolov was recently a visiting associate professor in the Department of Public Affairs at George Mason University and is an assistant professor at the Institute of Sociology of the Bulgarian Academy of Sciences. Prior to this, Nikolov taught at the Institute of Sociology in Sofia. He is a former news columnist and has been working in the field of American studies since 1977. Nikolov is the author of four books and approximately thirty articles on the American political process and decision making, which have been published in Bulgaria, the USSR, Czechoslovakia, East Germany, India, and Finland.

Contributors

Quintin Oliver is director of the Northern Ireland Council for
Voluntary Action, a nonprofit development agency committed
to social change by using community development strategies
in areas of deprivation. He chairs the program advisory committee of the European region of the International Council for
Social Welfare and its "Poverty in Europe" working party. He
has written widely on welfare rights, rural poverty, fuel poverty,
housing rights, and the role of the nongovernmental sector in
times of strife.

Karen Paul is an associate professor of management at Rochester
Institute of Technology. She has done research in problems of
economic development, intergroup relations, and business ethics.
As Peace fellow at the Bunting Institute of Radcliffe College and
as a Fulbright research fellow, she has done a major study of
the impact of the Sullivan signatory projects in South Africa.
Her most recent book is *Business Environment and Business Ethics:
The Social, Political, and Moral Dimensions of Management.* She has
published a number of articles on ethical investing and issues
involved in monitoring the social performance of multinational
corporations.

Onny S. Prijono is head of the Department for Socio-Cultural
Affairs and is on the board of directors of the Centre for Strategic and International Studies in Jakarta, Indonesia. Prijono
is presently conducting a study on voluntary organizations in
rural development. She has published articles on youth, women,
and delinquency and books on education in Indonesia.

Susan Saxon-Harrold is research manager at the Charities Aid
Foundation (CAF) in London, where she directs the research
program on philanthropy and the voluntary sector. CAF's annual publications include *Charity Trends,* the *Charity Household
Survey,* and *Corporate Support for the Voluntary Sector.* Prior to joining CAF, Saxon-Harrold worked on the "Markets and Voluntary
Action" project at the Management Centre, University of Brad-
ford. Her most recent activities include founding *Voluntas,* the
new international journal of voluntary sector research and the
annual publication of *Sources of Charity Finance.*

Wolfgang Seibel is a professor of political science at the University of Kassel, in Germany. Formerly, he was a member of the Institute for Advanced Study in Princeton, New Jersey. He is the author of three books and numerous articles on public administration, the nonprofit sector, and the problems of governability, and he coedited (with H. Anheir) *The Third Sector: Nonprofit Organizations in Comparative and International Perspectives.*

Russy D. Sumariwalla recently retired as vice president and senior fellow at the United Way Strategic Institute and he currently serves as a senior consultant to United Way and other organizations. Before he became vice president and senior fellow, he headed the Research, Development, and Program Evaluation division of United Way of America. Among several of his publications relating to the independent sector are *UWASIS II: Taxonomy of Social Goals and Human Services Programs,* the second edition of *UWASIS: United Way of America Services Identification System,* and the second revised edition of *Accounting and Financial Reporting: A Guide for United Ways and Not-for-Profit Human Services Organizations.* He is the principal author of the *National Taxonomy of Exempt Entities* and cosponsor of INDEPENDENT SECTOR's 1991 Spring Research Forum.

Andrés A. Thompson is senior researcher for Group of Analysis for Social and Institutional Development (GADIS). He was formerly a professor in the Department of History at the University of Buenos Aires and a fellow of the National Council of Scientific and Technological Research (CONICET) in Argentina. He was also an international fellow of the Center for the Study of Philanthropy at the City University of New York in 1989, where he wrote *The Voluntary Sector in Transition: The Case of Argentina.* His other publications include various articles and papers on nongovernmental organizations in Latin America and a forthcoming book entitled *Gobierno y Sindicatos en Argentina: Los Anos de Alfonsin.* Thompson has been guest researcher at the Transnational Institute and the Center for Study and Documentation on Latin America (CEDLA), both in Amsterdam.

Anna Maria Thränhardt is currently lecturer at the Heinrich-Heine University of Dusseldorf and member of the board of the Association of Social Science Research on Japan. She has done extensive research in Japan, and her publications include *Verbandliche Wohlfahrtspikege im internationalen Vergleich* (coedited with R. Bauer) and "Traditional Neighborhood Associations in Industrial Society — The Case of Japan" in H. Anheier and W. Seibel (eds.), *The Third Sector: Comparative Studies of Nonprofit Organizations.*

Tymen J. van der Ploeg is an associate professor of law on partnerships and legal persons (companies, associations, and foundations) at Vrije Universiteit in Amsterdam and substitute judge in the court of Haarlem. He is the author of several articles on the law of legal persons in general and on associations and foundation law in particular. In recent years, van der Ploeg has focused on comparative legal study in the field of voluntary organizations, especially on such organizations' relationships to their governments.

Burton A. Weisbrod is director of urban affairs and policy research and John Evans professor of economics at Northwestern University. He was the director of the Center for Health, Economics, and Law at the University of Wisconsin, Madison. Weisbrod is a former senior staff member of the Council of Economic Advisers to the president, former member of the executive committee of the American Economic Association, fellow of the American Association of Advancement of the Sciences, and former president of the Midwest Economics Association. His publications include *The Voluntary Nonprofit Sector, Economics and Medical Research,* and *The Nonprofit Economy.*

Tadashi Yamamoto is founder and president of the Japan Center for International Exchange (JCIE) in Tokyo. Founded in 1970, JCIE promotes international communication, stimulates research on international issues involving Japan, and encourages international exchange by private organizations. Yamamoto is currently a member and Japanese director of the Trilateral Commission, a member of both the U.K.–Japan 2000 Group and the Korea-Japan 21st Century Committee. He served as Japanese director of the U.S.-Japan Advisory Commission and is the coauthor of *Japanese Private Philanthropy in an Interdependent World.*

Junhai Zhang is at Case Western Reserve University and was formerly a junior fellow in international philanthropy at the Johns Hopkins University, Institute for Policy Studies. He is also the acting chief of the International Cooperations Section, where he has worked with the Red Cross Society of China for more than four years. As acting chief, Zhang is responsible for international cooperation projects and exchange programs.

THE
NONPROFIT
SECTOR IN
THE GLOBAL
COMMUNITY

Virginia A. Hodgkinson
Kathleen D. McCarthy

Chapter 1

The Voluntary Sector
in International Perspective:
An Overview

The final decades of the twentieth century have witnessed an extraordinary shift in the social and political geography of the world. In part, these developments represent a movement away from the monumental changes that marked the years immediately after the Second World War. The colonial devolution, the rise of growing welfare states, the spread of communism — each in turn bolstered the role of governmental responsibilities. More recently, Reagan administration initiatives, the push toward "privatization," the rapid efflorescence of nongovernmental organizations (NGOs) in developing nations, and the dismantling of many former communist regimes have combined to generate new interest in the efficacy of nonprofit organizations, both as service providers and as advocates for reform.

This volume provides tangible evidence of the breadth of interest in voluntary sector activities that currently exists outside the United States. Trends in almost thirty countries in Europe, Asia, Africa, Latin America, and Australia are surveyed, and most of the chapters have been written by non-U.S. authors. What began as a trickle of scholarly interest in the early 1980s has grown to genuinely global dimensions.

Several common themes emerge from the chapters of this volume relating to the roles and functions of the nonprofit sector, voluntary association, and individual, foundation, and corporate philanthropy. These include the common roles of voluntary associations, the structure and uses of voluntary associations and their relationships and uses by governments, and the distinction between voluntary associations and nonprofit service organizations. Other common themes are the role of governments in constraining, encouraging, or augmenting voluntary sector activities; the religious, ethical, and pluralistic values that either inspire or impede giving, voluntarism, and the development of nonprofit activities; and the role and practice of philanthropy. The differences that separate voluntary activities among developed nations, and between developed nations and those in developing areas, and past and present communist regimes are also explored. This chapter provides an overview of these major themes as well as surveys the authors' suggestions for future research and policy-making initiatives.

The Roles and Functions of Nonprofit Organizations

One of the major problems in discussing the voluntary or nonprofit sector of various societies is the difficulty in defining it. Efforts have been going on in the United States to define what the nonprofit sector is, to determine what organizations are included in this sector, and to describe how voluntary behavior is defined through voluntary association and individual giving and volunteering. Various umbrella terms have been suggested by American scholars, including philanthropy, voluntarism, voluntary action, and not-for-profit activity. The concept of a sector of activity that functions between the family and the larger bureaucratic sectors of for-profit business and government has variously been called the not-for-profit sector, the nonprofit sector, the voluntary sector, the third sector, or the nongovernmental sector (Hodgkinson, 1989; Payton, 1988; Van Til, 1990). While the type and scope of organizations included in the nonprofit or nongovernmental sector vary according to the laws of various nations, nonprofit organizations have certain characteristics in common: they are organizations formed to serve the public good, and income (or profits) from these organizations are not distributed to members or owners. The primary functions that the nonprofit or voluntary sector performs to a greater or lesser extent, depending on its legal status, are to serve underserved or neglected populations, to expand the freedom of or to empower people, to engage in advocacy for social change, and to provide services. All the authors of this volume describe nonprofit organizations that carry out these roles to a greater or lesser degree.

The structure of the nonprofit sector in different nations varies according to the historical development of the legal structure of those countries. Helmut Anheier (1990) has proposed four major structures of the voluntary sector based on the legal and constitutional structures of nations. The first major structure is determined by countries organized under civil or common law. These nations are primarily found in Western Europe, Australia, and North America. Nations such as France, Germany, and Italy have more a corporate structure within their states. These countries have been affected by the large corporate structure of the Catholic church in addition to the state. In these countries, legal and administrative powers, directly or indirectly through nongovernmental agencies created by the state, are given to nonprofit organizations. While nonprofit organizations have independence in such states, the distinction between governmental and nongovernmental institutions is blurred. In some countries, such as France, government delivery or control of services is more important than service delivery by nonprofit organizations, while in other countries, such as Germany, an elaborate system of pure nonprofit and quasi-governmental nonprofit administrative bodies deliver the bulk of social welfare services at regional and local levels, as described by Seibel (Chapter Eleven) and Bechmann (Chapter Twelve).

Another distinction within this structure of nonprofit organizations exists in common law countries such as Great Britain, the United States, and Australia. In these countries, the nonprofit sector is based on voluntarism, and organizations are more competitive. Thus they are more likely to resemble for-profit firms than government agencies. Even when the government supports social welfare in these nations, the tendency is not to enlarge government but to conduct service delivery through nonprofit organizations, as described by Saxon-Harrold (Chapter Eight) and Lyons (Chapter Fourteen). Anheier (1990) also includes within this structure, yet separate from the civil law countries, the socialist democratic governments found in the Scandinavian countries. Although they have for-profit sectors, these countries have moved beyond government subsidies of welfare provision to the concept that government support of welfare is a right. Here the nonprofit sector is not as highly developed in delivering programs as the government is; nor is the concept of volunteering to assist in the provision of some services highly developed, as described by Boli in Chapter Thirteen (Anheier, 1990).

The second type of nonprofit structure that Anheier characterizes is that of nonprofit organizations found in socialist nations, where the government is officially the only sector and nonprofit groups if they exist at all are totally controlled by the government. Descriptions of the limitations on the freedom of association and nonprofit organization in communist countries are provided by Hegyesi (Chapter Seventeen), Kapiszewski (Chapter Eighteen), Nikolov (Chapter Nineteen), and Belyaeva (Chapter Twenty). In Eastern and Central European countries, where there were formerly strong traditions of voluntarism and philanthropy, the transformation to a private sector and nonprofit provision of certain welfare services pose considerable challenges.

The third structure Anheier (1990) defines is comprised of the various structures of the nonprofit sector in developing countries. While this area is the least researched, there has been some growth in the nonprofit form, both for advocacy organizations and in development activities. The decentralization of development tasks has received increasing attention by the World Bank in recent years, because the bank believes that indigenous nongovernmental organizations have a better record in providing social services, engaging in community development, and helping as well as acting as advocates for the poor. Since 1988, the World Bank has tripled its support of projects involving NGOs in developing countries (Williams, 1990). The diversity and variety of nonprofit activity and advocacy movements are covered in Chapters Twenty-Two through Twenty-Seven. In Chapter Three, James and Birdsall argue that nonprofits can be more efficient and equitable in the provision of services to the most impoverished groups in society in developing nations. They demonstrate that government subsidy programs generally support the more affluent groups in society. Bechmann (Chapter Twelve) echoes this theme when she describes the situation of the truly poor in France, those who do not seem to get adequate government support. In this situation, voluntary organizations seem far greater advocates for the poor than government agencies or governmentally subsidized and regulated nonprofit organizations.

The fourth and final defining structure that Anheier (1990) proposes is the type of philanthropy found in Islamic countries. As Ibrahim describes in Chapter Twenty-Three, Islam calls for charity (*zakat*), or the contribution of 2.5 percent of one's income to serve the poor. However, charity for the most part remains at the individual level. Organized efforts at charity and the development of a nonprofit sector are not an intrinsic part of the Islamic culture and have been variously encouraged or discouraged by colonial and postcolonial governments. Similar to Islam, Judaism also has as part of its fundamental belief *tzedakah*, which requires that Jews give to the community and others as an act of social justice. Jews give both time and money and have a long history of providing services through the creation of nonprofit organizations. Such sophistication is evidenced by the role of nonprofit organizations among the ultra-Orthodox Jews in Israel who set up a parallel set of nonprofit institutions outside the government to maintain their independence and religious identity. Jaffe (Chapter Sixteen) discusses the ability of a minority group, through the nonprofit form, to control the majority in states such as Israel, where diversity among Jewish religious groups and various cultural traditions prevents the majority from exercising its will.

While the nonprofit sector and voluntarism are more likely to be more independent in common law states than in civil law states, the authors of this volume reveal that government and the structure of government affect the strength of the voluntary sector. They can also affect the culture of their citizenry. The giving of time and money is not as important in determining the role and functions of the nonprofit sector in most other nations of the world as it is in the United States, where philanthropy is regarded by citizens as a responsibility along with the responsibility of government (Hodgkinson and Weitzman, 1988) even though the government funds a larger proportion of social services than do citizens. However, several types of nonprofit organizations, such as religious organizations and to a lesser extent arts organizations, receive little or no government funding in the United States compared with other nations. In the United States, volunteering is regarded as a responsibility of active citizenship, whereas in many countries discussed in this volume, such behavior is reserved only for those groups that government neglects. In many of the advanced social welfare countries of Western Europe and in Japan, voluntarism is not regarded as an individual responsibility but rather as proof of charity. Thus, many authors in this volume focus on the roles and functions of the nonprofit institutional form rather than on the practice and contribution of individual giving and volunteering as part of the definition of a voluntary or nonprofit sector.

Historical Trends

One of the most striking themes to emerge from the chapters in this volume is the impact first of the expansion and then of the contraction of centralized governmental responsibilities on nonprofit activities. By 1990, voluntary associations were active in almost all the countries reviewed in this volume. Many of these groups were rooted in religious concerns, as surveyed by authors such as Eliezer D. Jaffe, Stephan Nikolov, and Barbara Lethem Ibrahim (Chapters Sixteen, Nineteen, and Twenty-Three). Ethnic, neighborhood, and village-based mutual aid have also played a role in generating new institutions, some of which are described by Anna Maria Thränhardt and Onny S. Prijono (Chapters Fifteen and Twenty-Five).

The Second World War recast the scope of these activities. In China and Eastern Europe, the immediate postwar years witnessed the introduction of Communist regimes that left little room for philanthropic initiatives, autonomous nonprofit organizations, or religious sentiment. These years were also marked by the rapid expansion of governmental services in the United States, Western Europe, Australia, and selected developing nations, where public authorities assumed a steadily increasing measure of responsibility for the provision of national health and educational, social welfare, and cultural services. The Marshall Plan, America's Great Society programs, and the rise of Cold War foreign aid policies all concentrated on building, strengthening, consolidating, and implementing governmental initiatives, casting nonprofit organizations into the role of gap fillers and junior partners in the welfare state. Yet, beginning in the mid 1960s, several factors began to enhance the importance of voluntary sector activities. In the United States, the drift toward "third-party government" ensured that many enlarged federal programs would be carried out by nonprofit organizations (Salamon, 1987). Australia and several Western European nations also evolved into what Ralph M. Kramer terms "contract states," in which government programs are carried out through nonprofit organizations (Chapters Five and Eleven). Student protests and the social movements of the 1960s and early 1970s gave rise to a host of new social activist and development groups in various parts of the world. At the same time, growing government corruption and difficulties in sustaining comprehensive, equitable social services and development campaigns generated an additional impetus to nonprofit development. Reaganomics, Thatcherism (Chapter Eight), the shifting priorities of the international donor community, and the crumbling of former Communist regimes all helped to highlight the role of giving, voluntarism, and nonprofit organizations in new ways.

The Growth of the Voluntary Sector

As scholars such as Estelle James, Ralph M. Kramer, and Burton A. Weisbrod have previously noted, several factors contribute to nonprofit development (James, 1987; Kramer, 1981; Weisbrod, 1975). Some of the key variables include the role of government, the available supply of private resources (surplus cash and time), religious and ethical values, and the degree of national heterogeneity. While governments can play a catalytic role by providing grants, contracts, legal sanctions, and tax incentives (which are discussed by Burton A. Weisbrod and Elizabeth Mauser in Chapter Two), they can also outlaw nonprofit initiatives or restrict them through legal and financial constraints. As a result, governmental initiatives play a major role in determining the strength and survival of voluntary sector activities within their borders.

Nongovernmental resources are equally important. The amount of surplus cash and time available to individuals or corporations (or foreign donors) is often a major determinant of the breadth and health of the nonprofit sector. The more diversified the spectrum of donors and volunteers, the greater the degree of control that nonprofits can exercise over their programs and policies.

Religious and ethical values also play a role. Christianity, Judaism, Islam, Hinduism, Parsiism have each contributed to the growth of philanthropy. Even in the United States, which many consider a relatively secular nation, over half of all funds donated are channeled into religious causes and institutions. As a result, religious diversity has helped to produce a varied array of Catholic, Protestant, and Muslim organizations in such diverse places as the Netherlands, Egypt, and Singapore (Chapters Ten, Twenty-Three, and Twenty-Six). This volume examines the impact of religion from a variety of perspectives, emphasizing its role in spurring individual generosity, promoting institutional elaboration, preserving group norms, and challenging and supplementing the role of the state.

Heterogeneity is yet another important variable in promoting nonprofit development. According to this hypothesis, while heterogeneous countries such as the United States and India have broadly based nonprofit sectors, more homogeneous nations such as Sweden and Japan have proven less hospitable to the development of nonprofits.

The chapters in this volume illustrate the diversity with which these factors — government, individual and corporate largesse, religious and ethical values, and degree of heterogeneity — have fostered nonprofit activities in different national settings. Indeed, not one but several types of nonprofit systems currently exist outside the United States, including those in developed nations in Western Europe, Asia, and the Pacific; those in developing countries; and those in current and former Communist states.

Western Europe and Australia

Because government funding plays a significant, sometimes an almost exclusive, role in supporting nonprofit activities, discussions of Western European and Australian trends have tended to focus on the dimensions of government-nonprofit collaboration. Australia and many of the countries in Western Europe began to feel the pinch of financial constraints in the 1980s. This in turn heightened public interest in the nonprofit sphere. In several nations, governmental retrenchment and a new interest in privatization helped to blur the traditional boundaries between the governmental, nonprofit, and commercial arenas. As a result, increased attention has been focused on nonprofits in and of themselves.

Although government initiatives form the *leitmotiv* for voluntary sector activities in these areas, there is considerable variation in the role allotted to nonprofits. Perhaps most atypical is the situation in Northern Ireland, described by Quintin Oliver in Chapter Nine. Here community groups were called upon to provide public services when government programs temporarily collapsed. In Holland and Australia, the growth of the voluntary sector paralleled that of the state. Indeed, the two were often intimately linked (see Chapters Five, Ten, and Fourteen). As in the United Kingdom, favorable legislation, capitalist economies, religious tolerance, and other long-standing traditions historically nurtured nonprofit activities in these countries. Ralph Kramer and Tymen van der Ploeg (Chapters Five and Ten) point out that government support for nonprofit services constitutes the backbone of Holland's social welfare system. By 1979, public welfare costs accounted for approximately 50 percent of the national budget, with Dutch nonprofits almost wholly dependent on government funding.

In other nations, such as Sweden, France, and Japan, centralized governments and the political philosophies that support them traditionally served to limit and constrain the growth of nonprofit activities. As Wolfgang Seibel points out in Chapter Eleven, a lingering mistrust of private associations has served to limit the growth of France's voluntary sector since the days of the French Revolution. Swedes have also been more comfortable with the notion of state sponsorship of domestic social services. Unlike the United States, where volunatry sector activities are legitimized by Lockean concepts of individual autonomy, Hobbesian political notions that stress the virtues of a strong, centralized government have served to circumscribe the role of Sweden's nonprofit sector. As a result, to quote John Boli (Chapter Thirteen), Sweden's "charitable activities are generally oriented outward; domestic social welfare is the responsibility of the state."

Yet even here, nonprofit organizations have achieved a measure of public responsibility. As Seibel explains in Chapter Eleven, nonprofit organizations are charged with providing an important share of health and welfare services in both Germany and France and are backed by public subsidies in both countries. Seibel contends that the German government has a more flexible policy toward NGOs than that of France. Voluntary agencies, including political pressure groups, "are a crucial element of German polity, whereas their role continues to be contested in France." Nonetheless, even France's socialist government began to foster nonprofit development in the early 1980s, and public subsidies now account for approximately 80 percent of the funding for health and social service agencies. Unlike Seibel, Dan Ferrand Bechmann concludes that French nonprofits have merged "into the mainstream of associations largely financed and controlled by public institutions" (Chapter Twelve).

Sweden lies at the far end of the European continuum, with a strong welfare state backed by public expenditures that account for 67 percent of the country's GNP, the highest figure in the noncommunist world. As John Boli explains in Chapter Thirteen, Swedish nonprofit organizations tend to be less autonomous than comparable institutions in many other nations because "the collectivist emphasis of Swedish culture has blurred the distinction between public and private to such an extent that the nonprofit sector's independence now seems highly questionable." Even nonprofits that have been established to promote the causes of special-interest groups are heavily dependent on governmental subsidies.

The Western European model is intimately linked to questions of government, with many nonprofits functioning as an extension of the state. Within this context, concerns have been voiced about the extent, nature, and impact of government funding; nonprofits' appropriate political roles; and the nature of government monitoring and control. Relations with the state, rather than institutional autonomy or philanthropic trends, are the key issue here. The one exception is Susan Saxon-Harrold's chapter (Chapter Eight), in which she presents the trends in philanthropy in Great Britain.

Developed Nations in Asia

While discussions on Western European trends focus on the state, the chapters on Asia's economic pacesetters concentrate instead on the pulse of giving and voluntarism. Ironically, each of these chapters deals, in part, with transplanted models. Paul Cheung provides an analysis of the impact of Singapore's Community Chest in Chapter Twenty-Six. Like Japan, Singapore has one of Asia's fastest-growing economies, which has acted as a spur to local generosity. By Cheung's estimate, the Community Chest of Singapore raised $14 million in 1988 alone. Yet, despite its success, this organization may ultimately discourage the development of other philanthropic initiatives by centralizing local giving in ways that threaten to make it the country's "only legitimate fund raiser." Thus, Cheung concludes that "the dominance of the Chest clearly has adversely affected the establishment of new philanthropic foundations for welfare activities."

He also addresses the issue of heterogeneity. Unlike Japan, Singapore is a highly heterogeneous culture, with a diverse population of Chinese, Malays, Indians, and Europeans. Both religious and ethnic groups have developed their own institutions, including Chinese clan, district, and dialect associations. Cheung's analysis suggests an important caveat about the extent to which heterogeneity alone promotes voluntary sector activity. As he points out, the Chinese clan associations "were tolerated by the colonial government as long as they did not constitute a threat to the established order." However, their efforts were curtailed in the 1960s, when they ran aground of the government's national integration efforts. The events in Singapore underscore the fact that governmental tolerance of pluralistic initiatives, as well as the mere fact of heterogeneity itself, determine the extent to which an ethnically or religiously diverse population will produce an equally diverse array of nonprofits. When separatist leanings clash with nationalistic imperatives, associations run the risk of being officially disbanded.

Japan is far more homogeneous and its government far more centralized. As such, public bodies provide the majority of services, with nonprofits accorded only a limited role. Tadashi Yamamoto, who was one of the pioneers in promoting corporate philanthropy in Japan, adopts a strong advocacy stance in Chapter Seven on Japanese trends. Yamamoto traces the rise of modern Japanese philanthropy to the 1970s, when the country's corporations first began to establish foundations in significant numbers. Ironically, despite the lack of tax incentives for donations made outside Japan, more of this largesse has been directed overseas than has been given by private foundations domestically. Indeed, Yamamoto notes a growing interest in Japanese corporate social responsibility, backed by the efforts of powerful organizations such as the Japan Federation of Economic Organizations (Keidaren). Although quick to caution that there is a need to distinguish between philanthropy and public relations, Yamamoto contends that such efforts, if properly conducted, will enable Japan to participate more effectively in international affairs.

Anna Maria Thränhardt, in Chapter Fifteen, shifts the discussion from donors to volunteers in Japan. Neighborhood associations reflect the traditional Japanese concern with hierarchy and group solidarity, as well as Confucian notions of the importance of collective cooperation, harmony, and aid. While these efforts have tended to be organized and funded by the government, cadres of more autonomous, more critical alternative groups emerged in the 1960s. Thränhardt notes that the number of alternative groups declined sharply after the early 1970s, in part because these organizations challenged the traditional values of individual conformity and collectivist norms.

In Singapore and Japan, therefore, rapid economic growth, demographic patterns, traditional values, and transplanted models have combined to shape the contours of local philanthropy. Giving rather than government has been the primary focus here.

Developing Areas in Other Parts of the World

Conditions in developing nations evince a more checkered approach to NGO-government relations and philanthropic trends. Organizations in these areas have developed from a series of cultural overlays, ranging from religious and ethnic institutions to colonial imports and social activist and development NGOs created over the past two decades with assistance from foreign donors. Here, too, there has been a growing dissatisfaction with governmental attempts to deliver comprehensive, equitable services and development plans. This has served to heighten the visibility and importance of NGOs and private funding. Indeed, Estelle James and Nancy Birdsall argue in Chapter Three that

these governments would do well do divest more of their responsibilities onto the voluntary sector in the name of increased equity
and efficiency.

Anil K. Gupta, in Chapter Twenty-Four, traces the development of India's NGOs in the 1960s and 1970s to four
sources: responses to natural disasters, man-made disasters, student protests, and the neo-Gandhian movement led by Jaya
Prakesh Narayan in the early 1970s. Much of this momentum
was lost during Indira Gandhi's "emergency" at mid-decade,
when voluntarism was stigmatized as "a sign of despicable deviance." Since then, the attention of the international donor community, some favorable domestic legislation, and the diversion
of former radical groups into development-oriented activities
have helped to rekindle the country's voluntary spirit.

Secular values have left an imprint as well. In India, the
concept of *aparigrah* emphasizes the worth of self-denial. Gupta
underscores the impact of this idea on Indian voluntarism, arguing that voluntary associations that ignore the role of cultural
roots and religious identities, and the philosophical basis of social
responsibility severely diminish their chances to develop successful programs among the poor.

Many of these organizations are caught in a "love-hate"
relationship with their host governments, working toward common development and humanitarian goals but often cast in an
adversarial stance, particularly when dealing with such volatile
issues as human rights, environmental concerns, and the mobilization of the poor. Some governments see NGOs as competitors for foreign funds; others view them as unwanted critics or
competitors for local power.

In Latin America's Southern Cone, for example, many
NGOs were created in response to the imposition of authoritarian rule, a situation discussed by Andrés A. Thompson in Chapter Twenty-Two. Perhaps the most vivid example of this type
of organization was Las Madres de la Plaza de Mayo, an Ar-
gentinian organization whose protests against government ab-
ductions garnered international attention.

As Barbara Lethem Ibrahim points out in Chapter Twenty-
Three, government efforts to control these activities often have

a stifling effect. Thus, Egyptian "PVOs face formidable red tape in order to register, security investigations, and requirements for elaborate record keeping." The Ministry of Social Affairs approves voluntary association programs, controls their fund raising, and often appoints its own personnel to run them, practices that have limited the development of Egyptian foundations and autonomous voluntary associations. Conversely, the absence of a recognized government on the West Bank spurred the growth of grass-roots organizations, many of which served as alternative service providers. Because these services helped to sustain resistance to Israeli rule, many Palestinian voluntary agencies have now been closed down by the Israeli military, and their leaders have been threatened with arrest or deportation.

Tensions between governments and Third World organizations are exacerbated by the fact that social activist and development NGOs often rely heavily on foreign funds because government, individual, and corporate giving tends to be minimal in many developing areas. This in turn can render such organizations politically suspect and threaten their programmatic autonomy. Although Julie Fisher argues in Chapter Four that local, state, and provincial governments are becoming increasingly receptive to NGO programs, many governments are clearly nervous about the growing crop of NGOs within their borders, initiating head counts, peering into nonprofit management, tightening regulatory controls, and in places such as the West Bank, outlawing their activities or harassing their leaders (McCarthy, 1988).

Another problem is that of scale. Because many NGOs work at the grass-roots level, the scope of their programs tends to be limited; this often isolates them from larger, national policy-making discussions. Onny S. Prijono notes in Chapter Twenty-Five, for example, that grass-roots organizations have had little input into Indonesia's national development programs despite their extensive experience at the local level — a problem echoed in many developing nations (McCarthy, 1988).

Funding can be an especially touchy issue. In Chapter Six, Karen Paul outlines the troubled philanthropic record of American multinationals in their attempts to aid South Africa.

In the wake of the Soweto riots of 1977 and intensifying domestic pressure to divest their South African holdings, a number of U.S. multinational corporations signed the Sullivan Principles, in which they vowed to support efforts to improve standards of living among the country's black, colored, and Asian populations. The corporations' efforts were complicated when a new plank pledging the signatories to work "to eliminate laws and customs that impede social and political justice" was added in 1985. According to Paul, this placed the companies in the uncomfortable position of "outright defiance of the South African government."

Despite their record of support for educational initiatives such as scholarships, equipment, and multiracial private schools, Paul contends that the corporations' programs have been increasingly politicized and poorly managed, which has ultimately served to discredit them. She also recommends that corporations conducting philanthropic programs in developing nations retain their normal standards of accountability and control in selecting and monitoring their grantees and work to "foster deep and extensive ties with existing community leaders."

Religion, as well as politics, has played a particularly important role in shaping institutional growth and individual beneficence in Asia, Africa, and Latin America. The advent of liberation theology thrust the Catholic church into the forefront of institutional development in Latin America, spawning a host of new organizations to help the poor and promote grass-roots reform. While Jaffe, Thompson, and Gupta analyze the role of religion in shaping voluntary activities and nonprofit development (Chapters Sixteen, Twenty-Two, and Twenty-Four), Ibrahim examines indigenous philanthropy (Chapter Twenty-Three). Ibrahim points out that *zakat* (a religiously based alms tax) lies at the heart of Arab philanthropy. According to this principle, every Moslem with surplus wealth beyond his or her immediate needs is expected to contribute a portion (usually 2.5 percent) of that surplus to the poor. This practice has helped to give a new slant to corporate, as well as individual, giving in Egypt, as modern businesses based on Islamic principles have begun to devote a share of their profits to charitable ends.

One of the most intriguing questions is whether a portion of this religiously inspired giving will be diverted from direct and often highly personal charitable projects to more development-oriented campaigns. Ibrahim notes that Jordan's religious leaders have begun to encourage the use of *zakat* donations for efforts to increase self-reliance among the poor, as well as simply providing relief. Similar changes are under discussion in several other Arab countries as well, marking a possible shift in the use of *zakat* donations from charitable to philanthropic ends.

Arab philanthropy has also played an important role in keeping voluntary associations alive on the West Bank. Ibrahim notes that contributions from Palestinian emigrés served an especially important role in supporting these institutions through foundations created by expatriates in the United States, Switzerland, and Holland.

Funding issues have assumed new importance with the growth of voluntary sector activities in Eastern Europe, adding a note of competition. As Thompson points out in Chapter Twenty-Two, many NGOs are "aware that the democratization processes that are taking place in Eastern Europe will certainly increase the competition for funds and reduce the interest of Western European development cooperation agencies in Latin America." NGO-government relations, the quest for policy-making parity, and the search for sustainability have all assumed heightened significance in recent years. Independence and equity are the *leitmotivs* here.

Current and Former Communist States

Current and former communist countries provide a far different model. In Eastern Europe, nonprofit organizations are just beginning to reappear after years of political repression. Religious organizations, which provided a wellspring for institutional development in other parts of the world, were persecuted and dismantled as communist governments consolidated their hold over Eastern Europe and China in the late 1940s, echoing Soviet patterns played out three decades earlier. Government expansion and centralization stifled nonprofit activities as some groups were taken over by the state and others were summarily disbanded.

As Gábor Hegyesi explains in Chapter Seventeen, under Stalinist control "every organization not managed by the state was banned, harassed, and dismantled." Religious, economic, cultural, and political organizations were all swept away in Eastern Europe after 1948. According to Hegyesi, only a fraction of Hungary's estimated 14,000 nonprofit organizations were allowed to remain in operation under Communist rule. A few survived covertly, nurtured by political protest and enduring traditions of mutual aid. Others, like the Red Cross, were sometimes kept alive as appendages of the state but were almost wholly dependent on government funds and managed by Communist party officials and appointees.

Ethical values played a powerful role in limiting the scope and nature of voluntary sector activities in these areas because communist systems emphasized that institutional development was a state responsibility rather than an individual responsibility. To quote Stephan Nikolov (Chapter Nineteen), socialism "is contradictory, noncompatible, and even hostile to the very idea of nonprofit charitable activity." In Bulgaria, this meant that charitable activities were either "outlawed, especially when performed by the church . . . or at least considered to be strongly suspicious and generally discouraged." As a result, "People were taught to believe that . . . they only had to take care of their own kitchen or bedroom. Volunteerism was still alive, but mainly among elderly people in the countryside."

Nevertheless, as Andrzej Kapiszewski notes in Chapter Eighteen, the sudden erosion of communist monopolies in Eastern Europe was accompanied by the "explosive reemergence of independent, voluntary, nonprofit organizations," trends that were particularly pronounced in Poland because of the enduring vitality of the Catholic church and the country's endemic opposition to Communist party rule. Within this milieu, Solidarity was both a leader and a harbinger in the rebirth of the nation's voluntary sector.

These developments have had both positive and negative implications. In Hungary, for example, "the state appears eager to withdraw from responsibilities and to rid itself of every type of financial burden. Of course, this dismantling of government responsibility is one of the reasons why the indebted states of Central and Eastern Europe are supporting the development of the nonprofit sector." In the process, Hungary's fledgling nonprofits have been encouraged to provide services without either the luxury of formal institutional backing or state subsidies (Chapter Seventeen).

Nikolov also emphasizes the "overall lack of funds" in his analysis of the Bulgarian situation in Chapter Nineteen. As he explains, "any nonprofit, charitable, or philanthropic activity presupposes the existence of personalities and institutions capable of donating resources to benefit all the population of deprived members of the community. There are simply no such individuals, organizations, or institutions under socialism other than the state itself." Even volunteer time is a scarce commodity: "overtime labor, the ordeal of getting daily supplies of food and basic commodities, and poor transportation to and from working places all curtail possibilities for contributions to the welfare and entertainment of others."

In Hungary, as in Bulgaria, state subsidies for nonprofit activities are very limited, and corporations and individuals have little disposable income. As a result, the country's nonprofit organizations are very poor. Nina Belyaeva, in Chapter Twenty, also points to "the absence of concentrated funds" as a major stumbling block to the development of sustainable voluntary sector activities in the Soviet Union. Possibilities for indigenous philanthropy are limited in countries such as the USSR, where the government still controls an estimated 95 percent of the nation's funds. (Deborah A. Brody and Elizabeth T. Boris provide a somewhat more optimistic reading of Soviet conditions in Chapter Twenty-One.)

The situation in China, which is described by Junhai Zhang in Chapter Twenty-Seven, reflects much the same history as that of Eastern Europe and the Soviet Union. Few private organizations survived China's Communist Revolution, and many of those that did were subsequently forced to disband during the Cultural Revolution. Here, as elsewhere, the government sought to assume complete responsibility for meeting the country's social needs. And here, as elsewhere, public demands for services exceeded governmental capacities to deliver them, spurring a new interest in philanthropy and the nonprofit sector. As a result, in China, as in the Soviet Union, government officials have demonstrated an increasing willingness to tolerate the existence of nonprofit activities. Yet here, as elsewhere, support for China's voluntary sector is severely limited by a lack of tax incentives, disposable income, or indigenous traditions of giving.

Although the 1980s witnessed a sudden efflorescence of nonprofit initiatives in these areas, voluntary associations continue to suffer from a lack of legal sanctions; private funding is extremely difficult to secure; voluntarism is often sporadic and limited; and efforts to develop programs outside the state have (until recently) run the risk of being deemed unethical. And because by their very existence these organizations afford mute testimony to popular efforts to challenge or augment the role of the state, their role may be far more politically oriented than comparable roles in other parts of the world. To quote Kapiszewski, "one of the key elements of democracy is freedom of association" (Chapter Eighteen). The full implications of these activities in Eastern Europe, China, and the Soviet Union remain to be seen.

Future Opportunities and Needs

Two types of needs are consistently cited by the authors in this volume: the need to strengthen the managerial capacities and political viability of nonprofit activities and the need to stimulate and strengthen nonprofit research. At the policy-making level, more money will certainly be needed if Eastern Europe's fledgling crop of nonprofits is to flourish and survive. At the same time, efforts will have to be made to ensure that activities in this region will not threaten the survival of NGO activities in Asia, Africa, and Latin America by siphoning off badly needed funds from these areas, which in turn suggests the need to cultivate new sources of philanthropic giving.

One of the major tasks facing Japan, according to Yamamoto (Chapter Seven) is for more "full-fledged nonprofit and governmental institutions" to help in Japan's "management of the interdependent relationship with the United States and other nations." The issues are somewhat different in developing areas, where NGOs are struggling to gain a greater voice in national decision-making processes. Thus, Prijono, in Chapter Twenty-Five, calls for the creation of new forums where NGOs might begin to forge their programs and firsthand experience at the grass-roots level into more effective national development campaigns. Thompson, in Chapter Twenty-Two, also underscores the need to link grass-roots social service and empowerment programs to more efficient advocacy techniques within government. Better managerial capacities are another oft-cited requirement, along with projects to promote indigenous philanthropy in order to strengthen social activist and development campaigns.

The policy-making agendas for Eastern Europe, the Soviet Union, and China are more basic, calling for more reliable sources of funding, increased legal sanctions, better models for institutional development and managerial techniques, and tax reforms to encourage nonprofit growth.

Research capacities need to be bolstered as well, in part as a means of promoting these policy-making ends. Thus, Weisbrod and Mauser (Chapter Two) call for increased efforts "to determine both the qualitative and quantitative consequences of the various ways that nonprofit organizations are defined, subsidized, and restricted." As Kramer points out in Chapter Five, attempts to assess the nature of these changes have been hampered by the "continuing absence of an accepted definition and typology of voluntary organizations."

As a result, the available figures on the dimensions of the "organizational explosion" remain relatively impressionistic but nonetheless impressive. Clearly, the number of nonprofit organizations is growing in many parts of the world, a development that merits further exploration. More precise methodological approaches are needed to ensure accurate comparisons across national frontiers, as well as sharper definitions to clarify the distinguishing features of nonprofit associations, NGOs, private voluntary organizations (PVOs), foundations, and traditional charities. In the process, the growing dimensions of the international voluntary sector will begin to emerge in sharper relief.

Beyond definitional issues, Kramer outlines an agenda for future research that includes international comparisons of government funding at the local and national levels, as well as the effects of these policies on service delivery. Several authors call for more comparative studies of nonprofit-government relations, giving, and voluntarism and for increased opportunities for networking among scholars and practitioners at the regional and global levels.

Beyond these specific recommendations, several larger themes for future research are suggested by the volume as a whole. Certainly more needs to be known about the scope and nature of giving, voluntarism, and nonprofit activities in a diverse array of national settings. Better theoretical constructs can help to illuminate the complex ways in which governmental policy-making, economic and demographic trends, and religious and ethical values interact to determine the contours of voluntary sector initiatives in a variety of nations. Greater attention also needs to be paid to the very different roles that philanthropy and nonprofit sector activities serve within differing political and economic systems. Perhaps most important, an enhanced sensitivity to the diversity, as well as the comparability, of voluntary sector activities must infuse future research if we are to comprehend fully the breadth and significance of these activities in various parts of the world. The chapters in this volume constitute a preliminary contribution toward these ends.

References

Anheier, H. K. "Themes in International Research on the Nonprofit Sector." *Nonprofit and Voluntary Sector Quarterly*, 1990, *19*, 371–391.

Hodgkinson, V. A. "Key Challenges Facing the Nonprofit Sector." In V. Hodgkinson and R. W. Lyman (eds.), *The Future of the Nonprofit Sector: Challenges, and Policy Considerations*. San Francisco: Jossey-Bass, 1989.

Hodgkinson, V. A., and Weitzman, M. S. *Giving and Volunteering in the United States.* A survey conducted by the Gallup Organization. Washington, D.C.: INDEPENDENT SECTOR, 1988.

James, E. "The Nonprofit Sector in Comparative Perspective." In W. W. Powell (ed.), *The Nonprofit Sector: A Research Handbook.* New Haven, Conn.: Yale University Press, 1987.

James, E. (ed.). *The Nonprofit Sector in International Perspective: Studies in Comparative Culture and Policy.* New York: Oxford University Press, 1989.

Kramer, R. *Voluntary Agencies in the Welfare State.* Berkeley: University of California Press, 1981.

McCarthy, K. "The Voluntary Sector Overseas: Notes from the Field." Working paper. New York: Center for the Study of Philanthropy, 1988.

Payton, R. L. *Philanthropy: Voluntary Action for the Public Good.* New York: Macmillan for the American Council on Education, 1988.

Salamon, L. M. "Partners in Public Service: The Scope and Theory of Government-Nonprofit Relations." In W. W. Powell (ed.), *The Nonprofit Sector: A Research Handbook.* New Haven, Conn.: Yale University Press, 1987.

Van Til, J. "Defining Philanthropy." In J. Van Til (ed.), *Critical Issues in American Philanthropy: Strengthening Theory and Practice.* San Francisco: Jossey-Bass, 1990.

Weisbrod, B. A. "Toward a Theory of the Voluntary Nonprofit Sector in a Three-Sector Economy." In E. Phelps (ed.), *Altruism, Morality and Economic Theory.* New York: Russell Sage Foundation, 1975.

Williams, A. "A Growing Role for NGOs in Development." *Finance and Development,* December 1990, pp. 31–33.

Global Comparisons

Part One presents a series of cross-cultural overviews of such issues as taxation and public subsidies to nonprofit organizations. Each focuses on apsects of nonprofit-government relations, ranging from government efforts to stimulate nonprofit growth to the ways in which nonprofits can help to maximize the efficiency and equity of publicly sponsored programs.

In Chapter Two, "Tax Policy Toward Nonprofit Organizations," Burton A. Weisbrod and Elizabeth Mauser analyze the role of tax incentives in encouraging or discouraging nonprofit activities in ten Asian and European countries. Cross-national similarities and differences are surveyed in terms of types of organizations and activities that qualify for tax exemption and those that are disallowed; administrative mechanisms for granting and regulating nonprofit status; the types of subsidies and tax incentives granted; and restrictions on for-profit activities.

In Chapter Three, "Public Versus Private Provision of Social Services: Is There an Efficiency-Equity Tradeoff?" Estelle James and Nancy Birdsall examine government programs for public health, education, and welfare services in developing nations, arguing that greater equity in social spending could also result in more efficient use of public moneys. The authors suggest that many current governmental responsibilities could be turned over to fee-charging nonprofits to achieve the same ends.

In Chapter Four, "Local Governments and the Independent Sector in the Third World," Julie Fisher explains that there has been an "organizational explosion" of nongovernmental organizations in developing nations over the past two decades. Although relations between these social activist and development groups and their host governments have sometimes been openly adversarial at the national level, Fisher sees evidence of greater power sharing between grass-roots organizations and local, provincial, and state governments.

Ralph M. Kramer shifts the focus to Western Europe in Chapter Five, "Privatization in the Personal Social Services in the United Kingdom, the Netherlands, and Italy." In it, he argues that many European welfare states are evolving into "contract states," in which governments have increasingly embraced nonprofit organizations as partners in the provision of local and national health, educational, and social welfare services. As a result, the nonprofit sector in each of these countries has grown rapidly, backed by public revenues and lively policy debates about the appropriate roles of government and the voluntary sector.

Karen Paul examines an aspect of foreign funding in "U.S. Corporate Philanthropy in South Africa, 1977–1989" in Chapter Six. She argues that poor planning and covert political agendas ultimately discredited the efforts of the Sullivan signatories to help South African blacks. In addition to surveying the reasons for the programs' failures, she suggests ways in which corporate giving programs might be strengthened in Third World countries.

In Chapter Seven, "Private Philanthropy as a Necessity in Our Interdependent World," Tadashi Yamamoto points out that although the growth of philanthropy was hampered by Japan's long-standing tradition of centralized government and its lack of a Judeo-Christian ethic, the country's rapid economic ascendance, its growing presence on the international scene, and its new interest in corporate social responsibility have helped to spur the growth of corporate giving. He argues the case for increased giving and nonprofit activity to help Japan adapt to its role as a major world power.

Burton A. Weisbrod
(with the assistance of
Elizabeth Mauser)

Chapter 2

Tax Policy Toward
Nonprofit Organizations:
A Ten-Country Survey

Every society has a continuing need to choose the forms of institutions through which it will seek to achieve its social and economic goals (Davis and North, 1971; Williamson, 1975; Buchanan, 1987; Wolf, 1988). Traditional analysis has focused on two types of institutions: the private market and government. In recent years, however, increased attention has been paid to a third class of institutions, private nonprofit organizations — hybrids that combine some characteristics of private enterprise

Note: We thank the Ford Foundation for financial support. We also thank those people who responded to the survey questionnaire: Christoph Badelt (Austria), Patrick De Bucquois (Belgium), Miklos Marschall (Hungary), Jimmy Weinblatt (Israel), Disiano Preite (Italy), Mark Robson (United Kingdom), Julia Montserrat

with other characteristics of government (Hansmann, 1980; Young, 1983; Rose-Ackerman, 1986; Weisbrod, 1977, 1978, 1988). Evidence on international differences in institutional mix is extremely limited (James, 1987; McCarthy, 1989). This chapter extends in one direction knowledge about the nonprofit sector in a comparative international perspective. The goal is limited: to describe a number of features of the tax systems of various countries as they relate to the encouragement or discouragement of nonprofit organizations. We highlight cross-national similarities and differences, and where differences are found, we comment on their significance. Careful analysis, however, of either the positive or normative significance of the differences and similarities is a subject for future research.

   Differences in the tax and subsidy treatment of nonprofit organizations relative to private firms affect the competitive position of each and thereby affect their relative strength within an industry. In the United States, for example, nonprofit organizations play a major competitive role in the health care industry, particularly in hospitals, nursing homes, and day-care centers. Private firms often claim that tax advantages permit nonprofits to compete "unfairly" (Business Coalition, 1985; U.S. Small Business Administration, 1983; Wellford and Gallagher, 1988).[1]

   Specifically, this chapter reports results from a survey designed to identify differences and similarities among countries in their tax policies toward nonprofit organizations.[2] The countries included in this survey are from Europe, Asia, and the Middle East. They do not constitute a systematic sample but represent countries with a variety of tax systems about which information could be obtained.

   This survey is but a first step, however, in a larger research process. Insofar as our research discloses large differences

(Spain), Ching-Chang Yen (Taiwan), Somchai Richupan (Thailand), and Wolfgang Seibel (West Germany). In addition, we benefited from reading draft papers by Frits W. Hondius (Council of Europe) and Sheila Avrin McLean (McLean & Co., Ltd.), both of whom have done related work on tax treatment of charities in various countries, and from comments by Christoph Franz on an earlier draft of this chapter.

among countries in their encouragement of the nonprofit sector, three questions will remain: Why do the differences exist? What are the consequences? Which policies are preferable in terms of efficient resource allocation and equity?

The Issues Surveyed

The questions addressed in the survey grow out of previous theorizing about which dimensions of public policy toward nonprofits are likely to affect the size of the nonprofit sector of an economy, the industries in which nonprofits are concentrated, and the economic choices made by the nonprofits.

The first question we sought to answer was whether "nonprofit" organizations are recognized under the law of each country. Thus,

> *Question 1:* Is there a class of organizations that is termed "nonprofit," "voluntary," "charitable," "philanthropic," "exempt," and so forth, which receives some special treatment under the tax laws of your country? If so, precisely what name is used to identify the class?

The definition of terms such as *nonprofit* could vary considerably among countries, perhaps encompassing a broad set of activities in one country, a far more restricted set in another. To get at this, two additional questions were asked:

> *Question 2:* What is the definition of those organizations — that is, what is the rationale for singling them out for special attention and tax treatment?

> *Question 3:* What kinds of activities may they engage in to qualify for the special status? (Is there a list of activities that qualify, at least potentially, for the special status?)

No matter how broadly or narrowly a country defines the permissible domain of nonprofit organizations, the actual size and scope of the nonprofit sector will depend on how the laws are administered. Some agency must decide whether a particular organization that proposes to engage in a particular set of activities does or does not qualify for nonprofit status under the law. We were especially interested in whether the administrative agency is purely governmental and whether the governmental role is played by the tax collection agency (the IRS in the United States) or by some other unit. This led to

> *Question 4:* What is the administrative mechanism by which a decision is made as to whether an organization qualifies for the special status? (For example, in the United States, the Internal Revenue Service makes the determination. In another country, both the tax authority and the government agency operating in the substantive area, such as health care or education, must approve. If the tax collection agency is involved, does that agency have a special division dealing with nonprofits?)

Admission of an organization to nonprofit status carries some favorable treatment. One issue, therefore, is whether the number of such organizations is limited in any way. Thus,

> *Question 5:* Are there any restrictions on the total number of organizations that may receive the special, nonprofit status?

Nonprofits could be given two classes of benefits: (a) the organization itself could receive subsidies (for example, reduced postal rates for exemption from taxes on property or value added), and (b) donors to the organization could receive subsidies for giving money, goods, or time. A question on each of these types of benefits was included. Of particular interest was anything that would give an advantage to a nonprofit organization in competition with a private firm.

> *Question 6:* If an organization qualifies for the special status, what specific subsidies or other favor-

able treatment does it receive *as an organization,* either through the tax system or in other ways? That is, does it have any tax or subsidy advantages over a private-sector firm? (For example: (1) Is it not subject to certain restrictions that exist for private firms, such as minimum wage law? (2) Does it receive direct monetary transfers from government or subsidies for specific purposes such as postal rates? (3) Is it exempt from any of a variety of taxes such as taxes on corporate profits, property, value added, and so forth?)

Question 7: Are private individuals or firms that *donate* to nonprofit organizations encouraged, through the tax systems or in other ways, to contribute to nonprofit-type organizations? (For example, are donations tax-deductible on individual and corporate income tax returns, and if so, at what rate? Are there lower or upper limits on the amount of an individual's contributions that are subsidized? Are there any special provisions of the law that deal with donations of goods by private firms to nonprofits— such as a cannery donating dented cans of food?)

Tax benefits often carry corresponding restrictions. To understand further the potential effects of nonprofit organizations on the private sector, two questions were asked about constraints on the nonprofits. The objective was to learn how nonprofits are restricted, what penalties are imposed on them for violating rules, and more particularly, what the consequences are— at least as stated officially— of a nonprofit engaging in an activity that lies beyond its nonprofit boundaries.

Question 8: Do nonprofit-type organizations face any *restrictions* that private-sector firms do not? (For example, are nonprofits permitted to engage in a "significant" amount of legislative "lobbying"? Are they prohibited from selling any goods or services that are *unrelated* to their official objectives? Are they prohibited from distributing any surplus or profit to anyone associated with the organization?)

Question 9: If an organization engages in any commercial activities that are outside the purpose for which it was established and approved, how is the revenue from such an activity treated for tax purposes? (In the United States, for example, such profits are essentially taxable as ordinary corporate profits, while in some other countries any such "unrelated business" activity is totally prohibited and would cause the loss of "nonprofit" legal status.)

A related matter not examined explicitly in this exploratory effort involves the definition of "the organization." For example, may a nonprofit organization form a for-profit subsidiary to engage in activities that are "unrelated" to the purposes for which that organization was granted nonprofit status? If it is permitted, are there restrictions on transactions between these "separate" but related organizations? Are there restrictions on the joint use of personnel or other resources? May the same people serve on both boards of directors? These matters are potentially important for determining whether nonprofit status can be used in unintended and perhaps undesirable ways to reallocate resources from socially desired ends to private benefits.

The Survey

The survey was sent to academicians and government officials in sixteen countries. Responses to the full questionnaire were received from ten countries: Austria, Belgium, Hungary, Israel, Italy, Spain, Taiwan, Thailand, the United Kingdom, and what was at the time West Germany. The initial responses were supplemented by further correspondence to clarify answers and to verify interpretations of the responses. The ten countries differ in level of economic development, size, and cultural diversity. They do not represent a scientific sample of either explicit randomization or stratification; the goal, after all, was simply to identify areas of diversity and of homogeneity across countries in the tax treatment of nonprofits.

Responses are summarized briefly, in the order of the questions.

Defining the Domain of "Nonprofit" Organizations (Questions 1-3)

Every country that participated in the study has provision for a class of organizations variously termed nonprofit, philanthropic, charity, voluntary, community oriented, public interest, and so on, and all convey some special encouragement to them. However, the breadth of activities subject to the subsidies and constraints varies enormously.

In Austria, a wide range of organizations can qualify for nonprofit status; they must be pursuing goals deemed to be community oriented, charitable, or church oriented. However, only a small subset of these organizations—specifically, those engaged in scientific research—have the advantage that gifts to them are tax deductible for donors. In the United Kingdom, the domain is at least as broad—a "charity" organization may be involved with the relief of poverty, the advancement of education or religion, or "other purposes beneficial to the community" (M. H. Robson, letters to the author, May and June 1988)—but in contrast to the situation in Austria, tax benefits are available to donors to all the nonprofit organizations.

In responses to questions 1-3, in general, nonprofits are authorized to operate in sectors similar to those in which governments typically are major providers, involving either public-type goods, such as scientific research (Weisbrod, 1977), or goods for which substantial informational asymmetries arguably exist, so that consumer protection beyond the level available through ordinary private markets is deemed appropriate—for example, health care, day care of children, and education (Hansmann, 1980; Weisbrod, 1988). Nonprofits are typically seen as alternatives to government in the sense that objectives other than profit maximization are assumed to be sought (Young, 1983); yet financing of the activities is substantially through voluntary, nontax mechanisms such as private donations or commercial sales and user fees.[3]

Who Decides Whether a Given Organization Qualifies for Nonprofit Status? (Question 4)

In every country surveyed there is some formal administrative mechanism for deciding whether an organization qualifies for the special tax status associated with being a nonprofit. In general, it is the government tax collection agency (analogous to the Internal Revenue Service in the United States and Inland Revenue in the United Kingdom) that makes the decision, although that decision is constrained in some countries by the requirement of approval from the government ministry whose substantive jurisdiction would be involved, for example, education or social welfare.

In Israel, Italy, Taiwan, Thailand, and what was formerly West Germany (as in the United States), only the tax collection agency must approve a nonprofit organization's legal eligibility for tax benefits. (In Israel, two such organizations are involved: the custom authorities, who are in charge of the value-added tax, and the income tax authorities, who are in charge of the taxes on income, property, land betterment, and so on.)

By contrast, in a number of other countries the tax collector (Revenue Department, Ministry of Finance) is not the sole decision maker. In Spain the tax agency makes the determination only after the nonprofit organization has been approved and registered by the ministry responsible for the particular area of activity. For example, philanthropic organizations have to be registered by the Direccion General de Accion Social (Director General of Social Action), within the Work and Social Security Ministry. Similarly, in Austria the tax authority determines an organization's eligibility for subsidies only after the organization has been approved by the Federal Ministry of Science and Research. In the United Kingdom the tax collection agency, Inland Revenue, has the final say in granting eligibility for tax benefits. However, in England and Wales (but not in Scotland or Northern Ireland) a separate body, the Charity Commission (or the Department of Education in the case of schools) also has a role by registering and monitoring all charities to prevent fraud.

The preeminent importance of tax considerations in the regulation of nonprofit organizations is striking. In most countries the tax collection agency is the only government agency responsible for determining whether a particular organization will be permitted to operate as a nonprofit, receiving the tax advantages but also subject to certain constraints. However, the presence, in some countries, of a decision role for another agency, whose perspective encompasses considerations other than taxation, is noteworthy. And in one country, Hungary, we find that the tax collection agency has no role in the decision to grant or not to grant legal recognition to a nonprofit; that decision is made solely by the government department responsible for the field in which the nonprofit would operate.

Even within the tax collection agencies of different countries there are differences in the administration of laws relating to nonprofits. In Taiwan, the United Kingdom, and the United States a special unit exists within the tax collection agency to deal with nonprofits.[4] In other countries — including Austria, Spain, and Germany — there is no such special unit. In Germany, for example, the tax department that is responsible for each specific form of tax (corporate income tax, property tax, and the like) deals with both for-profit and nonprofit organizations. Even though by law there is no special unit of the tax authority to deal with nonprofits, in practice larger local tax authorities have set up special units to handle nonprofit organizations. In addition to the tax authorities, special administrative units manage nonprofit housing corporations and foundations.

The consequences of these alternative administrative arrangements have not been studied. It seems likely, however, that decisions differ, depending on whether the administrative unit has a broader or narrower perspective, that is, whether it sees itself as responsible for nonprofit organizations in general or simply for a particular form of tax.[5] In most cases, an organization is eligible for nonprofit status at the time of its inception. There are, however, exceptions. In Austria and Germany, a determination is not made until the organization files its first tax return and claims that it is "community oriented" or of "public interest." In Thailand, the decision on granting nonprofit status is not made until the nonprofit has existed for at least three years in order to ensure that its activities are in the public interest. Such delays add to an organization's uncertainty and thus appear to discourage the formation of nonprofits.

Are There Any Restrictions on the Total Number of Nonprofits? (Question 5)

In none of the countries surveyed is there any limit on the number of nonprofits that can receive special tax treatment.

The desirability of limiting entry to the tax-privileged status of a nonprofit organization is not known. Entry restrictions are common in other realms, such as in public utilities that provide electric power and drinking water. In the case of nonprofits, an argument in favor of such restrictions comes from private firms in the United States, which are complaining increasingly that they are victims of "unfair competition" from nonprofit organizations (U.S. Small Business Administration, 1983; Business Coalition for Fair Competition, 1985).

While barriers to the entry of nonprofit organizations are apparently not established explicitly in any of the countries studied, concerns have been expressed about restricting entry of nonprofits that do not serve the public but that are "for-profits in disguise" (Weisbrod, 1988). In the United Kingdom, for example, a 1986 law gave the Inland Revenue and the Charity Commission new authority to "prevent the abuse of charitable status" (M. H. Robson, letter to the author, May 1988). In Germany, nonprofit organizations are prohibited from paying "disproportionate (high) remunerations"—a mechanism for distributing profit through higher wages.

What Favorable Treatment Do Nonprofits Receive? (Question 6)

In every country surveyed a nonprofit organization receives exemption from various taxes on business. Exemptions from taxation of profits, if any, and of real estate appear to be quite general. Other exemptions depend on the specific features of a particular country's tax system. In countries with a value-added tax, for example, nonprofits are given varying degrees of exemption from it. Full relief from the value-added tax (VAT) is granted to nonprofits in Austria, Italy, and Spain and to a subset of charities in the United Kingdom; reduced rates are granted in Hungary; and an alternative tax exists in Israel (nonprofits pay 6.25 percent of their VAT from wages plus 15 percent on purchased inputs in comparison to for-profits that pay 15 percent of their VAT but are granted a refund for their VAT on purchased inputs). In Hungary, where the status of nonprofit organizations was in flux even before the political events of late 1989, nonprofit organizations receive various kinds of direct, program-specific grants from government. In the United Kingdom, nonprofits are also exempt from tax on capital gains. Taiwan exempts nonprofits from the transportation license tax on vehicles owned by nonprofit educational, cultural, and health care organizations.

Nonprofits benefit not only from tax subsidies — exemption from various taxes levied on other organizations — but also from direct subsidies either in monetary form or as services available at below-market prices. In the United Kingdom nonprofits engaged in a construction activity can use unemployed young people who are receiving on-the-job training financed by the government training commissions. Private firms do not have access to this in-kind labor subsidy. Nonprofits in the United Kingdom also benefit from access to grants from other nonprofits, grants that are not available to private individuals or firms.

Exemption from taxation of real property (land and buildings) is extremely common across countries. While the responses from some countries were not entirely clear on this matter, it appears that every country provides nonprofits with at least partial exemption from property taxation.

With respect to subsidies for specific purposes such as postal rates — a major form of subsidy to nonprofits in the United States — it is interesting that not a single country surveyed reported having lower postal rates for nonprofits. Similarly, no country reported that nonprofits benefit from exemption from restrictions imposed on private firms—for example, from minimum-wage legislation—as they did in the United States until recently.

All of these exemptions from taxation or other restrictions that affect particular resource inputs—land and buildings, mail, vehicles, and low-wage labor—highlight an important dimension of public policy: in an attempt to stimulate the nonprofit form of organization in certain parts of the economy, public policy may distort the use of resources within the nonprofit sector. The point is that it is generally inefficient to subsidize the use of particular resources relatively more than others. Subsidies that are tied to nonprofits' use of certain inputs do not simply provide the organizations with more total resources; they also encourage the organization to use resources differently—to use more land and capital relative to labor, to engage in fund raising by using mailings relatively more and newspapers and television less, to own more vehicles rather than to lease them, and to use more low-wage labor than higher-wage labor (Weisbrod, 1988).

There is yet another potential dimension in terms of which nonprofits might benefit from public policy. There could be a policy that expresses a preference for nonprofit organizations over private firms in particular industries, with government grants in those industries going only to nonprofits. In Belgium, for example, government transfers to old people's homes and children's homes are conditional on their having nonprofit status.[6] Spain gives preference to nonprofit organizations for government grants and subsidies to hospitals and old people's homes, as does Germany for hospitals.

Do Individuals or Private Firms Receive Any Encouragement, Through the Tax System, to Donate Money or Goods to Nonprofit Organizations? (Question 7)

Donations of money are generally deductible on individual and corporate income tax returns. In Belgium, however, tax deductions are allowed only for a subset of nonprofits, as determined by the Ministry of Finance; political parties are included but churches are not, except for those church activities that involve outside, public-serving activities (and with a $25 per year minimum and a maximum of the lesser of 5 percent of net taxable income or the equivalent of approximately $250,000). Although Austria restricts tax-deductible donations to a small subset of nonprofits (those engaged in scientific research), business firms try to get around these restrictions by giving hidden grants to nonprofits and declaring them as business expenses. Spain has a very limited incentive for individuals to donate to nonprofits; only gifts to the Spanish Historical Society are deductible for individuals—20 percent of the gift, up to 30 percent of taxable income. Donations by businesses, however—in money, art, or other assets—are deductible up to a limit of 10 percent of a firm's net profits. In Italy, donations of appreciated property are exempt from the capital gains tax, and donations of up to 2 percent of taxable income by firms to organizations engaged in scientific research are tax deductible, as are donations by individuals to the Catholic church and to organizations engaged in Third World aid and in preservation of goods of artistic interest.

Tax deductibility provides a financial incentive to donate, but the magnitude of the incentive depends on the marginal tax rate to which the donor is subject and on any minimum or maximum limits on the amount of tax-deductible donations. In Hungary, top tax rates of 50 percent for businesses and more for individuals make the after-tax cost of donating quite low (and there is no upper limit on deductible donations). Taiwan limits deductibility to a maximum of 20 percent of the donor's gross income. Thailand's limit is 10 percent of taxable income for individuals and 1 percent of profits for firms. Germany's limit is 5 or 10 percent of income, depending on the organization to which the taxable donation is given.

The United Kingdom has a more complex system but one that appears to be equivalent to a tax-deductibility arrangement. To qualify for a tax deduction, a donor must "covenant" the donation for a minimum of four years. The donor deducts the "basic" income tax rate (now 25 percent) at the time of the donation, and if the donor is subject to a greater marginal tax rate, then the additional amount is refunded at the end of the tax year. The recipient "charity" reclaims from the Inland Revenue the 25 percent deducted by the donor. Until 1986 there was no tax incentive for donations involving less than the four-year commitment; since then, however, donations by firms not closely owned have become deductible provided they do not exceed 3 percent of dividends; employee donations, if deducted from payroll, are deductible up to about $800 (£480).

Allowing donations to be deducted as an expense on an income or profits tax return is the most common mechanism for encouraging donations to nonprofits. One country, however — Israel — uses a tax *credit* rather than a tax deduction. All donors may reduce their tax liability by 35 percent of donations, up to about $50,000 (95,000 N.S.) per year or 25 percent of taxable income, whichever is lower; there is also a minimum of $50 of donations (80 N.S.), below which no credit is allowed.

The difference between a tax deduction and a tax credit for donations is important because of the different incentive effects. With tax deductibility — which is the law in most countries surveyed, as well as in the United States — the tax reduction gained by a person who donates a given sum depends on two variables. One is whether the tax law distinguishes, as it does in the United States, between taxpayers who do and who do not "itemize" certain allowable expenses, including donations; the after-tax cost of donating depends on whether the taxpayer has enough total expenses to justify itemizing, and so the incentive to donate can differ among taxpayers who have identical incomes and who give identical sums. Second, in countries that have a progressive income tax system, tax deductibility makes the after-tax cost of donating a given sum lower for higher-income persons.

A tax credit, by contrast, has neither of these effects. The after-tax cost of donating is the same for all donors regardless of whether or not they itemize and regardless of their income level and its associated marginal tax rate. With a tax credit system, the after-tax cost of donating a given sum depends only on the tax-credit rate; with a 35 percent rate, for example, a $100 donation costs the donor $65 after the tax credit.

Donations may be not only in the form of money but also in the form of goods and services. Austria, the United Kingdom, Germany, and the United States permit deductibility of in-kind donations (as well as money donations) to nonprofits. Taiwan, however, does not provide for deductibility of donations of goods.

Wherever donations of goods are deductible, a serious administrative problem arises: how to place a value on the donated items. Depending on how this is resolved, firms and individuals will face differing profit incentives to give to nonprofits. Such administrative difficulties may help to explain why no country provides tax deductibility for donations of unpaid, volunteer time, although Germany allows "volunteers" for educational or social welfare organizations to be paid up to $1,400 per year income-tax free.[7]

Are Nonprofit Organizations Allowed to Engage in Commercial Activities, and Do the Organizations Face Other Restrictions That Private-Sector Firms Do Not? (Questions 8 and 9)

All countries appear to impose on nonprofit organizations a "non-distribution" constraint, a prohibition on paying profit or surplus to owners, trustees, or others associated with managing the organization. Thus, for example, Germany prohibits nonprofits from paying "disproportionate" (high) wages (W. Seibel, letter to the author, September 1988) as one element of the effort to prevent people associated with the organization from enjoying "any special monetary advantage." Taiwan prohibits nonprofits from "distributing any surplus or profit to anyone associated with the organization" (C. Yen, letter to the author, November 1988), as do Austria (C. Badelt, letter to the author, June 1988) and Hungary (M. Marschall, letter to the author, May 1989). In the United Kingdom and Spain, trustees of nonprofit organizations may not receive any remuneration at all; in Spain, however, this restriction applies only to trustees who are policymakers, not to the director or the manager of the organization (M. H. Robson, letter to the author, 1988; J. Montserrat, letter to the author, June 1989).

Thailand further restricts the allocation of a nonprofit organization's revenues. Expenditures must be at least 60 percent of total revenues for the year except when the nonprofit is saving for something such as a new building (S. Richupan, letter to the author, March 1989). Similarly, in Germany *all* revenues must be spent in the same fiscal year unless the nonprofit is saving for a specific approved purpose.

Recently, there has been growing attention to whether nonprofit organizations should be restricted in their participation in commercial activities — where they sell outputs, often competing with private firms — and what should be done if a nonprofit engages in activities that are beyond the bounds of its nonprofit charter or authorization. As nonprofits have encountered fiscal stresses, they have often engaged in commercial activity with the goal of obtaining profits with which to cross-subsidize their nonprofit activities.

Nearly all countries have policies toward nonprofits that reflect awareness that the organizations can use their subsidies in socially undesirable ways. Mechanisms for dealing with this problem, however, vary.

One approach is to distinguish between activities that are "appropriate" and those that are not and then to apply ordinary corporate tax treatment to the latter. This is the practice in Belgium, Italy, and Taiwan, where a nonprofit organization that engages in any activity not covered by the ruling granting it nonprofit status is permitted to do so but must pay ordinary corporate tax on any profits from those activities. In Germany, a nonprofit organization can engage in a commercial activity unrelated to its tax-exempt purposes as long as the activity does not dominate the nonprofit activity; however, the organization must pay ordinary corporate tax if the sale volume of the commercial activity is larger than $35,000. In Spain, profits derived from nonexempt activities are taxed but at a rate lower than that for ordinary corporate profits (J. Montserrat, letter to the author, July 1989).

In Austria, a nonprofit organization may only engage in commercial activities that do not "endanger the objectives laid out in the statutes." It must, however, pay ordinary tax on profits generated by those activities, and it does not receive relief from the value-added tax. The freedom to engage in commercial activities gives the nonprofits an advantage, since the first $12,000 of profit (A.S. 100,000) is not subject to corporate income tax (C. Badelt, letter to the author, June 1988).

The United Kingdom takes a stricter stance on commercial activities that lie outside a nonprofit's charitable purposes. A sharp distinction is drawn between the charitable activities and other activities that may provide funds for the charitable activities. A nonprofit may not engage in commercial efforts of the latter type except in two instances: (1) if the trade is exercised in the course of carrying out the charitable goals, or (2) if the individuals who carry on the trade are mainly the beneficiaries of the charity. However, a nonprofit may lawfully set up a "sister" organization without charitable status, and that organization may covenant profits to the charity (M. H. Robson, letter to the author, June 1988).

In Thailand, a nonprofit organization may not engage in any commercial activities that are not included in its original statute. If the organization does engage in such an activity, its charitable status will be taken away. Moreover, "[i]f that activity is damaging to the organization or the public, the person who is responsible in such an organization will be punished with imprisonment not exceeding two years or a fine not exceeding four thousand baht or both" (S. Richupan, letter to the author, March 1989). If a nonprofit organization is involved in a commercial enterprise that is consistent with its statute (charter), the organization is not exempt from taxes on these activities except by approval by the Ministry of Finance; however, if the organization is taxed, it is subject to a special tax rate.

In sharp contrast, Israel does not restrict the activities a nonprofit organization may engage in, and there is no special treatment of revenues from commercial activities. "If an affiliate or a subsidiary [of a nonprofit] engages in [commercial activity], it pays regular value-added tax, but the profits are usually not taxed by the income tax authorities since they are transferred to the parent nonprofit organization" (J. Weinblatt, letter to the author, May 1988).

Hungary is one country in which the law has not distinguished between appropriate and inappropriate activities of nonprofits. Nonprofits are not prohibited from operating for-profit businesses as long as the profits are used for the goals outlined in the organization's statutes. If the profits are used for other purposes, they are taxable. There is no concept analogous to the United States notion of an "unrelated business" activity. "There is no specific restriction on the kind of [commercial] activity a nonprofit may engage in" (M. Marschall, letter to the author, May 1989). The laws regarding nonprofit organizations in Hungary are just beginning to evolve as the country moves away from a highly centralized, government-run welfare system; consequently, the private delivery of public goods is still very new there.

Throughout the countries studied, difficult practical problems arise, including how strict to be in deciding whether an activity is outside the purpose for which the nonprofit organization was established and approved, and how to deal with a commercial organization that is legally distinct from a particular nonprofit but actually deeply entwined with it.

Conclusion

We have found both similarities and differences among the ten countries surveyed in the tax treatment of nonprofit organizations. The major findings may be summarized as follows: (1) The definition and scope of such organizations varies considerably. (2) Nonprofit organizations — however they are defined in a specific country — are typically regulated by the tax collection agency of government; in some countries, however, there is also some involvement, at least at the time of the initial grant of nonprofit status, of the government agency responsible for a particular realm of activity, such as health or education. (3) A wide variety of tax exemptions — sometimes termed tax "subsidies" — are offered to nonprofit organizations, with exemption from corporate profits tax being universal. Various subsidies are tied to specific resource inputs — for example, motor vehicles, land and buildings, and mail. In contrast to the exemption from profits tax, these subsidies have distortionary effects, encouraging nonprofit organizations to substitute more of the subsidized inputs for unsubsidized alternatives. (4) Almost every country places limits on nonprofit organizations that engage in activities that are "unrelated" to their nonprofit status; the mere fact that such an activity generates profit that is then used to finance the nonprofit organization's "principal" activities (or tax-exempt purpose) is generally not sufficient to permit that profit to go untaxed. The critical issue appears to be one of just how far from those principal activities a nonprofit should be permitted to go; a closely related matter, however — and a very complex one that is seldom addressed in the tax laws — is what relationships a nonprofit should be allowed to have with for-profit firms. (5) In addition to the direct subsidization of nonprofits through government grants and through tax subsidies, nonprofits also benefit from tax benefits to individual and corporate donors. Most countries permit donors to deduct donations of money (and in some cases, also goods and services) from taxable income, although there are typically both minimum and maximum limits on amounts that can be deducted. One country uses a tax credit rather than a tax deduction; with the credit, every donor has the same after-tax cost of donating a given sum.

The reasons for the differences and similarities uncovered in our survey remain subjects for future research. We have found that along some dimensions there is great variation across countries, while along others there is little or no variation. Apparently, countries differ in their desire to encourage nonprofits in general and in specific areas of activity. The reasons for those differences, however, may vary among countries, just as the forms of encouragement vary. One factor that may play an important role in shaping a country's policy toward nonprofits is the degree of heterogeneity of the population as that is reflected in the ability of government to satisfy citizen wants (Weisbrod, 1975). Research, however, on the factors that determine the relative size of the nonprofit sector in any economy, compared with the sizes of government and the proprietary sector, remains in its infancy (James, 1987).

What these findings point up is the need to determine both

the qualitative and quantitative consequences of the various ways that nonprofit organizations are defined, subsidized, and restricted. This is part of a larger task of understanding why such differences exist across countries and what the "appropriate" role of nonprofit organizations is in a modern mixed economy that also has private enterprise and public sectors.

Notes

1. Researchers who focus on the "privatization" of governmental activities as distinct from private nonprofit activities are raising analogous questions, for governmental enterprises also have a variety of tax and subsidy advantages over private firms (*Journal of Policy Analysis and Management*, 1987).
2. Examples for the United States are also presented, but the United States is not included in the survey.
3. Insofar as private donations reduce donors' tax liabilities, donations involve implicit grants from taxpayers, supplementing the donors' after-tax contribution.
4. In the United Kingdom, it is the Claims Branch, Charity Division, within the Inland Revenue. In the United States, it is the Exempt Organizations Branch, within the Internal Revenue Service.
5. For further discussion, see Weisbrod, 1988, especially Chap. 9.
6. For a discussion of the theoretic case for such a policy, see Weisbrod, 1988.
7. Even without deductibility for volunteer labor, a tax system that allows deductions for donations of money is actually neutral in the incentives provided to give money or time. A donor of an hour of time gives up the after-tax money that he or she could earn by working for pay instead of volunteering; that is, a donor gives up $W(1 - t)$, where W is the wage rate and t is the marginal tax rate. A person who donates W in money also gives up $W(1 - t)$ in after-tax income provided he or she itemizes. For nonitemizers, however, a tax-deduction system is not neutral between givers of money and givers of time; for nonitemizers, a donation of W dollars costs W after tax, while a

donation of an hour of time involves an after cost of $W(1 - t)$ (Long, 1977).

References

Buchanan, J. M. "The Constitution of Economic Policy." *American Economic Review,* 1987, *77,* 243–250.

Business Coalition for Fair Competition. *Unfair Competition in the United States.* Washington, D.C.: Business Coalition for Fair Competition, 1985.

Davis, L. E., and North, D. C. *Institutional Change and American Economic Growth.* Cambridge, England: Cambridge University Press, 1971.

Hansmann, H. B. "The Role of Non-Profit Enterprise." *Yale Law Journal,* 1980, *89,* 835–901.

James, E. "The Nonprofit Sector in Comparative Perspective." In W. W. Powell (ed.), *The Nonprofit Sector,* pp. 397–415. New Haven: Yale University Press, 1987.

Journal of Policy Analysis and Management, Special issue on privatization, 1987, *6* (entire issue).

Long, S. H. "Income Tax Effects on Donor Choice of Money and Time Contributions." *National Tax Journal,* 1977, *30,* 207–212.

McCarthy, K. D. *The Voluntary Sector Overseas.* New York: Center for the Study of Philanthropy, City University of New York, 1989.

Rose-Ackerman, S. (ed.). *The Economics of Nonprofit Institutions.* New York: Oxford University Press, 1986.

U.S. Small Business Administration. *Unfair Competition by Nonprofit Organizations with Small Business.* Washington, D.C.: U.S. Small Business Administration, 1983.

Weisbrod, B. A. "Towards a Theory of the Voluntary Non-profit Sector in a Three-Sector Economy." In E. Phelps (ed.), *Altruism, Morality and Economic Theory.* New York: Russell Sage Foundation, 1975.

Weisbrod, B. A. *The Voluntary Nonprofit Sector.* Lexington, Mass.: Lexington Books, 1977.

Weisbrod, B. A. "The Private Nonprofit Sector: Facts in Search of Theory." Discussion Paper 501. Madison: Institute for Research on Poverty, University of Wisconsin, 1978.

Weisbrod, B. A. *The Nonprofit Economy.* Cambridge, Mass.: Harvard University Press, 1988.

Wellford, W. H., and Gallagher, J. G. *Unfair Competition?* Washington, D.C.: National Assembly of National Voluntary Health and Social Welfare Organizations, 1988.

Williamson, O. E. *Markets and Hierarchies: Analysis and Antitrust Organization.* New York: Free Press, 1975.

Wolf, C., Jr. *Markets or Governments: Choosing Between Imperfect Alternatives.* Cambridge, Mass.: MIT Press, 1988.

Young, D. *If Not for Profit, for What?* Lexington, Mass.: Lexington Books, 1983.

Estelle James
Nancy Birdsall

Public Versus Private Provision of Social Services: Is There an Efficiency-Equity Tradeoff?

An important current issue in development economics concerns the appropriate degree of reliance on such measures as user charges for publicly provided health, education, and other social services and use of the private sector for the provision of these services. Proponents of user charges and greater privatization claim that these measures will conserve scarce public funds and promote efficiency in the sense of cost-effectiveness and responsiveness to consumer preferences. Opponents retort that because user charges rely on ability to pay as a rationing criterion, such charges for public services and privatization will have negative

Note: This chapter is reprinted by permission of the World Bank.

distributional effects that are likely to outweigh any efficiency gains. Most of the literature in this area implicitly accepts the existence of an efficiency-equity tradeoff, with some people choosing efficiency and others opting for equity.

In this chapter we argue that in many settings in the developing world, this presumption of a tradeoff between efficiency and equity is incorrect. We argue that, in fact, the current situation in many countries is inefficient in part because it is inequitable; greater equity in social spending would also be more efficient (in reducing mortality, for example, or in maximizing social returns to spending on education). Put another way, in these countries there exists an identifiable group of efficient reallocations that would simultaneously improve distribution. These reallocations often involve the delegation of certain responsibilities to the private nonprofit sector.

The first section of this chapter, "Theory," sets forth the theoretical reasons for predicting that the state will often finance a bundle of social services that is both inefficient and inequitable — inequitable in the sense that the upper and middle classes rather than lower-income groups will benefit therefrom. The second section, "Empirical Examples," presents a variety of such examples, from both developed and developing countries. The conclusion summarizes the crux of the political economy problem. Since we start with a model in which degree of efficiency and redistribution are endogenous, the real difficulty is, How do we break into the chain of causation and bring about a new equilibrium, more efficient and more redistributive, when this has apparently not been in the interest of the main actors or it would already have happened? A role for the nonprofit sector is proposed to help bring about this social change.

Theory

Welfare Theory

Classical welfare theory gives us a normative view of what government *should* do, focusing on efficiency rather than distributional considerations. The economic role of government is to correct market failure by funding public goods, by subsidizing goods that generate externalities, and by compensating for capital market or insurance market failure and otherwise simply to set the framework within which private enterprise will function. The standard approach is to assume that the efforts of government to correct for market failure in themselves introduce some efficiency losses because those efforts usually require taxes, and nondistorting lump-sum taxes are not feasible. The problem is, then, one of a tradeoff between the benefits and the costs of intervention.

With respect to distribution, government is viewed as benign or slightly benevolent, having some interest in equalizing income or opportunities. For example, people cannot be excluded from public goods, by definition, so the poor as well as the rich benefit therefrom. Some welfare theorists go further and argue that there exists a set of "merit goods" (health, education) that society does not wish to ration according to ability to pay; hence government steps in, on efficiency grounds, to impose some alternative criterion.

Finally, according to classical welfare theory, the "maximum" point of social welfare is acknowledged to depend on distribution as well as efficiency. Opinions vary on whether a "social welfare function" exists, what an "equitable" distribution might be, and how much the government should intervene to alter the distribution determined by pure market forces. Usually, however, the presumption is that if there is to be any politically determined redistribution, it should be from rich to poor and not vice versa. In this chapter we use the term *equity* as a shorthand term meaning "redistribution to the poor" while recognizing that this is a value-laden word that goes beyond standard welfare theory usage.

Public Choice Theory

A second, more recent and less benevolent view of government activities stems from public choice theory, which gives us a positive model of what the government *will* do, under the presumption that the chief agents act to maximize individual utility rather than social welfare. According to this theory, politicians do not seek to maximize efficiency but rather to maximize their own chances of getting reelected, and individuals use governments to maximize their real income via the creation of protected market positions and the direct provision of services and transfers.

Public policies designed to benefit powerful interest groups will not necessarily be inefficient. Indeed, these groups would have a potentially larger slice of the pie to capture if the Pareto frontier were reached. As one extreme example, the economy might operate with perfect efficiency, and poll taxes could then be imposed on some and transferred to others. However, the allocation of resources resulting from public choice politics often is inefficient, for the following reasons.

First, in a context of imperfect information, people may not know the degree and direction of redistribution that is occurring. If well-defined groups know that they are "losers," they are more likely to mobilize and foment opposition to existing policies; therefore, the "gainers" benefit from perpetuating a "veil of ignorance." Suppose that efficient transfers are also more obvious (for example, transfers in cash are more transparent than those in kind). In that case, efficiency imposes cost to the "gainers" by reducing the amount they will potentially be able to extract, and they are therefore likely to choose inefficient mechanisms. Most commonly, some private goods may be publicly provided and oversupplied because they benefit a politically influential group of people in a nonobvious way.

Second, and closely related to the first reason, imperfect information and uncertainty also surround the relationship between the tax structure and the bundle of public services provided. While these may be interdependent components of a long-term political equilibrium, they may appear independent of each other in the short term. In that case, some newly demanded public goods, merit goods, or quasi-public goods with large benefits will be undersupplied because their benefits accrue to widely dispersed, less influential individuals, and it is uncertain whether the tax burden of these groups will eventually be adjusted upward commensurately with their benefits. Similarly, some goods will be oversupplied because their chief beneficiaries are politically powerful if taxes are regarded as fixed.

Third, the real costs of publicly produced private goods may be above minimal levels because government imposes costs of bureaucracy and red tape (in part as a substitute for the profit motive), often lacks competitive pressures for internal efficiency (perhaps because politicians reap a surplus from monopolistic provision), and uses distortionary tax financing.

Fourth, the diversion of entrepreneurial energies toward extracting a surplus from public agencies rather than toward productivity-enhancing market activities also impedes private-sector efficiency and growth. Thus, not only are public resources misallocated, but private resources are misallocated as well, as a consequence of these rent-seeking activities.

The resulting distribution of real income will depend upon political power as well as market power. Political power, of course, will vary across societies and through time, depending on the size of different producer and consumer groups, the coalitions among them, and the long-term "rules of the game" that have been set up (through constitutions, for example) for allocating voting rights. Although we do not attempt to build a rigorous model of political power determination in this chapter, we do argue that the final distribution of real income is likely to be considered inequitable by standards that many people hold. For example, since producer groups are likely to be more concentrated and better organized than consumer groups and since upper- and middle-income groups are probably more articulate and politically active than poorer groups, public choice theory predicts that producer and upper-middle-class groups will benefit disproportionately from government policies.

This is not to say that there will be *no* redistribution to the poorer classes under public choice theory. In fact, we would expect to find some such redistribution on efficiency grounds because it makes everyone better off. For example, people voluntarily donate to beggars out of altruism and use the government as an efficient mechanism for transferring income to disadvantaged groups through welfare payments, disability compensation, and so on. Along similar lines, the extremes of poverty and socioeconomic immobility may raise fears of crime or revolution that will ultimately hurt the rich. Historically, the provision of certain merit goods to the poor (for example, basic education and unemployment and medical insurance) has been viewed as a particularly effective way of combating these problems.

Moreover, since there are more poor people than rich, the desire to constrain the popularity of opposition groups in a democracy leads to some distribution to lower-income groups on grounds of expediency. Out-of-power groups must be appeased by giving them "just enough" to prevent opposition parties from gaining strong support. Expenditures on high-quantity, low-cost primary and secondary school systems are familiar examples. But "just enough" may not be very much. We argue that in many situations, perverse distributional criteria rather than efficiency or equity criteria determine the allocation of government funds, and these criteria imply large benefits to powerful upper-income groups combined with small redistributions to the poor.

Social Choice About Social Services

The social service sector is an arena in which many of these forces play themselves out because it consists of a variety of quasi-public goods with different mixes of public and private benefits and different beneficiaries. The frequent designation of social services as "merit or externality-generating goods" provides ample justification for government intervention along welfare theory lines. Yet once this intervention begins, ostensibly to correct for market imperfections and benefit poor consumers, it is often seized by producer groups and the allocation of resources diverted to a more "private" service mix that predominantly benefits the rich, albeit in a somewhat disguised way, as public choice theory would predict. While the rhetoric stresses the importance of avoiding price rationing in order to provide access to the poor and thereby garner their support, alternative rationing mechanisms used by the government may be equally income biased. If this is the case, turning provision of these services over to the private sector, including the nonprofit sector, or reducing public expenditures on these services by greater reliance on user charges will not only encourage government to concentrate on the financing of goods with a larger "public" or "merit" component but will at the same time improve efficiency and combat poverty.

Empirical Examples

In this section we cite numerous examples, from developed and developing countries, that make it clear that allocations within the social service sector often disregard the tenets of welfare theory and instead fulfill the more pessimistic predictions of public choice theory. While these examples are not universal, they are very widespread. We also suggest the reallocations, involving a shift of some financing to private sources, that will increase efficiency and equity at the same time.

The efficiency and equity criteria discussed in the first section of this chapter and used by us in the second section deal mainly with the question of who *finances* quasi-public services. Another set of efficiency considerations deals with the questions of who *provides* these services and how much private choice and public controls are involved. Throughout this chapter we focus on the benefits of shifting some of the financing of quasi-public services to the private sector, irrespective of whether the private or public sector manages and provides the service. We also abstract from the possible links between financing and provision that can arise in the real world for institutional or political economy reasons. (For example, the amount raised via user charges may be greater if the provider retains control over the resources, private provision with partial public subsidy may be more sustainable politically than public provision with partial user charges, and public regulations may accompany public subsidies.)

Education

Education is a prime example of a quasi-public good, one that yields a combination of private and external (social) benefits. However, the mix of public and private benefits varies across educational products. In particular, primary and secondary education, which enhance basic literacy and numeric skills, probably provide larger externalities than undergraduate higher education and generally provide a larger social rate of return as well — an efficiency rationale for public spending. Specifically, the average rate of return in developing countries has been

estimated to be 24 percent at the primary level, 15 percent at
the secondary, and 13 percent at the higher education level
(Psacharopoulos, Tan, and Jimenez, 1986). Even if these rates
of return are upwardly biased by the absence of controls for student ability and school quality, the ranking of actual returns
across levels of education is probably correctly captured. Yet
many countries spend a disproportionate share of their total
educational budgets at the tertiary level. This is also the level
that heavily benefits upper-income groups. A large expenditure
is concentrated on a small number of advantaged students in
contrast to primary education, which disproportionately benefits the poor.

Public universities typically do not have price barriers to
entry. However, they have academic barriers, which are more
likely to be surmounted by high-income families whose children
complete primary school, attend a high-quality secondary school,
pay for after-school tutoring, and pass the entrance exam to the
prestigious public institution.

For example, Brazil spends only 9 percent of its public
education budget (including spending at the federal, state, and
local levels) on secondary education, but 23 percent on higher
education ($144 per student on the former and $2,536 on the
latter). Yet, 95 percent of all students at public universities come
from middle- and high-income families (World Bank, 1988).
In India, 19 percent of the total public educational budget is
spent on colleges and universities, while the majority of rural
children do not even finish primary school (Tan, 1989). In
Africa, 22 percent of the public educational budget is spent on
higher education, available to only 2 percent of the relevant age-
group. In Mexico, a person coming from a high-income family
is ten to twenty times more likely to attend a public university
than is an individual from a low-income family. In Costa Rica,
Chile, the Dominican Republic, and Uruguay the top-income
quintile receives more than 50 percent of higher education subsidies, while the bottom quintile receives less than 10 percent
(Winkler, 1988; Quintero, 1978; Petrei, 1987).

One of the most detailed studies of educational subsidies,
that for Colombia, showed that 60 percent of all higher educa-

tional subsidies are received by the top-income quintile, while only 6 percent goes to the bottom two quintiles, and these proportions are exactly reversed at the primary level. Overall, educational subsidy per household is approximately the same for all income groups. However, the rich receive most of their subsidies from attending a university, while the poor receive their educational subsidies at the primary level (Selowsky, 1979). Similarly, in Malaysia, 50 percent of postsecondary subsidies are received by the top quintile and 10 percent by the bottom two quintiles, the mirror image of the distribution pattern at the primary level (Meerman, 1979).

Within higher education there is an efficiency rationale for public funding of research and graduate training, whether at public or private institutions. These are the activities that yield externalities for society as a whole, that will not be funded privately. In addition, capital market failure may justify public funding for expensive scientific equipment and financial aid for low-income students. On the other hand, at the undergraduate level, private institutions and private funding of public institutions should be able to provide for instruction in the less-expensive labor-intensive fields (liberal arts, law, management) to middle- and upper-class students, where private benefits predominate and tuition can cover the costs.

Yet most public funds for higher education are spent on undergraduate instruction at public colleges and universities, and as just noted, most of these students come from middle- and upper-income families. Expenditures on research and graduate training in most developing countries are minuscule, and in only a few countries are student grants and loans specifically targeted at the poor (James, 1991; Levy, 1986; James and Benjamin, 1987). The beneficiaries of research are widely dispersed, and economically disadvantaged students are also likely to be politically disadvantaged, while middle-class parents clamor effectively for access to higher education for their children. Thus, this allocation of resources within higher education is more consistent with the pressure group predictions of public choice theory than with the efficiency or equity rationale of welfare theory.

A more efficient solution would delegate responsibility for undergraduate instruction to the fee-charging private sector, and fees would be charged at the small group of public institutions as well. The experience of many countries has shown that when the supply of public university slots is limited, private openings spring up to accommodate the excess demand. Public funds could then be reallocated to the primary and secondary levels or to research, scientific equipment, and financial aid for needy students at the higher level. Moreover, these funds could be awarded, on a competitive basis, to both public and private institutions. Indeed, elements of this pattern are found in countries such as Japan and Korea, which have thereby achieved high rates of educational attainment at low cost to the public treasury. In Korea, for example, only 9 percent of the public educational budget is spent at the higher level, but this is heavily supplemented by private resources from those who receive the private benefits.

The private provision of education is often criticized on grounds that it is income biased. However, as we have noted, public universities are also heavily income biased. In income-biased private sectors, the rich pay their own way, while in income-biased public sectors, they are subsidized by tax revenues that could more efficiently be spent in other ways. Moreover, to mitigate the distributional problem, private universities could be required to reserve some specified proportion of their student bodies for low-income students, and public student aid could also be provided for this purpose.

In countries where the private sector (often run by religious organizations) is also the elite, preferred sector (as in Peru, Ecuador, and Mexico, for instance), private institutions combine both academic and price barriers to entry and are therefore more income biased than public institutions (Levy, 1986; Winkler, 1988). In countries where the public sector is relatively elite and the private sector accommodates the large excess demand, however, academic barriers keep the poor out of public institutions, while price barriers restrict their access to private institutions. As a result, the two sectors are roughly equivalent in degree of income bias. For example, in Japan, where 90 percent of all undergraduates attend private colleges and universities, a student from a top-quintile family is roughly five times more likely to attend a university than is someone who comes from the bottom-income quintile in both sectors (James and Benjamin, 1987). We suspect that in a country such as Brazil, where public university slots are heavily rationed and most students attend private institutions, the public institutions are actually more income biased than private institutions.

In addition, analysis of higher education enrollment rates across twelve Asian countries showed these rates to be highest in countries with the largest private-sector share. Apparently, the constraints on quantity that stem from limited public resources are greater than those that stem from limited private resources. When the private sector is encouraged, private resources can be tapped. And since the poor are much more likely to have access to a large than to a small tertiary education sector, the distributional consequences are likely to be positive. We would predict that countries with large private sectors and high enrollment rates (for example, Brazil, Colombia, and Korea) also have high rates of participation by the poor. This shift of public/private responsibilities is not only efficient, it is equitable as well.

Health

In general, welfare economics criteria would dictate government expenditures to reduce communicable diseases, to carry out immunization campaigns and other preventive services, to improve the water supply, to spread information about life-styles that promote good health (for example, through anti-smoking and pro-nutrition campaigns), and to provide basic health services (a merit good) to (poorer) groups and (rural) regions that cannot support private medical services. Maternity and child care are particularly important examples of the latter since they affect the health of future generations, in which there should be a large social interest. It is probable that these services would raise health standards and reduce mortality in the most cost-effective manner because they would touch the lives of many people directly and through the externalities they would generate. Because these services have public-good characteristics and many of their beneficiaries are poor, they are not likely to be provided by the private market. Hence they are a logical candidate for public funding on efficiency grounds.

Nevertheless, in many countries, we observe relatively little public health money going to these cost-effective programs (where government intervention is warranted because of private market failure), and consequently population coverage is very limited. Instead, a large proportion of public health budgets is spent on hospitals, usually located in urban areas, even in countries where the vast majority of the population lives in rural areas, where there are high mortality rates caused by diseases that need not be treated in hospitals. In Bangladesh in 1986, hospitals consumed more than 80 percent of recurrent public health spending. In Brazil in 1982, 78 percent of public health funds were spent on high-technology hospital procedures (kidney dialysis, coronary bypass surgery, and Caesarian sections) for relatively small groups of urban patients, at least some of whom could afford to finance these services out of private medical insurance in fee-charging hospitals. In Zimbabwe, which has tried to make its health sector more egalitarian, two-thirds of the Ministry of Health expenditures are for hospital services, and 60 percent of these expenditures are absorbed by four hospitals in Harare. In Tanzania, which has made a special effort to improve rural clinics, 60 percent of the recurrent health budget was nevertheless spent on hospitals in 1983 and 1984 (Griffin, 1989; World Bank, 1988).

Government provision of hospital services is sometimes used as a justifiable alternative to health provision. One problem with this arrangement, however, is that once government undertakes the task of financing hospitals, a giant share of the public budget is absorbed (as in the examples just cited) because of the high cost of modern technology. Another problem is that these hospitals are (understandably) located in urban centers, and consequently they serve the urban middle class; superior public hospitals (for example, armed prison and social security hospitals) serve the elites; and the rural poor have much more limited access to health facilities.

Since hospital services are parceled out to their patients, they have a large private benefit component and could therefore be financed privately by middle- and upper-income groups, particularly those with access to insurance. However, government financing crowds out these private resources and also discourages the development of private insurance markets. Suppose, instead, that many public hospitals were turned over to private bodies, with fees covered by health insurance (which might be administered by the government but financed by premiums paid by the beneficiaries of their employers). Along similar lines, user charges could be instituted at the remaining public facilities. Public funds would then be freed up to provide the externality-generating health service noted above and also to subsidize health insurance for the poor — very likely bringing about a net improvement in health indicators.

Examples of countries with such systems are Zambia, where the university hospital at Lusaka is being turned into an institution that charges clients for services, with public funds thereby released to finance new maternal, child health, and family planning services; Zimbabwe, where a fee has been introduced for patients who bypass lower levels of the health system and those who want a private hospital room; and Gambia, where fees charged for drugs are turned over to village development councils for further health improvement (Akin, Birdsall, and de Ferranti, 1987). But privatization alone will not do the job unless public funds are deliberately reallocated. For example, in Brazil, about half of health care expenditures are private, many private hospitals do exist (70 percent of the total), and health maintenance organizations (HMOs) privately funded by workers and their employers are a rapidly growing urban phenomenon, thus demonstrating the viability of the market in health. Nevertheless, most of the public health funds are spent on expensive hospital procedures, with a large private benefit component for upper-income groups (World Bank, 1988).

Even if public funding continues, competition within the hospital sector and use of privately managed facilities might improve their cost-effectiveness. For example, costs declined when housekeeping and food services at public hospitals were contracted out to private firms in Jamaica. In Chile, increased reliance on private hospitals during the past decade was accompanied by a shift toward less expensive medical personnel (more nurses and midwives, fewer doctors), by structural changes to improve incentives, and by the targeting of government services toward primary health care and other services for the poor.

Moreover, if reliance on government funds has limited hospital expansion, access to private funds (including insurance reimbursement) may increase hospital services and thereby improve health indicators in a manner similar to the private-sector expansion in higher education described above. This occurred in the Philippines in the 1970s, and the greatest expansion of hospitals occurred in the most poorly served regions (Griffin, 1989). Access to private services for disadvantaged groups can be further encouraged by subsidizing facilities in low-income regions or by requiring hospitals to retain a specified proportion of their beds for charity patients.

The availability of medical insurance plays a key role in all these scenarios. Insurance, of course, raises the problem of moral hazard, hence overspending, which must be addressed or the efficiency gains just described will be wiped out. Indeed, uncontrolled private hospitals together with mandatory medical insurance may be the worst combination of all from this point of view. Common procedures for dealing with this problem are requiring co-insurance (for example, an annual deductible and/ or a copayment for each treatment), exempting small costs from coverage, paying hospitals on the basis of diagnosis rather than procedures, reviewing recommendations for surgery and unusually high surgical rates, and structuring in competition among insurance carriers — in general, greater reliance on market incentives to contain costs. At the same time, it must be recognized that cost escalation in the health field is a problem whose first-best solution has not yet been found in any country. Perhaps all that is possible is a second-best solution in which the burden does not fall on the public treasury or the lowest income groups in society.

In any event, the reallocation of public funds to public goods just described, together with a shift of responsibility for "private" services to the private sector, aided by privately financed medical insurance, holds out the promise of raising efficiency and health standards at the same time. The health gains should be particularly great for the poor. Once again, efficiency and equity seem to be complements rather than substitutes.

Social Security and Other Social Programs

Social security programs may be justified on efficiency grounds if the private savings discount rate exceeds the private, so that many people will not voluntarily save for their old age. Society may then make a collective decision requiring people to save to provide a minimum "safety net" for all. In order to provide the maximum of risk pooling, to avoid adverse selection, and to enable inflation insurance, the compulsory savings may be administered through a public social security program, as it is in most countries.

This "safety net" efficiency rationale for social security would dictate broad coverage, with benefits above subsistence levels but less than wages. The relationship between individual contributions and payouts would vary with life span (the insurance function), but the two would otherwise be closely related, unless redistribution was an explicit goal. If redistribution were desired, it would presumably be from rich to poor and not vice versa.

However, the pattern in some countries is quite different. In Brazil, for example, social security covers about half the population, mainly urban workers, and a high proportion (28 percent) of total benefits accrue to early retirees, many of whom are from upper-income groups and whose benefits are initially almost as high as their wages. (In time, the real value of benefits declines because of inflation.) As a result of these expenditures, in some recent years social security ran a deficit that had to be covered out of general tax revenues and it is in danger of doing so again (World Bank, 1988).

This is another instance where greater reliance on the private sector (personal saving and supplementary private pension plans for the small group of privileged early retirees) would relieve the pressure on the public treasury, permit "safety net" coverage for the masses, and hence be more efficient and equitable at the same time.

A similar pattern holds in housing, where public funds are sometimes (as in Brazil and the United States) used to subsidize construction or mortgage loans for middle-income housing, the benefits of which are largely private, while housing for the poor remains a major problem and the rental market is distorted by price controls. A reallocation of public funds to more public goods, while allowing the private market to operate freely to provide private goods such as middle-class housing and rental housing, is recommended on classical efficiency grounds and would also free up resources that could be used to benefit the poor.

Conclusion: Political Strategies

In this chapter we have argued for a policy that concentrates government funding on public goods and encourages the nonprofit and the for-profit market to do what it can do best: fund and produce private goods. A drift away from this policy in the social service sector of many developing countries in recent years has had, we believe, negative distributional as well as negative efficiency consequences. While efficiency and equity objectives do not always lead to the same set of actions, numerous examples suggest that the two do coincide in the education and health sectors of many countries today. These actions usually involve increased financial responsibilities for the private sector, both for-profit and nonprofit, combined with a reallocation of government funds within the public sector. In the absence of political change, however, the shift we are proposing will not be easy to accomplish because the current situation has come about precisely because people with political power have felt that they could benefit therefrom and will resist relinquishing the source of real income.

While these comments sound pessimistic, there are a few sources of hope. First, as discussed in the first section of this chapter, many of the inefficient and inequitable policies we have been discussing are stimulated and perpetuated by imperfect information. The "losers" do not always know how much they are losing, and the "winners" incur costs to hide information from the losers. Spreading more accurate information may then alter the feasible political equilibrium. Along similar lines, politicians do not know peoples' preferences or the intensity of those preferences with certainty. If politicians' perceptions of preferences are changed, the policies that they deem politically optimal will also change. Given the current fiscal crisis in many countries, politicians may be more willing to consider cost-effective reallocations.

In addition, the realignment of public and private responsibilities that we have been discussing constitutes a move toward efficiency. This move generates a productive surplus which can, at least theoretically, make everyone better off. If the surplus is distributed in such a way that there are more winners, including influential winners, than losers, this should help to offset the political resistance to change. The political strategy to follow, then, is one of slow increases in equity, with many groups benefitting but the poor benefitting most of all.

Finally, the power structure may be changed through the intervention of external actors such as local and international nonprofit nongovernmental organizations (NGOs), the World Bank, and other aid agencies—although the scope for action here is obviously limited.

Some examples of policies that might be adopted to facilitate change follow.

First, concerned internal and/or external actors could initiate a citizens' education campaign to make clear to lower-income groups that their needs are not being met and to the middle- and upper-income groups that if changes are not implemented, the country as a whole will face increasing costs, much of which they will have to pay. Examples of these costs are higher taxes, higher social security premiums, slower income growth, environmental problems, crime, and political instability.

Second, rather than withdrawing entirely from a service area (such as higher education or hospitals), governments should in many instances simply halt future expansion, leaving further increases in demand to be accommodated by the private sector. This too should minimize opposition among consumer groups.

Third, governments should be cautioned about starting up new service areas unless they meet a stringent public good test. It is easier not to start services than to cut off those already being provided. New social programs should be carefully scrutinized and should not be undertaken by the government unless it is clear that they (a) have a high social rate of return, (b) will not be undertaken by the private market, and (c) do not have perverse distributional effects.

Fourth, on the other hand, government spending should be encouraged for social services that yield a large public good component. If new spending is concentrated on public goods, the poor will automatically benefit even if they are not targeted. And since the rich also benefit they would be reluctant to oppose these programs, even though they prefer government spending on private services from which their benefits are larger.

Fifth, even where funding responsibility is retained by government, economies of competition may be attained if production and management responsibilities are shifted to the private sector (as in "contracting out" schemes, done on a competitive basis) or if market approaches are introduced into the public sector (as in voucher schemes, where funds follow students or patients within public institutions). These market elements should cut down on rents that often have a perverse distributional effect and should generate a surplus that can be spent in a more egalitarian manner. Once these possibilities are put on the agenda they may themselves generate new constitutions and coalitions (for example, from private sector organizations) that alter the political equilibrium. Agenda setting is thus a powerful tool.

Sixth, another way of economizing on costs, and thus permitting greater quantity for any given budget, is to give modest subsidies to NPOs that provide services to disadvantaged communities and are able to draw on donations of money, volunteer and quasi-volunteer labor. Perhaps more important, NPO advocacy groups might be used to play an important role as informational conduits to disadvantaged groups and as grassroots organizations that inform politicians of consumer preferences and stimulate the government to act. (This is the role NPOs play, for example, in Sweden, where they are built into the political process.) Thus, NPOs can help change the balance of political power, which is both a reason why some groups support them and why many influential groups oppose them.

References

Akin, J., Birdsall, N., and de Ferranti, D. *Financing Health in Developing Countries: An Agenda for Reform.* Washington, D.C.: World Bank, 1987.

Griffin, C. "Strengthening Health Services in Developing Countries Through the Private Sector." Draft report. Washington, D.C.: World Bank, 1989.

James, E. "Private Higher Education: The Philippines as a Prototype." *Higher Education,* 1991, *21,* 189–206.

James, E., and Benjamin, G. "Educational Distribution and Redistribution Through Education in Japan." *Journal of Human Resources,* 1987, *22,* 469–489.

Levy, D. *Higher Education and the State in Latin America.* Chicago: University of Chicago Press, 1986.

Meerman, J. *Public Expenditures in Malaysia: Who Benefits and Why.* New York: Oxford University Press, 1979.

Petrei, A. H. "El Gasto Publico Social y Suo Efectos Distributivos." Rio de Janeiro: ECIEL, 1987.

Psacharopoulos, G., Tan, J. P., and Jimenez, E. *Financing Education in Developing Countries: An Exploration of Policy Options.* Washington, D.C.: World Bank, 1986.

Quintero, H.J.L. "Metas de Igualdad y Efetos de Subsidio de la Educacion Superior Americana." *Revista del Centro de Estudios Efectivos,* 1978, 8.

Selowsky, M. *Who Benefits from Government Expenditure? A Case Study of Colombia.* Washington, D.C.: World Bank, 1979.

Tan, J. P. "Financing and Costs of Education in Asia." Draft report. Washington, D.C.: World Bank, 1989.

Winkler, D. "Efficiency and Equity in Latin American Higher Education." Draft report. Washington, D.C.: World Bank, 1988.

World Bank. "Brazil: Public Spending on Social Programs." Report No. 8147-BR (confidential draft). Oct. 30, 1988.

Local Governments
and the Independent Sector
in the Third World

There are certain things
I would not do if I were to start again.
One of them is the abolition of local government
and the other is the disbanding of local cooperatives.
We were impatient and ignorant.
— Julius Nyerere

Most of the indigenous development organizations founded in recent years in the Third World can be roughly divided into grass-roots organizations (GROs) and grass-roots support organizations (GRSOs). Grass-roots organizations have members and assist their own communities. Grass-roots support organizations are composed of paid professionals and assist communities other than their own by working with GROs. It is estimated that there are over 100,000 GROs and roughly 15,000 to 20,000 GRSOs in Asia, Africa, and Latin America, most of them organized since the early 1970s (Fisher, forthcoming). This chapter focuses on the relationships of these rapidly proliferating members of the independent sector to local, provincial, and state governments.

Beginning in the 1970s in Asia and Latin America and somewhat later in Africa, the availability of foreign assistance provided idealistic young professionals with an alternative to dead-end government jobs or migration to the developed countries. They were able, instead, to create thousands of GRSOs concerned with development, environment, the role of women, and primary health care. By working mainly through existing GROs, these professionals further stimulated organizational processes at the grass roots. GROs, however, have also become far more active on their own. Faced with the deterioration of their environment and the increasing impoverishment of the 1980s, they have organized horizontal networks among themselves. In some cases, they have created GRSOs from below by hiring their own expertise. GRSOs are also forming networks with each other as well as with GROs.

What will be the political impact of this organizational explosion? Although development organizations may have a long-term effect on macroeconomic and social development, their impact on political development is likely to be more direct since they represent a kind of nonpartisan political alternative or challenge to prevailing power monopolies. I have elsewhere (Fisher, forthcoming) defined political development as "an interactive public decision-making and learning process, based on power creation and dispersion, within and between governmental and nongovernmental groups. This process leads to increasing individual and group autonomy from below and more responsiveness from above." The purpose of discussing political development is not to argue that this process is inevitable given the growth of the independent sector. Rather, it is to enable the reader to recognize indicators of political development already occurring in some local spaces in the Third World because of the sector's rapid growth.

Because GROs and GRSOs are development organizations, they also embody the possibilities for mutual reinforcement between socioeconomic and political development. Through their influence on government policies, grass-roots support organizations interested in the environment, for example, can push governments toward environmentally sustainable development policies.

Decentralization

The theoretical focus of this discussion is decentralization, explored from both the governmental and independent sector perspectives. Although most scholars who discuss decentralization are genuinely interested in enhancing responsiveness and accountability to the local level and are not necessarily sympathetic to existing regimes, their discussions assume, almost exclusively, a governmental perspective (Rondinelli and Nellis, 1986). The underlying assumption in most of these discussions is that decentralization is, by definition, pushed down from above. Such discussions need to be juxtaposed with discussions of decentralization from the perspective of the independent sector because there is evidence that the interaction of local governments with GROs and GRSOs is creating new forms of local power at the local level. Interaction with the independent sector, in effect, allows local governments to assume new roles not being performed by national authorities. Looking at both the governmental and independent sector perspectives will clarify the interactive process of power dispersion and creation indicative of political development. It will also stimulate discussion of a process that may be planned or unplanned, active or reactive, with either government or the independent sector taking the initiative. Before proceeding with this discussion, however, two important definitional issues need to be explored.

As used here, the term *local government* includes all but national or federal governments. It may be that relationships between the independent sector and large provincial governments in India or Brazil more closely resemble this sector's relationships with national regimes or that decentralization from the provincial to the local level resembles national decentralization policies. Such distinctions, however, will have to await the results of more intensive field research. This discussion is based on the plausible assumption that local governments, whatever their size, are more susceptible to independent sector influence than are national regimes with more complex lobbying pressures from all sides.

A second, unresolved definitional issue is the distinction between local development associations (LDAs) and village or town government. Like other types of GROs (irrigators' associations or women's groups, for example), local development associations such as village councils and neighborhood improvement associations are usually considered part of the independent rather than the governmental sector. LDAs are membership organizations working to improve and develop their own communities. Only rarely are they recognized as the local authority by national, provincial, or even district governments.

On the other hand, LDAs are not an entirely new phenomenon in the Third World and may have evolved from the original governmental sector. Many of the tribal or village organizations that predated the development of local and national governments and functioned in their stead were eclipsed but not replaced as more "modern" forms of governance emerged. A historical study of a Peruvian highland community found that the members of local community organizations carried out thirty-seven major development projects, including the building of roads, schools, and irrigation ditches, between 1895 and 1967 (Fishel, 1979).

It is also true that LDAs can flourish where they assume quasi-governmental powers. Both squatter settlements and remote villages often lack official local governments, and local development associations fill the political vacuum. *Juntas de Vecinos* (neighborhood councils) in the Latin American squatter settlements often set aside land for public purposes during the invasion of unoccupied land and adjudicate disputes between residents (Fisher, 1984). In the Arab Republic of Yemen, the gradual assumption of a quasi-governmental role for LDAs has been officially sanctioned, even though they were created locally in response to the revolution of 1962 (Lutz, 1983).

Until such time as further research is done on LDAs, it probably makes sense to place them on the conceptual border between the independent and governmental sectors but to treat them as part of the independent sector for the purposes of this chapter since they interact with "official" local governments in many localities.

The Governmental Perspective: Forms of Decentralization

Rondinelli and Nellis (1986, p. 5) define decentralization as "the transfer of responsibility for planning, management, and the raising and allocation of resources from the central government and its agencies to field units of central government ministries or agencies, subordinate units or levels of government, semi-autonomous public authorities or corporations, areawide, regional or functional authorities, or *non-governmental private or voluntary organizations*" (italics added).

As a way of distinguishing between two major types of decentralization Uphoff (1986, p. 222) uses the matrix shown in Table 4.1.

Table 4.1. Centralization and Decentralization Alternatives.

Decision Makers Accountable:	Decision Makers Located:	
	CENTRALLY	DECENTRALLY
CENTRALLY	Centralization	Deconcentration
DECENTRALLY	Democratization	Devolution

Centralization and democratization are outside the scope of this chapter because decision makers are centrally located. Deconcentration, however, is a form of decentralization, even though local administrators remain centrally accountable. The following discussion of deconcentration to locally based administrators of a federal or national government can help clarify the more lengthy discussion of devolution that follows.

Deconcentration. Does relocating central decision makers to the provinces (deconcentration) have any impact at all? There are no simple answers, even to such a general question, nor are there generalizable differences between Asia, Africa, and Latin America. In Dharampur, India, a high rate of turnover and poor morale ultimately led to more effective deconcentration through service modules, and service modules in the barrios of Caracas streamlined the delivery of government service (Gupta, 1983; Gomez and Myers, 1983). Deconcentration has increased local community access to central resources in Morocco and, to some degree, in Algeria, Libya, and Tunisia (Rondinelli and Nellis, 1986). However, one Tunisian development project excluded local participation because local residents were supposedly represented by local party leaders and government administrators (Skinner, 1983, p. 146).

Nor is it clear whether deconcentration precludes devolution or makes it more likely. In India, according to Satia (1983), there is a "remarkably consistent view" that the job of the district-level administrators is to operate established facilities and procedures, not to survey local resources, including local institutions. Yet he also found local exceptions that could become more common with a little encouragement. As Tanzanian bureaucrats became more physically accessible to villagers, it became harder for them to avoid responding to questions in meetings (Maeda, 1983, p. 149).

Deconcentration can also provide increased space and more access points for the local independent sector. With the return to democracy in Chile, the government has established decentralized corporations to funnel loans and resources to indigenous communities. The system is headed by an anthropologist, with independent sector experience, who has been given a mandate to work closely with GRSOs (Wali, 1990, p. 20).

Because the evidence is scattered, however, international comparisons or even countrywide generalizations about the relationship of local administrative units of national governments to the independent sector are difficult at best. This research gap is perpetuated by the frequent tendency of those writing about development projects or processes to use the term *government* without clearly designating what level is involved. Given the complicated relationships among local governments, regional governments, local administration, GROs, and GRSOs, increased descriptive clarity would be very useful. Some GRSOs, for example, interact both with bureaucracies at the national level and with their local administrators at the local level. These interactions may have different results. In remote areas, GROs or GRSOs may have more influence on local administrators than do their governmental superiors in the capital.

Devolution, on the other hand, appears to be more powerful than deconcentration in terms of its impact on political development. Devolution differs from deconcentration in two important respects. First, it decentralizes accountability as well as the location of decision makers. Second, the devolution of power and responsibility may be pushed downward from higher levels of government or created, if not pulled down by the assumption of new powers by local governments, usually in conjunction with the independent sector.

The next part of this section is concerned with the impact of official devolution initiated by national governments. This is followed by a discussion of devolution initiated by GROs and GRSOs in relation to local government.

Devolution. Devolution initiated by national governments can be directed toward private enterprise (privatization), local governments, or the independent sector. Privatization will not be dealt with here; this discussion of governmental devolution will focus on devolution to local governments and to the independent sector.

Complicating the issue of devolution is the relationship between local governments and the independent sector. Official devolution to the independent sector may also strengthen local governments, just as devolution to local (including state or provincial) governments can lead indirectly to an increased role for the local independent sector.

Although authoritarian or dictatorial regimes are less likely to initiate devolutionary policies in the first place, there is little evidence linking the character of national regimes to the outcomes of devolutionary policies. A study of land reforms in sixteen countries found that the devolution of government responsibility to local organizations (governmental and nongovernmental) did not lead to the capture of benefits by local elites (Montgomery, 1972). In fact, the study concluded that the degree of benefits, measured in farmer income, participation, and tenure security, depended more on the active involvement of local organizations than on the previous degree of local inequality or the ideology of the national regime.

Nonetheless, devolution from national to local governments, like deconcentration, has variable results. In some cases it may actually strengthen local elites and lessen the potential impact of GROs and GRSOs on local policies. In Sudan, provincial councils and commissioners have been given the responsibility for nearly all public functions except national security, mail delivery, and foreign affairs. Since the councils grew out of the traditional rural chiefs left intact by the British, however, devolution has done little to open the political system to new players (Rondinelli and Nellis, 1986; Huntington, 1988, p. 90).

Observers of rural development have also noted the tendency for coalitions to develop between richer peasants active in local government and national government administrators. Local governments in India were elected and given community development functions by the central government in the 1960s. Yet devolution was not accompanied by any changes in the social and economic power structure. Panchayat elections became contests between elites (Tinker, 1968, p. 224). On the other hand, Adams's (1986) study of rural Egypt concludes that the lack of government resources can make official ties to local elites much less important.

Even if devolution to local governments strengthens local elites, moreover, the long-term results are not always predictable. Devolution of housing policy to city councils in Colombia varied from complete failure, where local elites used their new power to undermine a progressive mayor, to a major success, where local elites were civic minded and worked together successfully (Rothenberg, 1980).

Nor are the results of devolution always straightforward or easy to evaluate. Devolution of authority to the Tambon (subdistrict) governments in Thailand in the mid 1970s led to many accusations of corruption. Nonetheless, the $25,000 government grants led to many projects such as the digging of wells and building of roads that villagers can still identify. More important, the national government's Department of Community Development gained in competence and effectiveness as a result of this earlier initiative (Calavan, 1984, p. 236). By 1982, the department was supporting both local governments and GROs that were building libraries, roads, playgrounds, and medicine banks. It was also helping local groups make contacts with district and provincial officials.

Whether it is because local elites are not always as powerful as they appear or because devolution allows others to enter the local political arena, a number of studies have shown that turning over responsibility to local governments can increase local accountability as well as project efficiency (Hadden, 1980). Despite support from the Agency for International Development (AID), it was feared that the Egyptian government's Basic Village Service Project (BVSP) would move slowly because roads, sewage, and water projects were to be built by 480 local governments. Yet because the size of the tasks was kept manageable in each locality, BVSP was one of the few projects in Egypt to exceed the AID's implementation schedule. It built facilities worth more than $200 million, trained 5,000 project managers, and provided them with long-term practical experience (Uphoff, 1986, p. 223).

Even if devolution to local governments avoids capture by elites, it rarely includes the power to tax, and results may be less impressive without heavy outside financial support. In contrast, devolution to the independent sector can build effectively on local resources without necessarily requiring a major financial reform or commitment. In Nepal, bridge construction committees set up under local development associations built sixty-two bridges in four years with materials contributed by the national government. It is estimated that the total cost was one-fourth what it would have cost the government to do the job on its own (Uphoff, 1986, pp. 283–284). In Kwara State, Nigeria, "local self-help groups were able to raise [considerable funds] for health, education, and infrastructure projects, more than 90 percent of which came from local contributions and only about 8 percent from central or state governments" (Rondinelli and Nellis, 1986, p. 13).

Funding decisions that support the independent sector are being made in some countries, even though tax reform to strengthen local governments is still rare. In Tunisia and Pakistan, LDAs have been given a percentage of official taxes and have tended to perform better than local governments. The Ministry of Health in North Yemen gives grants to LDAs for constructing primary health care units, with the community contributing the balance of funds. In Oman, the village community development committees discuss possible projects with national government staff members, and responsibility and funding are then given to subcommittees of interested villagers. By the mid 1980s, the projects had reached 142 villages, and facilities constructed included wells, meeting halls, canals, and latrines (Uphoff, 1986, pp. 56, 249, 293).

Are there disadvantages for GROs in helping government implement development policies? It is true that LDAs, particularly village councils, have suffered from their identification and use by colonial regimes in Africa (Riggs, 1966; Hyden, 1983, p. 88). And village councils in Trinidad have been "subverted by the politics of welfare and patronage," according to Craig (1985, p. 191). However, Esman and Uphoff's (1984, p. 166) extensive literature search revealed that GROs are not "spoiled" by connections with governments and that those with no government connection at all did not perform any better. More important, they found that no locally established organization had become totally dominated by the government. Despite their problems, the Trinidadian councils represent "an undeniable potential case for popular participation in decision making and policy implementation at the local level. . . . [I]t is gratifying to record . . . the subtler aspects of the resistance from below to manipulation from above" (Craig, 1985, p. 191). Even neighborhood improvement organizations originally created by the Colombian government have become relatively autonomous (Fisher, 1984).

Officially sponsored devolution to the independent sector can also have a long-term influence on all levels of government. The *Delegado* system that links government to neighborhood associations in Mexico City has decreased the local power of the official Institutional Revolutionary Party (PRI), for example (Ward, 1981, p. 401). Officials of the Thai National Irrigation Association have shifted to a dramatically more participatory style through working with local farmer groups (Calavan, 1985, p. 225). Lesotho's previous experience with the independent sector is producing a network for change that embodies elements of both deconcentration and devolution. The National Environmental Council makes policy and coordinates activities of the national ministries at the central and local levels, but it also works through GRSOs such as the Lesotho Planned Parenthood Association, the private sector, and district and village councils (*Brundtland Bulletin,* 1990, p. 35).

State, provincial, and even district governments can also initiate "devolution" of their powers to lower levels of local government or to the independent sector. BENFAM, the largest Brazilian GRSO concentrating on population and family planning has entered into a number of contracts with both state and municipal governments.

Devolution can also be initiated from below. Local governments with no access to the resources of the independent sector may, in theory, assume new functions in the absence of the effective provision of national governmental services. However, it is the relationships between local governments and the independent sector that have made this form of devolution more prevalent in the Third World in recent years.

The Perspective of the Independent Sector: Devolution

Both GROs and GRSOs consciously and unconsciously pursue a number of strategies that influence government policies at all levels and may also lead to de facto devolution of governmental power to the independent sector. The massive increase in numbers of GROs and GRSOs is rearranging relationships between governments and the independent sector. As GROs and GRSOs become important local political actors, governments respond by adapting, co-opting, repressing, or even learning from them. They are less and less able to remain unconcerned about the activities of the GROs and GRSOs.

How do GROs and GRSOs first make their presence known to governments? A common strategy is direct organized

pressure by GROs or federations of GROs. Geographical proximity to the sources of power pushes squatter neighborhood organizations in Latin America into making demands and obtaining city government consideration as well as services (Fisher,
1984). In Madya Pradesh, India, a federation of women's GROs
called Mahila Mandals began pressuring men as a group on
the connections between domestic violence and drinking and
then successfully pressured the state government to reduce the
hours of state-owned liquor stores (Sadrin, 1989). Activists from
the Chipko movement in India are getting tree seedlings from
state government foresters (Rush, 1990, p. 235).

Grass-roots support organizations are also becoming politically significant. A Colombian GRSO, CRIC, has had to
battle the drug trade, guerrillas, the Colombian military, and
lumber and pulp companies to help GROs regain their land and
fight conversion of native species into pine forests (Macdonald,
1987). As early as 1970 the Malayan Nature Society waged a
successful media campaign against the Pahang state government's plan to initiate logging in a national park (Rush, 1990,
p. 194). An anticorruption center in Maharashtra supported
by a GRO network of farmer and youth groups investigates com-
plaints and pursues them through the courts. Eighteen months
of litigation in one case resulted in the dismissal of forty local
revenue officers. Good relationships have been established with
the state government, and the center is training people in other
areas to set up similar programs (Ashoka, n.d.).

While well-organized political protest is an essential first
step in many areas, the catastrophic dimensions of the poverty-
environment-population crisis in the Third World provide opportunities for the independent sector to assume greater power
and responsibility. Local governments, realizing that GROs and
GRSOs may be their only significant resource, are often eager
for assistance and cooperation.

Nowhere is such "devolution by default" more obvious
than in the cities of Brazil. Because of runaway inflation and
federal government paralysis, municipal governments in Rio,
São Paulo, Boa Esperanca, Santa Catarina, and many others
are working directly with both neighborhood associations and

GRSOs. In São Paulo, 1,300 neighborhood associations work with municipal authorities. Over 400 of these are involved in community garden projects, and 20 regularly sell fruit and vegetables grown on community plots at low prices to almost 200,000 people. The Public Enterprise of the State of Rio de Janeiro uses *mutirao* (self-help) in close cooperation with neighborhood associations to provide sewage facilities, water ducts, garbage collection, and biogas production. Initial activities of the neighborhood associations with the Water and Sewer Company of Rio reached 150,000 people. In Parana, many cooperatives of the unemployed are producing basic commodities and working for both the city and the private sector (Sachs, 1986; Aveline, 1985). With technical support from Brazilian GRSOs "Something entirely new is being born . . . self-management, decentralization, local alternatives, mutual help, and popular participation" (Aveline, 1985, p. 22).

This is happening in many other countries as well, particularly in urban areas. Human Settlements of Zambia (HUZA) works closely with the Lusaka Urban District Council on housing policy and helps select advisers to elected ward councillors (Rakodi, 1990). Neighborhood organizations in Lima are now formally incorporated into urban planning processes on such key issues as water. They have assisted the municipality in fixing up old tenements and distributing more than 1,000 titles (Pease, 1988). Bintari, a GRSO in North Sumatra, has organized squatters in Medan into a waste collecting and recycling service for the city (Ashoka, 1985).

There is also evidence of power sharing between GRSOs and provincial or state governments. Officials in the state of Rajasthan, India, meet monthly with GRSO representatives to review social development programs (Sethi, 1983). The State Forestry Department in West Bengal works closely with GRSOs, universities, and the Ford Foundation in developing joint management policies for forest reserves and degraded lands (Rush, 1990). On the island of Mindinao in the Philippines, the Development of People Foundation was founded by a medical school to give students experience in providing health care to nearby villages. The DPF soon realized, however, that the local

GROs were not only concerned with health and worked to create an enabling environment for other local initiatives by cooperating with government agencies at various levels in a variety of sectors. A senior DPF representative is a member of the regional development council — normally restricted to government officials (Organization for Economic Cooperation and Development, 1988, p. 69). GRO and GRSO networks in Mexico are working with state agencies and using state resources (Arruda, 1985). Whether this constitutes devolution, co-optation, or some evolving mix of the two is unknown but worthy of further study.

A third form of influence leading to devolution occurs through changes in local government personnel. Landless organizations in Bangladesh are winning elections to union councils and have formed their own union-level federation of village-level associations. One GRO-GRSO network in India has elected forty local associates to village councils. "Most of these people belong to the poorer families and are not typical of the kind of people who normally get elected to village councils" (Seva Mandir, 1988–89, p. 28).

Representatives or "alumni" of the independent sector are also entering local governments as professionals. In Peru, one-third of local governments have former staff members of GRSOs as employees, in conjunction with GRO leaders being elected as mayors of municipalities. As the late Mario Padron, a leader of a major Peruvian GRSO noted in a 1989 interview, "DESCO has not worked very much with governments, preferring to concentrate on the grass roots, but now we are confronted with the grass roots becoming the local government. DESCO had prepared alternative municipal programs such as how to recycle sixty tons of garbage in Lima that are now really affecting what is implemented."

GRSOs are also helping to train local officials. The Arab Urban Development Institute in Saudi Arabia teaches municipal officials about waste management and urban renewal (Cordoba-Novion and Sachs, 1987, p. 9). In Gadchiroli, a destitute tribal area in Southeast Maharashtra, Abhay and Rani Bang organized a national group of medical professionals concerned with the social dimensions of health care; that group is working with Gad-chiroli government workers to show how the massive public health system can do a better job (Ashoka, n.d.).

A fourth tactic to promote devolution is for GRSOs to act as brokers between local communities and local governments. In Colombia, one-half of a national sample of GRSOs was able to persuade governments (national and local) to provide services to the poor in their region. A business foundation called Fundacion Carvajal has persuaded municipal governments to give tax breaks to the small businesses it supports. On the other hand, GRSOs in Colombia have faced repression where they severely threaten the local status quo (Smith, 1990).

Conclusions and Recommendations

Although deconcentration is initiated from above and may have a more positive impact on social and economic development than on political change, it can sometimes undermine vested interests that inhibit increased local political development. There are cases where the independent sector is unable to challenge successfully powerful national vested interests but where local administrators of the national governments sponsor potential challengers to local elites. This was true with Saemaul Undong in Korea, the Farmer's and Irrigator's Associations in Taiwan, and the Small Farmer's Development Groups in Nepal.

Devolution probably has a more consistently powerful impact on political development, especially when it is initiated from below. However, the evidence indicates that even devolution pushed down from above can improve socioeconomic results and empower local actors. This is especially true when devolution is directed to the independent sector.

The rapid growth of the independent sector is already having a significant if widely varying impact on political development at the national as well as the local government level. Nevertheless, there are some contrasts between the local and national levels that make this discussion of local governments particularly important. Repressive policies against GRSOs and even GROs are increasingly common at the national level, at least in some Asian and African countries. In contrast, at the local level, it is sometimes easier for GROs and their GRSO allies to overcome vested interests, particularly if they have the support of local governments dependent on their expertise and popular support. Just as elite control has traditionally been tied to the general weakness of local government in many Third World countries, so too does this weakness expose them to the influence of growing numbers of GROs and GRSOs intent on defeating these interests to promote sustainable local development. Esman and Uphoff (1984, p. 205) found a number of cases where local elites had been converted or overcome by effective grass-roots organizing.

Nongovernmental organizations are also having an impact on local governments. In many cases these new political actors have initiated processes that force changes in government attitudes and behaviors and advance the processes of power creation and dispersion, as well as interactive learning between the independent and local governmental sectors. Although African evidence is both more scattered and problematic than that from Asia and Latin America and despite the fact that many countries in the Middle East remain relatively untouched by this organizational explosion, political development is occurring in many local spaces in the Third World.

The impact of GROs and GRSOs can be considerable if they assume a role in development evaluation, visit other villages and projects, and exchange catalogues of community resources. Nothing prevents local and national governments from listening to and learning from the people who will benefit from development and those who are already working hard to help them succeed.

Reforms at the national and local governmental levels could support this process of political development being initiated by the independent sector. Decentralization pushed down from above could be strengthened by tax reform as well as increased cooperation with the independent sector. Bureaucrats could be trained to identify and support local skills and organizations without smothering them and could be rewarded for learning from failure (Calavan, 1984). Foreign donors could fund such national governmental initiatives as well as support mapping of local institutional resources in relation to sustainable development priorities.

Although GROs and GRSOs are forming horizontal and vertical linkages in many countries, well-targeted international support could also enhance the likelihood that the process would increasingly include local representatives of national governments, as well as local governments. Interactions between the independent sector and local governments could become a major focus of the generally recognized need in the development community to move from project to process. "Economic development and foreign aid policies should be founded on the process of building up local and provincial-level organizations, both public and private, to the principal end that political maturity will gradually take root" (Goodell, 1984, p. 278).

References

Adams, R. H. "Bureaucrats, Peasants and the Dominant Coalition: An Egyptian Case Study." *Journal of Development Studies,* 1986, *22* (2), 336–354.

Arruda, M. *The Role of Latin American Non-Governmental Organizations in the Perspective of Participatory Democracy.* Third International Consultation, Freedom from Hunger Campaign/Action for Development. Rome: FAO, Sept. 3–6, 1985.

Ashoka. "The Evidence: Profiles of Early Ashoka Fellows." Unpublished paper. 4200 North Nash Street, Arlington, Virginia, n.d.

Ashoka. "The New Fellows—Early 1985." *Changemakers,* 1985.

Aveline, C. "Communitarian Alternatives for Brazilian Crisis." ISDA dossier, No. 45, 1985, 19–22.

Brundtland Bulletin, March 1990, *7.*

Calavan, M. "Appropriate Administration: Creating a 'Space' Where Local Initiative and Voluntarism Can Grow." In R. Gorman (ed.), *Private Voluntary Organizations as Agents of Development.* Boulder, Colo.: Westview Press, 1984.

Cordoba-Novion, C., and Sachs, C. *Urban Self-Reliance Directory.* Nyon, Switzerland: International Foundation for Development Alternatives, 1987.

Craig, S. "Political Patronage and Community Resistance: Village Councils in Trinidad and Tobago." In P. I. Gomes (ed.), *Rural Development in the Caribbean.* New York: St. Martin's Press, 1985.

Esman, M. J., and Uphoff, N. T. *Local Organizations: Intermediaries in Local Development.* Ithaca, N.Y.: Cornell University Press, 1984.

Fishel, J. T. "Political Participation in a Peruvian Highland District." In M. A. Seligson and J. A. Booth (eds.), *Political Participation in Latin America,* vol. 2. New York: Holmes and Meier, 1979.

Fisher, J. "Development from Below: Neighborhood Improvement Associations in the Latin American Squatter Settlements." *Studies in Comparative International Development,* 1984, *19* (1), 61–85.

Fisher, J. *The Quiet Revolution: Development Organizations of the Third World,* forthcoming.

Gomez, H., and Myers, R. A. "The Service Module as a Social Development Technology." In D. Korten and F. Alfonso (eds.), *Bureaucracy and the Poor.* West Hartford, Conn.: Kumarian Press, 1983.

Goodell, G. "Political Development and Social Welfare: A Conservative Perspective." In D. Korten and R. Klaus (eds.), *People Centered Development.* West Hartford, Conn.: Kumarian Press, 1984.

Gupta, R. "The Poverty Trap: Lessons from Dharampur." In D. Korten and F. Alfonso (eds.), *Bureaucracy and the Poor.* West Hartford, Conn.: Kumarian Press, 1983.

Hadden, S. G. "Controlled Decentralization and Policy Implementation: The Case of Rural Electrification in Rajasthan." In M. Grindle (ed.), *Politics and Policy Implementation in the Third World.* Princeton, N.J.: Princeton University Press, 1980.

Huntington, R. "Memories of Development: The Rise and Fall of a Participatory Project Among the Dinka, 1977–1981." In

D. W. Attwood, T. C. Bruneu, and J. G. Galaty (eds.), *Power and Poverty: Development and Development Projects in the Third World.* Boulder, Colo.: Westview Press, 1988.

Hyden, G. *No Shortcuts to Progress: African Development Management in Perspective.* Berkeley: University of California Press, 1983.

Lutz, E. "Die 'Local Development Associations' in der Jemenitischen Arabischen Republik" ["The 'Local Development Associations' in the Arab Republic of Yemen"]. *Orient,* 1983, *24.*

Macdonald, T. "Grassroots Development: Not Just Organic Farming and Good Faith." *Cultural Survival Quarterly,* 1987, *1* (1), 41–45.

Maeda, J. "Creating National Structures for People Centered Agrarian Development." In D. Korten and F. Alfonso (eds.), *Bureaucracy and the Poor.* West Hartford, Conn.: Kumarian Press, 1983.

Montgomery, J. D. "The Allocation of Authority in Land Reform Programs: A Comparative Study of Administrative Process and Outputs." *Administrative Science Quarterly,* 1972, *17* (1), 62–75.

Organization for Economic Cooperation and Development. *Voluntary Aid for Development: The Role of Non-Governmental Organizations.* Paris: Organization for Economic Cooperation and Development, 1988.

Pease, G. H. "Experiencias de Democracia Local y ONGD." In M. Padron (ed.), *Las Organizaciones no gubernamentales en el Peru.* Lima: Centro de Estudios y Promocion del Desarrollo, 1988.

Rakodi, C. "After the Project Has Ended: The Role of a Non-Governmental Organization in Improving the Conditions of the Urban Poor in Lusaka." *Community Development Journal,* 1990, *25* (1), 9–20.

Riggs, F. W. "Bureaucrats and Political Development: A Paradoxical View." In J. L. Finkle and R. W. Gable (eds.), *Political Development and Social Change.* New York: Wiley, 1966.

Rondinelli, D. A., and Nellis, J. R. "Assessing Decentralization Policies in Developing Countries: The Case for Cautious Optimism." *Development Policy Review,* 1986, *4* (1), 3–23.

Rothenberg, I. F. "Administrative Decentralization and the Implementation of Housing Policy in Colombia." In M. Grindle (ed.), *Politics and Policy Implementation in the Third World.* Princeton, N.J.: Princeton University Press, 1980.

Rush, J. Draft manuscript for Asia Society conference, 1990.

Sachs, C. "*Mutirao* in Brazil: Initiatives for Self-Reliance." *Development,* 1986, *4,* 65–70.

Sadrin, M. Talk given at the fourth conference of the Association for Women in Development, Washington, D.C., Nov. 17–19, 1989.

Satia, J. K. "Developmental Tasks and Middle Management Roles in Rural Development." In D. Korten and F. Alfonso (eds.), *Bureaucracy and the Poor.* West Hartford, Conn.: Kumarian Press, 1983.

Sethi, H. "Development Is Not a Politically Neutral Task." *Ceres,* 1983, *16* (3), 19–22.

Seva Mandir. Annual Report 1988–89. Udaipur, India.

Skinner, R. J. "Community Participation: Its Scope and Organization." In R. J. Skinner and M. J. Rodell (eds.), *People, Poverty and Shelter.* London and New York: Methuen, 1983.

Smith, B. H. *More Than Altruism: The Politics of Private Foreign Aid.* Princeton, N.J.: Princeton University Press, 1990.

Tinker, H. "Local Government and Politics, and Political and Social Theory in India." In M. J. Swartz (ed.), *Local Level Politics: Social and Cultural Perspectives.* Chicago: Aldine, 1968.

Uphoff, N. *Local Institutional Development: An Analytical Sourcebook with Cases.* West Hartford, Conn.: Kumarian Press, 1986.

Wali, A. "Living with the Land: Ethnicity and Development in Chile." *Grassroots Development,* 1990, *14* (9), 12–20.

Ward, P. "Political Pressure for Urban Services: The Response of Two Mexico City Administrations." *Development and Change,* 1981, *12,* 379–407.

Privatization in the Personal Social Services in the United Kingdom, the Netherlands, and Italy

This is the first account of the background, rationale, design, and some preliminary findings of a three-country study of trends and issues in government–nonprofit organization relationships, particularly those concerning funding in the personal social services (PSS).

Background

Since the mid 1970s there has been an astonishing upsurge of public interest in North America and Western Europe on the role of nonprofit organizations (NPOs) as an alternative to government in the provision of quasi-public services. Although the relationship between the state and voluntary associations is deeply rooted in history and, since de Tocqueville, in political theory, there has probably been more public discussion and research on the role of the voluntary sector in the last decade than in the previous fifty years. For example, a recent inventory of research since 1980 lists almost two thousand studies on the non-profit sector in the United States and in Europe (Anheier, 1986). Within the last few years, a dozen or more scholarly books have been published. In the last decade, six new research centers have been established in the United States and one at the London School of Economics, two new scholarly journals have been launched, and international conferences for researchers on NPOs have been held biennially since 1987.

What accounts for all this activity? Two related trends may explain this resurgence of interest, both of which are a response to the "crisis of the welfare state" after its unprecedented expansion during the last twenty-five years. The first is ideological, and as part of the effort to halt the expansion of the welfare state, there has been a rediscovery of the special virtues of voluntarism by both the right and the left. Voluntary organizations have come to be viewed as a bulwark against further governmental intervention or at least as an alternative to it if not a substitute for it. Some look upon the sector nostalgically, as a means of recovering a lost sense of community through voluntarism, self-help, and other forms of citizen participation (Janowitz, 1976; Hadley and Hatch, 1981). Hence, there is widespread support for privatization, partnerships, and welfare pluralism in the United Kingdom, and for empowerment and co-production in the United States. Incidentally, the proponents of these policies often fail to distinguish between different types of voluntarism; between volunteers as unpaid staff and as peer self-help; between mutual aid associations and neighborhood or community-based organizations, and service bureaucracies staffed by professionals. This confusion reflects the continuing absence of an accepted definition and typology of voluntary organizations except perhaps as "tax exempt entities" with a social purpose.

Related to ideology, but more instrumental, is the convergence of three policy trends conducive to the greater utilization of NPOs to implement public policy. They are governmental decentralization, deinstitutionalization, and the more selective targeting of services to specific needy groups. Thus, even though the welfare state may be perceived as being "dismantled," "in retreat," or "at an impasse"—at least, its growth has slowed—an entity called "the contract state" has rapidly emerged as NPOs have been used to deliver PSS to an evergrowing clientele for whom there is governmental responsibility. For example, the needy elderly, the mentally ill and retarded, the physically handicapped, and abused or neglected children may receive PSS such as day or institutional care, counseling, rehabilitation services, and so on. Through its grants, subsidies, and fee-for-service payments, the state has everywhere become a *partner, patron,* or *purchaser* of services for NPOs whose number increases each year. In fact, there is no country today where there is a substantial voluntary sector that is not dependent on governmental support to a greater or lesser degree (James, 1989). In the United States, governmental funds have become a more important source of revenue for NPOs than all private giving combined (Salamon, 1987). Similarly, in the United Kingdom, despite the slowdown and cutbacks in public expenditures since 1975, statutory fees and grants have been the fastest-growing source of voluntary sector income, almost doubling in amount and as a percentage of total income in the last fifteen years (Knapp and Saxon-Harrold, 1989).

The increased interdependency of government and the voluntary sector is recognized in the popular concept of a mixed economy, a pervasive and complex mingling of public and private funds and functions, producing quangos and paragovernmental organizations, with the consequent blurring of the traditional boundaries between the state, the market, and the "independent" or third sector (Hood and Schuppert, 1988).

In their separation of public financing from service provision, welfare states vary greatly in their dependence on NPOs. The Netherlands, where voluntary organizations are the primary service delivery system, stands at one end of a continuum; the government allocates 70 percent of the GNP, but it directly controls only 10 percent. Sweden, where practically no nongovernmental organizations are used—although some are subsidized for purposes of advocacy—stands at the other end. Closer to the Netherlands is Germany, where well over half of the social services are subsidized by government but provided by NPOs, some of which are indistinguishable from conglomerates or cartels. Other countries with similar patterns are Italy, Belgium, and Austria. Britain and Switzerland are closer to Sweden because of the dominance of their statutory systems, while France and Canada stand between them and the United States.

In each country, the particular division of responsibility between government and NPOs is not formalized but reflects a distinctive history and sociopolitical context. Yet they all share a basic perception of NPOs, which are expected to be innovative and flexible, to protect particularistic interests, to promote citizen participation, and to meet needs not met by government (Kramer, 1987, p. 241).

Generally, there is growing interdependence between the NPOs and the departments of central and local government that are involved in fiscal and, in varying degree, planning, coordinating, regulatory, legal, and political relationships. At the same time, there is enormous variation in these interorganizational relationships, few of which are standardized or even formalized. Of greater importance to NPOs than to government, such expenditures rarely exceed 3 percent of their budgets. Typically, there is coexistence and accommodation between them, with infrequent collaboration of partnerships but relatively little competition or conflict. Contrary to the conventional wisdom, there seem to be few successful attempts of the state to control, regulate, monitor, evaluate, or press for greater accountability. (These generalizations are based on a summary of papers from fourteen countries presented at the International Conference on Voluntarism, Nongovernmental Organizations, and Public Policy, held in Jerusalem, May 22–24, 1989.)

Despite the variations in their reliance on NPOs, all welfare states in the advanced industrial countries have encountered similar problems in their PSS: spiraling costs, over- or underuse, fragmentation of services, and other obstacles to access, planning, and coordination (Kahn and Kamerman, 1981).

At the same time, curiously, the standards of quality—insofar as we have data other than expenditures—do not seem to be markedly different in the Netherlands, Sweden, former West Germany, and Switzerland. This suggests that legal "ownership" of an organization may not be as important as organizational variables such as size, structure, degree of formalization, type of staff, and the like. *How* a service is delivered may be more important than *who* delivers it.

Although the blurring of the boundaries between the public and the private is widely acknowledged (Bozeman, 1987), there are still no generally accepted concepts, models, or theories to describe and explain this process of interpenetration of the state by the market and the voluntary sector (Streek and Schmitter, 1985). Instead, there are numerous labels such as the "new political economy," "welfare pluralism," and "shadow state"; "third-party government," "nonprofit federalism," and the "franchise state" in the United States; "indirect public administration" in Finland, Germany, and Denmark; and the "social economy" in France.

Rationale for a Comparative Study of NPOs in Western Europe

Most of the debate about the future of the welfare state and the desirability of NPOs as a means of privatizing the PSS is predominantly ideological and impressionistic. There is little empirical data on the trends, patterns, and consequences in different countries of utilizing NPOs as private, public service providers of various forms of social care (Knapp and others, 1990; Leat and others, 1986). Because NPOs have facilitated the expansion of the welfare state and are likely to assume a larger role in the provision of welfare services in the future, it is important to know what can be expected from them. Answers to questions such as the following would be desirable: Why are NPOs funded by government? To what extent are they more effective and cost-efficient instruments for the delivery of social services? Are NPOs, as is widely believed, more flexible, less bureaucractic, and more accessible to their clientele? What are the effects of governmental funding on NPO independence, advocacy, and accountability? On their governance and management? On the use of volunteers, and on organizational goals and priorities? Finally, what are some of the major consequences of public funding of NPOs for the governmental agency, for the service delivery system, and for consumers?

A cross-national study is particularly well suited to infuse the social policy debate about privatization with empirical data about the experience of three Western European countries with different patterns of relationships between government and NPOs. For example, the Netherlands is a classic prototype of privatization, with the longest post-World War II history of virtually 100 percent governmental subsidy of its 3,500 NPOs or "PIs" (private initiatives). Originally under the auspices of religio-political blocs (*zuilen*), they have become increasingly professionalized, bureaucratized, secularized, and the object of governmental pressures for greater coordination, efficiency, and accountability (Brenton, 1985). More reliance on NPOs instead of government, or "welfare pluralism," has been urged in England, where the local authority is the primary social service provider. A recently published white paper proposes major changes in organizational roles and urges the local authority to contract with NPOs for service delivery (National Council for Voluntary Organisations, 1989). The Dutch experience is cited by both supporters and opponents of a greater role for NPOs, but neither side has much evidence. In Italy, a latecomer to these issues, the relationship between government and NPOs has been changing rapidly, reflecting the rapidly growing number of voluntary associations, the shifting power relations between the Catholic church and the state, and the strong desire for regional and local independence. NPOs are seen as the basis for a new social policy in Italy, but there is concern about the capabilities and the preservation of their identity and autonomy if they become dependent on government support (Ascoli, 1987; Pasquinelli, 1987).

The current research has a macro and a micro dimension; only the former is the subject of this chapter, which analyzes some of the recent trends and issues in NPO-government relationships in the PSS, particularly as they concern funding in England, the Netherlands, and Italy. On the micro or interorganizational level, in each country there are in process case studies of a comparable sample of twenty national NPOs serving the physically and mentally handicapped; findings will be presented in future publications. [The research in the Netherlands is being conducted in collaboration with the Nederlands Instituut voor Maatschappelijk Werk Onderzoek (NIMAWO) with Willem Melief; in Italy, in cooperation with the Istituto per la Ricerca Sociale with Sergio Pasquinelli. In England, the project was assisted by the Centre for Voluntary Organisation, Dr. David Biliis, director, in the London School of Economics and Political Science. The three-country project was part of the Western European Regional Research Program of the Fulbright Commission for 1989–90.]

Some Preliminary Findings Concerning Trends and Issues in Government-NPO Relations

In all three countries — England, the Netherlands, and Italy — the decade of the eighties was one of significant change and growth in the number of NPOs of all types and in the size of their income from governmental sources. For example, UK estimates show aggregate increases in real income of 200 percent, with statutory fees and grants constituting the fastest-growing source of revenue, rising from about one-third in 1975 to two-thirds in 1987. Using a broader sample of voluntary organizations, there was a tenfold increase in grants from the Department of Health and Social Security from 1976–77 to 1985–86 (Knapp and others, 1990). The magnitude of growth in total and statutory income is also evident in the cohort of the twenty national agencies in the study whose payments and/or grants from government increased fivefold within the decade.

In all three countries, the necessity for reducing governmental expenditures was associated with the renewed interest in the voluntary sector; that is, this seemed to be the "real" reason — if there was a primary cause — with the ideology of voluntarism providing the "good" reasons. While the growth rate of public spending on social welfare started to decline in 1976,

NPOs had prospered during the expansion of the welfare state during the 1960s and 1970s; they continued to grow in number and size even under the more restrictive economic conditions that prevailed in the 1980s. In England and in the Netherlands, NPOs flourished under both Labor and then Conservative governments.

A second notable trend in these countries was an ongoing policy debate reevaluating the respective roles of government and NPOs. In contrast to the 1970s, when national commissions in many countries reviewed the prevailing division of responsibility, a similar process in the last decade was related to new public fiscal policies and the election of Conservative governments. Hence, the promotion of the virtues of the market, degovernmentalization, and privatization, as well as the search for greater efficiency and accountability. In England, this took the form of support for "welfare pluralism," a belief in the superiority of NPOs as service deliverers and the preference for contracting instead of grants-in-aid. In the Netherlands, where the social services were already privatized, the emphasis was on decentralization and deregulation. In Italy, where the NPOs were proliferating, there was interest in their serving as an alternative or substitute for government, not just as a supplement. This coincided with the development of a research interest in voluntary organizations for the first time (Pasquinelli, 1987). The following sections summarize some of the leading trends in each country.

The United Kingdom: Toward Privatization and a New Paradigm of the Welfare State

In the last fifteen or so years a series of remarkable developments have occurred in the voluntary sector, particularly among NPOs in the PSS. In addition to their increased number and growth in statutory income, other trends noted in a recent survey were the following: greater diversity in income sources, programs, and organizational complexity; enhanced advocacy; and more extensive media attention related to more professional fund raising, management, and use of marketing. There has been more involvement with government as reflected in proposed changes in charity law, in the introduction of tax concessions and payroll deductions, new requirements for residential care, and more joint projects and planning with local authorities (Knapp and Saxon-Harrold, 1989).

These changes should be viewed in the context of the emergence of a new, Conservative paradigm in the United Kingdom following an unprecedented and rapid succession of ten governmental reports and legislative initiatives since 1985. These involve major shifts in tax and income policy; in housing, education, and health; in the financing of local government; and in the delivery of PSS relating to community care. These changes represent a significant departure from a tradition of incrementalism and social reform, and they reverse expenditure trends of more than two decades (Glennester and others, 1989). The Thatcher government sought to break with the past in its determination to degovernmentalize the social services and other state enterprises (Le Grand and Robinson, 1984), replacing collective provision with more emphasis on voluntarism and charity. On the other hand, this reflected an ideology based upon a revival of nineteenth-century Liberalism in which reliance on market competition, individual responsibility, and private philanthropy replaces the role of the state. Other related nineteenth-century beliefs that have resurfaced include the residual philosophy of social welfare and its kin, the principle of subsidiarity; invidious stereotypes regarding the inherent virtues of voluntary organizations and the vices of government; and traditional fears about the dangers of government funding of voluntary organizations (Warner, 1894; Kramer, 1981).

Essentially, there is a lack of confidence in the ability of local government to directly provide cost-efficient services; rather, it is to be an enabler of voluntary and private provision, perhaps a monitor and regulator. As *Community Care: Agenda for Action* (1988) declares, "Local Authorities should be purchasers of care services and not monolithic providers." These proposed changes, set out in the white paper *Caring for People* (1989), went into effect in 1991; they give sweeping new powers to local authorities to support the voluntary and private sector but on different terms, namely, in the form of contracts, with their more explicit and rigorous criteria for funding (Demone and Gibelman, 1989; Kuttner and Martin, 1987). The increasingly uncertain environment of contracting will probably be more competitive, perhaps with a more active role for consumers, who may have more choices, but certainly with pressures on local government to function only as a funder and contract manager.

Throughout the 1990s, NPOs are likely to be viewed by the government as a substitute service provider or public agent; a preferred alternative rather than a supplement or complement to statutory provision, as set out in the earlier Wolfenden Report. Not long ago, the major concern of the voluntary sector was its declining role because statutory agencies had taken over so many PSS in the preceding decades. Now, in contrast, there is great unease because it may have an expanding role.

Different types of NPOs will, however, have different futures as they react in their own way to the "contract culture" that may emerge. For example, rate capping and the financial incentives for local authorities to divest themselves of residential facilities may be regarded as an opportunity to be seized by large national organizations, but as a dangerous threat to the survival of small, community-based organizations whose grants-in-aid may be eliminated or who may be unable or unwilling to compete for contracts because they cannot meet the requirements for greater specificity, accountability, and compliance with regulations. Then, too, local authorities also vary greatly, and depending on their history and politics, they may not be interested in "partnerships" with NPOs; some may be reluctant to invest resources in their development if, as is true in many communities, NPOs are too small and weak and lack the capacity to serve as contractees. Under these circumstances, local authorities may set up their own surrogates in the form of nonprofit trusts or limited companies or contract instead with the private sector. However NPOs may view contracting, it does change their relationship to local government: from supplicant-patron to supplier-purchaser, from asking for support to negotiating deals.

In some respects, it appears that the United Kingdom may move closer to the Dutch model, although for many this degree of privatization would represent a "worst case" scenario, particularly because of its anticipated constraints on equity, entitlement, and access (Kahn and Kamerman, 1981; National Council for Voluntary Organisations, 1989).

The 1990s, then, represent an unusual opportunity for researchers in the United Kingdom to study empirically the consequences of these new funding policies on the structure and roles of NPOs, the local authority social service departments, and the service delivery system and on consumers themselves. (Two independent studies of contracting in the personal social services in England are currently underway at the University of Birmingham's Institute of Local Government Studies and the Birmingham Settlement and at the Personal Social Services Research Unit of the University of Kent, Canterbury.)

The Netherlands: Decentralization and Restructuring

In the Netherlands, the relationship between government and NPOs is the reverse of the pattern in the United States, the United Kingdom, and most other European countries. A highly complex network of paragovernmental organizations, quangos, and voluntary nongovernmental organizations (PIs) almost completely financed by central government (Hood and Schuppert, 1980) provides virtually all health; education; PSS; housing, culture, and recreation services; mass media; transportation; and utilities.

Originating from the distinctive Dutch religiopolitical social structure, the division of responsibility between the state and NPOs has become part of the political debate only in the last decade. There had been mounting criticism of the lack of efficiency, coordination, and accountability since the mid 1970s, along with pressures from central government for mergers and elimination of duplicate services designed along sectarian lines. Formerly regarded as a virtual "prisoner of the PIs," the central government in the last few years has exerted an increasing measure of control over the PIs it funds. Culminating a long struggle, central government finally succeeded in 1989 in "hiving off" direct funding of the PSS to the municipal governments, as well as to the provincial governments for a small number of agencies that operate on a wider geographical basis.

The process of decentralization began slowly in the mid 1970s, when a precedent was established for municipal responsibility for certain social services for the handicapped if a PI agency was unwilling or unable to carry out the implementation of a facilities plan previously adopted. Another law was passed in 1984 giving additional resources to municipalities to provide more social services directly and not to have to rely exclusively on PIs. Subsequently, however, budget cuts by the central government reduced the incentive and the possibility of the municipalities taking a more active role in the direct provision of services.

Beginning in 1989, extensive local governmental discretion was, however, justified as a form of "deregulation" and is encouraged by block grants from central government to the municipalities, grants that may be allocated for any public purpose. (In this respect, the new Dutch pattern of financing is similar to what will evidently be the case in England, where designated funds or "ring fencing" was not proposed in the white paper on community care.) Among the motivations for this devolution of funding was the belief that it could lead to a reduction in expenditures for PSS, in addition to deflecting downward the political pressures of the PIs on the government. As a result, thousands of PIs that formerly received their annual subsidies directly from a ministry are now dependent on municipal or provincial government for funding on the basis of expenditure levels and criteria established by the central government.

This policy of decentralization has special—and confusing—implications for organizations serving the physically and mentally handicapped. Financing and supervision of services to the physically and mentally handicapped continue to be divided among five ministries. Although two ministries were combined in 1982 to create the Ministry of Welfare, Health, and Cultural Affairs (WVC), the two separate directorates still differ in their budgeting, financing, planning, policy-making processes, and relations to the municipalities, as well as in their ability to enforce compliance with standards. For example, all forms of institutional care for handicapped children and adults are the responsibility of the Health Directorate in WVC and receive social insurance funding, while the other social care services in the community are the responsibility of the municipal and provincial governments. Central government, however, has some control over the health services funded by social insurance, but it has no authority over the community-based PSS. Again, in sharp contrast to the situation in the United Kingdom, WVC has withdrawn from any direct control over the PSS except for allocations to the national agencies and restricts itself to support of research and development, service innovation, and professional development. Nevertheless, these latest changes have been criticized because they contribute little to more coherent funding, planning, and service delivery among the three levels of government and between health and welfare services. The Dutch system continues to fund organizations rather than individual needs, and there is still no single body in control or responsible for the whole process. It also seems to provide few incentives for the development of new or noninstitutional services on the part of the PIs.

In addition to the decentralization of funding, the government has also been able to accomplish another one of its longterm objectives, restructurization, by reducing the number of national organizations from ninety-five to thirty-five through mergers of formerly sectarian organizations, cessation of funding of organizations dominated by professionals and/or concerned primarily with planning, coordination or policy analysis, or other indirect service functions. In a series of unprecedented reorganizations and consolidation of organizations with similar purposes, the government exhibited a degree of power that few expected. After many years of domination by this "fifth power"—the national organizations—the government was able in the name of austerity and greater efficiency to mobilize sufficient pressure because of its control of funds to bring about these radical changes in the number, structure, and function of the national "roof" or "dome" organizations.

The corporatist character of the Dutch polity is illustrated in the government's determination to deal with one instead of three national organizations representing the disabled themselves. The government persisted for many years and ultimately was able in 1988 to bring about the establishment of a new Council of the Handicapped, consisting of a federation of sixty consumer organizations with advisory committees of provider organizations and professional associations. These "peak" associations or, as the Dutch refer to them, "dome" organizations are regularly consulted by the government when it is considering any legislation or formulating regulations that affect them.

In addition to decentralization and the devolution of funding authority to municipal and provincial governments, some deregulation, and the restructuring of national organizations, there were two other significant fiscal trends in the 1980s: (1) some retrenchment, for the first time, during 1981 and 1982; a no-growth budget for residential care during 1984, 1985, and 1986 and a transfer of 500 million guilder to community health and social care services; and (2) an accelerating trend since 1985 to shift from subsidies to inclusion of selected PSS in the social insurance programs of the Exceptional Medical Expenses Act (AWBZ). The latter now includes a wide array of institutional and other forms of care for the mentally handicapped. Because of its inclusion in the AWBZ for more than twenty-five years, mental handicap is defined as a medical condition, and it has been very difficult to shift funds from institutional care, the primary method of treatment, to various forms of community care.

In these ways, the Netherlands has evolved a corporatist system on the national level and a highly decentralized, pluralist pattern of PSS delivery in local communities. As in Sweden, advocacy organizations representing major service providers, consumers, and professionals have considerable influence on the policies of the national ministries on which they depend completely for their financial support. In practice this has meant that the primary sources of accountability and innovation are internal, residing mainly in the norms and incentives of professionals responsible for managing the PIs and providing the PSS.

Although the same neoconservative ideology is espoused in both Britain and the Netherlands, the political strategies were markedly different. In Britain, the Thatcher government sought to stimulate pluralism and competition but at the same time to reduce the powers of local government. In the Netherlands, on the other hand, the government had struggled for more than fifteen years to reduce the proliferation of PIs that they were more or less obligated to subsidize. Suffering from a surfeit of pluralism, subject to the multiple pressures of thousands of PIs and their national organizations, it was in the government's interest to decentralize funding and strengthen local government.

Italy: On the Threshold of a Partnership?

In the period from about 1977 to 1985, there was a very rapid increase in the number and variety of voluntary organizations in Italy. There is, of course, a long history of Catholic church sponsorship of health and welfare services in Italy. However, in 1977, after a century of persistent church-state conflict, most of the charities were put under municipal control. The growth of secular and local voluntary associations seems to have been inspired by the social ferment of the 1970s, which was marked by reforms in the laws pertaining to divorce and abortion, psychiatric care, public health, and drug abuse to name some of the most notable. There is extensive variability within and a high degree of autonomy between each level of government in Italy. As part of the country's strong drive toward decentralization, municipalities have been delegated responsibility for the PSS, with a historically weak central government providing most of the funding. Because the belief that the state must be the only social service provider is no longer accepted, many of the newer voluntary associations have obtained funds from provincial and local governments to offer a wide range of service programs for the physically and mentally handicapped.

There is, however, no policy either nationally or locally on the use of NPOs for public purposes. Decisions regarding financial support are made locally, usually on political and ideosyncratic grounds, reinforced by the prevailing, conventional beliefs about the special advantages of voluntary organizations over governmental organizations (that the former are more flexible, lest costly, less corrupt, and the like).

Under these circumstances, it is not surprising that most of the voluntary organizations have a comparatively low degree of bureaucratization and professionalization and that they are often regarded as amateurs by governmental officials. Yet the role of the voluntary agency as a new, third force in the debate about the future of the Italian welfare state has already emerged; it is perceived as a choice between a hands-off, laissez-faire government and an empowered, technocratic state system (Ascoli, 1986).

The type and frequency of contacts with government vary greatly, with Catholic organizations — and those in the more impoverished South — having far fewer contacts and being the least likely to receive public funding (Pasquinelli, 1987). The proportion of voluntary agencies' income derived from local government is much lower in Italy than in other European countries, but this may be due to the relative recency of these interorganizational relationships. For example, there is no Italian legislation pertaining to voluntary agencies or their tax exemption, although five current bills await discussion in Parliament. Yet there is already concern that more involvement with government might result in a loss of these agencies' distinctive identity. This is one of the signs that Italy may be on the threshold of an era of more intensive and frequent interaction between government and voluntary organizations for the implementation of public policy.

Conclusions

Influenced by similar ideological and pragmatic factors in an era of fiscal austerity, relationships between government and NPOs in the United Kingdom, the Netherlands, and Italy have changed, with increasing separation between funding and production of personal social services.

If the past is any indicator, the next phase of the welfare state will be characterized by an even greater use of NPOs as public service providers. Consequently, it is essential to learn more about these interorganizational relationships, how they actually work, and how to make them work better. Issues that need to be addressed pertain to autonomy, accountability, efficiency, and effectiveness.

Future research agendas should give more attention to international comparisons, on both the macro and micro levels, of the political economy of governmental funding of NPOs, the effects on the organizations involved, their strategies for dealing with interdependency, and the consequences of these policies on the service delivery system.

References

Anheier, H. K. *International Directory of Research on Nonprofit Organizations, Foundations and the Third Sector.* New Haven, Conn.: Institution for Social and Policy Studies, Program on Non-Profit Organizations, 1986.

Ascoli, V. "The Italian Welfare State: Between Incrementalism and Rationalism." In R. Friedmann, N. Gilbert, and M. Sherer (eds.), *Modern Welfare States.* Brighton, England: Wheatsheaf, 1987.

Bozeman, B. *All Organizations Are Public.* San Francisco: Jossey-Bass, 1987.

Brenton, M. *The Voluntary Sector in British Social Services.* London: Longman, 1985.

Caring for People — Community Care in the Next Decade and Beyond. White paper. London: HMSO 1989.

Community Care: Agenda for Action. The Griffiths Report. London: HMSO 1988.

Demone, H., and Gibelman, M. (eds.). *Services for Sale: Purchase of Service Contracting in Health and Human Services.* New Brunswick, N.J.: Rutgers University Press, 1989.

Glennester, H., and others. "New Enlightenment or New Leviathan?" Discussion Paper. Toyota-Suntory Programme on the Welfare State, London School of Economics and Political Science, 1989.

Hadley, R., and Hatch, S. *Social Welfare and the Failure of the State.* George Allen & Unwin, 1981.

Hood, C., and Schuppert, G. F. (eds.). *Delivering Public Services in Western Europe.* London: Sage, 1988.

James, E. (ed.). *The Nonprofit Sector in International Perspective: Studies in Cooperative Culture & Policy.* New York: Oxford University Press, 1989.

Janowitz, M. *Social Control of the Welfare State.* New York: Elsevier, 1976.

Kahn, A. J., and Kamerman, S. B. *Social Services in International Perspective: The Emergence of the Sixth System.* New Brunswick, N.J.: Rutgers University Press, 1981.

Knapp, M., and Saxon-Harrold, S. "The British Voluntary Sector." Discussion Paper 645, Personal Social Services Research Unit, University of Kent, Canterbury, July 1989.

Knapp, M., and others. "Public Funding, Nonprofit Production: Whose Welfare?" In H. K. Anheier and W. Seibel (eds.), *The Third Sector: Comparative Studies of Nonprofit Organizations.* Berlin: De Gruyter, 1990.

Kramer, R. *Voluntary Agencies in the Welfare State.* Berkeley: University of California Press, 1981.

Kramer, R. "Voluntary Agencies and the Personal Social Services." In W. W. Powell (ed.), *The Nonprofit Sector: A Research Handbook.* New Haven, Conn.: Yale University Press, 1987.

Kuttner, P., and Martin, L. *Purchase of Service Contracting.* Newbury Park, Calif.: Sage, 1987.

Leat, D., and others. *A Price Worth Paying? A Study of the Effects of Governmental Grant Aid to Voluntary Organizations.* London: Policy Studies Institute, 1986.

Le Grand, J., and Robinson, R. (eds.). *Privatization and the Welfare State.* London: George Allen & Unwin, 1984.

National Council for Voluntary Organisations. *The Contract Culture: The Challenge for Voluntary Organisations.* London: National Council for Voluntary Organizations, 1989.

Pasquinelli, S. "Voluntary and Public Agencies in the Welfare State: The Italian Case." In *Politics, Public Policy, and the Public Sector,* proceedings of the annual meeting of American Association of Voluntary Action Scholars, 1987.

Salamon, L. "Partners in Public Service: The Scope and Theory of Government-Nonprofit Relations." In W. M. Powell (ed.), *The Nonprofit Sector: A Research Handbook.* New Haven, Conn.: Yale University Press, 1987.

Streek, W., and Schmitter, R. "Community, Market, State, and Associations." In W. Streek and R. Schmitter (eds.), *Private Interest Government: Beyond Market and State.* London: Sage, 1985.

Warner, A. G. *American Charities: A Study in Philanthropy and Economics.* Boston, Mass.: Crowell, 1894.

Chapter 6

U.S. Corporate Philanthropy in South Africa, 1977–1989: The Impact of the Sullivan Signatories and Their Projects

In 1977, after the Soweto riots created intense pressure to disinvest from South Africa, U.S. multinationals joined in a cooperative effort to demonstrate that by their presence in that country they were not supporting apartheid but rather were helping blacks in South Africa. They were guided by the Sullivan Principles, which mandated a number of actions both in the workplace and outside the workplace, including the support of a variety of community development projects in the areas of housing, health, welfare, civic involvement, recreation, and assistance

Note: This research was supported by grants from the Fulbright Program, the Bunting Institute of Radcliffe College at Harvard University, the Center for the Study of Philanthropy at the City University of New York, and Rochester Institute of Technology.

to business owned by members of the black, colored, and Asian communities.[1] Between 1977 and 1989, U.S. companies in South Africa that have functioned under the auspices of the Sullivan Principles invested over $289 million in programs designed to improve the status of blacks in that country.[2]

This was the first time that external social forces effectively prescribed that corporations should engage themselves in a particular set of activities designed to achieve a social objective and should submit to social monitoring and public reporting.[3] The response of U.S. multinationals to domestic and international pressures to help bring about social change in South Africa provides a model for the development of corporate social monitoring systems that are now evolving as a guide to collective investor and consumer actions.[4]

Development of the Sullivan Principles

In the early 1970s General Motors was under special pressure to get out of South Africa as a result of Project GM, an effort by a group of lawyers and campus activists to "democratize the corporation" in 1970.[5] One demand was that the corporation withdraw from South Africa. A shareholders' resolution to this effect attracted little support, but the company did nominate a black clergyman from Philadelphia to sit on the board of directors. For five years this clergyman, Rev. Leon Sullivan, pressed General Motors to withdraw from South Africa.[6] Then he developed a unique system of corporate social monitoring to guide the U.S. companies in South Africa.

The Sullivan Principles, issued in March 1977, called on U.S. companies to follow these guidelines:

1. Nonsegregation of the races in all eating, comfort, and work facilities
2. Equal and fair employment practices for all employees
3. Equal pay for all employees doing equal or comparable work for the same period of time
4. Initiation of and development of training programs that will prepare, in substantial numbers, blacks and other non-

whites for supervisory, administrative, clerical, and technical jobs
5. Increasing the number of blacks and other non-whites in management and supervisory positions
6. Improving the quality of employees' lives outside the work environment in such areas as housing, transportation, schooling, recreation and health facilities

It was the last of these principles that provided the basis for the philanthropic activities of U.S. corporations in South Africa in the areas of housing, health and welfare, civic activities, recreation, and assistance to black-, colored-, and Asian-owned business.

The original signatories to the Sullivan Principles included GM, Union Carbide, Ford, Otis Elevator, 3M, IBM, International Harvester, American Cyanamid, Citibank, Burroughs, Mobil, and Caltex. Signatories were obliged to provide reports in which they detailed the extent of their efforts to comply with each of these principles. For the first ten years of the program, the Reverend Sullivan guided the process by which goals were set and ratings were compiled. Although the evaluation process was conducted and the reports issued by Arthur D. Little, Inc., a consulting firm, the project depended on data collected under the auspices fof the Industry Support Unit.

Three ratings were possible: "making good progress," "making progress," and "needs to become more active." Each company was assigned to one of these categories on the basis of data submitted in response to a questionnaire that was then analyzed by Arthur D. Little, Inc. The "goalposts" changed each year, and companies were evaluated in comparison to the entire set of signatories. While individual companies knew of the areas in which they achieved high and low markings in the evaluation process, for the outside public, the only information released was each company's final rating. In the 1977–1978 period, reports were issued on a six-month basis; thereafter annual reports were issued, with data collected from July 1 of one calendar year to June 30 of the next calendar year.

The Sullivan Principles were controversial when they were introduced in South Africa. First, they obligated the companies to undertake certain activities that went beyond normal employee practices and in many cases breached existing legal restrictions or social conventions in South Africa. For example, the second principle called for the representation of employees in trade unions, legal for whites but not legal for blacks at the time the principles were introduced. Second, they required businesses to undertake activities *outside* the plant, activities that involved not only their workers but the larger black community as well. Third, they subjected a company's social performance to outside auditors, public reporting, and disclosure.

The Sullivan Principles evolved over the years, with the Reverend Sullivan providing several amplifications that emphasized actions he thought U.S. companies should be taking. His first amplification, issued in 1978, called on companies to desegregate the workplace and all its facilities immediately. The second amplification, issued in 1979, stated that companies should support changes in influx control laws to provide for the right of black migrant workers to normal family life. (Influx control was a system of restrictions that required blacks to remain outside urban areas unless they could present proof of employment by means of a pass issued by employers.) The third amplification, issued in 1982, required that companies have several items verified by their own accounting firms.

However, the fourth amplification, dating from 1985, constituted a significant expansion in the activities expected from signatories. This amplification required that companies press the South African government to end the laws and regulations that constituted apartheid. This last amplification was institutionalized as a seventh principle, "Working to eliminate laws and customs that impede social and political justice" in the Tenth Report, issued in December 1986.

This final amplification put signatories in the position of outright defiance of the South African government. Normally, multinationals operating abroad are expected to stay out of politics, to refrain from attempting to exert undue influence on the government, to respect local laws and customs. But U.S. companies in South Africa were being asked to lobby actively to create pressure for changing South African laws, to support those who challenged the government, and to take a public stand on social issues — in short, to become an instrument for social change.

By the middle of the 1980s the majority of the approximately 350 U.S. companies in South Africa had joined the Sullivan program as signatories, with the number subscribing to the principles increasing to 184 in 1986. Many of the companies who joined the program during this period did so as a direct result of pressure brought to bear by the U.S. Department of State as President Reagan's policy of constructive engagement came under increasingly critical scrutiny in the face of intense township unrest and the imposition of a state of emergency by the South African government. According to the U.S. Department of State, only twenty-nine U.S. companies in South Africa remained outside the Sullivan program at the end of 1986.

However, the number of U.S. companies in the Sullivan program decreased to ninety-two by June 30, 1987, to seventy (including one non-U.S. signatory) by June 30, 1988, and to sixty-four on June 30, 1989. This drop in numbers was due mainly to the withdrawal of U.S. companies from South Africa, with mergers and acquisitions also causing some reduction in numbers.

Accomplishments of the Sullivan Signatories

The accomplishments of the Sullivan companies, later called the Signatory Association, may be considered as including three types of activities. These projects tended to be located in communities where the intended beneficiaries lived, but in some cases they were directed to ongoing research projects aimed at influencing government policy. The second type of accomplishment was more directly related to workplace activities. Included here were desegregation of the workplace, providing job training for blacks, supporting the activities of trade unions, and purchasing goods from black-, colored-, and Asian-owned business. Corporate support of housing, while classified under Principle

6, could consist of company support for employee housing either in the form of mortgages (bonds, in South African terminology) or in signing leases or purchase contracts for those employees who wished to live in locations other than where they were officially allowed to reside. The third type of accomplishment of the Sullivan companies involved taking a stand on policy issues such as the recognition of black trade unions, which the U.S. companies supported in the late 1970s, and the collection of rents through company payrolls, which the U.S. companies opposed in the mid 1980s.

In considering the philanthropic role of the signatory companies, the emphasis is on the first type of accomplishment, that resulting from support of projects aimed at improving black life in communities. Total spending of the signatory companies from 1976 (reporting period ending in 1977) through 1987 was a reported total of $230 million, as noted above. In addition, for the one-year reporting period ending June 30, 1988, total contributions were reported at R86 million, or about $30 million, and for the reporting period ending June 30, 1989, total contributions were reported at R83, or about $29 million, bringing the overall total from 1976 to 1989 to approximately $289 million.

The largest area of corporate philanthropy, as stated in the Sullivan reports or the signatory reports, was education. Included here were scholarships (bursaries, in South African terminology), adopt-a-school programs, donation of equipment to selected schools, and support of schools with special purposes, such as multiracial private schools and the secondary school known as Pace, located in the midst of Soweto. Other recipients of corporate philanthropy through the Signatory Association included recreation and sports projects, self-improvement programs, legal assistance projects, and support of community organizations.

During the first five years that the Sullivan Principles were in effect, 1977–1982, the program was widely respected in the communities of South Africa that supported improving the status of blacks and ending apartheid. The support provided by the signatories for the recognition of black trade unions was appreciated as one important element in persuading the government to recognize their legitimacy. The signatories' example in desegregating the workplace was followed by most other South African business and by changes in the law that removed the requirement to provide separate lunchrooms and lavatories for the four officially designated racial groups.

The philanthropic activities of the Sullivan companies were accorded a fair amount of respect in South Africa precisely because of the credibility of the program, which came from the leadership role of the Sullivan companies in taking a position that apartheid must be ended. The programs supported by the companies were fairly new and undeveloped and thus during these early years were not demonstrably failing to meet their objectives. Furthermore, the political atmosphere was such that it was possible to imagine that the South African government was on its way to making significant concessions to the black majority.

Paradoxically, the recognition of black trade unions provided a means of black empowerment that in some ways made the workplace reforms of the Sullivan companies, and by extension their philanthropic activities, of less relevance for the empowerment of blacks in South Africa. A trade union statement (that of the Motor and Components Workers) delivered in 1982 expresses this viewpoint, which was still emerging at that time but which gained currency in the years that followed: "The Sullivan Code is a toothless package that can be applied by US corporations operating in SA with ease, and is just piecemeal reform that allows this cruel system of apartheid to survive."

The next five-year period, 1983–1988, was a time of disillusion and despair on the part of the black community. Heightened political demands were being made by anti-apartheid activists both inside and outside South Africa, culminating with the African National Congress's call to make the country ungovernable in 1985. U.S. multinationals faced renewed demands to isolate South Africa through withdrawal and also faced a declining economy. In 1985 international banks led by U.S. banks refused to roll over existing loans, and the investment of new capital from abroad effectively ceased.

The role of the U.S. companies in enabling the South African government to maintain power came under intensified criticism by social activists in both South Africa and the United States. In the religious community, in universities, and in the political system, companies faced growing mobilization to impose penalties on U.S. companies maintaining business ties in South Africa. These pressures took several forms, including portfolio divestment, which came to include the $90 billion portfolio of the state of California, as well as many other state, trade union, university, and foundation investment funds.

An even more effective mechanism was the selective purchase ordinances that instructed municipalities to give preference to companies without ties to South Africa. In 1986 Fluor Corporation lost a $2.5 million contract with Los Angeles because of its ties to South Africa. Eastman Kodak found its position as a vendor of copying machines to New York City jeopardized by the fact that military posts in South Africa sold Kodak film. Bell & Howell cited concern for its microfilm and textbook lines of business in the United States as its prime consideration in withdrawing from South Africa.

The Comprehensive Anti-Apartheid Act of 1986, enacted over President Reagan's veto, while not as sweeping as activists would have liked, signified the deep support for the anti-apartheid movement that had been kindled in the United States as a result of the deterioration of the political situation in South Africa, as demonstrated by the township unrest that erupted in South Africa in 1985 and the declaration of a state of emergency by the government in 1986.

One further pressure to withdraw from South Africa was imposed by the Tax Reform Bill of 1986, which withdrew foreign tax credits for corporations in South Africa. This was the reason given by Mobil Corporation for its withdrawal in 1988, an event regarded as highly significant since Mobil was the U.S. company that had the largest presence in South Africa in terms of investment and number of employees and since Mobil had provided leadership for the Signatory Support Association in the United States.

In June 1987, the Reverend Sullivan called on U.S. multinationals to withdraw from South Africa. He followed through on the threat he had made two years earlier when he had said that if apartheid had not been dismantled by May of 1987, he would call for U.S. corporations to leave South Africa. Ironically, although the Reverend Sullivan dissociated himself from the monitoring process, the Sullivan Principles were now institutionalized in the Comprehensive Anti-Apartheid Bill. This legislation required U.S. companies remaining in South Africa to be monitored either through the Sullivan Principles or by the U.S. Department of State, which developed a similar set of guidelines.

The Signatory Association, now reduced in numbers, had to devise a new way of managing its social responsibility programs and of reporting its companies' ratings to the public. For the next year the companies agreed to work with what had been called the Sullivan Principles but now were known as the Signatory Principles. Arthur D. Little, Inc., agreed to continue to perform the monitoring function. However, the task forces that the Sullivan companies had formed in South Africa to work on various aspects of the principles ceased to function. The number of companies working in the Signatory Association was greatly reduced, and many companies were reexamining the extent of their future support of the projects they had previously supported. Some companies even looked at the possibility of opting for State Department monitoring, since this would reduce costs and since the demands being made under this system were considerably less than the demands that had been made in recent years under the Sullivan system.

Research Questions Concerning the Sullivan System

Difficulties in Identifying Appropriate Projects

Within the Signatory Association itself the emphasis was on demonstrating the extent to which each company had contributed to projects that would serve to gain points on the forms used by the evaluators to determine the ratings of the companies. Little discernable effort was made to assess the effectiveness or the efficiency of the projects supported by the U.S. companies.

Since companies were evaluated on the basis of inputs to the process rather than outputs, there was no external pressure to demonstrate that the resources devoted to the program were accomplishing the goals for which they were intended. Indeed, the way the monitoring system operated meant that both the companies and the external authorities that did the monitoring were continually focused on current efforts. Little future planning was done and little assessment of past activities was made.

The fact that compliance was largely a function of contributions made as compared to total number of employees of a particular company meant that program administrators were inclined to overcontribute to certain causes favored by program evaluators. Supporting many small projects requires more administrative effort than does support of a single large project. In many cases the degree of financial commitment the U.S. companies made was in excess of the need of the recipients and in excess of their capacity to use the funds well.

However, because the evaluations were conducted annually and on reports covering only the past year's activity, corporations received no special recognition for the long-term effectiveness of projects they supported. Hence, even favored projects faced uncertainty regarding continuing support.

Because the monitoring process was conducted on a timetable that did not correspond to the corporate planning and budgeting cycle, many of the projects developed to satisfy the requirements of the Sullivan Principles were created outside the normal corporate process for project development, implementation, and evaluation. The problem of time compression, compounded by the yearly change in targets and goals, made it difficult for companies to administer programs effectively.

The Sullivan signatories were continually torn between supporting projects that conformed to corporate assumptions about process and function and supporting projects that may have been more rooted in the local community but were less impressive from the corporate point of view. Indigenous projects that were rooted in the communities that the corporations wished to aid and that had the support of well-respected leaders in those communities were often overlooked.

Unfortunately, indigenous leaders sometimes lack the sophisticated communication and presentation skills that impress corporate decision makers, while indigenous individuals who become accomplished masters of flip charts and slide shows may lack credibility in the local community. Ironically, the very skills that tend to impress visiting dignitaries can sometimes signify distance from the community that is the target of the aid. Useful as such skills might be for corporate purposes, they should not be confused with actual leadership skills that can mobilize community support in the targeted areas or can effectively manage programs aimed at indigenous communities. Corporations, by allowing themselves to be taken advantage of by individuals who were perceived in the black community as inept at best and confidence artists at worst, actually did a great deal to discredit themselves in the eyes of their intended beneficiaries.

Methodological and Procedural Problems

Methodological problems were also raised about the reports. Data that formed the basis of the reports were represented as being "independently verified," but in reality only a very few items were verified, leaving unverified such critical items as the number of job vacancies in various categories, the total number of people in trainee positions, and the total number of blacks in various occupational categories, all critical factors in assessing whether or not blacks were being prepared for and moved into jobs requiring higher skills. Even if no intentional distortion were present, this system left much room for individual interpretation and hence inconsistency.

Because companies were evaluated on the basis of a check-off system that covered a myriad of areas, efforts tended to become fragmented. The yearly evaluation led many companies to make short-term donations rather than more enduring investments in social responsibility projects (Paul, 1986).

As mentioned above, the emphasis was on inputs to the process—the amount of expenditure on each item in this wide variety of categories—rather than on outcome. Companies tended to "throw money" at projects rather than to engage in careful planning, implementation, and evaluation since their rating points came from the donations they made rather than through the effectiveness of their projects. The timing of the monitoring process exacerbated this problem. Companies had to spend their target amounts very quickly in order to be able to report that they had met objectives.

Although the companies were obliged as a part of the monitoring process to inform employees of their rating categories and to review the implementation of the principles with employee groups several times a year, many black employees felt that they were not consulted adequately. Then, too, they sometimes resented the fact that the system was managed by white American management consultants from Arthur D. Little, Inc. Were no blacks qualified to do the monitoring? Why were black South Africans not represented in the process? Their exclusion made the monitoring system seem a paternalistic gesture on the part of U.S. business.

Questions About Basic Objectives

Critics charged that despite the efforts of U.S. companies to improve working conditions for blacks, the basic reality was that blacks had the lowest-paying jobs, few chances for advancement, and far from equal opportunity in the workplace. Furthermore, the conditions of life for blacks under apartheid remained oppressive. Questions began to be raised about the goals of the Sullivan Principles: Did they merely serve to promote incremental change which would make the conditions of work life more tolerable for blacks in South Africa? Would they never lead to fundamental change in the distribution of power or the recognition of basic human rights? (Schmidt, 1985). Another issue was whether South African blacks themselves were represented in the process or whether the companies instead formulated goals and objectives mainly on the basis of what made sense in boardrooms in the United States, with little attention to the actual needs defined by the victims of apartheid (Beaty and Harari, 1987).

Pressures on U.S. Companies

The creation of the Sullivan Principles effectively forestalled demands for company withdrawal from South Africa at the end of the 1970s and the beginning of the 1980s. The claim of the U.S. companies that they were doing good in South Africa was congruent with President Reagan's policy of constructive engagement, which did not lose favor until the township unrest of 1985. However, after widespread violence did erupt after the declaration of a state of emergency by the South African government, and after the detention of thousands of blacks, the companies faced considerable pressure from various constituencies to play a more active role in pressing for social and political change in South Africa. It was at this time that the Reverend Sullivan announced that if apartheid were not abolished by May of 1987, he would call upon U.S. companies to withdraw from South Africa.

One issue confronting U.S. corporations was how they could effectively challenge the government of a host country. In most situations, the posture of U.S. companies was to respect and to conform with the laws of the nation where subsidiary operations were located. However, in this case they had historically skirted the edge of legality, not obeying all apartheid laws, at least in the workplace. Now they were being called upon to do more, to go farther in defying the law. Second, U.S. companies wondered how they could do more given the system of economic, social, and political oppression that existed in South Africa. The Sullivan Principles required that they train and promote more black managers and supervisors, but the educational system of South Africa systematically failed to prepare blacks for these positions.

Another issue was whether or not it was worthwhile to put the necessary time, managerial attention, and investment into the compliance effort. The Reverend Sullivan was threatening to withdraw his own moral authority from the monitoring system he had created, and that would leave U.S. companies more exposed to charges of exploitation and propping up an illegitimate government. A number of cities and states had adopted resolutions putting restrictions on purchasing from companies with operations in South Africa. Cities and states buy a wide range of products — copiers, fleets of vehicles, computers, software, swimming pool chemicals, generators, food products — so these purchasing restrictions were of considerable importance.

The divestment movement was gathering momentum. Colleges and universities, labor unions, church groups, and a number of pension funds were joining the act. Resolutions to rid portfolios of holdings in companies doing business in South Africa would not in themselves depress stock prices; after all, if ready buyers came along at the going price, divestment would have no impact on stock prices. However, this was one more consideration for managers of U.S. companies.

Finally, there was a growing cynicism on the part of corporate decision makers about the usefulness of the programs they had created. The South African program recipients did not appear to recognize their merit sufficiently, and critics in the United States continued to point out deficiencies in these efforts (Paul, 1989).

The case of the Coalition on Southern Africa (COSA) demonstrates the extent to which U.S. companies, in an attempt to serve their own political agenda through their philanthropic activity, subjected themselves to exploitation and criticism. COSA was an organization made up largely of black U.S. ministers who were chosen on the basis of their not being aligned with the sanctions movement. The group was established in 1986 and authorized to assist black South Africans and incidentally to speak out against the movement to impose more extensive sanctions on U.S. companies. For example, early in 1988 the *Washington Post* ran an editorial opposing the Rangel Amendment, which would have extended sanctions against South Africa. Ten days later a letter to the editor appeared from Richard L. Fisher, presiding bishop of the A.M.E. Zion church and president of the Coalition on Southern Africa, supporting the position taken in the editorial. According to the Reverend Fisher: "In fact, the withdrawal of U.S. companies will mean abandoning thousands of black South Africans. . . . The Coalition on Southern Africa . . . believes that the eradication of apartheid must *not* be accomplished at the expense of black South Africans. The Rangel Amendment would do just that, and we agree with the *Post* that it is a mistake" (1988, p. A20).

Further news on the coalition indicates that the generous funds provided by U.S. companies produced little of value to the intended recipients:

> An audit being prepared for the multinational donors to the Coalition on SA (COSA) showed that less than 5 percent of the $765,000 donated by these companies went on the philanthropic activities in SA for which it was intended. The only money definitely known to have reached SA was $20,000 sent to Winnie Mandela for completion of her Soweto mansion and for other purposes of her choosing. Another $10,000 may also have reached SA.
>
> COSA acting executive director Frank Kent said some money had been spent sending used clothes to black South Africans. At least one container load was delivered to the Soweto Civic Association for distribution. An eye witness said the clothes were sold off by a well-known shebeen owner. Donors included Mobil Oil, Caltex, Johnson & Johnson, Pfizer, Combustion Engineering and Control Data. A report that a senior official at Mobil Oil had approved the donation to Winnie Mandela was strongly denied by the company (*South African Journal of Labour Relations,* 1989, p. 100).

This example demonstrates the problems that are almost certain to arise when corporate philanthropy becomes confused with corporate political action, especially when highly organized and mobilized external constituencies exist. Although many individual projects brought credit to the signatory companies, especially in the early years of the program, in the end the corporations discredited themselves by attempting to use the philanthropic program for their own political ends.

What Can Be Learned from the Sullivan Principles

Corporate philanthropy aimed at Third World recipients should retain conventional standards of accountability and control. To fail to do so invites abuse and diminishes credibility.

Corporate philanthropy should aim to accomplish ends that can be accomplished given the background of the recipients. Over-investment and overstated goals will lead to failure and disappointment on the part of both the corporation and the recipients.

Projects should be funded with limited amounts of resources but with some assurance of continued funding provided the project shows some degree of success. Then the donor should be prepared to devote whatever continued attention is required to make sure that the project continues to show some degree of success.

Corporations should be prepared to participate in lengthy processes of consultation and deliberation with the recipient community because it is through such processes that community support and mobilization can be created.

The process of consultation and deliberation should be ongoing because crises will occur, external circumstances will intrude, and the organization will develop a political dynamic of its own. Corporations should accept the unfolding nature of philanthropy aimed at creating social change and not expect final chapters to be written prematurely.

People who appear to have leadership qualities in the corporate setting may not have support in the communities for which aid is intended. For this reason, corporations must foster deep and extensive ties with existing community leaders.

Corporate philanthropy will sometimes, perhaps often, have a political impact in a Third World setting. However, putting forward a particular political agenda *camouflaged* as corporate philanthropy will tend to discredit both donor and recipient.

In the case of U.S. multinationals in South Africa, as long as their political agenda was open and acknowledged, as it was with regard to challenging apartheid, the sincerity of the effort was not in serious question, although its effectiveness was often challenged because it depended on a process of incremental change and because many of the projects supported turned out to be of little value to recipients. However, in the 1986–1989 period, when the U.S. companies attempted to fight increased sanctions in the U.S. by setting up the Coalition on South Africa, they exposed themselves to mistrust and even ridicule. Such efforts should be avoided in the future.

Notes

1. These are the official racial categories imposed by the South African legal system.
2. Total taken from the inside front cover of *Business Against Apartheid,* Revised Edition, edited by the Communications Task Group of the Sullivan Signatory Companies and published by the Industry Support Unit, 150 East 42nd Street, New York, New York, and the Twelfth Report (1988) and Thirteenth Report (1989) on the signatory companies to the Statement of Principles for South Africa, also published by the Industry Support Unit.
3. The Nestle boycott over the sale of infant formula to Third World countries may be considered another such example. However, it targeted only one corporation rather than a whole set, and the external critics aimed mainly to achieve a change in marketing and distribution of the infant formula product rather than broader social change. Engaging in corporate philanthropy was not an important part of the demands made on Nestle.
4. For example, a number of investment funds now use a social screen. Moreover, the Ceres Project in Boston has developed a code of environmental principles known as the Valdez Code that can be used as a guide for investors. For consumers, the Council on Economic Priorities has published a guide for supermarket shoppers to use in choosing products that are produced by companies that exhibit selected values. The *Green Consumer's Guide* has achieved wide distribution in Great Britain. In Germany, the sign of the blue angel denotes environmentally desirable goods. In Canada, a line of "green products" is now being marketed.

5. This effort was mobilized by the Project for Corporate Responsibility, an offshoot of the Center for the Study of Responsive Law in Washington, D.C., headed by Ralph Nader.

6. Rev. Leon Sullivan recounted his involvement in pressuring General Motors to exit South Africa, then in developing the Sullivan Principles, at the Sixth National Conference on Business Ethics at the Center for Business Ethics, Bentley College, Waltham, Massachusetts, Oct. 10–11, 1985, in a talk entitled "The Role of Multinational Corporations in Helping to Bring About Change in South Africa."

References

Beaty, D., and Harari, O. "Divestment and Disinvestment from South Africa: A Reappraisal." *California Management Review,* 1987, *29,* 31–50.

Fischer, R. Letter to the Editor. *Washington Post,* Jan. 13, 1988, p. A20.

Motor and Component Workers Union of SA. Statement quoted in (Johannesburg) *Financial Mail,* Feb. 19, 1982, p. 790.

Paul, K. "The Inadequacy of Sullivan Reporting." *Business and Society Review,* 1986, *57,* 61–65.

Paul, K. "Corporate Social Monitoring in South Africa: A Decade of Achievement, An Uncertain Future." *Journal of Business Ethics,* 1989, *8,* 463–469.

Schmidt, E. *One Step in the Wrong Direction: An Analysis of the Sullivan Principles as a Strategy for Opposing Apartheid.* New York: Episcopal Churchpeople for a Free South Africa, 1985.

South African Journal of Labour Relations, 1989, *13* (2), 100.

Chapter 7

Private Philanthropy
as a Necessity in
Our Interdependent World:
A Japanese Perspective

It is somewhat difficult to discuss the ways and means of promoting Japanese private philanthropy or "good corporate citizenship" with an American audience when there is increasing criticism, at least in some quarters in the United States, of Japan's "Yen for Power," or alleged Japanese efforts toward the "buying of America." In an article in the *New Republic* John B. Judis (1990, p. 20) quotes TRW Vice President Pat Choate from his forthcoming book as indicating that Japanese government agencies, corporations, and foundations spent $150 million in 1988 and $250 million in 1989 trying to win American "hearts and minds." Judis goes on to argue that "some of this money is directed toward what the Japanese call 'good corporate citizenship,' but much of it is aimed at reinforcing the viewpoint of the Japanese in the raging American debate over trade and foreign investments." Judis also argues that "unlike the funds spent by Canada and Great Britain and their companies, the Japanese contribution is part of a concerted political and economic strategy."

Such arguments remind one of a communist-inspired campaign in Japan in the post-World War II years that alleged that American foundation activities were a part of a concerted CIA strategy. (In fact, the Ford Foundation-supported Center for South East Asian Studies at Kyoto University had to be closed for some years because of this campaign.) Nevertheless, this chapter's analysis of Japan's philanthropic development may be credible to critics of Japan's money power because the author has been a vocal critic of the direct involvement of Japanese government agencies in the activities of third-sector institutions in the United States and of the unwise and unsophisticated patterns of Japanese corporate giving abroad. Thus, although some points made by John Judis and other critics of Japan are acceptable, one major disagreement lies in their assessment of the effectiveness of such "influence buying." If Japan has been so successful in buying the hearts and minds of Americans with money, why have we seen increasingly vehement conflicts over trade and investment between the United States and Japan in recent years? It would seem that much of the Japanese money has been wasted or that its use has been counterproductive, if indeed Japan's alleged strategy was to buy its way into American hearts and minds.

The recent criticisms of Japan's money power that fail to make a clear distinction between undesirable Japanese spending in the United States and the much more sincere efforts of philanthropic organizations and corporations are more worrisome. The activities criticized include those sincere efforts that are designed to develop a closer working relationship among research and other third-sector institutions in the United States, Japan, and other countries and those designed to help cope with a growing number of global issues that include maintaining the global free trading system and sustaining the global environment.

This chapter will show that the development of private philanthropy and third-sector institutions will be essential if Japan is to forge a truly cooperative relationship and to establish mutual trust and respect with the people of America, as well as with people of other countries. In order for Japan, as a major economic power, to establish a close relationship with all the nations of the world and to be seen not as a disruptive element but as a constructive partner, it is imperative that it develop full-fledged nonprofit and nongovernmental institutions. Such institutions will facilitate Japan's management of the interdependent relationship with the United States and other nations.

In an examination of private philanthropy from a cross-cultural perspective, Japan offers an interesting case. Through its "economic miracle," Japan has accumulated substantial wealth in the postwar period—a precondition for the development of private philanthropy. In the course of this rapid economic development, Japan has changed from a monolithic society to a society characterized by pluralism—another precondition for the development of private philanthropy. Since becoming a major economic power, Japan has come to be expected to shoulder greater international responsibilities and has thus come to be seen as a donor nation. In this process, not only is official-level cooperation toward development assistance and such global issues as the environment and population control expected to show a dramatic increase, but private-level international philanthropic activities are expected to do so as well. While Japan has thus become a nation that is considered capable of developing major philanthropic activities, there are legitimate questions as to whether a non-Western nation, with a tradition of governmental bureaucratic dominance in matters of public interest, without a Judeo-Christian tradition, and without a long history of democracy, can develop the kind of private philanthropy that has been seen primarily in the Western nations of North America and Europe. Perhaps, we may more readily identify some domestic constraints to this kind of philanthropic development as compared with the nations with longer histories of philanthropic tradition. As the nations in East Asia and the Pacific Basin continue to gain greater economic strength in the coming years, a similar set of questions may be asked about them.

As indicated above, this chapter will argue that growing interdependence has helped provide a new impetus for the growth of private philanthropy in Japan, though this development is frustratingly slow. The chapter will also suggest that this philanthropic development and the strengthening of third-sector institutions is a prerequisite for Japan to undertake global responsibilities appropriate to its status as a major economic power. A corollary to this contention is that the evolution of modern Asian philanthropy may take a similar form and that this development will be critical to the development of an Asian regional community, as well as to the full integration of East and Southeast Asia into the global system.

External Factors in the Evolution of Private Philanthropy in Japan

As discussed in detail in a paper for the International Symposium on Organized Private Philanthropy in East and Southeast Asia held in Bangkok, Thailand, in August 1989 (Yamamoto and Amenomori, 1989), there is a fairly long history to Japanese private philanthropy. It is generally understood that the very first organized philanthropy in Japan developed at the end of the Edo period. In 1829, a lay association called the Akita Kan'on Ko (*kan'on* roughly means "gratitude") was established by a group of merchants who catered to the needs of the lord of the Akita domain. Despite the early exceptional cases, the shogunate and the provincial lords of the Edo period were the main providers in the public interest. Their efforts were inspired by principles of rule based on morality rather than force, and the public looked to officialdom to meet their emergency needs. The highly centralized system of governance made private charity or philanthropy rather exceptional. This tradition persisted throughout the Meiji period and continued until very recently. On the other hand, it can be argued that even from these earlier periods, considerations of Japan's external relationship played a major role in stimulating private donations or philanthropic activities, as discussed below.

Private Donations for Efforts to Catch Up with the West

With the Meiji Restoration, the concerted modernization drive to catch up with the West that was begun in 1868, Japan began to adopt modern European and American legal, sociopolitical, economic, and educational institutions. Modern nonprofit public-interest corporations (*koeki hojin*), such as incorporated foundations and associations, were founded after the promulgation of the Civil Code in 1896; the basic framework of private foundations today still draws on the principles set down in that code.

In the ensuing modernization period, some large philanthropic organizations were created, but they were expected to follow the national priorities of science and technology development, industrialization, and educational advancement, which would enable Japan to maintain its independence and to cope with the Western powers. It is interesting to note that until very recently, tax incentives were largely limited to organizations dedicated to the promotion of science, technology, and industrial development. Private individuals and corporate groups that had accumulated financial resources in the course of Japan's earlier industrialization process seemed to feel the need, voluntarily, through peer pressure, or even through outright government pressure, to rechannel some of their wealth toward such national priorities.

Even in the post-World War II period, special incentives were provided for the establishment of science/technology-oriented foundations through the introduction of the Experimental Research Corporation System (*shiken kenkyu hojin*) in 1962, which provides tax exemption for donations to designated foundations that are "legal persons, the main purpose of whose activities is either to engage in experimental research in science and technology" or to provide financial support to such institutions.

Earlier Trade Conflicts and the Growth
of International Philanthropic Activities

A number of new private foundations were established in the early 1970s, primarily by corporations or corporate groups, and it is generally recognized that the period of the 1970s was the beginning of "modern" organized private philanthropy in Japan. These foundations, unlike their predecessors, were less concerned with overall national goals and instead followed their own goals, either in a spirit of enlightened self-interest or in defense of immediate corporate interests. By this time, the public had begun to be aware of the unfavorable aspects of economic growth, and the problems of environmental destruction and pollution came suddenly to the forefront of national issues. Corporations came under severe popular attack for lacking a sense of social responsibility. At the same time, this period saw the emergence of serious conflicts between Japan and its trading partners, and the calls grew louder for Japan to carry a greater share of global social responsibilities.

We cannot clearly assert that external factors played a more dominant role than indigenous factors in stimulating the establishment of larger foundations during this period, such as the Toyota Foundation, the Mitsubishi Foundation, the Japan Securities Scholarship Foundation, the Hoso Bunka Foundation, and others, but it is notable that many of these foundations did have plans from the outset for international activities, particularly in neighboring Asian countries. They have had to face somewhat exaggerated expectations from overseas academic and research institutions in spite of the limited financial resources at their disposal, and very few of them have been actually able to undertake international grant making.

The early 1970s also witnessed the beginning of overseas corporate giving programs. Faced with growing criticism of Japan's external economic activities, major corporations and corporate groups came to recognize their own vital stake in the maintenance of favorable relationships and contacts with other countries, and they started making direct international grants.

A precursor of this trend was the Mitsubishi Group of thirty-six Mitsubishi companies that contributed $1 million dollars to Harvard University Law School for the establishment of a Chair of Japanese Law. As discussed in detail in the aforementioned paper, a substantial number of contributions to American universities, research institutions, museums, and so on have been made since that time. It can be pointed out here that there has been more direct giving by corporations to overseas organizations than by private foundations in Japan.

Increasing International Economic
Interdependence and the Growth of
Good Corporate Citizenship Programs
and Japanese Overseas Foundations

As has been indicated, perhaps too simplistically, exogenous factors have helped the development of Japanese private philanthropy. One distinct recent development along this line is the keen interest in becoming "good corporate citizens," a development that has become increasingly evident in the Japanese corporate community in recent years, particularly in the United States. With greater economic interdependence and with the rapid increase of direct investment by Japanese corporations in the United States, together with some backlash against the strong presence of Japanese corporations in American communities, Japanese corporate managers have started to pay more attention to the American philanthropic tradition in general and to corporate philanthropy in particular. For example, over 5,000 copies of a memorandum on a fall 1988 study mission to the United States on "good corporate citizenship" (jointly organized by the Japan Federation of Economic Organizations (Keidanren) and the Japan Center for International Exchange (JCIE), with the help of the Council on Foundations, have been sold, and the memorandum has been widely quoted in newspapers and journals (Keidanren, 1990). A follow-up international symposium in November 1989 in Tokyo had the participation of several leaders in corporate philanthropy in the United States, including David Rockefeller, Reynold Levy of the AT&T Foundation, Peter Hutchinson of Dayton Hudson, Jim Shannon of the Council on Foundations, Al Scallon of IBM, Martin Walsh of the United Way, Michael Howard of Levi Strauss, and Mary Beth Salerno of American Express, and drew over 200 high-level participants and substantial media coverage.

One encouraging development in this field is that following up on a series of Keidanren-sponsored activities designed to promote "good corporate citizenship," the Keidanren adopted a resolution to "make 1990 an inaugural year for Japanese corporate philanthropy" (Keidanren, 1990, p. 2). The Keidanren also decided to push forward a proposal made by Natsuaki Fusano, managing director of the Keidanren, at the November symposium to create a "One Percent Club." Mr. Fusano had led the aforementioned study mission in the fall of 1988 and is a key figure in the Keidanren's efforts to promote corporate philanthropy. It should be noted that the Keidanren, recognizing that Japanese corporate philanthropy lags substantially behind that of the United States and other advanced democracies, organized an affiliate organization called the Council for Better Corporate Citizenship, which is headed by Akio Morita, chairman of Sony Corporation. This organization initiated programs to promote good corporate citizenship among Japanese corporations operating in the United States. In this connection, a new proposal to provide tax incentives for Japanese corporate contributions abroad has been approved by the Japanese government. It is not precisely clear how this system will work, but it is understood that contributions to organizations in foreign communities by corporate headquarters in Japan will be tax deductible if such funds are channeled through designated public-interest corporations. It is further understood that two newly established organizations, one affiliated with the Keidanren-sponsored Council for Better Corporate Citizenship and the MITI-affiliated Association for Communication of Transcultural Study will function as the channels for these contributions.

It is difficult to obtain an accurate estimate of total corporate giving overseas, but one indication of the size and scope of Japanese corporate giving is found in the fund raising for overseas institutions coordinated by the Keidanren, which

amounted to about ¥1.2 billion in 1987. Another indication of
the increasing Japanese corporate contributions for overseas organizations is seen in funds channeled through the Japan Foundation. Between 1972 and 1988, total Japanese grants channeled
through the Japan Foundation amounted to ¥29.7 billion. As
will be discussed later, until very recently Japanese donors were
not eligible for tax deductions on donations to overseas institutions unless they were channeled through the Japan Foundation.

One distinct development reflecting the need to respond
to the socioeconomic needs of foreign communities where the
Japanese corporate presence is growing is the emergence of
foreign-based Japanese foundations, many of which are operated by indigenous board members and well-experienced professional staff. Those established in the United States include the
Matsushita Foundation, the Hitachi Foundation, the Toyota
USA Foundation, the Subaru of America Foundation, the Honda
America Foundation, and the Sony Foundation. In Southeast
Asia as well, several Japanese corporations have begun to set
up foundations. Among them are the NEC Foundation in the
Philippines, the Toyota Astra Foundation, the Asahi Glass Foundation of Thailand, and Yayasan Asahi Glass Indonesia. These
foundations, as established by Japanese corporations, especially
when administered by local staff members, seem able to respond
to the needs of the regional communities where they are based and
can thus implement "good corporate citizenship" more effectively.
To reinforce the importance of exogenous influence, it should
be pointed out that the Japanese foundations based in the United
States with professional American staff members have been playing a catalytic role in encouraging Japanese executives and employees to undertake more positive philanthropic activities and
also in encouraging Japanese top management to develop a better understanding of corporate philanthropy in general.

*The Growing Need for External Linkages
in Private-Sector Institutions and Greater
Recognition of Third-Sector Institutions*

As Japan has become a major actor in the international community, its participation in the international intellectual net-

work of joint studies and dialogue on international political and security affairs, as well as economic relations, has become vital. Even government bureaucrats are beginning to recognize the dearth of Japanese nonprofit and nongovernmental institutions as waves of overseas approaches have started coming from independent research institutions proposing collaborative projects. There are hardly an appropriate number of Japanese counterpart organizations to form collaborative relationships with this kind of institution in the United States and other countries.

Yet the Japanese government has long neglected to encourage the development of such institutions that would be able to deal with issues of international affairs and with the growing number of global problems. As mentioned above, tax incentives for contributions have been available only to donors for contributions to organizations designated as "experimental research corporations" (*shiken kenkyu hojin*), which originally included only those involved in scientific research and academic institutions. After concerted efforts on the part of some in the private sector, the tax code was amended in April 1988 in order to grant the same privileges enjoyed by organizations designed as "experimental research bodies" to organizations promoting "international understanding" in Japan and abroad. In August 1988, the Japan Center for International Exchange became the first organization to receive this privilege, an epochal development in Japanese philanthropy. Although such a privilege cannot be made available automatically and most of the "private institutions" that have subsequently been given this privilege are subsidiaries of government agencies and rely heavily on governmental subsidies, the International House of Japan, which is another truly nongovernmental and nonprofit institution, also received this status in December 1989 after difficult negotiations.

Possible Role of Private Philanthropy in the Management of Interdependent Relationships — Opportunities and Constraints

The previous section described how the growing international interdependence now facing Japan has helped the development of "private philanthropy" in Japan. One could argue that as in many other situations, Japan would not move on its own without some external leverage, pressures, or even "bashing." On the other hand, one could also argue that the Japanese have become more sensitive to the necessity of developing private philanthropy and third-sector institutions in the international context rather than in a purely domestic context and that it is easier to mobilize Japanese private funding for causes related to Japan's external relationship.

The arguments to be considered and tested (thus offering a research agenda) are these:

1. External leverage is useful in raising the consciousness of the need, which can lead to some action if that leverage is not imposed but invited from within and is culturally sensitive.
2. External philanthropic activities are likely to meet with fewer domestic constraints and thus have a better chance of advancement.
3. Domestic constraints to the development of full-fledged private philanthropy can eventually be overcome (although it may be a very long process) through international collaboration among philanthropic organizations and third-sector institutions, especially through personal networks and institutional linkages.
4. At least in the past, the major constraints to the development of full-fledged philanthropic activities in Japan have been the bureaucratic dominance over the private sector on matters related to the public interest on one hand and the primacy of economic gains and economic efficiency in Japanese corporate culture on the other.
5. As a corollary to the previous point, another major constraint is the tendency in Japan to fail to distinguish between philanthropy and public relations efforts, for which managers expect direct and immediate results.
6. The development of both private philanthropy and third-sector institutions is essential if Japan is to participate effectively in joint international efforts to deal with common global environmental problems and the maintenance and promotion of the international free trading system.

7. The successful management of international interdependence will require domestic structural adjustments or systemic changes to make Japanese society compatible with the international environment, and private philanthropy and third-sector institutions are essential in generating domestic debates (nonideological), eventually generating support for changes (not in a revolutionary way), and overcoming domestic opposition.

8. The development of private philanthropy is essential in the reorientation of Japanese priorities from the exclusive focus on economic gains toward a more value-oriented approach that will allow Japan to take a leadership role in the formation of its own value judgments rather than just respond or react to foreign pressures.

9. Growing international interdependence has given rise to chauvinistic nationalism in many of the advanced industrial democracies, as well as in developing nations; third-sector institutions will play an essential role in countering this trend.

10. As a corollary to the previous point, a tighter collaborative network of private philanthropic institutions and third-sector institutions will be essential to the promotion of international cooperation among all nations to counter tendencies toward a nationalism and ethnocentric emphasis on the differences in values.

The designated length of this chapter does not allow an exhaustive treatment of the above points but does allow a discussion of some of the major elements that are most closely related to the full-fledged development of Japanese philanthropy and of Japan's role in improving its increasingly interdependent relationship with the outside world. As already discussed, there has been a steady growth of private philanthropy in Japan in recent years, largely in response to the country's changing relationship with the external world. Nevertheless, some of the constraints inherent in traditional patterns of Japanese sociocultural dynamics remain in the way of these changes. Thus, while one can be encouraged by statistical and recently evident Japanese philanthropic development, the effectiveness of such philanthropy and further philanthropic development may be impeded by persisting domestic constraints.

Needed Domestic Structural Reforms

One major domestic constraint to the full-fledged development of private philanthropy and third-sector institutions in Japan is government attitudes toward such activities, which reflect the traditional view of the bureaucracy as the sole guardian of public interest in Japan and the effective agent for change. It is ironic that Japan's phenomenal economic development has brought about a corresponding pluralism, in which bureaucrats, who function most effectively when national goals are clearly defined and public consensus is behind them, cease to be the agents of change. Instead, today's bureaucrats tend to be the guardians of narrowly defined interest groups and thus often constrain the changes that have the potential to adversely affect those interest groups. For Japan to respond to the changing international environment and to be able to manage its growing interdependent relationships with other nations, many domestic structural reforms are needed. Although the hastiness and high-handedness of the American government and Congress in pushing Japan to go through the Structural Impediment Initiatives (SII) might exacerbate the U.S.-Japan bilateral relationship, many Japanese are actually agreeable to the requested changes to Japan's sociocultural context, albeit in a slightly longer term perspective. The development of Japan's third-sector institutions, buttressed by the broader support of private philanthropy, is essential to the promotion of "enlightened" and "internationalist" points of view to mobilize support in Japan for such changes.

Similarly, Japan's traditional orientation, which gives priority to economic growth and industrialization, inhibits the "enlightened self-interest" approaches characteristic of private philanthropy and nonprofit nongovernmental institutions. Some Japanese corporations fail to distinguish between philanthropic activities and those public relations activities done for quick results. Public relations firms and lobbyists in the United States have become keenly interested in the recent surge of interest in "good corporate citizenship" among Japanese corporations and are trying to offer assistance to them. Although such firms and lobbyists can be useful in many ways, it is much more desirable for Japanese corporations to collaborate with nonprofit intermediary organizations such as the United Way and community foundations.

In short, these constraints can be removed by the further development of private philanthropy, and we are thus faced with a "chicken or egg" situation. Nevertheless, as argued before, the widespread recognition that Japan has to go through certain changes in order to "survive" is encouraging. Growing domestic discontent with the present sociopolitical arrangements, manifested in steep land prices and a growing gap between the "haves" and "have-nots" (particularly in terms of real estate and stocks), may provide further impetus for domestic support for such substantial changes in Japanese society to make it more compatible with the international environment. It is notable that the word *internationalization* is used more often in Japan than in any other country; we may be able to infuse the notion that internationalization in the present context requires an increased "value orientation" so that Japan can adopt a more enlightened self-interest approach in its relationship with the world outside. Thus, coming back full circle, a private philanthropy that is oriented toward values and enlightened self-interest would help Japan manage its interdependent international relationship.

The Necessity of Enhancing International Philanthropic Cooperation

International collaboration of philanthropic and third-sector institutions could play a very effective role in escaping the aforementioned "chicken or egg" situation. In this connection, it should be pointed out that the need for "internationalization" is shared by other countries as well. "Structural impediments" are not unique to Japan; rather, they are a common phenomenon of advanced industrialized societies that are pluralistic in nature. The difficulties of undergoing these structural reforms are shared by the United States and other democratic nations because they, too, have many domestic interest groups. One major difference may be found in the fact that the United States has many third-sector institutions that generate domestic debate on alternative approaches to solving problems, though the seemingly monolithic tone of American debate on trade issues fails to emphasize American domestic difficulties and thus diverges from the shining model of the pluralism of American democracy.

In light of international interdependence and the domestic constraints to adjusting to this new situation to be found in many nations, it seems clear that close collaboration among philanthropic and third-sector institutions around the world will be essential. Together, they can create a sense of "international common cause" that will serve to stimulate domestic change and to promote international cooperation.

Conditions for and Approaches to the Promotion of International Philanthropic Cooperation

Although international philanthropic cooperation is highly desirable in the increasingly interdependent global community, this kind of cooperation among institutions and individuals with such diverse historical, cultural, sociopolitical, and economic backgrounds is not easily achieved. Thus far in the course of Japan's philanthropic development, the various exchange and collaborative programs have operated in conjunction with primarily European and North American foundations, and other third-sector institutions have had considerable impact, as is described in detail in the previously cited "Japanese Private Philanthropy in an Interdependent World" (Yamamoto and Amenomori, 1989). The following observations regarding the conditions and approaches that may effectively promote this international philanthropic cooperation are based on this experience. Again, these points are tentative in nature and should be further examined.

1. It should be recognized that certain human values and aspirations are commonly shared even by people of nations with different sociocultural backgrounds. Some arguments ex-

pressed in the United States that Japan does not share the same values as the United States and other Western nations do not help philanthropic cooperation.

2. As a corollary to the above point, cultural sensitivity on the part of those working to promote international philanthropic cooperation is essential. There may be differences in the patterns of philanthropic development of different nations and there may even be diverse manifestations of the philanthropic instinct within one culture.

3. Although the essential elements of private philanthropy, particularly its independence from governmental and corporate intervention and influence, should be emphasized, it should also be recognized that the patterns of the relationships between the philanthropic organizations and government and business may vary in different countries. One Japanese working in the foundation field argues that there can be more "gray areas" in the relationships that Japan's philanthropic organizations maintain with government and business, especially given the relatively brief history of organized philanthropy in Japan. This point would be an interesting subject for cross-cultural discussion, although it should be pointed out that Japanese corporations are more "scrupulous" in that the boards of corporate foundations have very few representatives of the parent corporation (perhaps because of governmental administrative guidance!).

4. Cooperation with philanthropic organizations in other countries would provide effective leverage toward assuring the integrity and independence of philanthropic organizations in the domestic context. It could be argued that cooperation with major American foundations, not necessarily exclusively financial, has been essential for the JCIE to maintain its independence from government and business. This was particularly true in its earlier stages of development.

5. In terms of international grant making and other forms of philanthropy, cooperation among indigenous philanthropic organizations is often essential. At the least, it is very effective. If philanthropic organizations of advanced nations seek the cooperation of those in developing nations, they will succeed in circumventing the accusations of "cultural impe-

rialism." Furthermore, as discussed in the previous section, prospective Japanese grant makers, both private and corporate, can find assistance and expertise in American intermediary organizations such as the United Way and community foundations.

6. To continue this train of thought, joint funding and other forms of cooperation between nations with longer histories of private philanthropy, such as the United States, and those emerging economic powers with less of a philanthropic tradition, such as Japan, can be useful for many different reasons. For example, if private foundations and corporations in Japan could collaborate on joint funding projects with their North American and European counterparts, the newer Japanese organizations would have the advantage of the experienced professional grant-making staff, and the grants would certainly be more effective. Through such joint activities, grant makers in Japan and other newly emerging economic powers would learn to develop their own expertise. Furthermore, in some cases the pooling of financial resources would have a greater impact.

7. As a corollary to the above point, the professional staff of North American and European foundations can be effective catalysts in mobilizing human and financial resources of emerging economic powers such as Japan. Such activities can obviously be enhanced by cooperation with the indigenous third-sector institutions or individuals, as discussed earlier. Professional staffing of organized philanthropies in advanced countries can play an essential role in the philanthropic development of other nations and thus in promoting international philanthropic cooperation.

8. The increasing number of international conferences and collaborative research efforts of private philanthropy is evidence of the need to promote international philanthropic cooperation. In order to maximize the effectiveness of these efforts and to avoid unproductive duplications, their purposes should be clearly defined. The goals of these conferences and research should include the following: (a) to provide contacts and promote a sense of a collegial relationship

among those working in private philanthropy around the world; (b) to understand the philanthropic traditions of other countries and cultures, facilitating culturally sensitive cooperation; (c) to learn from each other while working toward a clearer understanding of one's own shortcomings in order to improve future philanthropic efforts; and (d) to provide opportunities for collaborative activities through the exchange of information and the joint exploration of pertinent issues. In addition to some of the current international efforts, such as conferences, seminars, and research projects, sustained support services such as organized networking of regional and national foundation information centers should be considered. The Foundation Center in the United States, with a long history, has recently been joined by both the European Foundation Center and the Foundation Library Center of Japan. Although they are in different stages of development and translation admittedly poses some constraints, the potential for closer cooperation should be explored.

9. International research activities should be action oriented, focusing on some area of possible philanthropic cooperation, such as our global environmental problems or the promotion of arms control. Undoubtedly, these conferences and joint research projects would still serve the purpose of "comparing notes" on the most effective ways to administrate grantmaking and other philanthropic programs while working toward the resolution of regional and global problems.

10. Networking efforts among foundations and philanthropic organizations in the Asia Pacific region, like those initiated by Barnett Baron, presently of Save the Children, provide interesting models for regional cooperation. Such Asia-Pacific-wide international philanthropic collaboration can provide valuable underpinnings for the emerging Pacific Basin community by forging noncommercial and nonpolitical links. Eventually, such regional philanthropic cooperation will allow interregional cooperation, providing a stronger base for global networking and international private philanthropy.

Japan's philanthropic development provides an interesting case for studies and discussions. Some of the points raised in this chapter written from the Japanese perspective may spur future international research and discussion. Above all, some may regard Japan's philanthropic development as a standard against which to judge whether Japan will become a truly great nation, with constructive contributions to the global community, or rather a destructive influence. The development of private philanthropy is a necessary condition for Japan to be able to proceed through needed domestic changes, including the promotion of internationalism as opposed to the possible rise of chauvinistic nationalism, the reorientation toward values as guidance for its international conduct, and the development of effective collaborative relationships with philanthropic institutions and individuals engaged in such activities in order to build strong underpinnings for a cohesive relationship with the nations of the world. Without philanthropic development, Japan's capacity to manage its interdependent relationship with the outside world will be substantially undermined. The challenge is enormous, but if there is any chance for Japan to develop its own private philanthropic tradition, it will be achieved only with the international cooperation of those institutions and people engaged in philanthropic activities in other nations.

References

Judis, J. B. "The Japanese Megaphone." *New Republic,* Jan. 22, 1990, p. 20.

Keidanren. "Keidanren no Katsudo Shishin" [Policy guidelines for Keidanren's (1990) activities]. Memorandum, Jan. 8, 1990, p. 2.

Yamamoto, T., and Amenomori, T. *Japanese Private Philanthropy in an Interdependent World.* Tokyo: Japan Center for International Exchange, 1989.

Part Two

Modern
Developed Democracies

Part Two examines trends in Australia, Israel, and nations in Western Europe. The push toward decentralization, privatization, and reduced governmental responsibilities has helped to highlight the role of the nonprofit sector here, as elsewhere. Each of the chapters in this section emphasizes the relationship between nonprofit organizations and government in the provision of health, education, and welfare services. The section also highlights the diversity of responses among these various democracies to relations between nonprofit organizations and government.

Susan Saxon-Harrold, in Chapter Eight, provides an overview of the voluntary sector in Great Britain from 1975

145

through 1989. She documents the move toward the privatization of welfare services through voluntary organizations. While government has gradually diverted funds for welfare services to voluntary and for-profit organizations, Saxon-Harrold also demonstrates that a commensurable growth in private philanthropy even with the liberalization of tax policies is a long-term effort.

In Chapter Nine, Quintin Oliver discusses the role of nonprofit organizations in Northern Ireland. Northern Ireland's nonprofits often work in a political vacuum, with community groups providing services when public programs have broken down. Although these groups have remained fairly neutral amid the country's political and religious rivalries, Oliver argues that they need to adopt more creative political roles in this deeply divided society.

In Chapter Ten, Tymen J. van der Ploeg examines changes in the relationship between private organizations and government in the Netherlands. Holland has a long tradition of nonprofit activity based on pluralistic notions of a "polarized" society in which Catholic, Protestant, and nonsectarian groups each developed their own institutional resources. This chapter describes the ways in which the Dutch government uses these institutions in the delivery of publicly financed social services.

Wolfgang Seibel, in Chapter Eleven, paints a somewhat different picture in his discussion of the relationship between government and the nonprofit sector in France and Germany. As he explains, the differing histories and political cultures of these two countries have left a strong imprint on the roles accorded their nonprofit organizations. Nonprofits in both countries provide an important share of health and social services and are heavily dependent on public subsidies. Yet although there has been a dramatic increase in the number of France's health and social welfare nonprofits since the mid 1970s, their role has been sharply limited by the inherent statism of French culture. Seibel concludes that the relationship between German government and nonprofits has tended to be more hospitable, stable, and conflict free.

In Chapter Twelve, Dan Ferrand Bechmann discusses the mission, purposes, and functions of nonprofit organizations in France. Despite the growth of a strong welfare state in the years after the Second World War, France has developed a number of powerful, publicly funded nonprofit organizations in the fields of social welfare and antipoverty efforts. She predicts that many of these organizations will increasingly be controlled by the state.

John Boli, in Chapter Thirteen, analyzes the nonprofit sector and the state in Sweden. He examines the strong ties that link Sweden's nonprofits to the state, including Hobbesian political notions that emphasize collectivism and centralized authority over individual and institutional autonomy. He then discusses the ways in which Sweden's nonprofits function as an extension of the state, by providing mechanisms for democratic policy formation and political debate.

Mark Lyons examines the role of government and the nonprofit sector in Australia in Chapter Fourteen. As he points out, governmental reliance on nonprofit organizations has increased significantly since the mid 1970s, as public support for Australia's nonprofits more than doubled (although he predicts that these public outlays will become more targeted in the future). In the process, the independence of some organizations has been lost, a theme echoed in several other chapters as well.

Anna Marie Thränhardt focuses on changing concepts of voluntarism in Japan in Chapter Fifteen. Two types of volunteer tradition now coexist in Japan: mutual aid efforts such as neighborhood associations that are rooted in Confucian models and East Asian traditions of group solidarity; and more critical, more individualistic alternative groups that emerged with the introduction of Western ideas after World War II. She examines the reasons why participation in alternative groups declined in the 1980s, as well as the ways in which neighborhood associations have continued to represent traditional values.

Finally, in Chapter Sixteen, Eliezer D. Jaffe explores the role of nonprofit organizations among the ultra-Orthodox Jewish community in Israel. Focusing on the impact of religious injunctions and self-help traditions in promoting nonprofit development among special-interest groups, Jaffe concludes by questioning where the state's responsibility and tolerance should begin and end regarding separatist religious and cultural minorities.

Chapter 8

The Voluntary Sector in Britain, 1975–1989: A Statistical Overview

The voluntary sector is a large and important part of British society. In 1980 and 1981, the income of registered charities was £7.3 billion, approximately 3 percent of the gross national product (GNP). By 1985, that figure had topped £12.6 billion, or 4.1 percent of the GNP (Posnett, 1987)—a rapid growth by any standards. Where does all this charitable money come from? This chapter will endeavor to outline the main components of the British voluntary sector's income. The scale and scope of voluntary activity over the past ten years will be examined, together with several issues for the 1990s.

     During the last few years, voluntary organizations have received more attention from government and the media than ever before. They are no longer obscure but at the front of public, political, and corporate awareness. Still, "charities are a second or third subject [with government]" (Brophy, 1989). Despite this prominence, few people can name more than two individual charities or know what they do (Saxon-Harrold, Carter, and Humble, 1987). All voluntary activity is important and worthwhile, but in reality, the vast majority of voluntary effort goes on unnoticed by donors.

It is easy to be confused about what role voluntary organizations play and how they are financed. Such organizations are not evenly dispersed across the country and can be complex in structure and operation. They have been viewed either as being synonymous with state provision or as being part of the private (for-profit sector). Whatever the perception, there can be no doubt that the growth of the voluntary sector has been encouraged over the last ten years by the Conservative government. The rationale has been that the state cannot and should not do everything. In 1979, the Conservative government pledged to support the voluntary sector, in particular, those organizations working in social services. One result has been that private institutions and voluntary organizations have been encouraged to provide and partly finance welfare services. Private giving was to be stimulated to help underpin this process, and payroll giving and more liberal tax concessions were introduced in 1986.

What of the future? It is likely that the 1990s will herald an increasingly stronger role for voluntary organizations. Proposed new legislation outlined in the government's white paper "Caring for People" (CM 849, 1989) requires that local authorities put welfare contracts out to tender among voluntary organizations and private firms. This, along with other legislation outlined below, is set to change the way voluntary organizations are funded at the local level.

However, with government policies of privatization and deregulation proceeding apace, the demands on the services of voluntary organizations are increasing. Concern is being raised as to whether the voluntary sector can secure sufficient resources to meet additional demands. What is known is that considerable opportunities exist for voluntary organizations to expand their operations. Before tackling these issues, a few points of definition are outlined.

Characteristics of Voluntary Organizations

This chapter uses the terms *voluntary organization* and *charity*. They are different species but have overlapping characteristics. Both can have no volunteers and rely totally on paid staff. Both can receive no income from voluntary donations. Some can receive a substantial part of their income from government sources but are not part of government. Others have trading outlets (shops) but are not for-profit firms. Therefore, it is misleading to assume synonymity between the terms *charity* and *voluntary organization*.

There are, however, some broad characteristics of "registered charities" and organizations that serve as an aid to definition. In general, we expect voluntary organizations to do the following:

1. Exist *independently* of the state
2. Be *self-governed* by an unpaid board of trustees
3. Benefit from philanthropy, gifts of cash, or time (volunteers) and be made up of individuals whose membership is not inherited or prescribed
4. Be instruments that produce *benefits* for others, benefits that are enjoyed outside membership of the organization (Guthrie, 1988; Kramer, 1981)
5. Be *nonprofit making,* and be "legally prohibited from distributing a monetary residual" (James, 1989)

The problems of definition span most countries that have any sort of "voluntary," "charitable," "nonprofit," "independent," or "third sector." To chart the size and scope of the British voluntary sector we have to start somewhere. A range of data sources are used, but these apply mainly to registered charities, and this, by definition, underestimates the total income of all voluntary organizations. The wide variety and shifting nature of voluntary activity make classification extremely difficult. Along with no common definitions, there is no unique classification of voluntary sector activity in Britain. Although no universal taxonomy exists, Charities Aid Foundation (1989a) uses the following fourteen-part classification: Animals, Arts, Community Improvement, Education, Employment, General Welfare, Housing, International Aid, Medicine and Health, Preservation of Heritage and Environment, Recreation and Leisure, Religion and Spiritual Development, Youth Development, Other.

An estimate in the late 1970s put the total number of voluntary bodies at 350,000 (Gerard, 1983), but because it included trade unions and schools, it must be treated with extreme caution. So what are registered charities?

What Is a Registered Charity?

A registered charity is an organization that is registered with the Charity Commission for England and Wales. Alternatively, it has been recognized as charitable by the Inland Revenue if based in Scotland or Northern Ireland. In order to be both registered and recognized, a prospective charity must satisfy the commissioners that it falls under one of the main headings of the charity. These categories were first outlined in the Preamble to the Statute of Charitable Uses, in 1601 (CM 43, Elizabeth I, C4). Case law has, over the years, altered the categories very slightly: the relief of the poor, the advancement of religion, the advancement of education, and other purpose beneficial to the community.

The first category includes the poor and destitute. However, old people's homes, hostels, and advice centers are all included in this category. The advancement of religion includes the promotion of all religions other than Christianity. The education category includes charitable schools, universities, colleges, and research institutes. The final category embraces a "rag bag" of purposes, including "the repair of bridges portes havens causewaies churches seabanks and highewaies . . . for marriages of poor maides, . . . and psons decayed" (CM43, Elizabeth I, C4, 1601).

At the end of 1988, a total of 164,534 charities were registered, 3,609 more than in 1987. The largest group of new registrations relate to social, cultural, and education purposes (Charity Commissioners, 1989).

The principal advantage of being a registered charity is that such an organization can gain a number of tax concessions. In 1987–1988, these tax concessions to charities in England and Wales cost the Treasury £639 million (Maslen, 1989).

Recipients of Voluntary Sector Income: Charities

Great advances have been made in the last several years in our understanding of the sources of voluntary sector income, but much remains uncharted territory. The use of charity data can prove difficult. The difficulties stem from (1) the considerable number of charities in existence and those with multiple objects, (2) the absence of a central register of charities, (3) the lack of standardization in the way financial information is outlined in charity accounts (Bird, 1985), (4) the absence of a market situation, and finally (5) the lack of a single output measure or prices to value goods and services (Knapp and Saxon-Harrold, 1990). The Charities Aid Foundation overcomes the first problem by confining surveys to the largest charities (that is, the top 400) or by using estimates of the incomes of charities based on samples of 500 charities drawn from the Charity Commission register, as in Posnett (1987).

Since 1977, the Charities Aid Foundation has published income and expenditure data for Britain's top 200 charities, and since 1986, the top 400. Size is defined by *total voluntary income,* or the sum of *voluntary income* (covenants, legacies, other gifts, and voluntary fund raising) and *other income* (trading, sales of goods and services, local and central government grants, rent and investment, and general income).

Table 8.1 shows the largest groups of charities and their total voluntary income in 1988 (adapted from Saxon-Harrold, 1989; Charities Aid Foundation, 1989a). The largest grouping is "Medicine and Health," with 155 charities. The majority of charities within this area offer direct services and support to particular groups — people with physical or mental handicaps (39),

Table 8.1. Top 400 Fund-Raising Charities, 1988.

Primary Area of Activity	No. of Charities	Total Voluntary Income (£ million)
Medicine and health	155	343
General welfare	95	268
International aid	47	193
Religious and missionary work	44	54
Animal protection	20	47
Preservation of heritage and environment	13	70
Youth and children	16	12
Arts	6	7
Education	4	2
	400	996

cancer sufferers (16), those who are blind (15), those with mental health problems (11), and those who are deaf (5). Companies also support medicine and health charities; 72 percent of companies (207) indicated that they supported medicine and health charities — some 149 organizations — to the tune of £6.3 million (23 percent of total usage) (Saxon-Harrold, 1989).

Rajan (1987) analyzed the trends in income of the top 200 charities between 1977 and 1989. She found that international aid charities (including Band-Aid), religious overseas aid, and arts charities all increased their share of total voluntary income over a ten-year period. On the other hand, charities dealing with cancer research, physical handicaps, the blind, the young and elderly, ex-servicemen, religious missionary support, and preservation of heritage and environment saw a decrease in total voluntary income. However, most organizations' total voluntary income increased in real terms between 1977 and 1986, and by a substantial amount in 1986.

A better indicator of total charity income is provided by a survey of 500 charities randomly selected from the register (Posnett, 1987). In 1985, this survey showed a total income figure of £12.65 billion, representing an increase in real terms of 32 percent since 1980 (see Table 8.2).

The largest increases came from grants (138 percent) and donations (116 percent). Grants from statutory bodies accounted

Table 8.2. The Income of Registered Charities in England and Wales, 1975–1985.

	1975–1976		1980–1981		1985–1986		%	Change in Real Income 1975–1985
	£m	%	£m	%	£m	%	1980–1985	%
Fund raising	683.6	28.4	890.6	12.2	1,925.3	15.2	116	+ 1.7
Fees and charges	821.5	34.1	4,802.6	65.9	7,672.3	60.7	60	+ 237.4
Rents and investment	523.3	21.7	886.3	12.2	1,398.4	11.1	58	− 3.5
Grants from statutory bodies	175.2	7.3	576.9	7.9	1,375.7	10.9	138	+ 183.7
Commercial activity and other	205.8	8.5	135.2	1.8	278.4	2.2	106	− 51.0
Total (£M)	2,409.4	100.0	7,291.6	100.0	12,650.1	100.0	73.5	+ 89.7

Source: Posnett, 1987.

for nearly 12 percent of the total income of all charities but 44 percent of the total income of all newly registered charities. Over a ten-year period, total net income increased by 89.7 percent. Part of this increase Posnett attributes to a 27 percent increase in the number of charities registered between 1975 and 1985. North American estimates suggest that nonprofit organizations comprise 4 percent of U.S. national income (Weisbrod, 1988), but this is only half the size of the nonprofit sector in Israel. The main reasons for the increase are attributed to increases in central and local government grants and income from fees and charges. Public-sector support is outlined below.

Public-Sector Support for Voluntary Organizations

Public-sector support for voluntary organizations is diverse and complex. The Charities Aid Foundation obtains information on this matter from seventeen central government departments and sixteen nondepartmental public bodies. Local and health authorities make payments across different departments and within each tier of administration. Financial arrangements can be in the form of grants or fees and charges, and the financing can be used for operating costs or for capital expenditure, as well as for diverse reasons set out in tightly worded agreements. Levels of accountability, amounts, and length of funding arrangements also vary. Public-sector support for voluntary organizations in 1988 is outlined in Table 8.3.

Table 8.3. Government Payments to the Voluntary Sector.

	£ 1987–1988
Government grants to housing associations and societies	1,138
Nondepartmental public bodies	926
Local authorities[a]	651
Tax concessions	639
Central government grants	293
Health authorities	33

[a]Figure for local authority support includes grants, fees, mandatory and discretionary rate relief.
Source: Charities Aid Foundation, 1989.

Less direct forms of support are fiscal concessions and rate relief (a reduction in property tax). Fiscal concessions are enjoyed by registered charities and by organizations recognized as charitable by the Inland Revenue if based in Scotland or Northern Ireland. Table 8.3 shows tax concessions given by central government in 1988. These totaled £639 million (£410 million in relief on covenanted gifts and £229 million in inheritance tax savings). This figure was up by £39 million in 1987. Rate relief was estimated to be £150.4 million in 1987–1988. Indirect assistance from local authorities to voluntary agencies (for example, secondment, cheap printing, and free legal and financial advice) was not costed by local authorities, but such support is acknowledged to be small.

Central Government Funding

The most recent available statistics of the components of public-sector support are based on official government figures and the analysis of the Charities Aid Foundation's own annual surveys. Over a ten-year period these surveys highlight the fact that income from central government, in its various forms, has shown the largest increase in recent years (see Table 8.4). It now stands at £290 million (1987–1988) up from £35.4 million in 1976–1977 (Wolfenden, 1987). This figure represents a 91.6 percent increase in real terms since 1979–1980. However, there has been a slowing down of this increase, and in 1987–1988 in real terms central government support was "static or even slightly falling" (Davis-Smith, 1989).

Another major, observable trend in the last decade or so has been the change in voluntary-statutory relationships. As central government has restricted local authority spending, local authority grant aid to voluntary groups has been replaced with money from the central government for special programs (for example, special employment measures) with fixed criteria of application. The problem for a great many voluntary bodies was that the employment field was an area with which many people were unfamiliar and found it difficult to cope with the goals and aspirations of the Training Commission (a nondepartmental public body described below).

Table 8.4. Central Government Grants to Voluntary Organizations.

	Total £000
1981-1982	140,984
1982-1983	150,970
1983-1984	182,270
1984-1985	224,411
1985-1986	267,777
1986-1987	279,499
1987-1988	292,916

Sources: Hansard, 1989; Charities Aid Foundation, 1989a.

Nondepartmental Public Bodies

The year 1976 saw the beginning of the quangos (nondepartmental public bodies, or NDPBs). Total funding in that year (excluding grants to housing associations) was £28 million (Hatch, 1983). By 1986-1987, the total reached £1.649 billion, almost six times more than total central government grants and three times more than local authority support. Figures for 1987-1988 show that quangos made payments of more than £920 million to the voluntary sector. The largest slice, £737.4 million, went to the Training Commission. The majority of this money was used to support employment schemes. The Community Programme received £564.4 million and the Youth Training Scheme, £118 million. The Arts Council was the next largest recipient, with an allocation of £135.9 million.

The prominence of the Training Commission (formerly the Manpower Services Commission, or MSC) since 1984 is highly significant. In 1983-1984, £285 million was devoted to MSC programs. By 1987-1988, that figure had reached £737.4 million, £86 million more than local authority funding. Within the Training Commission, the Community Programme alone multiplied its cash value more than ten times between 1982-1983 and 1987-1988. Until its wind down in 1989, this program accounted for 76 percent of Training Commission support and 61 percent of all quango (NDPB) funding. The dominance of MSC funding was particularly noticeable at the local level. MSC moneys gave rise to thousands of new voluntary organizations as staff and funding became available for a multiplicity of new projects. Despite huge increases in quango funding in the mid 1980s, the last two years' figures showed only a marginal increase in real terms. The troublesome trend to emerge from these figures is that central government funding and quango funding are stagnating at a time when charities and voluntary organizations are being asked to "take on an expanded role in the provision of welfare" (Davis-Smith, 1989).

Local and Health Authority Funding
(Including Fees and Charges)

During the 1970s and early 1980s voluntary organizations worked in "partnership" with local authorities in creating local services. There were exceptions to the rule, as noted by Leat, Smolka, and Unell (1981) and more recently by Unell (1989). In particular, statutory funding eroded strategic autonomy and flexibility in voluntary organizations. Even so, in 1976–1977 local authority finance was the largest source of statutory support for the voluntary sector. Wolfenden (1978) reported that local authorities spent £150 million on grants and fees via social services and education departments. Most of this money went to community development and urban regeneration (Mocroft, 1989b). Health authority funding was insignificant at this time, totaling £0.17 million in 1974–1975.

It is quite clear that by the end of the 1980s, while local authorities were an important source of funding for many voluntary organizations, they were not the largest. As other sources of public support have grown, local authorities have found it difficult to sustain their funding of voluntary agencies. From 1983 to 1988, cash support for voluntary organizations grew by 19 percent but declined overall to 97 percent of its 1983–1984 level of £500 million (Mocroft, 1989a). It must be noted that local authority support was truly overshadowed in the mid 1980s by the Manpower Services Commission (a quango). The MSC alone accounted for 97 percent of all local authority payments (Unell, 1989).

Health authority payments in the form of grants, fees, or joint payments with local authorities have continued to increase since 1974–1975, albeit from a very small base. Payments in 1986–1987 were £25.2 million, and in 1987–1988 they were £33 million, a 31 percent increase (Lehmann, 1989). The average value of grants rose by 59 percent to £15,900. This increase was partly accounted for by a decline in the number of grants of less than £500. Financial support is variable in terms of both levels of support and amounts across the country. Ninety-eight payments accounted for more than half the support in 1988. Hospices and terminal care received 18 percent of the total, and mental handicap and mental health received 14 percent and 12 percent, respectively. These areas witnessed a growth of fee payments that nearly doubled in 1987–1988. Currently, the National Health Service (NHS) is not a major source of support for the voluntary sector. However, it is likely that the government's white papers "Working for Patients" (CM 555, 1989) and "Caring for People" (CM 849, 1989) will quicken the trend toward voluntary organizations receiving a higher proportion of their income from fees and charges. Both pieces of proposed legislation would require local and health authorities to encourage the process of competitive tendering (started by the Local Government Act of 1988) and contract out services to the private sector (including voluntary organizations).

Leat (1990), in examining the composition of fees and charges among ten voluntary organizations, found them to be an important source of income for only 13 percent. This is in stark contrast to Posnett (1987), who found that in 1985, fees represented 60 percent of the total income of registered charities. (Later it was found that the inclusion of public schools and housing associations distorted this figure.) What we do know is that more voluntary organizations are receiving fee income — 42 percent of charities founded in the period 1980–1985 as opposed to 23 percent of charities founded before 1980. What is unclear, is whether the 1990s will see voluntary organizations in receipt of increased fee income or direct grant aid as a result of legislative changes.

Individual Donors

The Charity Household Survey (CHS) is the major source of information about charitable giving in Britain (Saxon-Harrold, Carter, and Humble, 1987). The primary aim of the survey is to obtain information on patterns of and motives for giving. In addition, information is collected on bequeathing and covenanting money to charity. Individual donations are not exempt from tax unless made under covenant for four years, by way of a trust, or through payroll deduction. Unlike the Internal Revenue Service (IRS) in the United States, the British Inland Revenue has no record of individual giving unless it is by one of the above methods.

Individual giving is a complex matter. For charities, the management and organization needed to obtain individual donations is critically important. Survival is at stake if resources are not obtained. Individual giving, like company giving (see below), can be broken down into three forms.

1. Gifts in kind can be given to charity. Gifts can range from giving blood to collecting silver paper, newspapers, or bottles. The extent of individual giving in kind is not known and would be extremely difficult to quantify.
2. Giving time, or volunteering, ranges from helping at a jumble (rummage) sale, collecting money for a flag day, looking after an elderly relative, and on through mountain or sea rescue. Again, measuring the extent of volunteering and the cost of these activities is a difficult problem.
3. Obviously, money can be given to charity. Quantifying how much money people give is easier than estimating the other two forms of giving.

The household survey shows that 80 percent of respondents reported that they gave money to charity in the month prior to interview, and 78 percent stated how much they gave (Halfpenny and Saxon-Harrold, 1990). The amount given per respondent ranged from nothing to £500 in the month preceding the interview. This includes all forms of giving asked about: covenants, payroll deduction, door-to-door and street collections, church collections, sponsorship, responding to appeal letters and advertisements, buying raffle tickets, and buying goods at bring-and-buy or jumble sales or in charity shops or through catalogues.

The distribution of giving was skewed, with many respondents giving nothing or very little and a few reporting very large contributions: 40 percent of respondents gave £1 per month or less, and only 8 percent gave more than £20 per month. The average (mean) amount given per respondent in the month prior to interview was £6.92 (95 percent confidence interval of £4.90 to £7.40). This represented 0.75 percent of average gross earnings. However, the median contribution is a less misleading typical value to quote for skewed distribution because it is unaffected by the size of large donations. The median monthly donation was £1.97 to £23.60 a year. The mean individual donation across the whole population lies somewhere in the range of £67 to £99. Total individual giving by 45.1 million adults in 1988–1989 was somewhere between £3 and 4.5 billion (95 percent confidence interval). At the highest point, this was one-and-a-half times more than total public-sector support.

The 1987 Charity Household Survey found that the mean amount given by each respondent in the month prior to interview was £6.10. This figure was 82p smaller than the mean of £6.92 in 1988–1989. *It is unlikely that this represents a real increase in giving from one year to the next.*

Donating money to charity through covenants and payroll deduction plans can be described as *planned giving*. In contrast, giving that is in response to appeals is called *prompted giving*. One percent of respondents reported that their charitable giving was exclusively planned, 71 percent that it was exclusively prompted, and 8 percent that it was a mixture of planned and prompted. In other words, three-quarters responded to giving when prompted, and less than one-tenth planned their giving.

The method of prompted giving most used in the month prior to the interview was door-to-door collection (35 percent), typically giving £6 per annum, followed by street collection (30 percent) and sponsoring someone in an event (30 percent). The least used methods were responding to an appeal advertisement (3 percent) or an appeal letter (2 percent). These *prompted philanthropic methods* (so called because the donor receives no material benefit) accounted for 31 percent of the total given.

Prompted purchases (from which the donor does receive a direct material benefit, such as buying goods through a shop or a catalogue) accounted for 45 percent of the total raised, although charities received a lower proportion of donations through purchases. *Planned giving* (for example, covenants and payroll) represented only 7 percent of total giving. Figures since 1985 (Saxon-Harrold, Carter, and Humble, 1987) show that charitable giving is overwhelmingly spontaneous rather than planned tax efficiently.

Individual giving does vary per annum by sex, age, social status, income, and so on, but only to a very minor extent. For example, a higher proportion of men than women gave nothing, and a lower proportion of men than women gave more than £100 per annum. Less than 2 percent of the variation in giving is explained by sex of donor. More people aged sixty-five and over gave nothing or small amounts, and more people in the age-group twenty-five to forty-four gave large amounts, but this relationship is also weak.

The most often named destination of prompted giving was the medical category, to which 25 percent of donations were made. This was followed by the category "other," which includes local charity (23 percent), and "general welfare" (20 percent).

Despite continued growth in statutory support, voluntary donations increased by 74 percent between 1980 and 1989. This was probably due to lower inflation, lower taxes, and a greater expectation among voluntary bodies about individual action. The growth was reflected (as outlined previously) in both the total and the voluntary income of the top 200 charities, rising, on average, by 30 percent and 27 percent, respectively, per year. This happened at a time when GNP was rising at a lesser rate. The 1989 individual giving figures showed no increase over the previous year. These figures are surprising given an increase in personal incomes in real terms by one-third. The troublesome aspect for charities is that the management of the gift relationship (between donor and charity) takes primacy over all other activities. All services, projects, and activities stem from the receipt of adequate resources, and it is well known that a charity cannot switch resource suppliers in the same easy manner that a business can (Hickson and others, 1986).

Planned Giving

For planned methods of giving—covenants and payroll deductions—the tax concessions have become more liberal since 1986. There is no upper limit on the amount given for four years by means of a covenant. Payroll deduction plans are a regular, tax-efficient form of giving. Deductions are taken from employees' pay by employers and passed to an "agency" charity, which distributes the money to charities registered with the plan. First introduced in 1986 with a maximum yearly donation of £120, the limit has since been steadily increased and now stands at £480 per annum. There were twelve active payroll agency charities in 1988–1989. The largest was "Give as You Earn" (G.A.Y.E.), operated by the Charities Aid Foundation with 1,957 employers and 90,700 employees contracted. According to Wickert (1989), just under £4 million was donated to charity, £2.7 million more than in 1987–1988 (the first full year of the plan's operation). The second year was disappointing. The number of donors doubled and the average donation increased, but "the growth disappointingly failed to achieve an annualized value of £10 million." According to the Charity Household Survey, the proportion of people who are aware of payroll giving and using that method to donate to charity increased in 1988–1989 over 1987–1988 by 31 percent. The median annual donation remained low, at £6, and the yield was very small, less than 1 percent of total giving (Halfpenny and Saxon-Harrold, 1990).

According to Maslen (1989), there were probably three million charitable covenants in 1987–1988, a million more than in 1986–1987. Tax relief on covenants in 1987–1988 amounted to £410 million. Fourteen percent of individuals in the 1988–1989 Charity Household Survey were aware of covenants and used this method to give (a lower percentage than for payroll deduction plans). In contrast to payroll, the median annual donation is higher (£36) and the yield considerable (7 percent of overall giving). Clearly, individual giving figures pose a challenge for charities and government in the 1990s to increase giving, both planned and prompted. Certainly, despite increased media attention individuals do not seem to be becoming more generous.

Legacies

Legacy giving is erratic, and the difficulty of measuring the value and assessing the content of a legacy should not be underestimated. In 1988-1989, the Charity Household Survey reveals, 30 percent of respondents had made a will (Halfpenny and Saxon-Harrold, 1990). As expected the proportion who had done so increased steadily with age and social status from 3 percent of those under the age of twenty-five to 55 percent of those sixty-five or older. Findings from previous surveys (Halfpenny and Saxon-Harrold, 1989; Smee and Ford, 1988) have revealed that only 3 percent of adults aged sixteen and older have made a will that includes a legacy to charity. Charities received £350 million from legacies in 1986 (Radcliffe, 1987). The figure is now probably between £500 and £600 million, although it probably varies from year to year (see Table 8.5). It is easy to underestimate the value of legacy giving for a number of reasons (Saxon-Harrold, 1988a). First, inheritance tax from estates where there is a liability has increased as a proportion of tax concessions. It accounted for £229 million in 1987-1988. Second, according to Smee and Ford (1988), the value of estates has increased; and third, the top 200 charities receive more than one-third of their voluntary income from this source (34 percent in 1987-1988 (Charities Aid Foundation, 1989a).

There is no doubt that charities could obtain a larger share of the legacy market. Demographic and economic changes suggest that there will be an elderly population owning more homes than ever before—a house being a substantial capital sum that could be donated to charity. Second, people are taking out private pensions and life assurance (insurance), which on maturity will leave individuals with a higher disposable income. During the 1990s charities will try to persuade the public to both make a will and leave a legacy to charity.

Table 8.5. Legacy Income as a Proportion of Voluntary and Total Income for the Top 200 Fund-Raising Charities, 1982–1983 Through 1987–1988.

	1982–1983	1983–1984	1984–1985	1985–1986	1986–1987	1987–1988
Percentage of voluntary income	32	33	28	33	36	34
Percentage of total income	17	18	16	18	19	18
Legacy income of top 200 fund-raising charities[a]	142,977	173,826	193,978	236,155	273,803	306,130

[a]Identifiable sums only.

Sources: Radcliffe, 1987, p. 116; Charities Aid Foundation, 1988, p. 114; Charities Aid Foundation, 1989a, p. 120.

Company Donations

Out of total income of £15 billion, large companies give only an estimated £200 million, or 1.6 percent, of that total. Even though corporate giving has trebled in real terms in the last ten years, both personal donations and central government grants have grown faster. In 1987–1988 the top 400 corporate donors made profits of £51.1 billion (Charities Aid Foundation, 1989a). Of this, £91.3 million went to charities and voluntary organizations in declared voluntary donations, or less than one-twentieth or one percent. The proportion of pretax profits donated gradually increased from 0.17 percent in 1977 to 0.24 percent in 1982. Since 1982, however, it has declined and was only 0.18 percent in 1988. The major trends since 1977 have been (1) substantial increases in voluntary donations, but donations of pretax profit stuck at 0.20 percent (Saxon-Harrold, 1989), and (2) increased gifts of noncash assistance (for example, secondment).

Voluntary corporate donations include cash donations but exclude many items of noncash assistance, such as secondment and sponsorship, and tend to underestimate total corporate support by large companies. Saxon-Harrold and Hunter (1987b) developed measures of cash and noncash assistance among large companies to gain a more realistic picture of company giving. Using these measures, we found that total corporate support in 1988 by 207 companies that gave over £20,000 per annum totaled £142 million (Saxon-Harrold, 1989). Cash contributions accounted for 43 percent of the total. In 1986–1987, 110 similar companies gave £98.1 million, £31.6 million of which was in cash contributions (or about 32 percent of the total) (Saxon-Harrold, 1989). A matched sample of ninety-four companies during 1987 and 1988 revealed a 1.8 percent increase in real terms in corporate support of £96.9 million and £104.4 million, respectively. The largest areas of noncash assistance in both 1987 and 1988 were sponsorship (£18.4 million) and secondment (£17.2 million). Cash donations ranged in size from nothing to £6.3 million. The largest category to benefit from these contributions was medicine and health, at £6.3 million (23 percent of the total), followed by community improvement at £4.1 million

(15 percent of total usage). Education accounted for £3.7 million (14 percent of total usage), and the arts accounted for £3.5 million (13 percent of total usage).

In 1988, a survey of 500 small companies defined as having a work force of fewer than 100 employees and a maximum turnover of £10 million, typically gave £200 per annum (median) to charity (Saxon-Harrold, 1988d). Assuming that these companies were representative of the total population, we can be 95 percent confident that the annual mean level of contributions was between £592 and £1,205 in 1987–1988. If we gross the total donations for the population of 800,000 companies, the result is between £474 million and £964 million, all made by small companies. If the median value of £200 is used, the total estimate is £160 million. Both figures show the small companies to be significant contributors overall. Small companies, like their large counterparts, support the community with cash and noncash assistance, albeit to a lesser extent.

Grant-Making Trusts

The top 400 grant-making trusts made grants of £234.7 million in 1987–1988, 82 percent of their total income, which was £30.5 million more than it was in 1986–1987. Grant-making trusts accounted for 1.5 percent of the total income of registered charities in 1985. Over a ten-year period the assets of such trusts have grown substantially. The real value of assets showed no growth between 1979 and 1982 (Saxon-Harrold and Hunter, 1987a) but have increased since. According to Lord (1989), trusts are triggering "a tendency for government departments to change from longer-term to short-term funding similar to trusts, and even setting up trusts to encourage this process for specific development." This has put pressure on grant-making trusts, which by nature, are conventional in their giving.

Into the Nineties: Possible Future Trends and Issues

If there is one theme throughout the presentation of these statistics, it is the sharply increasing rate and number of changes with which charities must cope—changes in fund sources, in organizational performance, and in terms of new charities entering the field. This section concentrates on issues of funding, relationships between the state and charity, and the need for increasing "professionalism" in charity management. First, here is an outline of forecasted demographic and social changes.

Demographic, Social and Economic Forecasts

The London Business School (1989) predicts that the economy will exhibit a slower rate of growth in the 1990s. Recession will continue to hit the inner cities, with semiskilled and unskilled individuals continuing to be the worst off. The largest population increases are expected to be among children and the very elderly (Office of Population Census and Surveys, 1989). The population aged eighty-five and older is projected to rise from 0.8 million in 1987 to 1.4 million by 2025 (Central Statistical Office, 1989). The number of people aged sixty-five and over is now more than 50 percent greater than it was in 1951. An aging population will mean increased demands for child care, sheltered housing, and health care. Finally, the "nuclear" family (typically two adults and two children) is expected to become a smaller percentage of all households.

A quarter of all households were one-person households in 1987, compared to about one-eighth in 1961. The impact of AIDS, changes in family structure, and attitudes toward the elderly will all be important in moderating future social and economic changes. Politically, it is expected that public expenditure will continue to be controlled. It is likely that money will be taken out of housing, agriculture, and industry and put into health, social services, social security, and law enforcement.

Patterns of Funding and Relationships

The problem of defining exactly what types of organizations are included makes it difficult to assign roles and responsibilities. Ambiguity in definition leaves the door wide open to determining the activities that serve the public interest and fulfill needs by both the government and private sector alike. This lack of clear definition of what voluntary organizations do and are causes problems for funders and voluntary organizations alike. For funders, the issue is how to allocate scarce resources to the best effect when voluntary organizations do not have adequate goal and mission statements. For voluntary organizations competing for funds, the problem is how to increase resources without changing purpose.

The nature of delivering welfare services will shift toward voluntary organizations and private companies in the 1990s. The changing nature of service delivery and funding will mean that partnership funding will be replaced by a more competitive model. In 1975 not many services were contracted to charities. In the future, government will view charities as an acceptable alternative for allocating resources. There has already been a shift from grant aid to contract-based arrangements, and the contracting of entire services is set to expand under the "Caring for People" and "Working for Patients" legislation.

From the government's point of view, if voluntary organizations can resettle the mentally handicapped in the community, a task previously undertaken by the state, state spending can be released for other purposes. This, in turn, will allow reductions in public expenditures and taxation. In theory, the government perceives charities as introducing greater flexibility allowing members of the public to have the choice of giving to causes most dear to them. These are the two criteria that charities will have to offer: flexibility and choice. The issue for managers will be to steer the charity "ship" through an increasingly more competitive operating and funding sea. During the last several years, tax incentives and quango funding have provided the underpinnings for this vision.

Will this shift of responsibility from government to voluntary organizations and toward commercial behavior lead to a rethinking of tax exemptions, as is occurring in the United States? (Hodgkinson, 1989). The diversification process will need to be handled competently if voluntary organizations are to maintain their objectives. New interorganization relationships will be of primary importance, if new skills and experience are to be shared. What is abundantly clear is that voluntary bodies are likely to diversify into a broader spectrum of activities and concerns than they exhibit at present. Certainly the new legislation and the AIDS challenge are likely to bring about a new partnership between the voluntary and statutory sectors and many opportunities in the field of health. It is likely that partnerships between health authorities and voluntary agencies to provide specific services will expand rapidly. In the past health authorities made small payments to a variety of services. In the future larger payments will probably be concentrated in areas of priority need. If voluntary organizations become the service providers, who will campaign for better standards of care? The answer to this question is unknown.

As already emphasized, securing a set of donors and convincing them of why they should give or give more is of strategic importance to charities. Companies are unlikely to give more in the 1990s unless they see central government and private individuals doing more. Noncash assistance will probably continue to be the growth area among larger companies. Given higher profits and a more favorable tax regime, the challenge for large companies is to give a higher proportion of pretax profits to charity.

The challenge for individuals is to give one percent of their income to charity (Patten, 1989), raising the average from £2 a month to £9.24 a month, which is the difference between current per capita giving and the amount needed to reach an average of 1 percent. Wealth is being amassed in certain quarters in Britain. The question is how people can be encouraged to give it away. One effort for the 1990s will certainly be for charities and government to persuade individuals and organizations to increase their level of personal giving and volunteering (Patten, 1989; Davis-Smith, 1989).

Professional Charity Management

Obviously, relationships between the state and the voluntary sector are set to change. The consequences of managing a multiplicity of funders means not only projecting an image of "professional" management but being more professional. Bound up with this concept already are administrative efficiency and concepts of effective management: low administrative costs and the development of professional management skills. Along with using professional management techniques, voluntary organizations must increasingly specialize as they become the sole providers of certain services. As a consequence each voluntary organization will want to preserve its own unique features as it faces competition for funds with other organizations in the same field. Will smaller charities be squeezed out? Will services only exist where charities have been able to compete and survive? Within ten years, we will know.

References

Bird, P. "The Charitable Treatment of Fundraising Expenses." Tonbridge, Kent, England: Charities Aid Foundation, 1985. (Mimeographed.)

Brophy, M. "The New 'Pharisees.'" (London) *Times*, Oct. 9, 1989.

Butler, R. J., and Wilson, D. C. *Voluntary and Nonprofit Organizations: Strategy and Structure.* London: Routledge, 1990.

Central Statistical Office. *Social Trends 19.* London: HMSO, 1989.

Charities Aid Foundation. *Charity Trends* (11th ed.). Tonbridge, Kent, England, 1988.

Charities Aid Foundation. "Internal Paper for 10 Downing Street Policy Unit." Unpublished paper, Oct. 1988.

Charities Aid Foundation. *Charity Trends* (12th ed.). Tonbridge, Kent, England, 1989a.

Charities Aid Foundation. "Research Methods." In *Charity Trends* (12th ed.). Tonbridge, Kent, England, 1989b.

Charity Commissioners. *Report of the Charity Commissioners for England and Wales for the Year 1988.* London: HMSO, 1989.

CM 43, Elizabeth I, C4. *The Preamble to the Statute of Charitable Uses.* Charitable Uses Act 1601.

CM 555. "Working for Patients." Command Paper 555. London: HMSO, 1989.

CM 849. "Caring for People: Community Care in the Next Decade and Beyond." Secretaries of State for Health, Social Security, Wales and Scotland. London: HMSO, 1989.

Davis-Smith, J. "Commentary." In *Charity Trends* (12th ed.). Tonbridge, Kent, England: Charities Aid Foundation, 1989.

Gerard, D. *Charities in Britain: Conservation or Change?* London: National Council for Voluntary Organizations, 1983.

Guthrie, R. *Charity and the Nation.* The Fifth Annual Arnold Goodman Charity Lecture. Tonbridge, Kent, England: Charities Aid Foundation, 1988.

Halfpenny, P., and Saxon-Harrold, S. K. E. *The Charity Household Survey 1987/88.* Tonbridge, Kent, England: Charities Aid Foundation, 1989.

Halfpenny, P. and Saxon-Harrold, S. K. E. *The Charity Household Survey, 1988/89.* Tonbridge, Kent, England: Charities Aid Foundation, 1990.

Hansard. London: HMSO, May 16, 1989.

Hatch, S. "Grants to Voluntary Organizations by Central Government 1976–1977 to 1981–1982." In *Charity Statistics 1982/83.* Tonbridge, Kent, England: Charities Aid Foundation, 1983.

Hickson, D. J., and others. *Top Decisions: Strategic Decision Making in Organizations.* San Francisco: Jossey-Bass, 1986.

Hodgkinson, V. A. "Major Changes Facing the Nonprofit Sector." Washington, D.C.: INDEPENDENT SECTOR, 1989. (Mimeographed.)

James, E. "Sources of Charity Finance and Policy Implications: A Comparative Analysis." In *Sources of Charity Finance.* Tonbridge, Kent, England: Charities Aid Foundation, 1989.

Knapp, M., and Saxon-Harrold, S. K. E. "The British Voluntary Sector." Discussion paper 645, Personal Social Services Unit, University of Kent at Canterbury, Olivetti Foundation, 1990.

Kramer, R. *Voluntary Agencies in the Welfare State.* Berkeley: University of California Press, 1981.

Leat, D. *Charities and Charging.* Tonbridge, Kent, England: Charities Aid Foundation, 1990.

Leat, D., Smolka, G., and Unell, J. *Voluntary and Statutory Collaboration: Rhetoric or Reality?* London: Bedford Square Press, 1981.

Lehman, M. "Health Authority Support for Charities and Voluntary Organizations." In *Charity Trends* (12th ed.). Tonbridge, Kent, England: Charities Aid Foundation, 1989.

London Business School. *The 1992 Myths and Realities.* London: London Business School, 1989.

Lord, G. "Grant Making Trusts in a Changing Society." In L. Fitzherbert and M. Eastwood (eds.), *A Guide to Major Trusts 1989.* London: Directory of Social Change, 1989.

Maslen, P. "Public Sector Support for Voluntary Organizations." In *Charity Trends* (12th ed.). Tonbridge, Kent, England: Charities Aid Foundation, 1989.

Mocroft, I. "Discussant's Comments on Unell Paper." In *Sources of Charity Finance.* Tonbridge, Kent, England: Charities Aid Foundation, 1989a.

Mocroft, I. "The Survey of Local Authority Payments to Voluntary and Charitable Organizations." In *Charity Trends* (12th ed.). Tonbridge, Kent, England: Charities Aid Foundation, 1989b.

Office of Population Census and Surveys. *Social Trends 21.* London, HMSO, 1989.

Patten, J. "Minister Aims to Encourage People's Charitable Instincts." *The Independent,* Dec. 28, 1989.

Posnett, J. "Trends in the Income of Registered Charities 1980–85." *Charity Trends* (10th ed.). Tonbridge, Kent, England: Charities Aid Foundation, 1987.

Posnett, J. "An Analysis of the Distribution of Charitable Donations from the 1984 Family Expenditure Survey." In *Charity Trends* (11th ed.). Tonbridge, Kent, England: Charities Aid Foundation, 1988.

Radcliffe, R. "Legacies." In *Charity Trends* (10th ed.). Tonbridge, Kent, England: Charities Aid Foundation, 1987.

Rajan, L. "Charity Statistics 1977–1986: An Analysis of Trends." In *Charity Trends* (10th ed.). Tonbridge, Kent, England: Charities Aid Foundation, 1987.

Saxon-Harrold, S. K. E. "Legacy Giving to Charity." In *Charity Trends* (11th ed.). Tonbridge, Kent, England: Charities Aid Foundation, 1988a.

Saxon-Harrold, S. K. E. "Annual Survey of Small Company Contributions." In *Charity Trends* (11th ed.). Tonbridge, Kent, England: Charities Aid Foundation, 1988b.

Saxon-Harrold, S. K. E. "Survey of Company Community Involvement." In *Charity Trends* (11th ed.). Tonbridge, Kent, England: Charities Aid Foundation, 1988c.

Saxon-Harrold, S. K. E. *Annual Survey of Small Company Contributions, 1988 Edition.* Tonbridge, Kent, England: Charities Aid Foundation, 1988d.

Saxon-Harrold, S. K. E. "Survey of Corporate Support for the Voluntary Sector." In *Charity Trends* (12th ed.). Tonbridge, Kent, England: Charities Aid Foundation, 1989.

Saxon-Harrold, S. K. E., Carter, J., and Humble, S. *The Charitable Behaviour of British People: A National Survey of Patterns and Attitudes to Charitable Giving.* Tonbridge, Kent, England: Charities Aid Foundation, 1987.

Saxon-Harrold, S. K. E., and Hunter, T. "Brief Notes on Trust Trends." In *Charity Trends* (10th ed.). Tonbridge, Kent, England: Charities Aid Foundation, 1987a.

Saxon-Harrold, S. K. E., and Hunter, T. "Trends in the Top 100 Company Donations to Charity." In *Charity Trends* (10th ed.). Tonbridge, Kent, England: Charities Aid Foundation, 1987b.

Smee, P., and Ford, D. *Statistical Survey of Charitable Wills: End of Year Summary 1987.* London: Smee and Ford, 1988.

Unell, J. "The Changing Pattern of Public Sector Support for Voluntary Organisations." In *Sources of Charity Finance.* Tonbridge, Kent, England: Charities Aid Foundation, 1989.

Weisbrod, B. *The Nonprofit Economy.* Cambridge, Mass.: Harvard University Press, 1988.

Wickert, D. "Payroll Deduction." In *Charity Trends* (12th ed.). Tonbridge, Kent, England: Charities Aid Foundation, 1989.

Wolfenden. *The Future of Voluntary Organisations: Report of the Wolfenden Committee.* London: Croom Helm, 1978.

The Role of
Nonprofit Organizations
in a Divided Society:
The Case of Northern Ireland

Nonprofit organizations in Northern Ireland share many of the characteristics of "voluntary" or "third sector" bodies in advanced European postwelfare-state societies. They are largely organized in three categories:

1. Mutual aid societies made up of members experiencing a problem and banding together for self-help
2. Service providers that offer facilities and services to the advantaged
3. Advisory bodies campaigning for social change

The current political and social unrest in Northern Ireland has spawned a growth in nonprofit activity, partly filling the

potential vacuum. This chapter examines this thesis and the issues of leadership and management in the vibrant community
sector. The roots of the Irish question run deep. In an *annus
mirabilis* of political change on a world scale, one of the areas
seemingly unaffected remains Ireland. The problems appear to
be inexplicable; they are also prone to misunderstanding and
often to deliberate obfuscation. Irish history tends not to travel
well.

In the opening lines of the introduction to his book *Divided
Ulster,* Liam de Paor offers this explanation: "In Northern Ireland
Catholics are Blacks who happen to have white skins. This is
not a truth. It is an oversimplification and too facile an anal-
ogy. But it is a better oversimplification than that which sees
the struggle and conflict in Northern Ireland in terms of religion.
Catholics and Protestants are not quarreling with one another
(most of them) because of matters of theology or faith. There
is no burning urge on either side to convert the other to the
one true faith, nor does a member of one side strike a member
of the other on the head with a club in the hope that he will
thereby be purged of his theological errors and become a better
candidate for heaven" (1971, p. i).

The intentions of this chapter are as follows: (1) to describe,
in simple terms, the background to the Northern Ireland conflict
and current governmental structures; (2) to undertake an analysis of the role of not-for-profit organizations in Northern Ireland; (3) to identify characteristics of voluntary action on both
sides of Northern Ireland's so-called religious divide; and (4)
to offer a development model for Northern Ireland's not-for-profit
sector in the 1990s.

Background

Northern Ireland has a population of 1.5 million, roughly one
million of whom are of Scottish or English descent, are broadly
Protestant by religion, and subscribe to continued union with
Great Britain; roughly half a million are of Irish lineage, are
broadly Catholic in religion, and aspire to a United Ireland.
The (Provisional) Irish Republican Army (the IRA) — whose political wing, Sinn Fein, garners up to 10 percent of the vote —

wages an armed struggle against the continued British presence. Just under 3,000 people have died in the latest round of political violence that erupted in 1968.

Since 1972, Northern Ireland has been governed by a Direct Rule administration from Britain, accountable to the British parliament. There is no locally elected political assembly or forum; services are provided by the local civil service, by appointed boards (covering education, housing, probation, health, social services, and other services), and by twenty-six elected local authorities whose powers only extend to leisure; the registration of births, deaths, and marriages; and garbage disposal. It is widely accepted that this form of government leaves much to be desired in terms of responsiveness, accountability, and participation. Williamson (1989, p. 7) describes it thus: "It does not command the affection of any section of the community; it is acknowledged to be unsatisfactory and was intended to be temporary."

Economically, Northern Ireland has rarely flourished; the traditional industries of ship-building, textiles, tobacco, and trade are in decline, there are few natural resources, and current image problems render it unattractive to foreign investors. The Single European Market of 1992 is thought likely to promote yet further centralization of the European economy away from the periphery, exacerbating Ireland's position as "une isle derrière une isle." Unemployment currently runs to 15 percent, with some pockets of multiple deprivation scoring at up to 60 percent. Historical imbalance in unemployment between Catholics and Protestants persists despite equal opportunity legislation, with rates in the former 2.5 times the Protestant figures. Derry poet Seamus Deane, in "Gradual Wars," has described the nearly hereditary joblessness of his city and its rioting: "The unemployment in our bones erupting on our hands in stones."

The Role of Not-for-Profit Organizations

At the height of the civil disturbances of 1972, when the Northern Ireland government was under such pressure locally and internationally that the British had to step in and suspend it, confidence in the minority (Catholic) community was at its highest. It was felt that new forms of community participation and accountability were emerging; the state was on the defensive, the people were on the march, the dream of people's power was close to reality. Donnison (1989, p. 210) describes it thus: "When disturbances in Belfast led to the temporary collapse of public services, and thousands of people were compelled by fear to move out of mixed areas into communities of their own faith, local groups took over many of the functions of government. They erected barriers at the entrances of their neighbourhoods and policed them for twenty-four hours a day. They allocated houses to the homeless, and provided relief for people who had lost all they possessed. They set up taxi services. If they had a bakery within their territory but no dairy, they bartered bread for milk with other community groups and distributed these things to the families in need of them."

Those special circumstances represent one moment in the development of the not-for-profit and community sectors of Northern Ireland. Assessing community action at the end of the 1970s in Northern Ireland, Eamonn Deane (1981, p. 49) records: "Then we believed that change was not only desirable, but that it was possible; now we are even more certain that it is desirable, but we are not so sure that it is possible."

How have things settled down? How does the voluntary, community sector see itself in the 1990s? How have twenty years of civil strife affected the aspirations of the dreamers of 1968? In an attempt to differentiate Northern Ireland's nonprofit sector from that operating in Great Britain and the rest of Ireland, this author (Oliver, 1988, p. 17) has identified ten such features:

1. *"Helicopter rule"* by government ministers elected by English constituencies, arriving — albeit for understandable security reasons — by helicopter, to dispense decisions from behind barbed wire creates an unusual and unnatural political environment that requires the exercise of special political skills by the community sector.

2. The *constitutional uncertainty* of the state has an
    unsettling effect on community activists and
    poses the dilemma of whether priority should
    be given to a political solution to the national
    question or whether a political solution will
    emerge from new community structures and
    models of operation.

3. The *removal of most powers from local government*
    has deepened the political vacuum; the creative
    tension between local and central governments
    (whatever their political colors) is absent; the
    scope for innovation and experiment falls to
    the community sector, in the face of overwhelm-
    ing state monopoly.

4. *Political stalemate among political parties* and their
    (understandable) obsession with the national
    question stifles democratic debate and deepens
    the atmosphere of sterility, enabling the com-
    munity sector to make much of the continu-
    ing social and economic policy debate. The
    checks and balances of plural democracy can
    be operated creatively and expressively by the
    third sector.

5. The *"troubles" and sectarian violence* on the streets
    of Northern Ireland present an atmosphere of
    tension and fear; the flight of the middle classes
    from political life leaves the community sector —
    as close to the ground, responsive, flexible, and
    committed groupings — in the front line as ser-
    vice providers and sometime arbitrators or
    negotiators between factions.

6. *Long-term and systemic deprivation* has left a mood
    of both bitterness and resignation, often fueled
    by perceived, if not real, grievance, providing
    fertile ground for the community activist but
    also for the illegal paramilitaries' recruiting
    sergeant.

7. *High-profile international media coverage* gives opportunities for the examination and scrutiny of issues, questions, and problems in the public domain. A caveat, however, is that the simplistic rose-tinted perspective of some of the media and their quest for one-dimensional answers hinders genuine debate and understanding.

8. The *claustrophobic hot-house environment* of Northern Ireland, constrained on the one hand by its border with the Republic of Ireland and on the other by the sea to Britain, causes frequent burnout in the community; the stakes are high, stress is endemic, opportunities for relaxation or relief are limited.

9. The *use of Northern Ireland as a test-bed for British legislation* elevates the significance of otherwise low-interest initiatives; the use of plastic and rubber bullets, punitive debt legislation, non-elected housing authorities, and political vetting of recipients of government grant aid have all had their origins in Northern Ireland.

10. The *suspension of some civil rights* is both an issue for the sector and itself a restriction; freedom of assembly, freedom of speech, the right to a trial by jury, access to the media, free association and freedom of movement have all been modified by special legislation for Northern Ireland, Britain, and Ireland, to different degrees.

The conclusion reached by most commentators is that the not-for-profit sector, taken in its broadest sense to include the community, voluntary, independent, and charitable activities of all organizations operating on a not-for-profit basis (as distinct from the state and private for-profit sectors), is large in volume by western European standards, similar in typology, but specially placed in its contribution to overarch the divided society. It has been described as a unique bridge in the community, drawing strength from its diversity, from its roots in both main communities, and from its stated neutrality in the formal political process. Unlike the extremes of division in South Africa, the occupied territories of the West Bank, or the Philippines, where the nongovernmental sector has found it necessary to ally irrevocably with the powerless and disenfranchised, the sector in Northern Ireland has, while identifying with the poor, preserved its place at the negotiating table; this reflects the nature of the Northern Ireland conflict as essentially one of identity rather than one of decolonization.

Characteristics of Voluntary Action

The premise on which this chapter is based is that the Northern Ireland conflict is not a religious one; this is merely a convenient label by which to describe a political struggle for identity and power between communities historically identified by their religious beliefs. Conventional religious practice, however, still persists in Northern Ireland: 75 percent of the adult population are regular churchgoers, as opposed to only 11 percent in Great Britain (Barker, 1989, p. 5). So what are the characteristics of the different communities? How do the religious predilections of the people manifest themselves?

Many community workers testify to the relative ease with which action can be stimulated in Catholic areas. This may be attributed to the historical experience of solidarity in adversity, folk memories of famine, collective response to problems, and the Catholic church's sense of community; further, the church is thought to have encouraged its politically alienated flock to develop a quasi-state under its wing and patronage — the principle of subsidiarity. Credit unions (cooperative associations that offer low-interest loans from members' savings) and extensive poor relief systems are good examples.

The Protestant tradition adheres to different values, which emphasize the individual and his or her relationship to God. The variety of Protestant sects — as opposed to the Catholic monolith — serves further to diminish on the Protestant side the strong collective bonds fostered in many Catholic areas. There is also some evidence that most Protestants are even more conservative than Catholics and therefore less likely to tackle social or economic issues; an opinion poll conducted by the *Belfast Telegraph* on October 4, 1988 showed that if the main British political parties put candidates forward for election in Northern Ireland, four times as many Protestants would vote for the Conservatives as would vote for Labor. Additionally, in Northern Ireland terms, the Protestants have little or no tradition of challenging the wisdom of the government, for fifty years "their" government — "a Protestant Parliament for a Protestant people" in the immortal words of a former Northern Ireland (Unionist) prime minister. This analysis reinforces the interlinking of religion and politics in the Northern Ireland context.

Some constraints also apply to the apparently fertile ground on the Catholic side. Although there is a tradition of collective action, the leadership of an impoverished and voiceless peasantry thrust on the nineteenth-century priesthood finds echoes today in Catholics' reluctance to challenge their erstwhile champions. Hence the influence exercised by the church over community action can counteract any emerging movement, unless sanctioned by the hierarchy. Second and perhaps even more problematic is the difficulty encountered when the social action necessitates engagement with the state; this either breeds apathy ("What is the point? The state — being Protestantism incarnate — is always against us") or cynicism (many believe that little will change until the national question is solved). Any interim engagement risks becoming part of the system or being reconciled to the status quo. Many also recognize, consciously or unconsciously, that if they did achieve success from constructive engagement with the state in redistribution of resources or power, this would conflict with, or seriously undermine, their basic belief in the impossibility of such an occurrence. Likewise on the Protestant side, being seen to challenge the state to which they are proclaiming political loyalty makes a mockery of that very loyalty.

On both sides, attitudes toward social issues are considerably less liberal than in most of western Europe; homosexual rights have been enforced in Northern Ireland and the Republic of Ireland only by European Court action; abortion in Northern Ireland is even more restricted than it is in Britain, while it is not only illegal but unconstitutional in the Republic of Ireland, as is divorce; contraception was only recently legalized and is still restricted. The Protestant and Catholic churches seem sometimes to unite only in their opposition to social progress.

McCartney (1989, p. 143) adds a further reason for the failure to encourage successful community development strategies: methodology of intervention. He questions whether sufficient account has been taken of "the normal processes of interactions which occur in local neighbourhoods" and suggests that professional values have been superimposed on working-class culture. Strikingly, he concludes: "It is interesting to note that paramilitary groups, especially in their formative period in the early seventies, were very much part of their area, and members were sensitive to the preferred styles of discourse and leadership. They had little outside advice, as community groups had from community workers, and this may have been significant in maintaining their roots in local culture."

The mushrooming of the community sector in the early seventies shares some of the U.S. experience as identified by Gerrard Suttles (1972, p. 156): "[T]he history of community organization in the United States is one of many small successes and several large failures. Where communities and neighbourhoods did unify themselves to some degree, their efforts were largely defensive and their successes measured largely by how well they withstood various forms of invasion from adjacent communities or neighbourhoods."

An extremely physical manifestation of these "various forms of invasion" was, of course, the very reason adduced by the emerging IRA for their legitimacy (De Baroid, 1989, p. 46). Similar observations have been made about community development in general in Northern Ireland (Frazer, 1981, p. 26).

Similarly, some striking individual successes have been built into general political change as in the growth of the religiously integrated voluntary schools movement, now government supported, and the widely accepted pivotal role of key women's organizations (Abbott and Frazer, 1985, p. 9).

The major difference from experiences elsewhere, however, lies in the nature of the complex interrelationship of religion and politics, under which the individual in Northern Ireland is born and which leads to a position on the other; not that this in itself is so different from the situation in, say, Sri Lanka or Israel, but in a western European liberal democracy it is unique. It is also unusual for the nongovernmental sector to have remained relatively neutral in terms of the formal political process. Finally, it is extremely unusual for the sector to have carved out for itself a central participatory role in the formal political vacuum as described. Acheson (1989, p. 31) argues that a new relationship between the sectors can be built on the old foundations, with recognition by each of the other's strengths.

A Development Model for the 1990s

For twenty years all parties to the Northern Ireland conflict have tended to see the British government as the ultimate power broker. On the one hand, the Republicans have subscribed to the nostrum that the British should withdraw from Ireland, describing it as a classic case of overdue decolonization; on the other hand, the Unionist majority has argued for the strengthening of British military forces to "root out terrorism" and either for greater political integration of Northern Ireland into U.K. structures or, alternatively, for devolution of power to a regional assembly, which they would dominate by virtue of an assured majority on the sectarian head-count basis of voting patterns.

Recently, however, some change has been noticed. The British secretary of state for Northern Ireland has admitted that the British cannot defeat an efficient and effective guerilla army by military or external political means alone; there must be an internal settlement. Sinn Fein, the political wing of the IRA, admits that it cannot win the military struggle alone either and that there must be constructive dialogue with Unionists prior to any settlement. Some Unionists also now recognize that an internal accommodation is needed and that they cannot continue simply to proclaim allegiance to a state from which they now feel fundamentally alienated. This was underlined by the United Kingdom's 1985 Anglo-Irish Agreement, an international treaty with the government of the Republic of Ireland, which gave consultative rights on Northern Ireland to that government. The agreement has been interpreted by Unionists as a "declaration of intent" to withdraw and by Republicans as "a cast-iron commitment to stay."

Mari Fitzduff (1989, p. 114) has expanded this analysis and argues that this scenario "may, eventually, provide fertile ground for the development of community politics where some of the old certainties are gone, and the "short, sharp shock" of military tactics has failed. . . . [T]he processes of community development work may begin to regenerate the energy, the enthusiasm, and the confidence of enough people to start some new and different balls rolling, both socially and, eventually, politically."

The clear link Fitzduff makes is to some in the more traditional voluntary sector an unpalatable one: that their role is inseparable from and integrally linked to the political process, especially in a region like Northern Ireland, where the constitutional question is so central and where the avowed nonpolitical stance of the sector has been so cherished. The challenge, however, is to find new models of operation that will enable the traditional value base of the sector — for example, the use of participatory models, innovation, accountability, equal opportunities, representation of minorities, bias in favor of the disadvantaged and of customer involvement — to be translated into new political forms without threatening or compromising the sector's perceived nonpartisan role.

The task, therefore, for the nonprofit sector in relation to Northern Ireland's seemingly intractable problems may be clear; if it offers one of the strategic neutral forums, overarching local sectional interests, as it claims, then it would be negligent not to make the connection between community development and the political process.

For example, a local community action group in other circumstances might lobby local politicians for better educational provision in its area; it would use traditional techniques of information dissemination, advocacy, petitions, letter writing, pickets of council meetings, and so forth, to secure a changed decision from local policymakers. However, in Northern Ireland those policymakers will be appointed officials accountable to central government rather than locally elected. Second, they will be operating within strongly centralized constraints and guidelines. Third, education, like so many issues in Northern Ireland, is heavily politicized and will probably require the political involvement of government ministers. The not-for-profit sector has, in this case, demonstrated its ability to move from meeting community needs (for example, for a religiously integrated school system) to causing significant structural changes in the organization of state education through state subsidy of the new integrated schools. There are similar examples in the fields of housing, training and employment, social services, and health provision.

The Community Relations Council, established in 1990 as a nonprofit independent organization developing activities in the field of relationships between the two main communities in Northern Ireland, has developed a further typology of community relations and community development work. It moves on a continuum from work designed to promote mutual understanding and respect, to prejudice reduction work with local communities, to work with churches on reconciliation of differences, to more positively antisectarian work designed to challenge institutional discrimination, to work designed to promote justice and rights for all communities, leading to discussion of alternatives and different political structures within which the governance of Northern Ireland might be accommodated. This typology again underlines the importance of community development as a process of empowering local groups to identify and meet community needs, its link to community relations work within the Northern Ireland context, and its irrevocable movement toward political systems and structures as an outcome of the expression of community need. In Northern Ireland terms, community development is described as a process of empowerment of individuals and groups, through work toward (1) raising awareness and understanding of advantage and disadvantage, wealth and poverty, and power and powerlessness; (2) promoting the interests of the disadvantaged, poor, and powerless by advocacy, representation, and jointly working with those organizations and groups that wish to defend and articulate the views of such sectors of society; (3) changing attitudes, policies, and structures of power in such a way as to promote understanding and respect; and (4) promoting democratic and participative models of organization. Community development therefore includes community action, community service, and community endeavor, whether geographically or issue based, with a propensity toward the disadvantaged, impoverished, and powerless within society.

With such opportunities, with such understanding, and with such enthusiasm and vitality as is present within the Northern Ireland not-for-profit sector, there is much that can and may be achieved. Let us remember, however, Hegel's caveat: "What experience and history teach us is—that people and governments have never learned anything from history, or acted on principles deduced from it."

References

Abbott, M., and Frazer, H. *Women and Community Work in Northern Ireland.* Belfast: Farset Press, 1985.

Acheson, N. *Voluntary Action and the State.* Belfast: Northern Ireland Council for Voluntary Action, 1989.

Barker, C. "Commentary." In Charities Aid Society, *Charity Trends* (12th ed.). Tonbridge, Kent, England: Charities Aid Society, 1989.

Deane, E. Quoted by P. Waddington in "Some Issues and Dilemmas." In *Community Work in a Divided Society.* Belfast: Farset Press, 1981.

De Baroid, C. *Ballymurphy and the Irish War.* Dublin: Aisling, 1989.

Donnison, D., Bulmer, M., Lewis, J., and Piachaud, D. (eds.). *The Goals of Social Policy.* London: Unwin Hyman, 1989.

Fitzduff, M. "Political Exigencies and Community Development—Conflicting or Connecting." In *Lost Horizons: New Horizons.* Belfast: Workers' Educational Association, 1989.

Frazer, H. "Community Work into the 80s." In *Community Work in a Divided Society.* Belfast: Farset Press, 1981.

McCartney, C. "Community Development: Working with or Against the Community?" In *Lost Horizons: New Horizons*. Belfast: Workers' Educational Association, 1989.

Oliver, Q. "Northern Ireland—A Relic of the Sixties or a Vision of the Nineties?" In *The Voluntary Sector in 1988*. London: National Council of Voluntary Organizations, 1988.

de Paor, L. *Divided Ulster*. Harmondsworth, Ireland: Penguin, 1971.

Suttles, G. *The Social Construction of Reality*. Chicago: University of Chicago Press, 1972.

Williamson, A. "Voluntary Organizations and Government in a Setting of Political and Ethnic Dissonance: Themes from the Experience of Northern Ireland." Paper presented at the conference "Voluntarism, Nongovernmental Organizations and Public Policy," Israel, May 1989.

Chapter 10

Changing Relationships
Between Private Organizations
and Government
in the Netherlands

Voluntary organizations have provided the bulk of social services in the Netherlands for nearly 150 years. In fact, the majority of public social services are provided by nongovernmental or quasi-governmental organizations, including health insurance, social security associations, housing societies, and regional institutions for outpatient mental health care. For many services, few people are able to distinguish whether the organizations that are providing the services are primarily governmental or nongovernmental in legal status (Aquina, 1988, pp. 94ff.; Baakman, 1988, pp. 51ff.). One could say that the old societal pattern that existed before the French occupation, in which there was no clear distinction between the responsibilities of government on the one hand or of the church and private citizens on the other hand, is in some ways still in operation. The reality is that in order to maintain public support and trust, government uses or creates private organizational forms to deliver social services. Because there is a high level of public trust in existing voluntary organizations, government entrusts these organizations with public tasks and authority. In both cases, whether these organizations are governmental or nongovernmental, government nearly fully finances them.

The involvement of private voluntary organizations in social welfare has always been important. Government involvement has been increasing since 1952, especially in the areas of coordination, planning, and financing. There are private voluntary organizations that do not receive government funding, but they are not important in the provision of social welfare. Since 1965, with the passage of the General Relief Act, government has had the primary responsibility for providing public relief. As a result of this act and the accumulation of a number of social security acts legislated since 1901, victims of all sorts of personal disasters have been guaranteed financial support. Therefore, private voluntary organizations only provide financial support in a few exceptional cases that are not covered by social insurance funds.

To provide some context for the relationship between the provision of social welfare and nongovernmental organizations, it is instructive to compare the dramatic changes that have taken place since 1854. In 1854, the population of the Netherlands was around 3.5 million people; in 1978, it was nearly 14.5 million. In 1854, there was no social insurance; in 1977, approximately 30 percent of the national income was spent on social security, including public relief (2 percent). Welfare costs for the state in 1979 accounted for nearly half of the total budget (48 billion Dfl.). In 1977, 4.6 billion Dfl. of the national budget was spent on public relief, and 6 billion Dfl. was spent for subsidies to private voluntary organizations (Reinders, 1981, pp. 21ff.).

In the Netherlands, social welfare includes health care for both medical and mental health and support for youth, prisoners on probation, all forms of education, the arts, sports, and the mass media. My focus in this chapter does not include education since this area has a specific constitutionally recognized status with special laws; nor do I go into detail in regard to specific fields of welfare because every area has more or less specific sociological and legal characteristics. Rather, my specific focus is on the ways that government and private organizations work together in the area of social welfare and how this cooperative interaction was made into public policy and put into specific legislation.

The following discussion is divided into three sections. The first presents the historical background of social welfare activities before 1952 and includes a discussion of major social welfare policy since the establishment of the Department of Social Welfare in 1952. The second section focuses on the philosophy and practice of decentralization of government support to nonprofit organizations. The final section examines the Welfare Act of 1988 and its implications for the relationship between government and private nonprofit organizations.

Historical Background of Social Welfare in the Netherlands

In the centuries preceding the major changes of 1952, care for the poor was undertaken by the churches and so-called civil institutions. In the constitutions of 1814 and 1815, the duty to provide for the poor by the churches and civil institutions was laid down, and the king was charged with the responsibility of reporting annually to parliament on the condition of this care of the poor. The renewed and modern constitution of 1848 (which was prepared under the guidance of the famous liberal statesman Thorbecke) called for legislation governing the care of the poor. This became the *Poor Act (Armenwet) of 1854*. The stipulations of this act were (1) that the church and private institutions should be free to care for the poor in their own ways and on their own conditions as long as they did not damage the interests of the state; (2) that these institutions should be required to report regularly to the central government and that other legal requirements would be put in place to ensure the efficient use of money by these organizations at both the national and local levels of government; and (3) that since care for the poor was in principle a matter for the churches and private organizations, governmental relief to poor people would only be given to those who could provide proof that nongovernmental agencies had not helped them.

Governmental help to the poor had the character of a police service: begging was not allowed and starvation was not acceptable. In fact, many local governments actually became administrators of private foundations (*stichtingen*) for the poor. These institutions were not governmental "in the true sense," because they were established by citizens of the community during the fifteenth to the eighteenth centuries. The founders of these organizations left their administration to local governments after their death. Thus, over a long period of time, local governments took over the administration of numerous private foundations (*fondsen*).

During this same period, the passage of the Association and Public Meeting Act in 1855 made it possible to establish legally incorporated associations (with royal consent). As a consequence of this act, in addition to the establishment of foundations, other associations were established for various purposes. One group included associations for voluntary poor relief and was modeled after the Charity Organization Societies of England and the United States. These associations tried to coordinate various services to people in poverty, to fight against abusive practices, and to provide assistance to the poor in programs modeled on those developed in England, the United States, and Germany.

At the end of the nineteenth century, the nongovernmental initiatives that emphasized greater unity and coordination among voluntary organizations providing poor relief led to important legislative changes in the Poor Act. The *Poor Act of 1912* gave the responsibility of coordinating poor relief activities to a Poor Council (*Armenraad*): this was an agency of the local government but was only installed in a community at the request of private organizations to the minister of inland affairs. This subtle connection between private organizations and their request to governmental authority is a good example of the continuous interactions between government and private organizations in the Netherlands. Depending on the period, the advocacy role of private voluntary organizations sometimes predominated, while at other times their role as service providers predominated.

For over a century, private organizations in the Netherlands were the sole or most important group of service providers in many fields of social welfare. The financing of their services was channeled through the central government and eventually through provincial and local governments (van Wersch, 1979).

During the last part of the nineteenth century and the first half of the twentieth century, Dutch society was characterized in nearly all areas by "pillarization," or the separate but equal systems among various groups (Goudsblom, 1967). The diversity of religious motives and political ideologies led to the formation of Roman Catholic, Protestant (Calvinistic), socialistic, and nonsectarian humanistic organizations like separate pillars in an edifice. Thus, the whole society was structured by these religious and ideological organizations. This "pillarization" was for the most part as true in politics as in the sphere of delivering nonprofit services (van Daalen, 1970).

Combined with this religious and political differentiation of organizations is the long tradition of "weak" central government, that is, a government that does not want to make all the decisions, but only those that apparently cannot be made at any other ("lower") level (Adriani, 1923; Aquina, 1988). Such a tradition stems from the fact that there is no political party in the Netherlands that can rule on its own; there have always been party combinations in government. As a result this system of significant private organizational influence and a weak government is in the interest of all the various influential groups in society and, therefore, thought to be in the general interest.

Thus it is not surprising that the major ideological or political groups in the Netherlands accept this structure of society, although for different reasons. The Roman Catholics accept the structure on the basis of the subsidiary principle that supports state responsibility for social services only when religious or private voluntary organizations fail to provide them. The Calvinists support the structure on the basis of the principle of sovereignty in every sphere; that is, according to this principle, the state does not have total responsibility but rather that responsibility depends on the nature of the "sphere." The socialists support the theory of functional decentralization, which maintains that government is in principle responsible for social welfare but that such tasks are best accomplished at the local level. Liberals support the current structure on the basis of the theory that society is stronger with a separation of powers (checks and balances).

Interestingly, although the Netherlands has a liberal constitution, liberal principles are not very popular in politics. The liberals, who share a political party with the conservatives, only garner about 10 percent of the votes. One reason for this phenomenon is that the Dutch are used to individual freedom.

After World War II, exclusiveness of the different groups in society declined, and a new openness began. For a long period of time, private organizations became less dependent on their traditional clients, because they felt less threatened by asking for a service from a group other than the one to which they belonged. In fact, professionals in such organizations were the first to switch among competing organizations.

In 1952 the Department of Welfare was established. The first minister (the Catholic Van Thiel) underlined the differences between poor relief and welfare work. Poor relief had to do with helping people to stay alive by any means at hand. Welfare work involved the provision of an array of services to help people maintain themselves in society. In 1965, when the General Relief Act took effect, separation between poor relief and welfare work formally became a fact.

From the beginning of its existence, the Department for Welfare Work had to think about its relations with private organizations (in Dutch, usually abbreviated as *p.i.*, or *particulier initiatief*). During the decade of the 1950s, the initial tendency was to stimulate private organizations to conduct welfare work and eventually to encourage the establishment of private organizations in fields where none existed. During the 1960s, govern-

ment policy changed somewhat. Rather than encourage the
founding of new private organizations, the department suggested
that gaps in welfare service should be filled by government at
the local level, which delivered some welfare services. There was
no central planning for social welfare until the end of the 1960s.
All the department did was to subsidize private organizations
and local governments.

The Philosophy and Practice
of Government Subsidization

The legal basis for public subsidies depended on the area of welfare work. For some areas the basis was an act, such as the
Library Act or the Probation Act. In most areas specific legislation was lacking. Therefore, other social welfare programs were
given legal status when the annual budget of the Department
for Welfare work was approved by parliament. The amounts
of subsidies were calculated in many different ways.

In several areas, the department that subsidized a particular program would publish its rules for providing government subsidies in the *Official Gazette*. These rules were not real
legislation because they had not been accepted by parliament;
rather, they were ministerial decrees that functioned as "pseu-
dolegislation." Once the rules were published, however, the
bureaucracy of the department was bound to follow these decrees.
Applicants could also appeal decisions from departments on the
ground that the decisions were contrary to the published rules.
Although many decrees were not based on real legislation, ministerial decrees governing the allocation of government subsidies
did have the force of law.

Government support in the Netherlands is not regarded
as a form of generosity but rather as a responsibility of the state
for society. Through such responsibility, government can steer
development within society. For example, the rights of clients
of private organizations can be (and are) imposed on such organizations through requirements for government support. It
is, therefore, not surprising that an important issue in the theory and practice of government subsidizing is just how much

government regulation is possible without infringing upon the autonomy/identity of the private organization (Hirsch Ballin, 1988).

In 1973, in the *Knelpuntennota* [Note of Bottlenecks], the Dutch government tried for the first time to formulate an over-all welfare policy. In this document, the concept of "basic provisions" was introduced. It stated what government support ought to be available to everyone on the basis of basic constitutional rights and democratic decision making. According to this note, it was the responsibility of central government to ensure the quality of services and to see to it that organizations that rendered the services behaved democratically. These democratic goals fitted very well in the dominant philosophy of social work professionals, who had, since the 1960s, promoted democratic participation as the major purpose of welfare work. They also supported the movement of society toward total democratic rule.

Beginning in 1973, the Note of Bottlenecks had a major influence on welfare policy. In the Subsidy Rules (or the Rules on Support by Central Government), two principles were manifest: the principle of *decentralization* and the principle of *democratization*. Decentralization meant in this case that local governments were the channels for distributing government support but that they could only get money (support) from central government when they had an official local ruling on subsidies. Such local rulings had to be approved by the local council that also approved the annual welfare plan. The local plan was, of course, restricted to a certain financial limit by the central government. Furthermore, according to the Rule of the Minister, these local subsidy rulings had to include the requirement that private organizations have as part of their regulations some form of participation by workers and clients in the administration of those organizations.

Considering its impact, the Knelpuntennota can be viewed as a semiofficial governmental declaration that turned nonprofit organizations that received public support into de facto agencies. It is not by accident that this happened, because a socialist Christian Democratic party government was in power. Nevertheless, this tendency toward decentralized administration and wide democratic participation was rather broadly supported. By this time, private organizations that were governmentally financed had lost a good deal of contact with their old supporters, and they were increasingly regulated by government. Most of the private organizations lacked active controlling bodies, and the requirement of democratic participation was an attempt to compensate for this weakness. Thus, the Knelpuntennota reestablished in the Netherlands the original situation in which the people who demanded a service, organized it and made important decisions about it.

Two trends have occurred to blur the distinction between government and nonprofit organizations. One trend is giving private organizations such as the health insurance and social insurance associations legal tasks and obligatory participation; clients have no free choice, and the funds have no free decisions. The associations are considered independent governmental agencies. This trend pervades other areas of welfare where clients, not organizations, have free choice. Nonprofit organizations are "governmentalized" (*verstatelijkt*). The other trend is that governments at all levels establish, alone or with other governments or with nonprofit organizations, organizations of civil law. These organizations can be either independent governmental bodies or "private nonprofit" organizations without governmental authority. Because this pattern has a long tradition, the actual term *privatizing* is not as new as it seems.

In social science theory, both of these types of organizations are called paragovernmental organizations (Aquina, 1988, chap. 1; see also Baakman, 1988, pp. 6/ff.). For legal theory or practice, these categories of paragovernmental organizations and private nonprofit organizations are not adequately distinguished. In any case, the phenomenon of governmentalizing private nonprofit organizations has been the subject of many sociological and policy studies, as is evident from the back files of the magazine *Beleid en Maatschappi* (policy and society) in the period from 1970 to 1980.

This governmentalizing of private organizations has also had a side effect. The financing of private nonprofit organizations by government is treated like the financing of governmental activities. One of the existing failures of governmental finance is the lack of control on the efficiency of spending after the budget has been set. Such lack of control has meant that private organizations can receive more money than they actually need. This practice has led to the building of reserve or support funds that are either not known about or not taken into account by the subsidizing government. The vision of private organizations as functional, decentralized governmental agencies, however, is not shared in practice by the boards of private organizations when it comes to the administration of money.

In many cases clients of nonprofit services do not know whether the organization that renders the service is governmental or private. In fact, employees are not always certain whether their agency is governmental or a private nonprofit organization. In many areas, the treatment of and regulations affecting employees are, by law, the same for governmental employees and employees of private organizations.

In order to provide a legal foundation for the decentralization of welfare services, the concept of Act Kaderwet Specifiek Welzijn (framework act for specific welfare) was introduced in 1977. Such legislation relating to the efficient and democratic functioning of nonprofit organizations would have provided a framework for all social welfare services. The idea was, on the one hand, to create an overall act on planning and financing of welfare work and, on the other hand, to decentralize and make planning dependent on decisions at the lowest level possible. Furthermore, the issue of democratization was taken up at this same time. A governmental committee issued a report with an overview on the condition of the nonprofit sector, including a vision of the future called "Efficient and Democratic Functioning of Subsidized Institutions." This report stimulated discussion in government, parliament, and the literature about what kind of legislation was needed to assure the efficient and democratic functioning of nonprofit institutions (see van Wersch, 1979). But the problem of finding a balance between the requirements of democracy for private organizations and their right to their own identity continued. After ten years, this issue of democratizing organizations in a uniform way eventually lost its attractiveness, and the government did not propose an act.

In the meantime, the government operated on the basis of the Knelpuntennota and its Rules for National Support. In practice, the disadvantages of a welfare policy with planned decentralization and compulsory democracy in voluntary organizations became very clear and made these goals less attractive (Bartels, 1984, p. 26). For instance, the disadvantages were felt in the processes of merging of private organizations that government asked for because of efficiency. Decentralization of planning and the democratizing of private organizations were also expensive operations. Decentralization therefore had to be combined with restrictions on separate operations by private organizations engaging in the same activities. This caused and still causes many joint operations and the merging of organizations on both the regional and national levels. These mergers have meant the loss of jobs for professionals in the affected organizations. Democracy rule within the organizations had given these professionals a formal voice in decisions concerning these operations, and this caused the professionals conflict between their function as professional workers and their function as decision makers in policy matters and the future of the organizations in general. Democracy rule related to clients also worked against plans directed toward the efficient provision of services. The participation of clients in governmentally financed organizations, furthermore, led to the clients' dependence on the existence of the organizations for their social status. Therefore, although the Kaderwet Specifiek Welzijn was accepted by parliament in 1982, it never was put into effect and eventually was repealed.

In 1981 a Socialist-Christian Democratic government was succeeded by a Christian Democratic–liberal/conservative government. Although concrete legislation on democratization and the central planning of decentralization failed in parliament, in 1983 the introduction of social rights into the constitution was accepted by parliament. This had its effect in the area of social welfare. The constitutional "care for poor-law administration" in the older versions of the constitution was replaced by the rule that "government creates the conditions for social and cultural development and for recreation." One has to keep in mind that these so-called social rights do not mean individual rights for citizens but are considered as instructions to government. As such, they provide wide freedoms for government and legislators to make policies (see Lunshof, 1989, pp. 224ff).

Also in 1983, legislative activities began for a new omnibus Welfare Act. These efforts were successful, and the act has been in force since 1988. According to this act, decentralization is not pyramidal as it was in the Kaderwet; instead, national, provincial, and local governments have been given responsibilities for specific fields of welfare. The national government, for instance, has responsibility for libraries for the blind and for sailors and for other special libraries; for national organizations for youth; and for regional translator centers for refugees. The provinces are responsible for the support of local libraries, sociocultural activities, emancipation activities, and telephone aid services. Local communities have responsibility for neighborhood work, specialized activities for the mentally handicapped, youth centers, a center for voluntary workers, and coordinated services for elderly people.

In two places this legislation sets out the relationship of government to private organizations: Section 6 of the Welfare Act states that provincial and local governments must take into account as much as possible in their decision making (policy) the pluralism of society and that they should support the initiative and responsibility of citizens, while observing guarantees for the quality, efficiency, and democratic functioning of these activities. Although private organizations are not specifically mentioned, it is clear that the initiative of the citizens is supposed to be channeled through private organizing (private "initiative").

Section 35 states that the provincial council and the community council are responsible for making regulations for the involvement of citizens and private nonprofit institutions within those areas that are included in the preparation of the policy plan and decision making relating to the provincial or local provisions of welfare. At each governmental level, an annual plan is prepared and published. In this plan those private organizations that will receive government support are to be mentioned. The local and provincial governments are responsible for providing accounts for expenditures to the minister of welfare work.

With these legislative requirements incorporating the involvement of private nonprofit organizations, it is not surprising that a professor in public law, who became the minister of justice in 1989, could declare that the realization of social rights is only possible with a vital sector of private organizations (Hirsch Ballin, 1988, p. 40). Another jurist went further (Bartels, 1984, p. 25) and stated that governmental responsibility for social welfare through this legislation in the Netherlands is translated into the guarantee of governmental protection for citizens against the governmentally subsidized private organizations through quality requirements and democratic participation in decision making. While this statement is not far from reality, it is, perhaps, too absolute.

Welfare social policy at the present time is quite different from what it was ten to fifteen years ago. It is less ideological, and economic arguments are now more likely to play a role. Viewed from a distance, one could say that the socialist concept of functional decentralization has been replaced by the concepts of the Catholic, Protestant, and liberal traditions. Apparently, clients prefer good services over the democratizing of organizations. This trend is leading to a more market-oriented nonprofit service sector.

Another clear trend is the privatizing of government agencies. While this does not necessarily mean the loss of governmental control—because there are many ways to guarantee such control in the regulatory statutes of civil law organizations—it does allow for more competition among older private nonprofit organizations. This trend toward privatization further bolsters a more market-oriented nonprofit sector.

These trends, however, will probably not lead to a completely market-oriented nonprofit sector. The main reason for this is that the clients and the organizations are, in practice, not equal partners; and some legal protection for clients is guaranteed (Bartels, 1984, p. 50). This market orientation will mean that organizations will have to legitimate their existence to clients as well as to the government. Thus more mergers will occur, reducing competition but also accentuating the particular identities of nonprofit organizations.

Conclusions

Like most Dutch observers, I do not think that the situation of an important place for private organizations made possible only by governmental recognition and support for them in the welfare area (or in other areas) of society will change or should be changed, although such liaisons do have their drawbacks. However, there are also arguments and drawbacks for a strong position of private voluntary initiative, even when financed by the government (van Wersch, 1979, chap. 2; Baakman, 1988, pp. 196ff.). While our model may not serve for universal use because systems emerge from cultural histories, its advantage is that it does not depend on continuity in the power of certain groups. Furthermore, in the increasing development of a pluralistic rather than a "pillarized" society that the Netherlands is becoming, I presume, like Aquina (1988, p. 106), that this interaction of private nonprofit initiative and government can and will be continued.

References

Adriani, J. H. *Voorlezingen over armenzorg en maatschappelijk werk* [Lectures about poor law and social work]. Utrecht: Ruys, 1923.

Aquina, H. "PGOs in the Netherlands." In C. Hood and G. F. Schuppert, *Delivering Public Service in Western Europe*. London: Sage, 1988.

Baakman, N.A.A. "Transformatie van overheid en maatschappij" [Transformation of government and society]. In J.G.A. van Mierlo and L. G. Gerrichhauzen (eds.), *Het particulier initiatief in de Nederlandse verzorgingsmaatschappij; een bestuurskundige benadering,* pp. 51–74. Lochem: De Tijdstroom, 1988.

Bartels, J.A.C. "Hulpverleningsrecht" [Law concerning medical and social assistance]. Dissertation, R. U. Utrecht, Kluwer, Deventer, 1984.

van Daalen, P. *Wij Nederlanders, een sociologische verkenning* [We Dutch people: a sociological survey]. Utrecht: Het Spectrum, 1970.

Goudsblom, J. *Dutch Society.* New York: Random House, 1967.

Hirsch Ballin, E. H. *Rechtsstaat, grondrechten en subsidieverhoudingen, preadvies Vereniging voor Administratief Recht* [Constitutional state, civil rights, and subsidy relationships: report for the association of administrative law]. Alphen aan den Rijn: Samsom, 1988.

Lunshof, H. R. "Welzijn, wet, wetgever; op zoek naar de taak van de wetgever" [Welfare, law, legislator: in search of the task of the legislator]. Dissertation, R. U. Utrecht, W. E. J. Tjeenk Willink, Zwolle, 1989.

Reinders, A. *Subsidiëring van instellingen* [Subsidizing of institutions]. Van Loghum Slaterus, Deventer, W. E. J. Tjeenk Willink, Zwolle, 1981.

van Wersch, P.J.M. "Democratisering van het bestuur van nonprofit instellingen" [Democratizing of the management of nonprofit institutions]. Dissertation, K. U. Nijmegen, Alphen aan den Rijn: Samsom, 1979.

Government-Nonprofit Relationships in a Comparative Perspective: The Cases of France and Germany

On Terminology

Though it is widely agreed that organizations between the market and the state represent an institutional universe in their own, deserving an appropriate scholarly treatment, descriptive terminology is still diverse and inconsistent. Concepts such as the nonprofit sector, the private voluntary sector, the nongovernmental sector, and the nonstatutory sector apparently cover more or less the same type of institutions; they do so, however, with different connotations. The terms *nonprofit* and *nongovernmental* implicitly emphasize the difference from either private enterprises or public bureaucracies. The terms *private voluntary* and *nonstatutory* emphasize a particular rationale of organizational constituencies and a specific regulatory environment, respectively.

For both pragmatic and theoretical reasons it might be helpful to escape from this puzzle by using the term *third sector* (Etzioni, 1973; Levitt, 1973) as a solution and, at the same time, as an appropriate analytical concept. Terminologically, denoting a group of organizations as a "third" institutional type avoids problems of cross-national comparison, at least as long as the organizational composition of the intermediary zone between the market and the state in different countries remains relatively unexplored. Analytically, this assumes a "third" type of organization, with a different style of organizational behavior as compared with private business or state bureaucracy. Therefore, the "third sector" seems to be an appropriate denotation for a special institutional form common to all Western democracies but substantially different in terms of organizational constituencies and relationship with government.

The Relationship Between Government and the Third Sector

The relationship between government and the third sector is usually reviewed from three different perspectives. The first one focuses on resource flows between government and third-sector organizations in terms of funding (Salamon, 1987, 1990). The second one focuses on the interorganizational relationship between government and, primarily, private voluntary organizations in terms of interaction styles (Lloyd, 1990). The third approach tries to identify the peculiarity of both statutory and third-sector organizations as service providers in terms of mutual competitive advantages (Rose-Ackerman, 1986; Weisbrod, 1988).

Not surprisingly, these approaches have some shortcomings with respect to potential generalization. Resource flows may indicate shifting involvements of the public versus the third sector in the provision of public goods, but they do not reveal the actors involved or the decisions they make. Analyses of interaction styles necessarily identify those actors but they usually do not consider the historical evolvement of their relationship. Economic models of mutual competitive advantages of public, private, and third-sector institutions implicitly assume that competition is also the general characteristic of the relationship between government and the third sector; this is not, however, necessarily the case.

This chapter emphasizes political and administrative culture as a crucial variable in explaining different national patterns of the relationship between government and the third sector. I will try to illustrate that government and third-sector agencies alike cannot escape from institutional setting and national styles of politics and policy that are imposed by national history and endorsed by appropriate patterns of ideological justification. Thus far, the relationship between government and the third sector is far less flexible in terms of mutual substitution than economic models might lead us to believe. Moreover, it is not competitive behavior that characterizes the interaction between government and the third sector in many European countries. We may observe stable group coalitions and strong ideologies supporting the use of a third sector that provides public goods as well as governmental ignorance vis-à-vis intermediary organizations and a spirit of etatism. Within this prefiguration, however, political regimes display different degrees of elasticity once the need for nongovernmental provision of public goods appears on the political agenda.

Some Basic Statistics

We have no reliable data on the scope and dimension of the third sector in France or what was formerly West Germany. Nor have we sufficient information about the flows of resources between the public and the third sector. Additional problems occur when it comes to cross-national comparative research. If there are any data, they are hardly compatible or comparable. Nonetheless, what is available in terms of statistics should be mentioned here even if it must be handled with care.

In France, there are 90,000 *voluntary associations* active in the fields of health care and social services. However, only 7,000 (or 8 percent) of them are service-providing institutions. These 7,000 voluntary associations provide a 51.6 percent share of all health and social services. This figure is broken down as follows (Inspection Generale des Affaires Sociales, 1984; Thery, 1986):

86 percent of services for the handicapped
70 percent of home-care services (for the sick, the handicapped, the elderly)
28 percent of old people's homes
 6 percent of day care for the elderly
80 percent of family vacation centers
68 percent of centers of social advocacy and advice
18 percent of child day care
17.5 percent of all the hospitals, but
   50 percent of hospitals with fewer than 150 beds
   75 percent of hospitals with fewer than 100 beds
   40 percent of all spa and recovery hospitals

As to the budget situation, data are only available for the
social services delivered by voluntary associations. In 1983, this
budget totaled 30 billion French francs or the equivalent of $6
billion: $2.7 billion in public subsidies (state and local), $2.1
billion in social insurance transfers, and $1.2 billion in fees and
charges (Thery, 1986).

Thus, 80 percent of the budget for social services delivered by voluntary associations consists of public subsidies and
social insurance transfers, in other words, of public or quasi-
public money. Moreover, French welfare associations in the area
of social services have a total of 230,000 employees.

Statistics are also available for the quantitative development of French voluntary associations in general. The "birth
rate" of associations dramatically increased, from 22,000 in 1974
to 47,000 new associations in 1983. While during the same
period the annual rate of increase for all French voluntary organizations was 20 percent, it was 29 percent for associations
in the category of social services (Archambault, 1985).

Another indicator of disproportional growth of the voluntary sector is the countercyclic development of employment.
Whereas employment was in stagnation in the French public
and private sectors in the early 1980s, the average annual increase for all voluntary associations from 1982 to 1984 was 4.5
percent. In 1984, voluntary associations of all kinds (not only
welfare associations) had 770,000 full-time employees (or 4 percent of the employed national work force) (Thery, 1986).

For Germany, there are no fully compatible data. Most figures that are available are for West Germany before unification. Data from what was East Germany are not yet available. According to the meritorious survey compiled by Helmut Anheier (1990), in terms of nonprofit institutions, the third sector holds a share of 33 percent of the hospital industry by hospital units, 37 percent of the hospital industry by beds, 9 percent of the schools by unit, and 7 percent of the schools by students.

As to employment, the third sector in Germany displays á similar countercyclical feature to its French counterpart. While general employment decreased slightly between 1982 and 1985, the nonprofit sector's share of total employment increased from 1.62 percent in 1982 to 1.88 percent in 1985 (Anheier, 1990).

German welfare associations in particular run more than 60,000 units that provide health care and social services. This represents, according to Anheier (1990), a share of 70 percent of all family services, 60 percent of all services for the elderly, 40 percent of all hospital beds, and 90 percent of all employment for the handicapped.

The three major welfare associations alone employ approximately 580,000 people (or 2.7 percent of the employed national work force) full-time. Investment in this segment closely followed the cycles of investment expenditures in the public sector from 1960 to 1984: it increased from 7 to 11.5 billion deutsche marks (compared to the public sector's 45 to 103 billion deutsche marks) and slowly but surely fell to 10 billion in 1980 (compared to the public sector's 101 billion) and then to 9 billion in 1984 (compared to the public sector's 74 billion) (Anheier, 1990).

The Twin Functions of Third-Sector Organizations and the Nature of the Relationship Between Government and the Third Sector

More information about the size and dimension of a given third sector as well as about resource flows between the public sector and the third sector remains a crucial prerequisite for further comparative research. However, no matter how precise statistical descriptions may be, they will not tell us anything special about the inner nature of the relationship between government and the third sector. The substantial dependence of both the French and the German third sector on public subsidies masks rather than reveals the important differences in the relationship of government and the third sector in the two countries.

It would be misleading to assume that the sectors (the public, the private, and the third) are black boxes that contain organizations with a given behavior (for example, more or less competitive). This would assume that the relationship between government and the third sector was more or less competitive, too, and that the consumer or voter was the sovereign decision maker. The respective importance of the public sector and the third sector could then be interpreted as an equilibrium of institutional choice according to the competitive advantages of each sector in terms of quality and efficiency.

In a comparative perspective, however, this assumption is hardly justified. In many countries we cannot observe a competitive relationship between government and the third sector. Whereas this relationship in the United States is, indeed, characterized by a relatively high degree of competitiveness in the commodity market as well as in the political market (this might explain why American scholars are inclined to assume competitiveness as a basic pattern of organizational behavior in the third sector), it may be characterized by consensus or coercion in other countries. Furthermore, there are good reasons to assume that third-sector organizations are less likely than other institutional forms to display competitive behavior in terms of quality and efficiency.

What makes third-sector organizations different from private firms and public bureaucracies are their special sociopolitical and economic *twin functions,* which presumably cannot be decomposed without affecting their raison d'être, or their stability. These twin functions are a consequence of the special *resource dependency* of organizations that belong neither to the for-profit nor to the public sector. Third-sector organizations have both an allocative and an integrative function. Since profit making and regular public financing as resource generators are absent, fund raising and volunteerism are the vital functions of third-sector organizations. Consider private or corporate giving, public subsidies, or a voluntary work force: since there is no remuneration of labor and no legal obligation of funding and since funding through fees is principally limited, resource mobilization is heavily dependent on the *nonmonetary rewards* the organization can provide. These rewards typically consist of reputation, network benefits, a sense of community, or similar types of ideological well-being. They are typically provided through membership on boards of trustees or directors and through volunteerism. Consequently, foundations, nonprofit hospitals, voluntary associations that provide social services, and similar organizations are not only providers of goods and services but important factors of social and political coordination.

The boards of trustees or boards of directors of these organizations do more than just control organizational performance. It is even questionable whether performance control is a board's primary function (Middleton, 1987). Boards act as the knots within networks of reputational, financial, and power elites. Mutual interests are balanced through this arrangement. From the organization's point of view, rich, influential, and reputable persons on the board of trustees are a prerequisite for successful fund raising; at the same time, being a member of a board brings one an increase in reputation and reinforces old networks and knits new networks of interpersonal relationships. Therefore, third-sector organizations have an unusual structure that might be called, according to sociologist Mark Granovetter (1985), "embeddedness."

There are, at least, two consequences of this special type of embeddedness. First, no mechanism, such as profit through consumer decisions, endorsement through voter commitment, or hierarchical auditing from outside the organization, links organizational performance and rewards for board members and volunteers. Board members may use their network connections and volunteers may enjoy community life despite organizational inefficiency. Since these rewards are relatively independent of organizational performance, third-sector organizations are rather unlikely to have a competitive advantage relative to public or for-profit institutions in terms of allocative efficiency. Second, since resources are not primarily mobilized through market transactions but through personal relationships among board members and their reference groups, the nature of social and political coordination exerted by a board presumably significantly shapes the relationship between government and the third sector.

Thus patterns of the relationship do not necessarily follow the logic of superiority in terms of quality and efficiency. Third-sector organizations exhibit a broad spectrum of organizational behavior that ranges from the efficient provision of public goods to the relatively inefficient (in economic terms) provision of outlets or structural filters for social and political tensions (Seibel, 1989). Whatever the function of third-sector organizations is, it is shaped by the structure of their embeddedness in a given social and political environment. Accordingly, it is sensible to assume that the relationship between government and the third sector is especially shaped by this embeddedness, which at the same time is shaping the way that third-sector organizations may be used for different purposes under different political circumstances.

The French and German situations display special patterns of this relationship, patterns that are characterized by different embeddedness structures in their respective third-sector organizations (welfare associations) and that provide different options for the use of the third sector as a tool of governmental action. The remainder of this chapter focuses on the historical evolvement of the relationship of government and the third sector in France and Germany, how their structures may be generalized, and what the impact of these structures on the current role of their respective third sectors may be.

Historical Roots of the Relationship
Between Government and the Third Sector
in France and Germany

In France, all kinds of "intermediary organizations" have been under fundamental attack since the revolution of 1789. As described by Tocqueville, the French Revolution executed the dissolution of the corporation order of the nobility and the clergy, already prepared by the absolutism. The famous *Loi Le Chapelier* (1791) and the *Code Penal* (1810) solemnly interdicted any intermediary institution to stand between the citizen and his republic. Accordingly, both the new civic order and historical progress could be identified with the centralized state. The general right of free association in France was enacted only in 1901. However, political and ideological perceptions of associations remained ambiguous. The Jacobinic tradition in France is still alive, and suspicion of the associations, most of them still close to the Catholic laic movement, has never completely disappeared. It was also sustained through efforts during the Vichy era of German occupation to rebuild a nondemocratic corporatist regime (Passaris and Raffi, 1984; Debbasch and Bourdon, 1987).

In Germany, the beginning of associational life in the eighteenth century was clearly marked by anticorporatist elements. The explicit purpose was to assemble people regardless of their position within the ranks of the nobiliary order of society. Until the end of the nineteenth century, however, associations displayed multiple patterns of purpose and political behavior, especially regarding their relationship with the state. In many fields where the role of the feudal state (especially in Prussia) as the principal agent of modernization coincided with the interest of the bourgeoisie in education, free trade, and economic development, there was early cooperation between the state and associations concerned with related issues. On the other hand, during the course of the nineteenth century, associations became the elementary form of political opposition against the state; after the failed revolution of 1848, they also became a surrogate for the democracy that had not been achieved within the state order itself. Therefore, today there is not only a tradition of cooperation between the state and voluntary associations in the provision of public services but also an inclination, especially on the part of the political left, to identify democracy with an attitude of anti-etatism and ignorance vis-à-vis a democratic structure of the state itself (Mueller, 1965; Wurzbacher, 1971).

Consequently, intermediary organizations of all types — including associations as political pressure groups and, especially, political parties — are a crucial element of German polity, whereas their role continues to be contested in France. Thus, the relationship between government and the third sector is stable and more or less conflict free in Germany, but it is contradictious and sometimes under tension in France. The division of labor between the state and private voluntary associations is one of the crucial elements of political common sense in German social policy (Katzenstein, 1987). In France, there is no such consensus; associations and private voluntary organization as providers of social services, health care (including hospitals), and private education are tolerated by government. This relationship, however, is relatively unstable (Meny, 1985; Goetschy, 1987).

A Scheme of the Relationship Between Government and the Third Sector: State Autonomy, Dominant Actors, and Styles of Linkage

For a systemization of the relationship between government and the third sector I use a scheme of different linkage patterns. This scheme is based on the distinction of different degrees of *state autonomy* (Nordlinger, 1981; Skocpol, 1985), different types of *dominant actors,* and different *styles of interaction* between these actors. The dominant actors may be differentiated along a continuum from local to national; the style of their interaction may be differentiated along a continuum of noncompetitive to competitive behavior (Richardson, 1982; Wildavsky, 1987).

Consider the board of trustees or board of directors of a given third-sector organization as a starting point for an analysis of its "embeddedness." On the one hand, the behavior of board members is shaped by mere affiliation with the board. As mere board members, these people form what William Ouchi (1980) has termed a *clan:* a system of mutual dependency in terms of power and/or expert knowledge and/or reputation. On the other hand, board members may represent within the board other types of so-called corporate actors (Mayntz, 1986). This is significant for both the French and German situations.

Whereas the *clan* structure is one component of the embeddedness structure of a third-sector organization and thus has a limited *local* scope of action, *peak associations* have a *nationwide* scope of action. They coordinate service provision in terms of general policy, and they are recognized as lobbyists vis-à-vis the government.

In both France and Germany the association is a general legal form for any type of civic or commercial activity (eingetragener Verein [e.V.], association declaree [AD]). What is peculiar to French and German welfare associations, however, is their dual character as service-providing organizations and peak associations (in France, L'union nationale interfederale des oeuvres prives sanitaires et sociales [UNIOPSS]; in Germany, Caritas, Diakonisches Werk, Arbeiterwohlfahrt, Zentralwohlfahrtsstelle der Juden in Deutschland). The local organization, close to the service-providing units, consists of a legally independent association. Within its board of directors, board members act as both controllers of the staff and representatives of the peak or national umbrella association.

Whereas the clan pattern and association pattern of embeddedness are common to both French and German welfare associations, the German situation is especially characterized by the strength of both peak associations and political parties as dominant actors. The relationship between government and the third sector in Germany is to a large extent the relationship between political parties and welfare associations. The autonomy of the state itself is relatively weak. In general, the micro-organizational embeddedness of a given third-sector organization at the local level, including the clan structure of the board network, is superimposed by the interaction between associations and parties at the national level. However, without the party system as a sort of political booster, the welfare associations would be mere lobbyists and therefore relatively ineffective.

The strength of parties and peak associations as dominant actors in the German welfare state also shapes the style of interaction in the relationship between government and the third sector. The pervasive role of the party system in Germany does *not* mean that there is a competitive style of interaction. On the contrary, the German political system systematically exempts important policy fields from political competition (Dyson, 1982).

This is especially true for the fields of industrial relations and social policy. The parties, especially the two most important ones, the Christian Democrats and the Social Democrats, are the principal coordinators of an arrangement between the state, all kinds of associations (including the unions), and the parties themselves.

Accordingly, Germany is a prime example of what is called a neocorporatist regime. However, neocorporatism, as a sort of preliberal or postliberal (depending on one's point of view) model of political stabilization is not based on competition but on what has been called in German political language (and also in the international literature) *concertation* as the dominant style of interaction (Lehmbruch, 1984). Concertation means a noncompetitive, concerted repartition of tasks and competencies through permanent bargaining. Social policy in particular is a prominent area of noncompetitive concertation between state authorities, the political parties, and the welfare associations. The result is a balanced division of labor between government and welfare associations, a division that is generally endorsed through legal approval (especially the basic Social Help Act, or Bundessozialhilfegesetz) and high-court judicial decisions. The concertational style itself is supported by a strong consensus that social welfare belongs among the grounding ideas of German statehood.

Unlike its German counterpart, the French welfare state really deserves its name (Ashford, 1986). *Welfare etatism* is the dominant pattern. Unlike the German welfare associations, the French associations are not only independent from government but exist in a certain competition with government in terms of both politics and service provision. Government exerts general legal control over all private institutions that provide social and health services, but there is no organized repartition of tasks and competencies as in the German case. Like their German counterparts, French welfare associations have a consultative status vis-à-vis the government, especially since the parapublic Conseil national de la vie associative was set up by the government in 1982. Unlike German peak associations, however, the French ones do not belong to the permanent system of governmental decision making. In other words, there is no neocorporatism in France but instead a relatively high degree of state autonomy.

There is, however, the so-called *tissu associatif* (Palard, 1981). This is a network of reputational and power elites, sociologically belonging to the middle class, with the associations as the structural basis, and the associations do exert a remarkable influence on local politics. Moreover, a particular feature of French polity is the cumulation of offices and parliamentary seats along the levels of state and municipal administration. Members of the national assembly and the national parliament, as well as acting state ministers, insist on being or remaining mayors (even in the tiniest villages) and/or members of the parliaments or quasi-parliaments at the regional level. The combination of municipal and state government offices and parliamentary seats and a personal embeddedness in the local *tissu associatif* is the basic resource of individual political influence. In addition, those in the leading circles of the national peak associations of private voluntary social and health services, close to the Catholic milieu, have always had a solid place in this network.

Nevertheless, the relationship between government and the third sector in France differs substantially from that in Germany. The relationship principally remains within the clan pattern. The dominant actors who link government and welfare associations are dignitaries in the traditional sense rather than rational networkers or sober bargaining partners. Despite the vertical linkage of local networks and central government, the influence and scope of action of those dignitaries (in French, *les notables*) are especially important only at the local level. They do not play a decisive role in the relationship between higher levels of government and the third sector. The simple reason is that in the provinces, those holding multiple offices are representing Paris, but in Paris they belong to the crowd of provincials. A more substantial reason can be understood through a comparison with the German situation. Whereas the strength of the German party system compensates for the disadvantages of a decentralized public administration, the linkage of central and local governments through the cumulation of offices and parliamentary seats in France compensates for the disadvantages of a centralized state structure (Gremion, 1974). Nevertheless, the natural advantage of centrality in terms of coordination capacity and power, which strengthen the position of the parties in Germany, is the natural strength of the state in France. Whereas German political parties are the crucial coordinators within the trilateral arrangement between the state, the peak associations, and the parties themselves, the party system in the French republic is relatively weak.

Accordingly, French representatives of the private voluntary sector, even when they are recognized by government as influential big shots, usually do not enjoy the additional advantage of strong party support that would make them really powerful. In Germany, by contrast, one hardly could imagine any powerful association leader without strong party connections. And whereas any major German nonprofit organization has its party representative on the board of trustees, the boards in France usually are intended to represent the local dignitaries without special respect to party membership (Heran, 1988), or they even have an ideologically homogenous composition (as for example, in the case of church-run organizations).

These differences are the result of the different embeddedness structures of the third sectors in both countries. In France, the dominant actors linking private voluntary organizations with their sociopolitico environment are clans and peak associations, both having a limited, basically local scope of action. In Germany, peak associations and political parties as dominant actors have a national scope of action. Consequently, the vertical linkage in the relationship between the local and central levels of government and the third sector is based on individual actors—dignitaries as cumulative officeholders—in France but on corporate actors—associations and parties—in Germany. Accordingly, the institutional autonomy of the state is strong in France but weak in Germany. The style of interaction between government and the third sector is slightly competitive but mainly, as far as government's behavior is concerned, manipulative in France, but it is based on conflict-free concertation in Germany. Finally, the ideological patterns of justification are also different in the two countries. In France, a high degree of state autonomy and the weak position of any intermediary organizations between the individual citizen and the government is justified, according to the Jacobinic state tradition, through the constitutional formula of the one and undivided republic (la republique une et indivisible). In Germany, the exemption of social policy from political competition is justified as a compromise of classic capitalism and a collective social welfare system, denoted by the formula of a social market economy (soziale Marktwirtschaft). The role of intermediary organizations as providers of social services and health care and a merely "subsidiary" role of the state are historically routinized and legally approved. (See Table 11.1.)

The Relationship Between Government and the Third Sector in France and Germany and the Dynamics of the Welfare State

Much of the political and scholarly interest devoted to the third sector has been stimulated by the economic and ideological

*

Table 11.1. Third-Sector Embeddedness Structures in France and Germany.

	France	Germany
General Pattern	Etatism	Neocorporatism
Dominant Actors	Clans	Peak associations, political parties
Scope of Action	Local	National
Vertical Linkage	Through individual actors	Through corporate actors
Degree of State Autonomy	High	Low
Style of Government/ Third-Sector Interaction	Competition, manipulation	Consensus, concertation
Justifying Ideology	La republique une et indivisible	Soziale Marktwirtschaft, subsidiaritaetsprinzip

challenges to the welfare states of the Western democratic type since the mid 1970s. From this normative point of view, the third sector appears as a tool to reduce the overload of government while mitigating the less desirable effects of simple privatization. The question is to what extent the relationships between the government and the third sector in France and Germany are likely to endorse this assumption.

In France, socialist government since 1981 has fostered the third sector's role through general rhetoric (*economie sociale*) and the establishment of governmental and paragovernmental offices concerned with the third sector: an undersecretary for the so-called "social economy" (which includes the cooperatives, the mutual insurance companies, and the welfare associations), attached to the prime minister and the already mentioned National Council for the Associational Life, both founded in 1983. The official justification for this new governmental policy in regard to the private voluntary sector has been to accentuate the general efforts of the socialist government to decentralize French public administration. Other governmental initiatives have included two major reports on behalf of the ministry for labor and social affairs on the role of the welfare associations in the French system of social welfare and the establishment of the position of undersecretary for the social economy (Inspection Generale des Affaires Sociales, 1984; Thery, 1986).

Beyond rhetoric and symbolic action, the socialist party has tried to alter the relationship between government and the third sector, especially at the local level, in response to the financial crisis in the municipalities that is threatening social services. Conservative and liberal local governments often do not hesitate to cancel social services, and communist municipalities have tried to maintain public control over service delivery, if necessary, through deficit spending. Socialist local governments, however, often subsidize private voluntary associations that provide social services. One example involves efforts to control unemployment of young unskilled workers (Marchal, 1986), where socialist local governments are eager to establish employment policy in close collaboration with voluntary associations. However, these associations are often artificial creatures — animated by the local socialist party and their clientele and financed through state money—that are organized by socialists who hold multiple offices and connect local and central government.

On the other hand, by far the most important effort of the socialist government in terms of institutional innovation has been the decentralization of French public administration. Despite the official version, state decentralization as it has been exhibited in France in recent years is apparently not compatible with the pronounced policy regarding the private voluntary sector. As the report on the role of the welfare associations in the French social security system reveals (Thery, 1986), the strengthening of governmental authorities at the regional level is likely to increase rather than lessen state control over private voluntary organizations. Significantly, especially when compared with the German situation, the report criticizes the government for refusing to implement concertation between state authorities and the welfare associations. It also deplores the fact that decentralization has straightened out—to the detriment of the welfare associations—a rather chaotic structure of public subsidies that had previously enabled the associations to milk several public authorities at the same time.

Although French socialists, obviously, are determined to enhance the third sector's role within the French welfare state, they cannot escape from the general patterns of political and institutional culture. Attempts to improve the elasticity of the given institutional setting of the relationship between government and the third sector have been distorted by the intrinsic etatism of French political culture and the incapacity of both the party system and the third-sector agencies themselves to transform political rhetoric into effective governmental action. The resulting tension between rhetoric and reality is likely to provoke perverse effects. Neither arrangements between the state and associations nor active involvement of political parties in administrative affairs has a stable tradition and routine patterns. Therefore, the attempt to promote such arrangements through party activism reinforces etatism and manipulation as the prevailing style of linkage between government and the third sector.

Generally, the relationship between government and the

third sector in Germany seems to be more elastic than its French counterpart. However, whereas the strength of the state seems to be the crucial weakness of French politics and polity, the strength of the German party system also reveals some intrinsic weaknesses. Political stability through party systems is principally dependent on fairly stable voter alignments. In addition, in the special case of German neocorporatism, the capacity of the party system to maintain and control the trilateral relationship between parties, the state, and the third sector is of crucial importance. The institutional elasticity that is provided through this arrangement works optimally when new issues on the political agenda can be processed by those combinations of parties and third-sector organizations that already exist, as has been the case with the welfare associations.

On the other hand, the role of the party system in Germany principally encourages the formation of *new* parties, not the search for alternative institutional solutions, when significant political issues seem not to be treated sufficiently by the existing parties. Nevertheless, political stabilization through the party system has worked relatively successfully in Germany until recently, especially when the new left-wing political party, the so-called "Greens," turned out to be a factor in successful political integration. This party also has its ideological counterparts within the third sector, especially self-help groups and a so-called "alternative economy" (small firms with no hierarchy and no personal profit acquisition as ideological guidelines). This arrangement absorbed much of frustration and potential political protest among the relatively well-skilled and educated young people who had been the main beneficiaries of the previous enhancement of the German education system but then were hit by the repercussions of the economic crisis in the mid 1970s.

The situation may change substantially when voter alignment and the availability of party-controlled third-sector organizations are no longer guaranteed. Because of the general effects of modernization, especially in terms of the vanishing role of religious confession and a growing new middle class with a high degree of sociological mobility, voter alignment to political parties is increasingly unstable in Germany. This is an additional incentive for the formation of new parties.

The situation is even more difficult when a social problem becomes a political issue without finding its addressees in
the party system and the third sector. Because of a high level
of enduring unemployment and a wave of immigration never
before known in German history, today housing, with all its
side aspects, is such a problem. Obviously, this issue has not
been sufficiently dealt with by the existing parties. Consequently,
the political system again answers with the formation of a new
political party — this time, however, an extreme right one.

Yet the threat to political stability, at least in terms of
governability, does not stem exclusively from the newly established political radicalism with its historical precedents. Another
reason is the partial inability of the third sector to respond to
the housing issue. The most important union-owned nonprofit
housing corporation, Neue Heimat, was involved in a corruption scandal (Deutscher Bundestag, 1987). The conservative-
liberal government did not hesitate to exploit the scandal during the national election campaign 1986–87 as an example of
socialist mismanagement. This clearly was an offense against
the basic rule of the corporatist consensus protecting the third
sector against the risks of political competition. It occurred because at the time no one expected housing to become a central
issue of domestic policy. As a result, the position of the nonprofit housing industry was generally shattered. However, the
blurring of the housing industry's corporatist embeddedness was
immediately punished. Only a few years later, government itself had to react in response to the housing crisis, with its incal-
culable risks in terms of legitimacy.

Conclusion

Welfare associations in France and Germany provide an important share of health care and social services. Moreover, in
both countries the associations depend heavily on public subsidies. Despite this similarity,the different histories of the two states
and the different intermediary organizations in France and Germany have shaped different relationships between government
and the third sector. Whereas the autonomy of the state is great
in France, it is slight in Germany. In France, linkage between

government and the third sector is based on actors with a small-scale scope of action, primarily on local elites with personal links to the central government. In Germany, corporate actors, primarily peak association and political parties, have a large-scale scope of action. Whereas the style of interaction between government and welfare associations in France is slightly competitive or, with respect to the government's behavior, manipulative, in Germany the style is noncompetitive, concertational, and consensus oriented.

Structural weaknesses of the two national patterns of relationship between government and the third sector are caused by the relative strength of the state (France) and by the relative strength of the party system (Germany). Whereas French state-centered society impedes balanced partnerships between government and the third sector, the party system in Germany impedes institutional innovation through third-sector agencies beyond party control.

In general, the capacity of political regimes to rely on a third sector as an alternative to government apparently depends on the stability of group coalitions interested in the mere existence of intermediary organizations and on the strength of ideologies that justify a nonstatutory form of social welfare production. In the German case both prerequisites exist. In France, however, they are only partially guaranteed.

State autonomy, therefore, may be identified as a crucial variable. However, even if the French and German situations seem to be complementary in terms of state autonomy, any generalization must be carefully considered. Corporatism, with its accompanying low degree of state autonomy, seems to be the general phenomenon in Germany, and *etatism* appears to be the general phenomenon in France. But autonomy of the state does not mean strong government, and corporatism does not imply weak government. In terms of governability, German corporatism is relatively successful. French government, on the other hand, obviously fails not only when it tries to strengthen but also when it tries to weaken the stable linkage patterns between the state apparatus and private intermediary organizations (Suleiman, 1987). However, autonomy of the state is a meaningful concept if an autonomous *"Logic* of the State" (Birn-baum, 1982) is acknowledged, meaning that the state appara-tus itself is autonomous in terms of maintaining its own style of behavior regardless of changing governments or changing in-terest groups. That statist style exists in France but never de-veloped in Germany.

In general, substitution of the nonprofit, government, and for-profit organization as institutional forms is subject to more or less substantial institutional inertia and, therefore, is far less flexible than economic models of institutional choice presume. This is due to the sociopolitico embeddedness of third-sector or-ganizations that allows a broad range of organizational behavior, including "permanent failure" (Meyer and Zucker, 1989) in terms of performance, manipulation of performance criteria, ideological protection against public criticism, and so on. We must therefore assume that the existing flexibility of institutional choice is dependent upon different patterns of third-sector embeddedness that can be revealed through cross-national com-parative research.

Future research, therefore, should continue to take the third sector seriously. There are good reasons to assume an al-ternative to for-profit enterprises and public administration to be a prerequisite to a balanced provision of goods and services as well as to social integration and political stability. However, the rationale of the third sector's persistence in all Western de-mocracies is not necessarily based on competitive advantages in terms of quality or efficiency or on superiority in terms of pluralism and democratic decision making. There is also a sym-bolic use of institutions, and the third sector, in many cases, may serve as a structural filter that enables market economies and democratic regimes to cope with social and political prob-lems that are hard to solve (Seibel, 1989, 1990).

On the other hand, though it makes sense to acknowledge a special "sector" relative to private economy and public bureau-cracies, its boundaries are blurring and its organizational con-stituencies are in a stage of permanent development. To assume different "embeddedness" patterns within the third sector also means to acknowledge different patterns of potential adaptation in terms of organizational behavior (Powell and Friedkin, 1987). With respect to government, third-sector organizations may maintain their autonomy only while being commercialized. This seems to be the case in many areas of the American third sector (Salamon, 1987). Or they may survive only while being publicly subsidized—and bureaucratized—which seems to be the prevailing pattern in both France and Germany. Finally, the third sector continues to be replenished through new grass-roots initiatives and all kinds of voluntary associations, many of which vanish after a short while but some of which persist and evolve with peculiar patterns of organizational behavior and adaptation to their environment. In short, one may conceive the third sector as a sort of amoeba, undoubtedly a species in itself, but continuously changing its phenotype.

References

Anheier, H. K. "A Profile of the Third Sector in West Germany." In H. K. Anheier and W. Seibel (eds.), *The Third Sector: Nonprofit Organizations in Comparative and International Perspectives.* New York: De Gruyter, 1990.

Archambault, E. "Les associations en chiffre." *Revue des etudes cooperatives,* 1985, 10–50.

Archambault, E. "Public Authorities and the Nonprofit Sector in France." In H. K. Anheier and W. Seibel (eds.), *The Third Sector: Nonprofit Organizations in Comparative and International Perspectives.* New York: De Gruyter, 1990.

Ashford, D. E. *The Emergence of the Welfare States.* Oxford: Blackwell, 1986.

Birnbaum, P. *La logique de l'etat.* Paris: Fayard, 1982.

Debbasch, C., and Bourdon, J. *Les associations.* Paris: Fayard, 1987.

Deutscher Bundestag. Drucksache 10/6779, Jan. 7, 1987, Beschlupempfehlung und Bericht des 3. Untersuchungsausschusses "Neue Heimat."

Dyson, K. "West Germany: The Search for a Rationalist Consensus." In J. Richardson (ed.), *Policy Styles in Western Europe.* London: George Allen & Unwin, 1982.

Etzioni, A. "The Third Sector and Domestic Missions." *Public Administration Review*, 1973, 314–323.

Goetschy, J. "The Neo-Corporatist Issue in France." In I. Scholten (ed.), *Political Stability and Neo-Corporatism: Corporatist Integration and Societal Cleavages in Western Europe.* Newbury Park, Calif.: Sage, 1987.

Granovetter, M. "Economic Action and Social Structure: The Problem of Embeddedness." *American Journal of Sociology*, 1985, *91*, 481–510.

Gremion, P. *Le pouvoir peripherique: Bureaucrates et notables dan le systeme politique francais.* Paris: Seuil, 1974.

Heran, F. "Un Monde Selectif: les associations." *Economie et Statistique*, 1988 (208), 17–31.

Inspection Generale des Affaires Sociales (ed.). *La politique sociale et les associations.* Paris: La Documentation Francaise, 1984.

Katzenstein, P. *Politics and Policy in West Germany: The Growth of a Semi-Sovereign State.* Ithaca, N.Y.: Cornell University Press, 1987.

Lehmbruch, G. "Concertation and the Structure of Neo-Corporatist Networks." In J. H. Goldthorpe (ed.), *Order and Conflict in Contemporary Capitalism.* Oxford: Clarendon Press, 1984.

Levitt, T. *The Third Sector: New Tactics for a Responsive Society.* New York: AMACOM, 1973.

Lloyd, P. C. "The Relationship Between Voluntary Associations and State Agencies in the Provision of Social Services at the Local Level." In H. K. Anheier and W. Seibel (eds.), *The Third Sector: Nonprofit Organizations in Comparative and International Perspectives.* New York: De Gruyter, 1990.

Marchal, E. "La participation des associations au programme des Travaux d'Utilite Collective," Enquete, presentee au colloque de L'Association pour le Developpement de la Documentation sur l'Economie Sociale (ADDES), June 17, 1986. (Mimeographed.)

Mayntz, R. "Corporate Actors in Public Policy: Changing Perspectives in Political Analysis." *Norsk Statsvitenskapeling Tidsskrift*, 1986, *3*, 7–25.

Meny, Y. "La legitimation des groupes d'interet par l'adminis-tration francaise." Rapport pour le Congres International de Sciences Politique, Paris, July 1985 (Mimeographed.)

Meyer, M., and Zucker, L. *Permanently Failing Organizations.* Newbury Park, Calif.: Sage, 1989.

Middleton, M. "Nonprofit's Board of Directors: Beyond the Governance Function." In W. W. Powell (ed.), *The Nonprofit Sector: A Research Handbook.* New Haven, Conn.: Yale University Press, 1987.

Mueller, F. *Korporation und Assoziation. Zur Geschichte der Vereinigungsfreiheit im deutschen Vormaerz.* Berlin: Duncker und Humbolt, 1965.

Nordlinger, E. *On the Autonomy of the Democratic State.* Cambridge, Mass.: Harvard University Press, 1981.

Ouchi, W. "Markets, Bureaucracies, and Clans." *Administrative Science Quarterly,* 1980, *25,* 129–141.

Palard, J. "Le mouvement associatif et le systeme politique local en France: Discours et pratiques." *Sociologica Internationalis,* 1981, *19,* 213–232.

Passaris, S. G., and Raffi, G. *Les Associations.* Paris, 1984.

Powell, W. W., and Friedkin, R. "Organizational Change in Nonprofit Organizations." In W. W. Powell (ed.), *The Nonprofit Sector: A Research Handbook.* New Haven, Conn.: Yale University Press, 1987.

Richardson, J. (ed.). *Policy Styles in Western Europe.* London: George Allen & Unwin, 1982.

Rose-Ackerman, S. (ed.). *The Economics of Nonprofit Institutions. Studies in Structure and Policy.* New York: Oxford University Press, 1986.

Salamon. L. M. "Partners in Public Service: The Scope and Theory of Government Nonprofit Relations." In W. W. Powell (ed.), *The Nonprofit Sector: A Research Handbook.* New Haven, Conn.: Yale University Press, 1987.

Salamon, L. M. "The Nonprofit Sector and Government: The American Experience in Theory and Practice." In H. K. Anheier and W. Seibel (eds.), *The Third Sector: Nonprofit Organizations in Comparative and International Perspectives.* New York: De Gruyter, 1990.

Seibel, W. "The Function of Mellow Weakness: Nonprofit Organizations as Problem-Non-Solvers in Germany." In E. James (ed.), *The Nonprofit Sector: Studies in Comparative Culture and Policy.* New York: Oxford University Press, 1989.

Seibel, W. "Organizational Behavior and Organizational Function: Toward a Micro-Macro Theory of the Third Sector." In H. K. Anheier and W. Seibel (eds.), *The Third Sector: Nonprofit Organizations in Comparative and International Perspectives.* New York: De Gruyter, 1990.

Skocpol, T. "Bringing the State Back In: Strategies of Analysis in Current Research." In P. Evans, D. Rueschemeyer, and T. Skocpol (eds.), *Bringing the State Back In.* New York: Cambridge University Press, 1985.

Suleiman, E. N. *Politics, Power and Bureaucracy in France: The Administrative Elite.* Princeton, N.J.: Princeton University Press, 1974.

Suleiman, E. N. *Private Power and Centralization in France: The Notaires and the State.* Princeton, N.J.: Princeton University Press, 1987.

Thery, H. "La place et le role du secteur associatif dans le developpement de la politique d'action educative, sanitaire et sociale. Rapport presente au nom du conseil economique et social." *Journal Officiel de la Republique Francaise,* July 29, 1986.

Weisbrod, B. *The Nonprofit Economy.* Cambridge, Mass.: Harvard University Press, 1988.

Wildavsky, A. "Choosing Preferences by Constructing Institutions: A Cultural Theory of Preference Formation." *American Political Science Review,* 1987, *81,* 3–21.

Wurzbacher, G. "Die oeffentliche freie Vereinigung als Faktor soziokulturellen, insbesondere emanzipatorischen Wandels im 19. Jahrhundert." In W. Rueegg and O. Neuloh (eds.), *Zur soziologischen Theorie und Analyse des 19. Jahrhunderts.* Goettingen: Vandenhoeck und Rupprecht, 1971.

Chapter 12

The Mission, Purposes, and Functions of Nonprofit Organizations in France

This chapter will discuss the new trends and new roles of non-profit organizations (NPOs) in France. It focuses on NPOs in the field of social services and more precisely on those that play a role in the fight against poverty. The attempt to address this important issue of poverty has changed the role of many NPOs, giving them a new image. There was little interaction between social and economic policy-making until the 1980 crisis, which instigated a greater concern for socioeconomic analysis, in which NPOs have a crucial role. Less value is now placed on techno-logical and scientific progress since their effects on unemployment appear to be increasingly disastrous in economic terms. The in-crease of social inequality and vulnerability through so-called progress is no longer ignored by NPOs, whose ideology favors greater equality and social justice. The stigmatization of social groups, age-groups, and ethnic groups is the dubious result of the development of an advanced, technological society in which NPOs are attempting to sustain more human and democratic values.

Historical Background

There are two different sectors in France: the private sector and the public sector. Within the private sector is the nonprofit sector, which is firmly rooted in the French history of self-help groups, labor movements, and religious institutions. Very early in the nineteenth century, there were discussions about social problems and many actions were taken. During this period, members of parliament as well as well-known writers, such as Tocqueville, Sand, Zola, Hugo, de Gerando, Villerme, and so on, spoke about poverty.

Pensions, insurance, and security against illness or accident were all provided by private bodies. The municipalities and the state still had a social welfare role, such as lodging and feeding paupers in huge hospitals and homes. Their aims were selective and their treatments limited to the needs of people lacking education, the elderly, the handicapped, and those living alone. These activities to alleviate extreme poverty were essential.

The division of functions between the state and private bodies at the time can be explained, perhaps, on the basis of unemployment or work. Those who were working received assistance through their colleagues or employers; those who were not working were dependent upon the state or charitable organizations. Religious organizations were responsible especially for children. New legislation was brought about by breakdowns in the system during wars and revolutions. People with handicaps acquired a new status, and new legislation was enacted after World War I because of the number of war-related injuries.

To understand the nature of the services and the division of labor among the various institutions in France, one needs to know the historical background. The roles of education and health, the financial role of the provision of benefits, and the types of control depended upon the ideology, and thus the ensuing legislation and regulations, of either liberal or radical parties. However, it was not clearly established that the homeless, indigents, and people at risk were in their situations because of a social flaw. During this period, the NPOs and social organizations tried to reinforce and initiate ideas of tolerance and obligation for compensation. Instilling notions of human solidarity and self-esteem was the responsibility of NPOs.

After the Second World War, the cohesion of society was reinforced. Following the British example of the Health Service and the National Social Security system, France's welfare state began to grow. The state became the principal and first provider of security and insurance, as recommended by Titmuss and Beveridge. But the welfare state continued to exist within a for-profit market of social services. Some of these services were managed by religious and nonreligious organizations that were often linked to political groups or trade unions. These organizations still had a role in improving the system, influencing legislation, and obtaining funds. Many of them strongly resembled for-profit organizations and were on the boundary of the market.

Informal solidarities began to be the victim of this dual public-private system of social service delivery. Outside the market, they were at risk of being underused and undersustained by formal institutions. For years, the idea of the disappearing role of the family and community was a fashionable way to explain the feeble role of community action. Far from business interests, far from community action, it was the moment of the rise of the welfare state and services, so-called private but financed with public money.

Some organizations argued that society has the responsibility to correct the undesirable and disturbing effects of the market economy. "Ought we to give to every poor person? The rule of Saint Benoit had made a clear distinction between the real and the unreal poor people" (Sassier, 1990). It was not until thirty years later, when a new socialist prime minister of solidarity tried to change the system into a more egalitarian one, that this idea was incorporated into the core of the system. Mrs.

Questiaux introduced new legislation to improve the welfare state. In neglected areas of industrialized democracies, people continued to suffer in a medieval state of misery despite thirty years of the welfare state.

Many authors, such as Donzelot, criticized the welfare state for being a compromise between political imagination and the realities of everyday life. Long-range plans were central to the French model, and the Sixth and Seventh Plans gave more power to private organizations through three new trends and sectors: employment, environment and urban life, and social protection. After 1968, the policy was to give more management power and assistance to the private sector in order to avoid too much bureaucratization. Illich's theory for explaining the role of institutions was very important and widely discussed (Donzelot, 1984).

A Social but Bureaucratized Machine

The French administrative machine is a huge bureaucracy. The local, regional, and national administrations do provide a safety net, but the different types of legislation, the number of intermediaries, the effects of an overly democratic and generous system that attempts to be fair are all responsible for many problems. NPOs play a very important role in achieving social welfare objectives. The nonprofit sector has a more flexible system, is closer to the communities and the people, and is better able to meet social demands. This sector can react quickly to problems in the fields of services, insurance, and care. It is the only sector that is able to involve volunteers. Its role in preserving values, especially pluralistic values, has been accepted. There is no longer any question of recognition and accountability, and the work of NPOs in improving the quality of life and empowerment is widely accepted. This sector creates more freedom for marginalized groups and initiates many social experiments. It tries to combat social isolation and offers new noninstitutional approaches and community care. This sector encourages self-help and self-confidence and promotes solidarity and the integration of marginal populations.

However, because of the increasing power of NPOs, this sector is also becoming a second safety net and a welfare bureaucracy. Many organizations such as those in the poverty program also have local, regional, and national structures. They are also beginning to increase the number of intermediaries. They have elected boards that are in many cases less and less representative of their members and donors and that often function to consolidate their own power and bureaucracies. Having to obtain as much money as possible from the state, some NPOs forget that their first goal is to carry out the objectives developed by public institutions. They use the same tools of communication as those in the public sector use: administrative questionnaires and brochures. As a result, NPOs have not really succeeded in reducing the gap between institutions and citizens. Their function as mediating structures is no longer clear.

Professionals and Volunteers Face to Face

Both volunteers and paid professionals work together in NPOs, joining altruism and professionalism. The two groups often have different motivations and attitudes as they work together with the same clients. Opportunities, salaries, and methods of recognition are different for the two groups. Because a number of senior citizens are volunteers, this situation is not too bad. In the area of poverty, however, both volunteers and professionals have similar motivations: to combat extreme poverty, to promote greater social justice, and to provide alternatives for changes in the welfare state.

Professionals, with state-recognized diplomas, have specific careers inside private institutions. Those who are in charge of handicapped children or adults or young people at risk enjoy a good system of salaries compared to that of other family or community social workers. Their careers and system of promotion are not to be compared to those who are in the public sector, such as the justice educators. It appears quite difficult to go from one sector to another, though their tasks are similar even if the clients are slightly different.

Volunteers are more numerous and have a better image

than they had earlier. The last decades have seen the explosion of volunteers in new fields, and they have created new jobs (Cheroutre, 1989). They are the unique work force of NPOs. Volunteers are both freer and more powerful because of their volunteer service, but they are less qualified and less able to act because of their lack of professional training. Volunteers revitalize the sector; they make a human contribution not only in quantitative terms but also in qualitative terms. For example, they are innovative and flexible and have a direct relationship with the most deprived groups; because many of the volunteers also have a foot in another professional network, they serve as important and effective liaisons. The value of time given by volunteers is difficult to evaluate. The nature of voluntarism in France remains complex and rooted in a long history. It is looking for new models abroad but continues to follow specific patterns because of the growth of the welfare state and the influence of important leaders.

The Role of Leaders

Abbe Pierre's speech against poverty in 1954 constituted a step in the social cohesion of a changing society. "Je n'ai rien a te donner mais j'ai besoin de toi . . . a-t-il dit a la premiere personne qu'il a rencontree dans sa mission." Emmaus, the NPO that he founded, is a model of a new modern charity. The famous priest Abbe Pierre is still alive and periodically gives important speeches against poverty and encourages altruism: "Il faut declarer la guerre a la miser!" Abbe Pierre asks why rich democratic countries forget the poor; why the whole world forgets poverty. He admonishes individuals to get angry at such poverty and calls upon them to struggle against inequality. For him, Europe should be a new model in creating better welfare.

Another former leader who was also a priest, J. Wresinsky, was in charge of an important study that has perhpas been as important as the Beveridge report. Entitled "Grande Pauvrete et Precarite Economique et Sociale," it has significantly changed the image of the NPO. From an NPO himself, Wresinsky analyzed the economic and social conditions in France. His report reinforced the role of NPOs in the welfare state and also recommended the establishment of a network. He lived with poor families and worked for the improvement of their situation. The international movement ATD Fourth World was created by Wresinsky in a shantytown near Paris. J. Rosenfeld (1989) describes the movement this way: teams of volunteers live in the most neglected parts of cities, devoting themselves to the families and playing an educational role. Wresinsky was a leader in the struggle for the right of Fourth World families. He was joined by many intellectuals, and a monument has been erected in the Troacadero, facing the Eiffel Tower, to commemorate the rights of the poor. One of the leaders of this movement is Madame De Gaulle.

The third important leader was the actor Coluch, who died a few years ago. He was very active in the Restaurants du Coeur, a sort of soup kitchen that provided millions of meals to poor people in cities and rural areas. His provocative manner and generosity created scandals and public reaction. However, almost every political leader was obliged to participate in television shows with Coluch. Even the prime minister of finance sold his straps to sustain the Restaurants du Coeur! Politicians from both the left and the right took part in these discussions because Coluch was able to trap them in debates dangerous for their images. Coluch was against exclusion but focused on the problem of hunger in a rich society and instigated a major public action that still remains effective despite new benefits for the poor. His charismatic leadership inspired new volunteerism among younger generations and among entrepreneurs and corporate leaders in food businesses, who felt obliged to give their share to these restaurants. Even the European Commission used to deliver millions of pounds of butter and vegetables to them. Coluch also championed a law to increase fiscal incentives for generous organizations. Although the law was never passed as he formulated it, he has had an impact on creating fiscal incentives for philanthropic action. Coluch's generosity stemmed from his poor origins and his strong feelings for solidarity. His dedication and contributions to this field have significantly changed our society. The most famous singers, actors, and artists struggle for more solidarity and philanthropy and have an enormous impact upon the public. They give large sums of money and time but also change public attitudes and increase individual obligation. Our democracy has been influenced by these actions.

The welfare state appears sometimes to have a large complementary role to that of individual generosity, broadening the field of services. These three leaders have tied together the links of brotherhood and have changed the attitude of the public toward the welfare state.

A Dual System

After a review of the research on NPOs, it appears that the poorest remain the primary targets of those engaged in anti-poverty programs (Ferrand Bechmann, 1989). The homeless, the indigent, the long-term unemployed, and isolated men are the main clients of these private organizations. Through a wide range of services, the average social institution of the nonprofit private sector provides services to various categories of people with handicaps as well as to the needs of specific age-groups. There are two categories of clients: the very poor and the normal beneficiaries of social action. The very poor were excluded from the usual avenues of social protection. They were homeless, had no protection from cold winters, and received no care and no money. Only the large institutions in the private sector tried to face these problems, forcing the statutory sector to react and to manifest solidarity in concrete actions such as the provision of food, lodging, and money. "On a multiplie par 3 les personnes qui se sont adressees a nous" (personal interview of an association director, autumn 1988). Lobbying for their clients, they have had a major impact. The public institutions are dependent on the social action of NPOs and respect them as consultants and co-decision makers. Some NPOs complain about their ancillary role as food providers to former Eastern bloc countries after the events of December 1989 or act as emergency lodging providers in France. They are seeking an expanded role and new functions, where they will not be solely servants or totally apart from social responsibilities. They advocate specific ethics toward specific groups and clients, and this selectivity is difficult to lobby for in our modern social welfare system.

Among the other social organizations targeted specifically for groups with various handicaps, the problem is slightly different. With the assistance of their clients' representatives and families, these organizations are providing paid services to clients. Their finances are public and they serve as administrators for the state, which remains the primary decision maker because it is the money provider. The French voluntary spirit is not evident in this sector, which is a quasi-entrepreneurial one that produces social goods. Organizations in this sector tend to choose between goals and leaders because of common opportunities and reject philanthropy. As such, they remain a second arm of the state. They are confronted with normal restrictions but also face the realities of cost effectiveness and market mechanisms. While their boards remain in favor of lobbying, they are more or less active, depending on the problems. For example, new issues, such as the problem of AIDS, mobilize new actors and greater participation. They create new attitudes and new techniques and values through a French pattern of self-help. Similar points must be noted in the field of battered women. Nevertheless, the quality of care, the low level of involvement, and a high percentage of public money remain characteristic of this quasi-public system. Such organizations are not redundant to the public services. They are not real for-profit institutions such as more recent organizations created for senior citizens, but they are an alternative system in between statutory and private nonprofit organizations. They do not manifest themselves against bureaucracies because they are themselves bureaucratic. They do not involve citizen participation and are less radical than the self-help movement in the Netherlands.

French Mechanisms, French Altruism

Inside the redistributive system, the NPOs concerned with poverty are very open to new clients and new trends. "Il y a une organisation sociale qui n'est pas adaptee a une realite nouvelle d'une pauvrete qui est partout prete a se rendre visible" (author's interview of a Catholic association leader, 1988). New ideas and practices from across the Atlantic have helped to change our French model of the welfare state. The range of ideological positions among NPOs is wide, but in time they will move from this innovative model toward a more bureaucratic one. Still sponsored by churches, some of them are quite wealthy, and others receive a great deal of financial support because they have set up a large network of donors. The emphasis given to them in television and the press helps them increase their power. Their basic objectives are relevant to many middle-class members, and they have prospects for support from a larger proportion of the population. Yet one can predict that the French mechanism of the welfare state will eventually push these organizations into the mainstream of associations largely financed and controlled by public institutions, and they will have to face crucial choices between freedom and security.

The other social service NPOs do not change because they must conform to political goals and financial restrictions. They are a part of the social bureaucracy. They have prospered for thirty years as social services providers, and they attempt to resist the changing situation. They try not to be heretical or too heterogeneous in relation to their original goals. They still try to maintain their number of employees, while attempting to adjust to the new values of community action and global interests. They are pluralist but promote the rights of the groups they serve. They have numerous critics, and a variety of views are accepted among their members, but they are becoming more and more professional, even as preservers of values.

References

Cheroutre, M. T. *Essor du Benevolat Rapport.* Paris: Conseil Economique et Sociale, 1989.

Donzelot, J. *L'Invention du Social.* Paris: Fayard, 1984.

Ferrand Bechmann, D. (ed.). *Qui sont les tres pauvres?* Paris: Ministere d'Affaires Sociale, 1989.

Rosenfeld, J. *Emergence from Extreme Poverty.* Paris: Aide a Toute Ditresse, 1989.

Sassier, P. *Du bon usage des Pauvres.* Paris: Fayard, 1990.

Chapter 13

The Ties That Bind:
The Nonprofit Sector
and the State in Sweden

The Individual and the Collectivity
in Sweden and the United States

The nonprofit sector in Sweden has the following general characteristics:

1. It is among the largest in the world on a per capita basis, comprising some 200,000 organizations with more than 31 million members in a population of 8.3 million people (Statens Offentliga Utredningar, 1987, p. 33).
2. The organizations that comprise it engage in three main activities: social reform, recreation and personal development, and the promotion and protection of organized interests.

3. Nonprofit organizations operate very few facilities for schooling, health care, social assistance, and the like.
4. Most charity and assistance efforts are directed to poor countries in Africa and Asia rather than to poor people within Sweden.
5. Nonprofit organizations work closely with national and local government agencies.
6. The nonprofit sector is heavily dependent on government subsidies and receives relatively little financial support from the private sector.

The only characteristic that the Swedish nonprofit sector shares with its American counterpart is its large per capita size. Otherwise, the American nonprofit sector presents striking contrasts. In the United States, the nonprofit sector operates a large share of all educational and health facilities. Most charity and assistance efforts are domestically oriented. Interest-group organizations are in effect excluded from the nonprofit sector because of the American belief that voluntary activity should serve the common good, not "special interests." The sector's relationship with government tends to be uneasy and conflict-ridden; government subsidies are viewed with suspicion. Private-sector subsidies may also be regarded as dubious, but they are nonetheless extremely important.

In my view these contrasts are due to differences in fundamental cultural conceptions in the two societies. I see Sweden and the United States as lying at opposite ends of a major axis of Western social organization, the dialectic between the individual and the national collectivity. Both societies are individualistic, and both have bureaucratic central authority structures that are charged with the overall management of society. However, American culture rests on a Lockean conception of society as being "nothing but" individuals. Individuals create voluntary associations (including business enterprises and government) through which autonomous individual action is channeled, and the result is (assumed to be) optimal collective welfare. Swedish culture, like that of most continental countries, is constructed around a more Hobbesian model. Society is composed of individuals, but individual autonomy must be guided and regulated by central authority if the welfare of some is not to preclude the welfare of all.

In schematic form, the American model thus posits a highly autonomous individual and a voluntary collectivity that has no authority other than that granted by its members. The Swedish model posits a more dependent individual and a more compulsory collectivity that has considerable authority independent of its members. Neither country represents a truly extreme position in the individual-collectivity dialectic — nineteenth-century American frontier society and twentieth-century Communist party–dominated countries are much closer to the opposite poles — but they are probably as far apart as any other pair of highly developed Western countries.

In this chapter I will analyze the Swedish nonprofit sector in light of this general cultural characterization. The next section describes the nonprofit sector in recent decades. The third section describes societal trends in the postwar period that have shaped the nonprofit sector's development and then reviews the multiple and complex ties between the nonprofit sector and government. Here I try to show how the collectivist emphasis of Swedish culture has blurred the distinction between public and private to such an extent that the nonprofit sector's independence now seems highly questionable. The last section discusses several countertrends that may indicate greater independence of the nonprofit sector in coming years.

The Swedish Nonprofit Sector

Cooperative organizations of producers and consumers head the list of nonprofit voluntary organizations in terms of membership followed by sports and recreation groups, labor unions, political organizations, and cultural and adult education bodies. There are nearly four memberships per capita, a very high figure in comparative terms. Between 80 and 90 percent of the population belong to at least one association (Westerstahl and Johansson, 1981; Vestlund, 1981).

Although many charitable organizations exist in Sweden — the Salvation Army has been active for over eighty years, for example—they typically are assigned to the "international" category. Charitable activities are generally oriented outward; domestic social welfare is the responsibility of the state.

How active are all these members? Nearly 40 percent of the 1978 population claimed active participation in an organization, fully 23 percent held an official position, and more than 60 percent had attended at least one meeting during the previous year. However, members of consumer organizations are, as a rule, quite passive, as are members of tenant and labor unions. The most active members are found in "local action" groups that focus on such specific issues as parking or pollution from a specific factory.

In the literature this active organizational engagement is invariably described in positive terms. The prevailing view is that a plethora of organizations and multiple memberships by much of the population are crucial for the health of Swedish democracy. Yet concern is often expressed that the organizations have become too big and bureaucratic and that there is little room for individual members to "make a difference." Thus many organizations have entirely lost their "movement" character (Vestlund, 1981; Lindroth, 1975).

Another concern is that many of the functions that were once served by the voluntary organizations have been taken over by the government. This was the central point of a 1974 "manifesto" produced by the Swedish Social Democratic Youth League (1975); see also Isling, 1978; Lindholm, 1983. This document led to a major debate about the organizations' goals and relationship to the state. The Youth League's manifesto envisioned a society in which the organizations would essentially meld with the state, taking over a wide range of activities that had become governmental functions but doing so under state guidance and by means of state moneys. Critics of this proposal complained that the Social Democrats were attempting to co-opt the organizations as political instruments. A healthy democracy requires, they argued, that voluntary organizations keep the state at arm's length.

The primary outcomes of the debate were typical of the Swedish system: first, the issue was researched to death for the next dozen years by a large number of state study commissions; second, state and local government agencies enormously expanded their subsidiaries to nonprofit organizations. These outcomes will be discussed below.

Volunteerism Inside the State

Before proceeding, a terminological discussion is needed. I have used the term *organizations* rather than *associations* to translate the Swedish terms *folkrorelser* and *foreningar*. Important nuances are at stake. *Folkrorelser,* or "popular movements," refers to the free-church, temperance, and labor union movements that emerged in the latter part of the nineteenth century. *Folk,* like the German *Volk,* designates "people" in the sense of "nation." The term thus indicates that these three movements have a *nationally collective character;* they are not viewed as a multitude of local, independent efforts. *Forening* (singular form), a more recent and broader term, means "a uniting" or, as in chemistry, "compound": two or more entities become one. For both terms, the connotative emphasis lies more on the collectivity than on the individuals who join together — on the Hobbesian rather than the Lockean version of the social contract. In what follows I will employ *foreningar* rather than *voluntary associations* to describe the nonprofit sector. I hope that this term will keep readers in mind of a more collectivist conception.

A second terminological issue is Swedish usage of the terms *stat* ("state") and *samhalle* ("society"). In American English these terms are clearly distinct: society is other than the state; it "contains" or is "governed" by the state. In Swedish the two terms are often used synonymously. Hence, when the term *welfare state* became common coinage in the 1960s, Swedish analysts began to speak of *det starka samhallet,* the "strong society," to designate the highly expanded public sector that ensured the rights and material well-being of the population.

Both of these terminological peculiarities are symptomatic of Swedish culture. We cannot speak of voluntary associations in Sweden, even though the *foreningar* are voluntary and associational, for these organizations have a unifying, national, almost compulsory tinge to them. The flip side of this observation is that the boundary between state and society is nebulous, not only empirically but also conceptually. It is therefore revealing that a Swedish equivalent to the term *nonprofit sector* is entirely lacking. One can speak of *folkrorelser*, of *foreningar,* and of *organisationer* (organizations), but the Anglo-Saxon concept of a nonprofit sector that is distinct from both the political sector and the economic sector is not directly applicable to Swedish social organization.

To put the nonprofit into perspective I will use the next part of this section to describe the larger context in which *foreningar* have developed during the past few decades.

Etatization and Politicization

During the twentieth century the government's role in Sweden has expanded tremendously. By 1985 total government spending had reached about 67 percent of GNP, government consumption was over 30 percent of GNP, and government employment had reached 38 percent of the labor force (Rodriguez, 1980; Statistiska Centralbayran, 1985; Furaker, 1987). All of these figures are the highest in the noncommunist world. However, this extraordinary expansion of government has not involved the nationalization of private enterprise; the state has never controlled more than about 10 percent of industry. Sweden has a *welfare,* not socialist, state. On the other hand, the high figures for government employment and consumption indicate the emergence of a large socialized segment of the economy. Carlsson (1987) reports that 49 percent of all paid labor hours in 1983 were in the public sector.

The rapid expansion of governmental authority in society has been accompanied by comprehensive party politicization. Parties first became the dominant vehicles for political action in the 1920s; more recently, party politics has entered the local government arena. Through the 1960s most municipalities operated on a nonparty basis, but by the 1980s, municipal elections were organized around distinct party lists, and the composition of municipal councils was determined in accordance with strict proportional representational principles. The various parties now write local political programs, mass media coverage of municipal elections has increased dramatically, and committee and administrative appointments have become explicitly political issues (Asp, 1987; Birgersson and Westerstahl, 1987; Statens Offentliga Utredningar, 1975: 46).

Additional politicization has occurred outside the party system. Beginning in the 1960s with the movement against American involvement in Vietnam, extra-party activity became an established feature of Swedish political life by the 1970s. Studies of local political activity suggest that the proportion of individuals who contacted officials directly to deal with their problems more than doubled between the 1960s and the 1980s. Citizens are now more likely to join local action groups or contact officials directly than to participate in party activities (Westerstahl and Johansson, 1981).

Implications for the Folkrorelser and Foreningar: Knotty Ties

The twin trends of etatization and politicization have greatly increased the ties between government and the *foreningar*. Important developments include the following:

1. Public support of the *foreningar* has increased enormously.
2. *Forening* participation in central authority has expanded.
3. The *foreningar* have come to be seen as agents of the collectivity.
4. Many *foreningar* are as much creations of the central authority structure as are voluntary initiatives of individuals.

Public funding of the *foreningar* began early in the century, but until the 1960s subsidies were few in number and quite limited (Statens Offentliga Utredningar, 1988: 39). The first major form of support was that given to the political parties, initially in the form of press subsidies and, after 1966, as direct cash payments (Hadenius and Weibull, 1985; Back, 1980). A 1969 law extended the right to grant party subsidies to local government units. By 1986 total party subsidies amounted to more than 355 million crowns. Over half of all party revenues are now publicly supplied (Gidlund, 1988; Birgersson and Westerstahl, 1987; Statens Offentliga Utredningar, 1988: 47).

Since the early 1970s public subsidies to *foreningar* of all sorts have increased rapidly. One study (Riksrevisionsverket, 1987) found that state agencies dispensed a total of almost 5 billion crowns in budget year 1985–86. County council subsidies totaled more than 200 million crowns, and municipal subsidies about 3.6 billion crowns (Statens Offentliga Utredningar, 1987: 33). Altogether, public subsidies to *foreningar* thus equaled almost 9 billion crowns, or roughly 300 crowns for each of the 331 million memberships in *foreningar*.

The most comprehensive estimate available suggests that some 30,000 organizations are the happy recipients of this remarkable public largesse. They range from the largest national organizations to local theater arts groups of half a dozen performers (Riksrevisionsverket, 1986, 1987). No comprehensive figures are available regarding the extent of *forening* dependence on public subsidies, so a few examples will have to suffice. In 1986–87 the adult education associations derived 70 percent of their revenues from public subsidies and the Red Cross received 46 percent of its cash revenues from public subsidies (Skoloverstyrelsen, 1988; Jansson, 1986). At the local level, a 1980 survey of six municipalities found that public subsidies accounted for 29 percent of the budgets of sports organizations, 43 percent of scouting groups, 51 percent of temperance societies, and 25 percent of religious groups, a mean of 30 percent (Statens ungdomsrad, 1980).

The granting of public subsidies has not occurred haphazardly. On the contrary, at least twenty-seven state subsidies and reports have considered policy in this area. Their recommendations have almost invariably supported public support of the *foreningar* (Statens Offentliga Utredningar, 1988: 39). The dangers of increased *forening* dependence on the state have often been discussed, but the argument that government has a responsibility to promote the *foreningar* because of the positive benefits they bring to society has usually won the day.

The *foreningar* are not simply passive recipients of public support. They have become active participants in the formulation and execution of public policy as well. Here we begin to see how indeterminate the line between central authority and the nonprofit sector really is.

I will begin with the state study commissions. Representatives of *foreningar* make up only about 10 percent of commission members (Birgersson and Westerstahl, 1987), but the *foreningar* themselves view state commissions as their most important means of influencing policy (Elvander, 1966). Study commissions usually circulate preliminary reports to relevant organizations for commentary and evaluation before preparing their final product. Proposals are often modified considerably in accordance with the weight of *forening* opinion.

A second formal channel for *forening* participation in central authority structure is provided by "layman supervisory boards" that are attached to nearly all state administrative agencies. *Forening* representatives comprised about 35 percent of all board members in 1987. The Advisory Delegation for the National Traffic Safety Office, for instance, includes representatives from fifteen organizations, including the Home and School Association (PTA), the Abstaining Motorists' Association, and the Federation of Swedish Farmers (Andersson, Melbourn, and Skogo, 1978). Though the degree to which the boards steer the agencies they oversee is debatable (Statens Offentliga Utredningar, 1985: 40; Andersson, Melbourn, and Skogo, 1978), they clearly strengthen the ties between *foreningar* and central authority.

A third channel is in some respects the most extreme. Beginning with the Labor Court in 1929, three types of specialized courts have been established to deal with civil cases in particular social sectors. The Labor Court, which handles disputes regarding collective bargaining agreements, was joined by the Market Court in 1971 and the Housing Court in 1975. All three courts consist of panels of judges and lay assessors, the latter being representatives of the major *foreningar* in the social sector in question. The Housing Court, for example, has six assessors from tenant organizations and six from landlord groups.

All three courts have final jurisdiction. Hence, in the Swedish system *forening* representatives are brought into the very heart of the authority structure as quasi-judges whose decisions cannot be appealed.

At the municipal level we find a dense web of formal and informal ties between the *foreningar* and government. A 1977 survey found that 80 percent of the municipalities maintain a permanent liaison office to manage municipality-*forening* relationships. About 90 percent of the municipalities have both an Advisory Council for Disabled Persons and an Advisory Council for Pensioners. Such councils always include representatives from the relevant nonprofit organizations. In addition, in most municipalities the *foreningar* work jointly with city officials in the operation of recreation programs and meeting facilities (Kommundepartementet, 1978; Referensgruppen for folkrorelserfragor, 1980).

"Interest group" associations (discussed below) are usually absorbed into the political structure directly. Tenants' unions routinely negotiate rents with landlord associations, which include municipalities as prominent members (some 38 percent of all rental units are publicly or quasi-publicly owned; Statistiska Centralbyran, 1982a). The Federation of Disabled Persons is regularly consulted when major construction projects are being planned. Local bowling clubs take part in the planning process for a new municipal bowling hall. *Foreningar* are brought into the central authority decision process in a wide variety of ways and very much as a matter of course (Gidlund and others, 1982; Statistiska Centralbyran, 1987).

Though public support of the *foreningar* is supplied with few strings attached, in the literature one often encounters the attitude that the *foreningar* are important to democracy not only as channels for input to the political system but also as vehicles for the implementation of state policy. For example, the participation of *foreningar* on the Advisory Delegation of the National Traffic Safety Office is seen as a plus because a number of these *foreningar* faithfully participate in safety campaigns initiated by the agency.

This sort of *forening* execution of public policy is wide-

250   The Nonprofit Sector in the Global Community

spread. Here are some additional examples: The Swedish International Development Agency channels much of its foreign assistance through *foreningar* that organize projects and disaster relief in poor countries. The National Social Welfare Board grants money to some three dozen *foreningar* to enlist them in its campaigns against drug and alcohol abuse. The Environmental Protection Agency subsidizes the magazines produced by conservation associations to encourage the dissemination of information on environmental issues (Riksrevisionsverket, 1986). Public support is thus used to bring central authority directly into society.

References

Andersson, S., Melbourn, A., and Skogo, I. *Myndigheten i samhallet* [Public Agencies in Society]. Stockholm: Liber, 1978.

Asp, K. "Rikspolitik och kommunalpolitik—valrorelsernas utrymme i svensk dagspress 1956–85" [National politics and local politics—Coverage of election campaigns in Swedish dailies, 1956–85]. In Statens Offentliga Utredningar, *Ju mer vi ar tillsammans (del 1)* [The more we are together, Part 1], pp. 353–370. Stockholm: Civildepartmentet, 1987: 6.

Back, M. Partier och organisationer i Sverige [Parties and organizations in Sweden]. Stockholm: Liber, 1980.

Birgersson, B. O., and Westerstahl, J. *Den svenska folkstyrelsen* [The Swedish system of popular rule]. Stockholm: Liber, 1987.

Carlsson, B. *Hur stor ar egentligen den offentliga sektorn?* [How big is the public sector?]. Stockholm: Bratt, 1987.

Elvander, N. *Intresseorganisationerna i dagens Sverige* [Interest organizations in contemporary Sweden]. Lund: Gleerup, 1966.

Furaker, B. *Stat och offentlig sektor* [State and public sector]. Stockholm: Raben and Sjogren, 1987.

Gidlund, G. "Tendenser i svensk partifinansiering" [Trends in Swedish party financing]. In Statens Offentliga Utredningar, *Mal och resultat—nya principer for det statliga stodet till foreningslivet*, pp. 115–138. Stockholm: Civildepartmentet, 1988: 47.

Gidlund, J., Engberg, J., Hallin, U-B., and Lidstrom, A.

Folkrorelser och kommunalpolitik [Popular movements and municipal politics]. Report 12 from the Research Group on Municipal Democracy, DsKn 1982:3. Stockholm: Kommundepartementet, 1982.

Hadenius, S., and Weibull, L. *Mass medier. En bok om Press, Radio & TV* [Mass media: A book on the press, radio & TV]. Stockholm: Bonniers, 1985.

Holmberg, S., and Gilljam, M. *Valjare och val i Sverige* [Voters and Elections in Sweden]. Stockholm: Bonnier, 1987.

Holmberg, C-G., Oscarsson, I., and Ryden, P. *En svensk presshistoria* [A Swedish history of the press]. Stockholm: Esselte, 1983.

Isling, A. *Folkrorelserna i nv roll?* [The popular movements in a new role?]. Stockholm: Sober, 1978.

Jansson, M. *Om Roda korset. Insamling och kassan* [On the Red Cross: Fund-raising and finances]. n.p.: Roda korset, 1986.

Johansson, F. "Delad rostning" [Split-ticket Voting]. In Statens Offentliga Utredningar, *Ju mer vi ar tillsammans (del 1)* [The more we are together, Part 1], pp. 323–341. Stockholm: Civildepartmentet, 1987: 6.

Kommunalt stod till de politiska patierna [Municipal subsidies for the political parties]. Stockholm: Civildepartmentet, 1988: 45.

Kommundepartementet. *Kommunerna och foreningslivet: redovisning av en enkatundersokning* [The municipalities and the voluntary organizations: Presentation of a questionnaire survey]. DsKn 1978:4. Stockholm: Kommundepartementet, 1978.

Lindholm, B. *Rorelsen och folkhemmet. Valfardsstaten, den kommunala demokratin och medborgarmedverkan* [The movement and the people's home: The welfare state, local democracy, and citizen influence]. Stockholm: Raben and Sjorgren, 1983.

Lindroth, B. *Bingo! En kritisk granskning av folkrorelserna i Sverige 1850–1975* [Bingo! A critical look at the popular movements in Sweden 1850–1975]. Uppsala: Prisma and Foreningen Verdandi, 1975.

Referensgruppen for folkrorelserfragor. *Folkrorelserna och demokratin* [The popular movements and democracy]. Stockholm: Kommundepartementet, 1980.

Riksrevisionsverket. *Det statliga stodet till folkrorelserna — en kartlagg-*

252   The Nonprofit Sector in the Global Community

ning [Public subsidies to the popular movements — A survey].
Dept. no 1986: 554. Stockholm: Riksrevisionsverket, 1986.
Riksrevisionsverket. *Det statliga stodet till folkrorelserna* [Public subsidies to the popular movements]. Stockholm: Civiltryck, 1987.
Rodriguez, E. *Offentlig inkomstexpansion* [The expansion of public revenues]. Lund: Gleerup, 1980.
Skoloverstyrelsen. *Studieforbunden infor 90-talet* [The adult education associations face the 1990s]. R 88:31. Stockholm: Skoloverstyrelsen, 1988.
Statens Offentliga Utredningar [Public State Report]. *Kommunal organization och information.* [Municipal organization and information]. Stockholm: Kommundepartementet, 1975: 46.
Statens Offentliga Utredningar. *Regeringen, myndigheterna och myndigheternas ledning* [The government, state administrative agencies, and the management of state administration]. Stockholm: Civildepartmentet, 1985: 40.
Statens Offentliga Utredningar. *Ju mer vi ar tillsammans (del 1)* [The more we are together, Part 1]. Stockholm: Civildepartmentet, 1987: 33.
Statens Offentliga Utredningar. *Mal och resultat — nya principer for det statliga stodet till foreningslivet* (Goals and results — New principles for state subsidization of voluntary organizations]. Stockholm: Civildepartmentet, 1988: 39.
Statens ungdomsrad. *Massor i rorelse. Foreningarna i Sverige* [Masses in movement: The associations in Sweden]. Stockholm: Liber, 1980.
Statistiska Centralbyran [Central Bureau of Statistics]. *Perspectives on Swedish Welfare in 1982.* Living Conditions Report no. 33. Stockholm: Statistiska Centralbyran, 1982a.
Statistiska Centralbyran. *Politiska resurser 1978* [Political resources 1978]. Report no. 31. Stockholm: Statistiska Centralbyran, 1982b.
Statistiska Centralbyran. *Offentliga sektorn: utveckling och nulage* [The public sector: Development and current status]. Stockholm: Statistiska Centralbyran, 1985.
Statistiska Centralbyran. *Foreningslivets engagemang inom offentlig verksamhet* [Association involvement in government activity]. Dnr 378:87. Stockholm: Statistiska Centralbyran, 1987.

Swedish Social Democratic Youth League. "Tillsammans for en ide" [Together for an idea]. In *Utblick* nr 36, "Fakta om folkrorelserna." Johannishov: Frihets Forlag, 1975.

Vestlund, G. *Hur vardar vi var demokrati?* [How do we preserve our democracy?]. Research on Education Report no. 43. Stockholm: Skoloverstyrelsen and Liber, 1981.

Westerstahl, J., and Johansson, R. *Medborgarna och kommun. Studier av medborgerlig aktivitet och representativ folkstyrelse* [Citizens and the municipality: Studies of citizen activity and representative popular government]. Report no. 5 of the Research Group on Municipal Democracy. Stockholm: Kommundepartementet, 1981.

Chapter 14

Government and the
Nonprofit Sector in Australia

This chapter begins with an overview of the private not-for-profit sector in Australia. It then focuses on the relationship between private nonprofit organizations and governments, drawing on two research projects in progress. The first part of this section delineates growing government financial support for nonprofit organizations as well as a growing government dependence on nonprofits. The second part takes a longer perspective and traces major shifts in the pattern of relations between government and nonprofit organizations over the past 200 years. This section concludes by examining the changing pattern of relationships over the last decade and identifying likely future developments. The chapter ends with brief suggestions for future research.

Overview of the Nonprofit Sector in Australia

Organizations that are neither governmental nor organized for profit play an important part in many aspects of Australian life today. In some cases, they play a dominant part. Yet this fact is hardly recognized, and these organizations are rarely studied.

In education, a little over a quarter of primary and secondary school pupils attend private nonprofit schools, mostly Catholic; the remainder attend government schools. The percentage attending private schools is growing. Preschool education reflects a similar distribution, but long-day child care is divided three to one between nonprofit and commercial provision, respectively. In the health sector, most older hospitals started out as nonprofit organizations, but many have come to be run by state government health departments and for years have been known as public hospitals. Nonetheless, in 1986, private hospitals supplied 23 percent of all hospital beds; 50 percent of these were provided by nonprofit hospitals, mostly religious and charitable organizations but some community based. Other private hospitals are operated for a profit. One-third of nursing home beds are provided by nonprofit organizations compared with 46 percent that are operated for a profit. The remainder are directly operated by state governments. Reflecting their origins as friendly or mutual benefit societies, many private health insurance providers are nonprofit organizations. These are credit unions that provide almost 20 percent of personal and consumer finance. Indeed, Australia's largest life insurance company, the AMP Society, is still, formally, a mutual benefit or nonprofit organization.

More than half of all welfare services are provided by nonprofit organizations. These include family support services, emergency accommodations, hostel accommodations for older people, and services to people with disabilities (the only exception begin services for the severely mentally ill, which are provided by state government). A vast array of self-help and advocacy organizations lobby government in the health and welfare fields. Some housing finance is provided by nonprofit building societies. A huge network of sociality/fund-raising bodies, loosely called community service organizations, of which Rotary and Lions clubs are perhaps the best known, provide funds and labor to various local projects. The burgeoning green or environment movement is entirely nongovernmental and not-for-profit. Almost all sports, from little athletics to horse racing and the major national football competitions are organized by nonprofit organizations. So too are other recreational pursuits, from bush walking to bridge. Registered clubs, a major recreational resource for many Australians, are also nonprofit, as are many bodies that cater to young people, such as scouts. Surf lifesaving clubs, an important part of Australia's coastal culture, are similarly nonprofit organizations. So too are bush or country fire brigades and many small cultural organizations, such as drama clubs and local history societies. By contrast, most large cultural organizations are government bodies. In the field of industrial relations, trades unions and employer associations are nonprofit, as are many of the organizations that provide training and work experience to the long-term unemployed. Private nonprofit organizations play an important part in the provision of Australia's overseas aid, but they are overshadowed by government efforts.

In few fields are nonprofit organizations the only providers. In some, they exist alongside government providers; in others, next to commercial or for-profit organizations. In many fields, all three types of organizations operate, sometimes in distinctive niches, sometimes in competition.

In most of the fields mentioned above, nonprofit organizations receive some form of assistance from government. Most will pay no tax on their income; donations to some will reduce the donors' taxable income; many local bodies will pay no or low rates (local taxes) and may receive facilities rent free from local governments. Direct subsidies from all three levels of government abound. Subsidies usually entail some degree of government direction, but even unsubsidized organizations will have their activities regulated in some manner, though rarely with any sort of rigor.

In some fields, the existence of nonprofit organizations was once the source of great controversy. The 1870s decision by the Catholic bishops in Australia to pursue a separate school system was a cause of deep social division for another ninety years. Only in the past twenty-five years have governments subsidized Catholic schools. Many health insurance organizations were once friendly societies, employing general practitioners to provide medical services to their members via a lodge system. But fifty years of campaigning by doctors against these arrangements culminated in the destruction of the lodges and a new role for the friendly societies as providers of health insurance. Two housing booms in Australia, in the period immediately after World War II and in the 1960s, were largely financed by nonprofit bodies. The first was facilitated by cooperative housing societies, mutual benefit organizations that, with a government guarantee, borrowed funds from the banks and lent them to their members. The second was facilitated by permanent building societies — which were established by the cooperative societies — taking deposits from the general public and lending them out as housing loans. Some producer cooperatives still exist in the rural and fishing industries, but neither producer nor consumer cooperatives have the importance they had fifty years ago.

Finally, while many nonprofit organizations are managed and their services provided by paid staff, the great majority employ the services of volunteers in some ways. Some, particularly those in the recreation field, depend entirely on volunteer labor. However, in some fields, government organizations also use volunteers: for fund raising, as guides, or to provide personal support.

Not much is known about nonprofit organizations in Australia. The regular government statistical collections provide little help. The Australian Bureau of Statistics (ABS) records government grants to nonprofit organizations by government purpose but does not clearly distinguish between the levels of government making the grant. National Account figures lump nonprofit organizations with unincorporated for-profit organizations as part of the household sector. Labor force data either do not distinguish the characteristics of the employing organization or lump "nonprofit" with "for-profit" in a grab bag "private" category. As well, the classification of industry subdivisions is such that while one subdivision (Welfare and Religious Institutions) can be identified as almost entirely occupied by nonprofit employees, that covers only a part of the nonprofit work force.

Better-quality data are available for certain fields where nonprofit organizations play a prominent part, largely because the commonwealth government subsidizes all (or almost all) organizations in those fields. Information exists for hospitals, nursing homes, schools, and child-care centers, but it is mostly unpublished.

Occasional or one-time surveys of nonprofit organizations in particular fields of endeavor provide additional information, often in great detail. However, such surveys are difficult to generalize from as they create their own classification schemes, which invariably are incompatible and cut across categories used by the ABS.

The most important of these studies was conducted by the Social Welfare Research Centre (SWRC), based at the University of New South Wales and funded by the commonwealth government, in August 1981 (Milligan, Hardwick, and Graycar, 1984; Graycar and Jamrozik, 1989). It surveyed a national sample of nearly 2,000 nongovernmental welfare organizations and received responses from almost 600. It defined welfare very broadly, to include large areas of health and housing, but excluded schools, hospitals, and most organizations that provide cultural and recreation services. Much of the study was devoted to exploring differences among categories of organizations and among states, but it made an attempt to determine some national estimates of the size of the nongovernmental welfare sector. However, its sampling was flawed in an important respect, inflating its estimates of the size of the nonprofit work force and its level of government support by a factor of three. Nevertheless, the study provides a valuable guide to a set of nonprofit organizations, and some use will be made of it below.

Overall, about 370,000 Australians are employed, full-time and part-time, by private nonprofit organizations. This estimate is derived from ABS labor force data (Australian Bureau of Statistics, 1989). This is a little less than 5 percent of the work force. By comparison, one-quarter of the Australian work force is employed by government departments or public trading enterprises. Nonprofit organizations also draw heavily on volunteers. The organizations in the SWRC sample employed almost twice as many volunteers as paid staff members, but for an average of only four hours per week. No data are available on the extent of volunteer effort mobilized by all nonprofit organizations. It is clearly considerable, however, and an important resource that must be taken into account in any estimate of the economic contribution of nonprofit organizations.

Nonprofit institutions receive funds from a variety of sources. For the sample of organizations in the SWRC study, 36 percent of income came from governments, 25 percent from donations and public appeals, 10 percent from user fees, and 12 percent from membership fees. In Australia, donations to many (but by no means all) nonprofit organizations are deductible from the donor's taxable income. Estimates by the Australian Treasury put the revenue foregone from that source at $83 million in 1986–1987 (The Treasury, 1988). The Australian Treasury does not provide a figure for the actual size of donations for which tax deductions were claimed. An average tax rate of about 25 percent would suggest a figure of some $330 million. One survey estimated that in 1988 Australians gave $869 million to charities (Milburn, 1989). Many of these donations would not have been tax deductible.

The SWRC study demonstrated that corporate philanthropy is relatively unimportant for most welfare organizations, constituting only one percent of the sample's total income. A recent survey that solicited information from the top fifty Australian companies on the size of their corporate donations received a positive response from only twenty-five. Some refused to provide information on the grounds that they did not wish their generosity to be known; they claimed to fear an avalanche of requests for help. Those who did reply claimed that they donated a total of $18 million (Bagwell, 1989). This figure was certainly inflated by bicentennary-induced generosity. It included some very large single donation items and some sponsorship arrangements. Corporate sponsorship is probably a more important source of funds for nonprofit organizations than is corporate philanthropy, but such sponsorship is concentrated almost entirely on the arts and sporting events. The Australian Opera alone received $2.3 million in corporate sponsorship in 1987–1988 (Roach and Eccles, 1988), but it is sports that benefits most from corporate sponsorship, with more than $2 million being given to the Victorian Racing Club by a brewing company to spend on the famous Melbourne and Caufield Cup horse races. An estimated $70 million a year was spent by corporations on sports sponsorship in 1988 (Neales, 1988).

The SWRC study indicated that government subsidies provided 36 percent of organizations' income. However, 37 percent of organizations received no government support and of the 63 percent that did, that support constituted almost 60 percent of their income. Estimates based on ABS government finance data for 1978–1979 suggest that the total income of what the SWRC study defined as nonprofit "welfare" organizations was $1 billion. This would be more than $2 billion in current values. It is not possible to estimate the total income of all nonprofit organizations. However, in 1986–1987, government grants to nonprofit organizations totaled $3.4 billion, or a little over 3 percent of all government outlays.

Little research has been done on the management of nonprofit organizations in Australia. A distinction most frequently drawn in Australia is between community-managed and traditional organizations. It is at best a fuzzy distinction but points to some important differences.

Community-managed organizations are mostly small and locally based. Boards are sometimes elected by users and sometimes by any members of the local community who attend the organization's annual meeting. Sometimes they are appointed by a local council or by a local clergyman. Sometimes they are self-perpetuating. A constant theme of popular writing about community organizations is the tension between the volunteer board and the usually paid staff. Pressure from governments and from insurance companies (as a condition for obtaining public liability insurance) means that almost all community-managed organizations are incorporated. Some are required to have a government nominee on their board; many have public servants in a voluntary capacity anyway. Some local organizations operate more as branches of a statewide body. Such parent organizations are usually traditional.

Organizations that are called traditional are usually at least thirty years old and are generally quite large. Most are incorporated, some by their own act of parliament. Their boards are more likely to be self-appointed, although some are elected by their membership. Many have links to religious denominations that control or influence appointments. Traditional organizations are usually organized along traditional bureaucratic lines; the management of some is quite autocratic.

Relationships Between Governments and Nonprofit Organizations

In several Australian service industries, private nonprofit organizations are significant providers alongside for-profit firms. The most notable of these industries are health (especially the hospital sector), aged care, leisure, child care, and personal and housing finance. In the first three cases, governments are significant providers as well. For the most part, relations between for-profit and not-for-profit organizations are distant; in some fields (such as child care), they are hostile. In many cases commercial providers were active before nonprofits, but they provided a service that was inaccessible to many classes of people and that was thought to be of low quality as well as exploitative.

By contrast, in all fields where nonprofit organizations are active, they interact with government agencies that regulate and frequently subsidize them. In a few cases (for example, schooling) they compete with government providers; in other instances they are closely controlled, even exploited by government officials; in most cases the relationship is based on a reluctant recognition of mutual interdependence.

The precise character of the relationship between government and private nonprofit organizations varies among fields of service (or industries) and even within fields. Relationships depend on many factors peculiar to the field, including the type of service, the extent to which each side depends on the other, the activities of other groups, and the recent history of those relationships. Consequently, it is difficult to generalize about relationships between governments and nonprofit organizations across fields of service. However, the pattern of relationships within each field is affected by significant events and movements that are external to the field and that shape the perceptions and activities of those within it. Thus, wars and depressions, the changing preoccupations and priorities of governments, the emergence of social movements, and secular demographic and economic changes can all produce more general changes in the pattern of government/nonprofit relationships. Generally, those external factors are mediated by actors within particular fields, but it is sometimes possible to identify similar forces for change at work in several fields at the same time.

There are many ways of identifying salient features in the changing pattern of relations between governments and nonprofit organizations. One way is to analyze patterns of government support for nonprofit organizations. This enables research at least to begin with a useful degree of specificity and provides a helpful sense of proportion. It is difficult, though, to obtain comparable data for more than the last twenty years, and this limits analysis to the recent past. Another method overcomes that problem. It uses the conventional historian's survey, detecting patterns from the 200-year sweep of history since European settlement. For much of the period, it relies on secondary sources, reporting patches of research rather than a systematic study. It can, however, provide a useful corrective to any tendency to believe that current developments are unique or that past times were a golden age.

Direct Government Support for Nonprofit Organizations

Initial work on ABS government finance data suggests that over the decade between 1976–1977 and 1986–1987 direct support for nonprofit organizations by all levels of government in Australia more than doubled in real terms. Table 14.1 provides data for eight fields, which account for 95 percent of all government

Table 14.1.

Field	1976-1977		1986-1987		Increase 1976-1977 to 1986-1987 (%)
	Govt. Support for NPOs ($ millions)	Govt. Support for NPOs (constant 1984-1985 values)	Govt. Support for NPOs ($ millions)	Govt. Support for NPOs (constant 1984-1985 values)	
Primary/secondary education	300	602.4	1300	1148.4	91
Health	140	281	550	486	73
Welfare services	90	181	630	556.5	208
Community development	13	26	15	13.3	-49
Recreation and culture	85	171	392	346	103
Employment and training	0.7	1.4	170	150	10,614
Research	13	26	120	106	308
Foreign aid	0.6	1.2	8	7	483
All fields	695	1,396	3,360	2,968	213%

Source: Unpublished Australian Bureau of Statistics government finance data.

support for nonprofit organizations. The data show considerable variations among fields, with the most spectacular being in employment and training, but from a very low base in 1976–1977. Of those fields with significant levels of expenditure in 1976–1977, welfare services saw the greatest increase, tripling in value over the decade, whereas recreation and culture doubled.

These figures, however, do not tell us whether governments came to rely more heavily on nonprofits in these or other fields over the decade. Table 14.2 shows for each field, government support for nonprofit organizations as a percentage of total government outlays in that field. From this, we can see that governments came to rely only a little more on nonprofit providers in the field of welfare services and recreation and culture. That is, big percentage increases in government grants to nonprofit organizations in those fields over the decade were matched by large increases overall in government expenditure. Of the high-expenditure fields, it was in schooling that governments came to significantly rely more on nonprofit organizations. Overall, though, employment and training experienced the largest increase, reflecting the commonwealth government's heavy dependence on community organizations for the extensive and relatively expensive work experience programs it started in the aftermath of the 1982–1983 recession.

Changing Pattern of Relationships Between Government and Nonprofit Organizations

Patterns of government financial support for nonprofit organizations, while interesting, leave many questions unanswered. One set of such questions concerns the longer-term pattern of relationships between government and nonprofit organizations: the changing characteristics of these relationships and the factors that shape them. Such questions require research that combines historical methods with contemporary political and organizational analysis. A preliminary survey suggests that it is possible to identify six phases in the pattern of relations between government and nonprofit organizations in Australia since the beginning of European settlement.

Table 14.2.

Field	1976–1977			1986–1987		
	Total Govt. Spending	Govt. Support to Nonprofit Organizations		Total Govt. Spending	Govt. Support to Nonprofit Organizations	
	($ millions)	Amount	% of Total Govt. Expenditure	($ millions)	Amount	% of Total Govt. Expenditure
Primary/secondary education	3,000	300	10	8,200	1,300	16
Health	4,100	140	3.4	14,000	550	4
Welfare services	400	90	22.5	2,500	630	25.2
Community development	230	13	5.7	260	15	5.8
Recreation and culture	730	85	12	3,030	392	13
Employment and training	230	0.7	.18	1,200	170	14
Research	180	13	7	900	120	13
Foreign aid	400	0.6	.15	807	8	1

Source: Unpublished Australian Bureau of Statistics government finance data.

From the early 1800s to the 1860s, nonprofit organizations concentrated on the relief of poverty and distress and on the provision of schooling. Organizations that pursued the former goal were started by members of the social elite; those that pursued the latter were initiated by the major religious denominations. All were subsidized by government, but by the 1850s most colonial governments had begun their own system of schools because of the inefficiency of denominational provision.

From the 1870s to World War I, governments took over most nonprofit organizations that they had previously subsidized, but at the same time there was a flourishing of nonprofit activity in the same fields and elsewhere. Governments took over most denominational schools, partly from a desire to achieve efficiencies and partly to remove what they saw as a major source of sectarian discord. However, the Catholic bishops refused to cooperate and kept their schools independent of government systems and without government subsidy (Gregory, 1973). In the field of charitable relief, governments took over those residential facilities for the indigent and aged or for young children that they had previously subsidized. In the latter case they closed down the institutions, initially putting children into foster care. In New South Wales, at least, governments soon began to pay a regular stipend to the child's natural mother (Dickey, 1987).

Similarly, by the turn of the century, most Australian states had introduced pensions for the aged and for people with disabilities (Kewley, 1973). The provision of income support, effectively as a right to certain classes of people, was a development only a government could initiate. Nonetheless, for some, it was inadequate. Government-provided residential accommodations for the chronically ill aged remained but did not expand. It was left to nonprofit organizations to meet the slowly increasing demand. Nonprofit children's homes expanded more rapidly to provide a service to mothers who were unable to keep a child but did not want the child in a foster home. Both of these nonprofit initiatives were without government subsidy until the next period. They were mainly a product of the religious denominations (O'Brien, 1988). By contrast with other residential services, hospitals, also the product of initiatives by the social elite or religious denominations, remained nonprofit but experienced increasing government control in return for increasing levels of subsidy (Dickey, 1987).

In addition to a flowering of denominationally based initiatives in the charitable sector, the period saw a flourishing of mutual aid organizations that drew their membership from the middle and respectable working classes. Based on British models, friendly societies enrolled up to 40 percent of the population, providing in return for membership, free medical care, sickness benefits, and funeral benefits. Each local branch or lodge contracted with doctors to provide medical services to lodge members (Green and Cromwell, 1984). Often contracts were let after competitive tendering. This practice was strongly opposed by doctors' organizations, which for eighty years conducted a campaign against the lodges. Flourishing, too, from the 1870s until the long depression of the 1890s, were building societies organized along mutual benefit lines (Butlin, 1964). Governments largely stayed clear of the mutual aid developments except to insist on actuarily sound management practices. The mutual aid organizations flourished at a time when Australia's per capita income was the highest in the world and when the emergence of trade unions and employer associations prefigured the formation of class-based party politics in the first decade of the 1900s.

From the 1920s to World War II, the only change in the pattern of relations between governments and nonprofit organizations was an increasing preparedness by state governments to provide modest subsidies to nonprofit organizations that offered charitable relief and residential support. The commonwealth government provided little support to nonprofit organizations. The period saw a conservative middle class come to dominate Australian political life and the foundation and flourishing of nonprofit community service organizations such as Rotary, Lions, and Apex clubs. It also saw a state government initiative to revitalize housing finance by encouraging the formation of mutual aid or cooperative building societies, providing them with a government guarantee, and encouraging the banks and insurance companies to lend them money that would then be distributed among their low- to middle-income members to be repaid over twenty years. It proved a highly successful initiative (Lyons, 1988).

From 1946 to the 1960s, the commonwealth government, which had emerged from World War II fiscally dominant over the states, began to subsidize certain nonprofit initiatives in an increasingly generous way, but not before destroying the lodge system of medical provision in the interest of fee-for-service medicine. The major objects of commonwealth subsidies were schools; aged persons' accommodations, including nursing home care; and hospitals. In the case of the schools, the commonwealth government succumbed to state government exhortations to help fund a massive expansion of secondary schooling and university education, but in quest of Catholic votes, it also made non-government — mostly Catholic — schools eligible. In the cases of aged persons' accommodations and hospitals, commercial providers also were eligible for government subsidies and flourished as a consequence. The major nonprofit initiative in the period was the formation of a large number of new organizations that provided care for people with certain disabilities. These were usually formed by parents of children with particular types of disability. The new organizations soon received support from state and commonwealth governments.

The late 1960s through the 1970s saw a thriving of community-managed organizations. These were supposed to return power to ordinary people and were formed as a protest against a perceived professional and bureaucratic dominance of many services. Community organizations were also said to be more cost-effective than governments. The sources of these community initiatives were mostly university-educated young people, the first products of the massive expansion of universities in the 1960s. Many found employment in government departments and encouraged government support for, even sponsorship of, community initiatives. These initiatives were successful in many fields, and the period witnessed a great expansion of community-based child-care centers, neighborhood centers, health centers, and the like. It also saw a considerable growth in government subsidies to nonprofit organizations (Birkett and Montgomery,

1977). Moreover, during this period there emerged articulate groups of consumers of health and welfare services who demanded special services or services shaped by their values. Most prominent were women's groups that demanded refuges and women's health centers and organizations of people with disabilities.

However, other forces were also at work. In the field of schooling, two developments occurred that became more widespread in the 1980s: government takeovers and targeting. In several states, governments took over a number of previously nonprofit government-subsidized special schools (for children with disabilities). The commonwealth government significantly expanded its subsidies for nongovernment schools, simultaneously adjusting the way it made funds available. Schools were graded according to the quality of their facilities and their ability to raise income by fees. Per-pupil grants were adjusted to give larger amounts to poorer schools.

Governments also indicated a preference for subsidizing nonprofit rather than for-profit providers. In the early 1970s, concerned about the rapidly increasing cost of nursing home subsidies that were going largely to a rapidly expanding commercial sector, the commonwealth government offered to underwrite all the costs of nonprofit organizations if they would expand their provision of nursing home beds. The government believed that nonprofits would provide high-quality care at lower costs, but they did not (Kewley, 1980). In 1972 the commonwealth government began to offer subsidies to nonprofit organizations to start child-care centers. One reason was to provide competition to commercial centers and force them to raise the quality of their care. These subsidies encouraged a considerable expansion in the number of child-care places. Only in 1990, after a long campaign and support from certain influential groups within the commonwealth bureaucracy, have commercial child-care centers won the right to obtain government subsidies to enable them to reduce the fees charged to low-income users.

The late 1970s saw growing criticism of the size and scope of governments. For a time, this helped nonprofit organizations and their supporters within government. They were encouraged to expand their services in lieu of government provision, but by the 1980s, government support was becoming more selective.

During the 1980s, relations between government and non-profit organizations were shaped by major attempts to reduce the scope of government and recast its management. Nonetheless, possibly because Labor governments were in office nationally and in most states during the period, Australia did not experience the dramatic cuts in government support for welfare programs or nonprofit subsidies that seem to have occurred in the United States (Salamon, 1989). Government social expenditure was not reduced, but it was, in the prevailing discourse, more closely "targeted" toward those with low incomes. Relations between governments and nonprofit organizations were characterized by increasing attempts by governments to exercise control, although more from a desire to see government funds used more efficiently, effectively, and equitably than from a desire to exert control as such.

Nonetheless, the independence of some nonprofit organizations was extinguished. The slow process that had begun a century earlier, of bringing government-subsidized nonprofit hospitals (the so-called public hospitals) under direct government control reached its culmination, while all direct government subsidies to private hospitals (both commercial and nonprofit) were withdrawn. In New South Wales, a network of community-based organizations that provided domiciliary care services was taken over by the state government, which along with the commonwealth government had been financing a massive expansion in its services. As noted above, the same state government a decade earlier had taken over a number of nonprofit, government-subsidized special schools in order to encourage the movement of many children into mainstream schools. Responding to similar pressure from professionals and consumer advocates, the commonwealth government considerably expanded its subsidies to nonprofit organizations that provide services to people with disabilities but required in turn massive changes in the provision of those services in the direction of deinstitutionalization and normalization. Methods for determining subsidies for nursing homes were changed to make them uniform across the country. These methods applied to for-profit and nonprofit homes alike. Organizations that wish to receive subsidies have had to guarantee a minimum set of residents' rights and admission procedures designed to ensure that only people who need a high level of care are placed in nursing homes.

While continuing to encourage nonprofit initiative in fields that had become their preserve, governments in the 1980s moved to adopt a more planned approach. In the 1970s, organizations that wished to receive government capital and recurrent subsidies to provide a service simply made a submission and were funded on a first-come, first-served basis. In the 1980s, governments became more precise about where they wished to fund new services and tried to target them in areas of high demand and low supply. This was particularly true of commonwealth government programs. More generally, governments increasingly came to organize their variety of subsidies into programs with specific objectives and set out their expectations of the nonprofit organizations that they subsidized in the form of contracts. However, they did not seek to award contracts by competitive tender. This is possibly because to have done so might have forced them to pay the full cost of the service. In most cases, governments still relied on nonprofit organizations to contribute some resources of their own, either financial or voluntary work time.

In some services, child care and nursing home care in particular, contradictory pressures acting on the commonwealth government caught providers in something of a bind in the 1980s. The government wished to provide a limited subsidy only, allowing the provider to cover most of its costs from fees; on the other hand, the government felt obliged by fiscal and electoral pressures to prevent providers from charging too high a user fee. Some interests within the commonwealth government suggested resolving the impasse by subsidizing consumers rather than providers by way of means-tested vouchers. This would enable the government to avoid intruding too deeply into the market for these services. However, other interests warned that to cease regulating fees would cause them to skyrocket and, as a consequence, considerably increase the cost to the government of its vouchers. Thus far these more prudent interests have prevailed.

At a more general level, the movement to reform the management of government organizations via corporate management techniques had ramifications for relations between government and nonprofit organizations (Considine, 1988a, 1988b). These reforms sought to bring the vast array of government activities under closer ministerial control by utilizing such techniques as corporate planning, program evaluation, and performance appraisal. Incidentally, the reformers sought to reach out to impose their view of order on the vast array of nonprofit organizations that are in some ways sustained by government. This was most pronounced at the state level, where over the decade there were at least a dozen inquiries into the funding of nonprofit agencies. Most of these recommend greater accountability to government by nonprofits and the wider use of performance indicators and evaluation. In practice, however, little changed. Not many government employees were expert in the new management techniques, and nonprofit agencies were adept at resisting too much control.

In the future, tendencies noted in the 1980s, such as the increasing use of managerialist techniques and greater targeting of government subsidies, will continue. The capacity of consumer groups to influence governments to pressure nonprofit, government-subsidized providers to change their ways — already seen in the disability services and aged-care fields — is likely to continue and to produce a growing tension between those two products of the 1970s: consumerism and community management. This is because consumers are coming to demand readily available, good-quality services. There is a growing belief that these are likely to be provided by larger organizations that can hire more specialized staff members and offer them further training and a career path.

This pressure is reinforced by two other developments. The first is the hostility of feminists to the continuing exploitation of women in the health, education, and community service industries. The work force in these industries is predominantly female but the management is mostly male; the wages

are generally low, skills are often underrecognized or unrecog-
nized, and work is often available only on a part-time basis
(Wheeler, 1986; Walker, Manning, and Howe, 1987). The second development is a new interest by sections of the trade union
movement in those industries in which nonprofit organizations
are well represented. This interest has two aspects. Partly in
response to the growth of community services such as child care
and aged care over the past decade, trade unions are moving
to obtain industrial awards for those large sectors of the community service industry that have been award free. Industrial
awards set standards of pay and other working conditions that
are mandatory for employers. They cover most sectors of the
work force, even where union membership is low. At the same
time, the whole of the Australian trade union movement, to
which more than 40 percent of the work force belong, is actively
seeking the review and reorganization of all industrial awards.
This movement, known as award restructuring, began as a plan
to revitalize Australia's ailing manufacturing industry and has
spread to the whole work force. Its essential aim is to produce
a better-trained and more broadly skilled work force in each
major industry sector. However, in those industries that pay
low wages, employers will have to increase pay rates over the
next three to four years, in some cases by as much as 40 percent. The trade union movement has identified health services
and child care as two priority areas for award restructuring.

     These factors, taken together, are likely to transform sig-
nificantly the structure and management of nonprofit organizations. Superficially, they would appear to encourage the expansion of existing large organizations and the amalgamation
of smaller bodies. There are some signs that this is beginning
to happen. Sometimes with government encouragement, larger
traditional welfare organizations are beginning slowly to expand
into fields of service such as tenants' advice, previously the preserve of smaller community-managed organizations. To counter
these pressures, many in the so-called community sector, who
strongly desire to maintain its more innovative, participative
forms of community management, are talking of improving
the sector's efficiency by developing loose forms of cooperative

networking, along with regional management service units to provide training and consulting services.

One thing is certain. Wage rates will rise and with them the cost of nonprofit service provision. Governments may increase their subsidies, but they are more likely to target them even more precisely, requiring providers to rely more on raising fees from those who can afford them.

Research Agenda

The importance of private nonprofit organizations in contemporary Australian life and Australian history has been largely ignored. What work there is focuses on particular fields of service or industries and does not recognize the existence of similar organizations in other fields. Three overlapping research agendas suggest themselves.

First of all, there is a need for more comprehensive and reliable data on nonprofit organizations. Data are needed on the number and size of organizations, the characteristics of their work force and management, and the source and allocation of their funds. Some of this information could come from current data collections such as those conducted by the ABS, but at present ABS data is of little value as it does not identify nonprofit organizations in its data collections. To fill in gaps, we need detailed surveys of nonprofit organizations, such as the SWRC study, but perhaps before commencing a project as ambitious as that, we need surveys of more limited scope, surveys designed to provide an indication of the wider picture. Even reliable data on corporate and government support for nonprofit organizations, such as the data provided for Great Britain by the Charities Aid Foundation, would be helpful. Unfortunately, Australian companies appear reluctant to provide such data.

Second, we need studies of industries in which nonprofit organizations are significant participants, studies that would focus on the interaction of nonprofits with governments and for-profit organizations. Such studies should seek to estimate the economic contribution of nonprofit organizations, including their voluntary work force. They should describe and seek to evaluate the organizational forms and management practices that predominate among the nonprofits in each industry. They should also have a historical dimension and throw light on questions such as the reason for the formation of nonprofit providers and why and how they have continued. In time, the collection of such studies will enable an adequate history of nonprofit endeavors in Australia to be written.

Third, and drawing on the first two agendas, we need as far as possible to adopt a comparative perspective in Australian studies or, putting it another way, to include Australia in cross-national studies of nonprofit organizations. Australia's inclusion in the Luxembourg income study has produced illuminating evidence that in comparison with like countries, Australia is characterized by significant inequalities and a miserly welfare system (Saunders, Hobbes, and Stott, 1989). This evidence powerfully contradicts the conventional wisdom. Conventional wisdom also has it that Australia has a very small voluntary or nonprofit sector (largely because it has a very strong government sector). Evidence on that point will also help in the important task of reassessing Australia's history and future policy options.

References

Australian Bureau of Statistics. *Labour Force: August, 1989.* Canberra: Australian Bureau of Statistics, 1989.

Bagwell, S. "Corporate Charity Feels the Squeeze." *Australian Financial Review,* Oct. 25, 1989.

Birkett, W. P., and Montgomery, K. *Government Financing of Non-Government Welfare Agencies 1970/71–1974/75.* Sydney: Kuringai College of Advanced Education, 1977.

Butlin, N. G. *Investment in Australian Economic Development, 1861–1900.* Cambridge: Cambridge University Press, 1964.

Considine, M. "The Corporate Management Framework." *Australian Journal of Public Administration,* 1988a, *47* (1), 4–18.

Considine, M. "The Costs of Increased Control: Corporate Management and Australian Community Organisations." *Australian Social Work,* 1988b, *41* (3), 17–25.

Dickey, B. *No Charity There: A Short History of Social Welfare in Australia* (2nd ed.). North Sydney: Allen and Unwin, 1987.

Graycar, A., and Jamrozik, A. *How Australians Live: Social Policy in Theory and Practice.* South Melbourne: Macmillan, 1989.

Green, D., and Cromwell, L. *Mutual Aid or Welfare State: Australian Friendly Societies.* North Sydney: Allen and Unwin, 1984.

Gregory, J. S. *Church and State.* Melbourne: Cassell Australia, 1973.

Kewley, T. H. *Social Security in Australia, 1990* (2nd ed.). Sydney: Sydney University Press, 1973.

Kewley, T. H. *Australian Social Security Today: Major Developments from 1900 to 1978.* Sydney: Sydney University Press, 1980.

Lyons, M. "Ted Tytherleigh." In R. T. Appleyard and B. Schedvim (eds.), *Australian Financiers: Biographical Essays.* South Melbourne: Macmillan, 1988.

Milburn, C. "Australians Give $869M a Year, Poll Finds." *Age,* Dec. 12, 1989.

Millgan, V., Hardwick, S., and Graycar, A. *Non-Government Welfare Organisations in Australia: A National Classification.* SWRC R&P No. 51. Sydney: Social Welfare Research Centre, 1984.

Neales, S. "Corporate Cunning Powers Our Sport." *Australian Financial Review,* Aug. 25, 1988.

O'Brien, A. *Poverty's Prison: The Poor in New South Wales, 1880–1918.* Melbourne: Melbourne University Press, 1988.

Roach, P., and Eccles, J. "How Our Top Guns Put on the Show." *Australian Financial Review,* Aug. 26, 1988.

Salamon, L. M. "The Voluntary Sector and the Future of the Welfare State." *Nonprofit and Voluntary Sector Quarterly,* 1989, *18* (1), 11–24.

Saunders, P., Hobbes, G., and Stott, H. "Income Inequality and Redistribution in Australia and New Zealand: An International and Comparative Analysis." In P. Saunders and A. Jamrozik (eds.), *Social Policy and Inequality in Australia and New Zealand.* SWRC R&P No. 78. Sydney: Social Welfare Research Centre, 1989.

The Treasury. *Tax Expenditures Statement.* Canberra: Australian Government Publishing Service, 1988.

Walker, J., Manning, I., and Howe, A. *The Identification of Priority Training Needs in the Human Services Sector.* Melbourne: National Institute of Economic and Industry Research, 1987.

Wheeler, L. *Close to Home: The Community Services Industry, New South Wales.* NCOSS Issues Paper No. 7. Sydney: Council of Social Service of New South Wales, 1986.

Changing Concepts
of Voluntarism in Japan

Social values in modern Japan are shaped by opposing traditions. On the one hand, East Asian traditions that center around
the group and put great emphasis on group solidarity continue
to exist. On the other hand, since the beginning of modernization, especially since World War II, Western ideas together with
the impact of industrialization and economic success have gradually changed basic social conceptions in the direction of more
individualism. Although this development has taken place at
a far slower pace than the adherents of modernization theories
expected, its consequences have been noticeable since the second half of the 1960s. This had led to a diversification of the
forms of and motives for voluntary work in Japan. It is on the

local level where the integration of the different groups of volunteers must be achieved: the more traditional neighborhood associations (*chōnaikai* or *jichikai*) and appointed community welfare commissioners (*minsei-iin*) on the one side, and the newly developed *borantia* movement (a Japanese adaptation of the English "volunteer") and various more autonomous alternative groups (*jūmin-undō*) on the other.

Traditional Noninstitutionalized Volunteers: Neighborhood Associations (*Chōnaikai/Jichikai*)[1]

Neighborhood associations consist of the inhabitants of a locally defined area, ranging between 180 and 400 households. Their average size of about 200 households (or 800 individuals) allows the establishment of good face-to-face communication. In densely inhabited Tokyo, approximately that many people live in an area of about 200 by 400 meters.

Jichikai are not institutionalized parts of the welfare system (Thränhardt, 1990), but they play an active role in the social life of present-day Japan. Their origins are said to be connected to the necessity of cooperation in a rice-paddy culture, but neighborhood associations existed in the urban centers of premodern Japan as well. They had important functions in the exercise of collective responsibilities and rights.[2]

Social Functions of Jichikai

Although neighborhood associations are multifunctional units that exercise both economic and administrative functions (Shinseikatsu, 1982), I shall concentrate here on the social aspects.

The vitality and creative force of *jichikai* for the "maintenance of the fabric of local social life" in downtown Tokyo has been shown in a fascinating case study (Bestor, 1985, p. 128). Central to *jichikai* activities are help to neighbors and people in the ward who are in need because of an accident, illness, death of a family member, and so on. An often related case is cooperative help in rebuilding the house of a neighbor after it has burned down. Most *jichikai* own a meeting place and give shelter to homeless families in cases of need. The meeting place is usually the center for various hobby groups, such as flower-arrangement clubs, chorus singers, folk dancers, and similar groups that involve, particularly, neighborhood women (they are comparable to social activities offered by Christian parishes in Western countries).

There are organized excursions to playgrounds for children or the inspection of all neighborhood bicycles. Once a year a trip to a sightseeing spot or to one of the popular hot springs, with its relaxed, sociable atmosphere, is organized. In more traditional neighborhood associations, the festival of the local Shinto shrine is a high point of communal activity, and virtually all members are involved in the festival's preparation and performance. On this occasion, a portable shrine is carried through the neighborhood, the boundaries of which are to be regarded carefully. Trespassing into the territory of an adjacent *jichikai* must be negotiated beforehand, and even unplanned detours by any member into "foreign" territory are expected to be followed by an apology from the festival committee. This shows the highly symbolic value of this parade as an occasion for local identification (Bestor, 1985).

Voluntarism and Confucian Values

The grass-roots character of *jichikai* justifies its inclusion in a discussion of third-sector groups. However, an application of the Western concept of voluntarism does not adequately describe the motivational forces for activity in neighborhood associations. Membership in *jichikai* might be called automatic and obligatory rather than voluntary in our sense. Despite this fact, the degree to which the members engage themselves in the neighborhood astonishes Western observers. An explanation for this must be given in terms of Confucian values such as the feeling of *indebtedness to other people in one's group* (*giri*) and the importance of *harmony* (*wa*). Within this system of values, abstinence from communal action would violate the principle of harmony that is at the center of the classical Confucian worldview. Furthermore, Confucianism, especially in its neo-Confucian version as it was developed in Tokugawa Japan, includes a strong element of hierarchical thinking that also exists in *jichikai*.

In connection with the social functions of *jichikai*, another Confucian value is important: neighborly love (*ninjo*), which motivates the members of the neighborhood to help one another. It must be stressed, however, that this love is particularized and restricted to the small group for which in-group feelings are developed; it is not universal and valid for all humankind as in the Christian command "love thy neighbor" (Dore, 1958).

In the wider context of social work this severely restricts the social impetus of *jichikai* and tends to exclude members of out-groups, such as the discriminated against *buraku* minority,[3] Koreans, or atomic bomb victims (*hibakusha*). A field study carried out in two Japanese and two West German communities demonstrated the relevance of such in-group/out-group categories in the social conscience of the members of city councils in Japan (Kevenhörster and Uppendahl, 1987).

Jichikai *in the Political Network*

The amazing fact is that this social unit, based on traditional Confucian values, has survived until today in large parts of highly industrialized Japan. A number of studies have shown its important functions for the residential (*jumin-unde*) and environmental movements of the 1970s. Margaret McKean has shown that environmental protection groups, especially in rural regions, usually have been successful once the support of local neighborhood associations has been secured. In this case, the *social acceptance* and *identification of the individual with the group* enable traditionally conservative people to oppose otherwise accepted authorities (McKean, 1976).

This is in contrast to the historical role of the *jichikai* or *chōnaikai*. In the Japanese authoritarian state of the 1930s and 1940s, they were used as an element of governmental control of the people, down to the very foundation of society. In a way, this was more successful than the single-party system in Italy or Germany during the same period because of the traditional legitimacy of group thinking and group organization. For that

reason, the *jichikai* were made illegal by the American occupation authorities, although some officers saw a source of possible
democratic revival in this grass-roots organization.

Traditional Institutionalized Volunteers: Appointed Community Welfare Commissioners (*Minsei-iin*)

The system of appointed voluntary community welfare commissioners has a history of more than seventy years. It is interesting to look back at its origins because this helps to explain
the high prestige that this category of officials enjoys up to the
present. In 1916, Emperor Taisho asked the governor of the
province of Okayama about the living conditions of the poor
in his prefecture. At that time of mounting inflation, the question of pauperization of the agrarian population had become
increasingly significant. Imperial concern led to intensive investigations by the governor of Okayama on his return home.
After having installed a committee that studied the systems of
charity in various countries (for example England, the United
States, China, and Germany), a model was developed based
on the German *Elberfelder System,* an institution similar to the
"friendly visitors" in Anglo-American countries. This model,
developed in the second half of the nineteenth century in the
textile city of Elberfeld (now Wuppertal) in Germany, was the
first *systematic* attempt to control poverty on the communal level.
The system divided urban areas into welfare wards, each under
the supervision of appointed honorary welfare commissioners
(*ehrenamtliche Bezirkswohlfabrtspfleger*). The mostly local notables
decided on the provision of money in cases of acute need such
as sickness of the breadwinner or unemployment. Their main
emphasis, however, was on counseling and helping people find
their way back to a "decent life." This institution was introduced
into the province of Okayama. A smilar system was started in
the Osaka prefecture in 1918. Gradually, this system found acceptance in the other parts of Japan as well, and by 1929 it
existed nationwide (Thränhardt, 1987).

National Establishment of Minsei-iin

During the Great Depression of the early 1930s, the problems of social deprivation and hunger, especially in agrarian regions, became more and more serious. This led the community welfare commissioners, who up to that time had acted independently and were largely integrated into the local structures, to initiate a common *demarche* for adequate poor relief regulation at the central level. After preparing several petitions and legal intiatives, which were unsuccessful, a group of 1,116 community welfare commissioners ventured to do the almost unthinkable: to petition the emperor (*jikiso*) directly. It was this audacious act that finally led to success: the promulgation of a new Poor Relief and Protection Law (1932), in which for the first time the central government accepted financial responsibility by assuming 50 percent of the costs of operation (incidentally, this was to be financed by national horse race revenue). The other 50 percent was to be paid by prefectures, municipalities, and towns.

This victory of the community welfare commissioners provided the basis for their sense of importance and self-esteem, which is expressed in the following passage taken from the preface of their self-description: "In the following is presented the progress and present work of the system of community volunteers — a system based on Eastern philosophy, born and cultivated through Japanese culture, and found nowhere else in the world but in Japan" (Japanese National Committee of Social Welfare, 1979). Certain nationalistic overtones cannot be overlooked in this statement.

Structure and Functions of Minsei-iin Today

With the introduction of professional welfare workers after World War II, the *minsei-iin* had to define their duties anew, in concert with the new concept of professionalism. The *minsei-iin* see themselves as mediators between clients and welfare offices. Their firm embeddedness in the locality for which they are responsible leads to detailed knowledge about their district. These districts are comparatively small, as Table 15.1 shows.

Table 15.1.

Area Division	Distribution Density
Tokyo and specified cities	1 minsei-iin for every 270 families
Cities with populations over 100,000	1 minsei-iin for every 200 families
Cities with populations under 100,000	1 minsei-iin for every 170 families
Towns and villages	1 minsei-iin for every 120 families

Source: Japanese National Committee of Social Welfare, 1979.

At present approximately 176,000 *minsei-iin* are distributed throughout Japan in a firmly institutionalized structure. Besides making home visits and giving advice on social welfare programs in counseling centers (*shimpaigoto sedansho*), the *minsei-iin* devote a great part of their activity to the preparation of statistical data, concerning, for instance, the situation of elderly people or health problems.

Almost 60 percent of *minsei-iin* are men, but the number of women is increasing steadily. The average age is fifty-eight years, with people engaged in agriculture as the largest vocational group (27.6 percent versus 17.9 percent self-employed and 9.7 percent company employees). Only 2.4 percent have registered themselves as religiously affiliated (Japanese National Council of Minsei-iin, 1986).

According to law, the system is autonomous but under the supervision of the Ministry of Health and Welfare (Koseisho). The appointment of *minsei-iin* by the governors of the provinces takes place every three years, and reappointment is frequent. The candidates are proposed by welfare committees on the local level. In fact these committees often turn to the leaders of neighborhood associations for nominations (Thränhardt, 1987).

Minsei-iin *and the Concept of Voluntarism*

The above-cited self-definition of *minsei-iin* as a system based on Eastern philosophy clearly shows that Confucian thinking is taken as the basis of the work of the appointed community commissioners. In many cases the same persons act as leaders of neighborhood associations and as *minsei-iin*. This underlines the similarity of these two groups of volunteers. The occupational structure of *minsei-iin*, with the predominance of people engaged in agriculture, and the comparatively high average age of *minsei-iin* are further proofs of their basically traditional inclinations.

Nevertheless, the gradual changes in the mentality of the whole of Japanese society have not remained without influence on *minsei-iin*. During recent years, a tendency for younger volunteers, a steadily mounting percentage of women, and a changed concept of voluntarism have been observed.[4]

Newly Institutionalized Volunteers: *Borantia-katsudō* (The Volunteer Movement)

In the 1960s there developed a new type of volunteer, whose work is more similar to Western counterparts, as the name *borantia* (volunteer) shows. In contrast to the *minsei-iin*, who feel responsible for *all* social problems in their quarter, the *borantia* take over special tasks according to the extent of their free time. Coordination of this voluntary work — mainly help in old people's homes, institutions for those with handicaps, and orphanages or youth welfare centers — is organized by bureaus, which were originally called goodwill banks (*zeni ginkō*) and later on, volunteer centers or volunteer activity centers.

This change of name signals an important element of the Japanese *borantia katsudō*'s character: the deliberate attempt by the government to strengthen the "spirit of voluntarism." Since 1973, the Ministry of Health and Welfare has provided "promotional funds for volunteer activity" (*shakai hoshi katsudō ikusei jigyo josei-hi*), the main objectives of which are "to develop and organize public goodwill for welfare activities" and "to develop and support volunteer groups" (Japanese National Committee of the International Council on Social Welfare, 1976). The government continued to enlarge and build up the structure of volunteer centers on the prefectural as well as the central level. The total number of volunteers, according to official statistics in 1986, was 2,875,812, the majority of whom were affiliated with volunteer groups such as the Senior Citizens' Club, Red Cross volunteers, and the Mothers' Club (*haha-oya kurabu*).

A breakdown of these volunteers by age and sex categories shows a picture different from that of *minsei-iin*. The majority of borantia are middle-aged women (Kōseisho, 1988). Their pattern of regional distribution is also markedly different: their centers lie in the metropolitan areas.

Noninstitutionalized Volunteers: *Jūmin-undō* (The Residential Movement) and Other Alternative Groups

In contrast to the *borantia-katsudō*, which is organized and subsidized by state funds, a number of autonomous alternative groups that were critical of government policy, misuse of power, or the negative aspects of capitalism developed. These groups, called *jūmin-undō* (citizen movement) or *shimin-undō* for the more experienced groups (*shimin* means "the inhabitants of cities") existed only for a limited period and did not keep records of their membership. Starting in the 1960s, they peaked in the 1970s. According to a report of the big daily newspaper *Asahi shimbun,* there were several thousand such groups in 1973. In the 1980s the upward trend did not continue, and the number of groups decreased.

The range of activities of these groups naturally goes beyond social work as narrowly defined, with the main emphasis being on consumer and environmental problems. But groups such as the "*Sanya sōgidan*" (Sanya-strikers), who strive for better conditions in the Sanya district, a slum in the Northern part of Tokyo where about 7,000 to 8,000 day laborers—mostly *buraku* (of Korean origin)—fight against social discrimination of a minority, a situation only very inadequately taken care of by established social welfare programs.

The case of this *Sanya sōgidan,* which has become more radicalized recently, clearly shows the difficult situation that Japanese alternative groups face. Yoshikazu Ikeda, in his interesting article "Warum es Alternative in Japan schwerer haben" ("Why Alternative Groups Have More Problems in Japan"), stresses the fact that alternative thinking in Japan violates the deeply seated wish of most Japanese to identify with the whole (Ikeda, 1988) and therefore exposes the volunteers in the alternative movement to an enormous degree of stress.

In this connection, it is interesting that women play a decisive role in the alternative movement. This seems to be due to the fact that they are not as tightly bound by the principles of social hierarchy and political-economic dependence as Japanese men are.

Notes

1. Neighborhood associations exist under different names, the most popular of which are *chōnaikai* (urban ward associations), founded before World War II, and *jichikai* (self-governing associations) for groups organized after the war. Some of the older organizations changed their names to *jichikai* after the war because of the more democratic connotations of this expression. I shall use this term throughout the chapter even if the actual name of the neighborhood association I refer to is different.

2. A detailed discussion of historical, legal, and social aspects of the neighborhood associations is given in Steiner, 1980, Chap. 10.

3. Burakumin (ghetto people) are the largest Japanese minority group, which is comprised of between two and three million people. They live in separate quarters in all parts of Japan except Hokkaido. Although they are not distinct from the Japanese racially or culturally, they are subject to severe discrimination, especially in terms of employment. Their political organization in the *Buraku Kaiho Domei* (Buraku Liberation League) resulted in a special antidiscrimination policy in effect since 1969. This has led to considerable improvements in their housing and educational situations, but discrimination in private companies continues (Cornell, 1967; Kaneko, 1981).

4. According to the estimate of Professor Y. Kojima (Japan Women's University, Tokyo), who is in charge of training *minsei-iin* in the Tokyo area, about half of today's *minsei-iin* think within more individualized terms of voluntarism (personal interview in April 1988).

References

Bestor, T. C. "Mimyamoto-chō: The Social Organization of a Tokyo Neighborhood." Unpublished doctoral dissertation, Stanford University, 1983.

Bestor, T. C. "Tradition and Japanese Social Organization: Institutional Development in a Tokyo Neighborhood." *Ethnology*, 1985, *24* (2).

Chiiki-Shakai-kenkyūsho (ed.). *Chōnaikai.* Vol. 79: Series Komyuniti. Tokyo: Dainippon-insatsu-kabushiki-kaisha, 1987.

Cornell, J. B. "Individual Mobility and Group Membership: The Case of the Burakumin." In R. P. Dore (ed.), *Aspects of Social Change in Modern Japan.* Princeton, N.J.: Princeton University Press, 1967.

Curtis, G. L. *Election Campaigning Japanese Style.* Tokyo: Kodansha, 1983.

Dore, R. P. *City Life in Japan.* Berkeley: University of California Press, 1958.

Ikeda, Y. "Warum es Alternative in Japan schwerer haben" [Why Alternative Groups Have More Problems in Japan]. In G. Hackner (ed.), *Die anderen Japaner — Vom Protest zur Alternative* [The Other Japanese: From Protest to Alternative]. Munich: Judicium Verlag, 1988.

Japanese National Committee of the International Council on Social Welfare. *Fact Sheet.* No. 6. Tokyo: Japanese National Committee of the International Council on Social Welfare, July 1976.

Japanese National Committee of Social Welfare/Japanese National Community and Child Welfare Volunteers (eds.). *Minsei-iin: The System of Community Volunteers in Japan.* Tokyo: Zenkoku-minsei-iin jido-iin kyogikai, 1979.

Japanese National Council of Minsei-iin Community/Child Welfare Volunteers. *Minsei-iin.* Tokyo: Japanese National Council of Social Welfare, 1986.

Kaneko, M. "Demokratieverständnis und Demokratieentwicklung in Japan am Beispiel der Minderheitenpolitik: Die Dōwa-Politik und die Buraku-Befreiungsbewegung" [Comprehension and Development of Democracy in Japan in the Example of the Politics of Minorities: The Dōwa Politics and the

Buraku Freedom Movement]. In G. Foljanty-Jost, S.-J. Park, and W. Seifert (eds.), *Japans Sozial-und Wirtschaftentwicklung im internationalen Kontext* [Japan's Social and Economic Development in the International Context]. Frankfurt: Campus Verlag, 1981.

Kevenhörster, P., and Uppendahl, H. *Gemeindedemokratie in Gefahr? — Zentralisierung und Dezentralisierung als Herausforderung lokaler Demokratie in Japan und der Bundesrepublik Deutschland* [Community Democracy in Danger? Centralization and Decentralization as a Result of Local Democracy in Japan and in the German Federal Republic]. Baden-Baden: Nomos-Verlag, 1987.

Kōseisho. *Kōsei hakusho 1987*. Tokyo: Kabushiki-kaisha kōseidō, 1988.

McKean, M. A. "Citizens' Movements in Urban and Rural Japan." In J. White and F. Munger (eds.), *Social Change and Community Politics in Urban Japan*. Chapel Hill: University of North Carolina, 1976.

McKean, M. A. *Environmental Protest and Citizen and Politics in Japan*. Berkeley: University of California Press, 1981.

National Volunteer Activity Promotion Center. *The Japanese Volunteer 1986*. Tokyo: National Volunteer Activity Promotion Center, 1986.

Shinseikatsu, undō kyōkai. *Jichikai, chōnaikai nado no genjō to tembō*. Tokyo: Yugengaisha, 1982.

Steiner, K. *Local Government in Japan*. Stanford, Calif.: Stanford University Press, 1980.

Thränhardt, A. "Organisierte Freiwilligkeit — Ehrenamtlich-keit als tragende Struktur des japanischen Sozialwesens." In R. Bauer and A. M. Thränhardt (eds.), *Verbandliche Wohlfahrtspflege im internationalen Vergleich*. Opladen: Westdeutscher Verlag, 1987.

Thränhardt, A. "Traditional Neighborhood Associations in Industrial Society: The Case of Japan." In H. K. Anheier and W. Seibel (eds), *The Third Sector: Comparative Studies of Nonprofit Organizations*. Berlin: De Gruyter, 1990.

The Role of
Nonprofit Organizations Within
the Ultra-Orthodox Community
in Israel

The ultra-Orthodox Jewish community in Israel includes approximately 25 percent of all Israelis. It is a highly visible, politically active, tight-knit community that has developed astounding self-help, nonprofit networks and fund-raising mechanisms to preserve its cultural separateness and identity within the larger secular Israeli society.

This chapter describes some of the background and workings of the haredi nonprofit system, its functional role, and its interaction with Israeli government as well as Jewish Diaspora institutions. It is a case in point as to how minority groups and subcultures guarantee continuity through nonprofit associations and has relevance for understanding subcultures in other communities.

Religious Groups in Israel

It is impossible to discuss the "haredi" (that is, the "fearful") Jews without some background about the Israeli religious spectrum. Most Israeli Jews can be roughly classified in terms of their religious beliefs and practices as being secular, traditional, or Orthodox. In Israel, these groups are referred to in Hebrew as *chiloni, masorti,* and *dati.* The dati group believes in the existence of God and "perceives the observance of Jewish law (*halacha*) as fulfilling God's commands" (Liebeman and Don-Yehiya, 1984). Although approximately 80 percent of the secularists also observe some selective Jewish rites, they do so as part of their own identity and personal understanding about being Jewish or out of respect for family tradition and custom.

The masorti Jews belong to the liberal wing of the religious population, since they acknowledge the existence of God, but they selectively practice parts of the halacha. Traditional and Orthodox Jews comprise nearly 30 percent of the population, and about 25 percent are Orthodox. (For comparative data on American Jews, see Huberman, 1989).

Perhaps the major variable that distinguishes between the masorti and dati groups is the degree of freedom that they take (or do not take) in interpreting and changing the halacha. For the Orthodox and ultra-Orthodox, the halacha cannot ever be changed because it was handed down to the Jews from God to Moses, then to the prophets, to the elders, and then codified in the Mishna, the Talmud, and other writings, where it essentially became finalized and frozen in perpetuity. The rabbis of the liberal religious groups (that is, those of the American Reform and the Conservative movements, also known in Israel as the Progressive and Traditional movements, respectively) have taken the liberty of modernizing the halacha "to keep it in touch with modern lives" (Liebeman and Don-Yehiya, 1984). For example, riding on the Sabbath, operating electrical equipment, or using fire on that day are normative and acceptable to those in the liberal movements, but they are totally inconceivable breaches of halacha to the Orthodox.

In principle, for dati Jews, observance of halacha is a way of life, a personal imperative and the single guide to all behavior and values. Nevertheless, within the dati (Orthodox) sector are a variety of groups, including the modern Orthodox, the haredi, and the ultra-Orthodox. These groupings will be somewhat further refined, but a full discussion can be found in other publications (see Liebeman and Don-Yehiya, 1984).

Origins of the Haredi Community in Israel

Contemporary ultra-Orthodox Jews have their roots in the great Diaspora of Jews who were taken captive by the Romans, exiled, and dispersed throughout Europe and who later migrated to North and South America and to Australia, South Africa, and other lands. More precisely, the European Jewish settlements and ghettos in Poland, Lithuania, Hungary, and Russia gave rise to great rabbinical dynasties after the Talmudic era that developed the major norms for haredi religious behavior and authority. Jews who immigrated to Palestine from Europe between the thirteenth and early nineteenth centuries brought with them and re-created entire communities in the Holy Land, communities based on the Diaspora religious norms of their time (Bahat and others, 1978). When the secular young Zionists arrived in Palestine from Europe in the late 1800s to establish their kibbutzim, there already existed a relatively large veteran religious population that was quickly labeled "the Old Yishuv" (that is, community). The new "pioneers" called themselves "the New Yishuv" and wrote off the pious haredim as an anachronistic, fatalistic Diaspora phenomenon.

The old Yishuv, which for over 100 years was settled primarily in Bnei Brak, Tiberias, Safed, and particularly Jerusalem, became the nucleus for the haredi community in Israel today. Since then, new Orthodox immigrants from Europe and America and very high birth rates (contraception is religiously unacceptable to them) have led to a dramatic rise in this population. One is immediately reminded of the European shtetl origins of many haredi Jews when strolling through the haredi Meah Shearim neighborhood of Jerusalem today and seeing most of the people garbed in the same clothing of the shtetl from the early 1880s. Today there are clearly defined geographical concentrations of haredi residents, mostly continuous neighborhoods such as Mattersdorf, Unsdorf, Bar Ilan, Sanhedria, Ma'alot Dafna, Shmuel Hanavi, Geula, and Meah Shearim in Jerusalem. These stretch from the western entrance to the city in a belt along the entire northern half of the city, ending at the Jaffa Gate entrance to the Old City and a short walk from the Western Wall of the Second Temple mount.

The compactness of this "belt," with overcrowding as families grow, also encourages and allows for intensive socialization and personalization of relationships and extensive self-help activity. This intense communal life is usually enhanced by synagogue worship (daily morning, afternoon, and evening prayers and Sabbath and holiday services) and by almost universal voluntary identification and affiliation with some particular rabbinical figure or dynasty. For example, hundreds of thousands of haredi Jews from all walks of life and socioeconomic statuses accept the religious authority of the Gerrer Rebbe (rabbi), the Satmar Rebbe, the Bobover Rebbe, or the Lubavitcher Rebbe, to name only a few.

These affiliations and loyalty to the Rebbe often dictate residence, synagogue affiliation, marriage matches, educational facilities, income opportunities, outlook on life, and style of dress. Some of the rabbinic leaders do not even live in Israel, but in Brooklyn, New York, or in New Jersey, yet their "kingdom" has no geographical boundaries (Kahan, 1988). Most of them are the offspring of fabled and famous rabbis from European towns, who lived over a century ago. The power of the rabbi is inconceivable, and disciples flock to his "table" on the Sabbath and weekdays and seek advice, comfort, and blessings about basic decisions and problems concerning their lives and their families. The rabbi is revered and respected, and the Lubavitcher followers frequently refer to their rebbe, Rabbi Menachem Mendel Schneersohn, as the contemporary equal of the biblical Moses.

The above description is primarily relevant for the hasidic wing of haredi Judaism. The more conservative mitnaged (that is, anti-hassidic) wing, originally created by mostly Lithuanian and German rabbis, abhor "the idol worship" of the hasidic groups and their overemotional, "less erudite" approach to Judaism.

Nevertheless, the mitnaged leaders, such as Rabbi Eliezer Menachem Shach, have also fostered many disciples and ardent adherents, but they do not foster the same dependency and expectations as the hasidic rabbis. On various occasions rivalry breaks out among the faithful in the hasidic and mitnaged camps, leading even to violence.

The central concerns of the haredi community are Torah learning, all sectors of worship, and Jewish family life. They believe that too much contact and involvement with the "outside" secular and Zionist community could lead to cultural "contamination" and is a threat to their values and religious way of life. This isolation not only perpetuates the faith but fosters many low-income, large families struggling to obtain basic health, education, and welfare services. University education and any forms of mixed (male/female) education or social contacts are totally unacceptable to the hard-core haredi.

Self-Help and Communal Services

In view of obvious socioeconomic needs in the haredi comunity, a sophisticated, intensive, social service network of private nonprofit organizations (NPOs) has been created by and for the haredi population. All of these organizations are anchored in Torah values, historic models from Jewish tradition, and necessity. The infrastructure is also functionally important since it provides employment, income, status, and power to haredi individuals, including haredi women teachers and other service providers.

Self-help activity was always an integral part of the Diaspora Jewish community everywhere, including Palestine. The haredi community, too, observed biblical injunctions to help the needy, clothe the poor, protect the orphan and widow, and do good deeds. The institution of *gemilut-chasadim* (deeds of loving kindness) found expression in interest-free loan funds, free meals, marital matchmaking, and tending to the sick, the dying, and the dead (Jaffe and others, 1989). In every Jewish community these institutions were developed to preserve Jewish life, education, and separate identity (Jaffe, 1982). They became nonprofit social services of the modern Jewish community around the world.

   In Israel, separate nonprofit services were created especially for the haredi population, usually located in close proximity to the recipients. The network is offered by a series of provider agencies, and each relates to segments of the user's life needs, sometimes in competition with each other. For example, there are numerous indigenous neighborhood-based nonprofit services. Jaffe and colleagues (1989) found that 55 percent of all interest-free loan funds in Jerusalem were established by haredi individuals or institutions and another 21 percent by religious Zionist individuals. In his research, Jaffe located 485 free-loan funds in Jerusalem, and he estimated that this represented only about one-third of the total. Most of the free-loan funds (71 percent) were located in private homes, and only 8 percent had an office. Seventy-two percent served only dati applicants. Sixty percent of the funds provided many loans, and 40 percent lent a variety of goods, including medicines, furniture, silverware, wedding dresses, pacifiers and baby equipment, medical and orthopedic equipment, pots and pans, and a long, imaginative list of other items (Jaffe and others, 1989). Other neighborhood-based services include day care, baby-sitting, personal counseling, shopping advice, home bazaars and street sales, and personal support in times of crisis.

   Another source of help results from one's religious affiliation. The various hasidic and mitnaged groups work extremely hard to secure resources for providing their followers with education, health, and welfare services. Each affinity group is helped with day care, early Torah education, Yeshiva education, maintenance stipends, matchmaking, and many other services. The rabbi of the community, whether in Israel or abroad, has a personal interest in seeing to the well-being of his disciples and their families.

   Many independent general haredi nonprofit associations also operate for the haredi sector. These involve private haredi individuals or organizations that have taken upon themselves the task of raising funds to provide low-cost, sector-wide goods and services, such as dental and medical care, family counseling, food coops, remedial education, dowries, mortage loans, school supplies, used clothing, books, scholarships, eyeglasses, "orphan" homes, programs for born-again Jews, overseas students, and newspapers.

At another level, and best-funded of all, are nonprofit services provided by the haredi (and other) religious parties. These political organizations provide many of the educational services (including boarding schools, educational services, kindergarten vocational schools, day-care centers, and so on) that the state provides to the secular population from the taxes, as well as services specific to the haredi community, such as yeshivot and Torah-learning schools, youth centers, and academies. The scope of these latter services and the access to funds for their support are directly related to the haredi relationship with the state and Zionism and the politicization of religion in Israel.

Before we move on to these issues, it is important to note that the indigenous self-help network of the haredi community is generally a very caring, individualized, friendly, personal phenomenon, very different from the isolation and anomie of urban secular neighborhoods and cities. In social work terms, these personal relationships reflect outreach activities and family adoption, often focused on family life-cycle celebrations that emphasize sensory experiences and are geared to reinforcing haredi Jewish identity and values. They are proactive and reactive and highly personalized. They are not premediated as a rule but spontaneous interactions with religious kin. This personalization reflects the Jewish religious philosophy that life is a short-term gift to be used for the benefit of others (Talmud, Psalm 49; Harofeh, ms. 1298).

The Messiah, Zionism, and Self-Help

The negative attitude of the Old Yishuv Jews toward the secular settlers was anchored in two basic principles: the settlers' rejection of the religious rituals and beliefs of their fathers and, most important of all, the attempt to create a Jewish state *without waiting for the Messiah* to do this. In the eyes of the ultra-Orthodox, this latter blasphemy is inexcusable and sinful. For them, Zionism is against God. They are living in exile in Zion. One scholar defines the haredi as whoever views and experiences life in the Jewish state as exile (Ravitzky, 1989).

The modern Orthodox Jew, however, also stems from a group of European rabbis such as Zvi Hirsch Kalischer (1798–1898), who preached that human efforts are absolutely legitimate and necessary to gradually bring about the final Redemption and the messianic era. They interpreted Jewish law, the halacha, as commanding Jewish settlement and the creation of a Jewish state, and they saw Zionism, political emancipation, and the return to Zion as a divine signal and necessary step toward the Redemption (Jung, 1958; Katz, 1973; Vital, 1978). This rabbinical school led to the creation of the religious Zionist movement, and to the modern orthodox, nationalist Jewish community in Israel, which became full partners with the secularists in the establishment of the state. One of its major leaders was Rabbi Zvi Yehuda Kook, who founded a major Yeshiva and a network of related educational institutions. His disciples founded the contemporary Gush Emunim settler movement (Doron, 1988).

This basic conception of the relationship between the Messiah, the Redemption, and the state has direct implications for self-help activities, funding for these activities, and the ways in which funds are secured.

The Politicization of Religion

Even before the founding of the State of Israel, in 1948, the religious Zionists established a political party in Israel, the Hapoel Hamizrachi, to deal with the secular establishment. They felt that this was necessary to secure funds for the nonprofit educational, religious, and welfare services for their constituents. After the state was established, the National Religious party (the NRP) constantly played its role in return for providing the swing seats in the Knesset (parliament) to one of the two larger parties (that is, Labor or Likud), enabling it to form a coalition government (Caspi and others, 1984). As part of the bargain, NRP members were given cabinet portfolios (that is, ministerial responsibilities) as well as massive funding for the party's extensive nonprofit educational and welfare organizations. But the most important concessions of all, agreed upon by David Ben Gurion, Israel's first prime minister, was a separate national religious public school system (alongside the secular system), and kosher food in all government institutions, including the army.

Another religious haredi group to the right of the NRP decided to run in the elections as well and exercise its swing seats in the Knesset to extract funding for its extensive religious and welfare nonprofit service networks. However, unlike the NRP, the Agudat Yisrael party did not accept the idea that the state was "the beginning of the Redemption." Nevertheless, since the state was the work of Jews and should be guided lest it go too far astray and since coalition bargaining could reap huge patronage for the Aguda network, thus promoting more religion in the state, the Aguda rabbis and their political servants do participate in national elections and in the Knesset. In order to avoid the Zionist stigma, however, they have never accepted a seat in the cabinet or a ministerial portfolio. Their only interest is obtaining funds from general revenue for their vast yeshiva, day school, seminary, kindergarten, and welfare program network, which will strengthen and enlarge the haredi population (Kahan, 1988; Krivine, 1989). They did exactly the same thing in the Sejim, the pre-World War II Polish parliament.

Two other dati parties, Shas, which consists of Jews who immigrated from the Moslem countries (Sepharadim) and is a mirror image of the NRP, and Degel Hatora, which is closer to the Agudat Yisrael, also participate actively in coalition bargaining in order to win resources for their own educational and social service networks.

Figure 16.1 clearly shows the critical importance of the religious parties in helping either Labor or the Likud to form a coalition cabinet. (Note: None of the larger parties seek the non-Zionist Arab party or Communist party as a coalition partner.)

The only religious groups that have not joined the political-patronage system are the smaller ultra-Orthodox sects that totally reject the Jewish state as a sin against God and will have

Figure 16.1. Potential Coalition Partners.

Total number of Knesset seats is 120, and 51 percent are needed to rule.

nothing to do with it or its institutions. Thus the Neturei Karta community, numbering several hundreds of families, lives almost entirely on donations, self-help, and self-taxation (Birnbaum, 1970).

Functions and Funding Sources
of the Haredi NPO Network

The major function of haredi institutions is to perpetuate Torah learning and observance of the halachic way of life. This goal requires providing employment for its members and the skills to maintain basic income. This is often provided by means of stipends for learning Torah (as in the Kollel or higher-learning academies) since learning is categorized as work.

Beyond the mainstay patronage steered to the community as a result of coalition agreements, huge amounts of money are collected for the various NPOs by their rabbinical leaders from among obedient and faithful disciples of these dynasties in Israel and especially abroad. Many of these institutions are named after the founding rabbi or after the European town he lived in, such as the Ruzhiver Yeshiva, the Mir Yeshiva, the Karlin-Stolin institutions, the Belz institutions, the Hebron Yeshiva, the Beth Zvul institutions, and the Erlog institutions, to name only a few.

Many donations also come from secular Jews abroad who symphasize with the haredi way of life but have little knowledge about their non-Zionist or anti-Zionist ideology. However, because of the "Who is a Jew" controversy, this laissez-faire attitude is rapidly changing. Until 1987, the Jewish Agency for Israel, which receives 50 percent of all United Jewish Appeal (UJA) funds, also provided significant funding to haredi nonprofit organizations. In 1987, the American Reform and Conservative delegates to the agency succeeded in blocking any further grants to non-Zionist haredi institutions. The American Jewish Joint Distribution Committee has a special grant-making department and budget to support 120 yeshivot in Israel, serving 32,407 students, 22 percent of whom are married. Several Jewish community federations in America also provide financial support through their Central Fund for Traditional Institutions (Jewish Community Federation of Cleveland, 1985).

No one in Israel knows the *true* extent of donor patronage to haredi institutions, including the Ministry of Finance. Soliciting from abroad is often very sophisticated, including lobbying and logrolling among political candidates and their haredi constituents, looking for resources from foreign governments for their Israeli compatriots in return for votes. Less sophisticated and smaller-scale solicitation takes place, door-to-door, in hundreds of American communities by hundreds of private and official *shlichim* (emissaries) sent from Israel. These efforts are supplemented by numerous mass mailing solicitations sent abroad, mostly during key Jewish holidays, as well as by public appeals in synagogues and newspaper advertisements and at donor dinners and more recently, by foundation grants.

Above all, however, Israeli government patronage to the haredi political parties is the most important source of funds, and the transfer of ministry funds to party-affiliated institutions is the norm rather than the exception (Horovitz, 1989).

Future Trends and Questions

The haredi case study suggests that NPO activity flourishes most when a political symbiosis is achieved with national and local government. The politicization of religion in Israel has produced huge resources for haredi nonprofit work. In the future, haredi demands will probably include the establishment of a third haredi public school system, thus freeing private philanthropy and other patronage for even greater nonprofit activity in the areas of housing, vocational training, higher Yeshiva education, and health and social services.

All this may change, however, in the event of a change in the Israeli electoral system. If the threshold for obtaining one Knesset seat is raised from the present 1 percent of all votes, to 4 or 5 percent of the votes, this will mean less clout for the smaller parties and the disappearance of some. It may also mean that one of the larger parties may succeed in obtaining a majority of the votes and an end to coalition government (Petreanu, 1989).

Everything depends on how much patronage the secular parties are willing to pay in order to rule, without risking electoral change.

Pluralistic social democracies pride themselves on the right of minorities to preserve their culture and traditions. But what do we really know about the barriers minority groups face, whether self-made or otherwise, in relating to the services of the dominant culture? What do we know of their problems and efforts to provide indigenous, often competitive services and to recruit resources while maintaining communal independence and control? What about the quality of minority religious non-profit social services as compared to public, for-profit, and secular nonprofit services? Where does the state's responsibility begin and end regarding separatist religious and cultural minorities and their services? The answers to these questions may help us better understand the relationship between secular and religious groups and nonprofit activity as well as the complicated operational variations of pluralism.

References

Bahat, D., and others. *The Continuity of the Jewish Settlement in the Land of Israel.* Tel Aviv: Israel Ministry of Defense, 1978.

Birnbaum, E. *The Politics of Compromise: State and Religion in Israel.* Teaneck, N.J.: Fairleigh Dickinson University Press, 1970.

Caspi, D., and others. *The Roots of Begin's Success: The 1981 Israeli Elections.* New York: St. Martin's Press, 1984.

Doron, A. *The State of Israel and the Land of Israel.* Kfar Saba: Beit Berl College, 1988.

Harofeh, Rabbi Yechiel ben Yekutiel ben Benjamin. *Ma'alot Hamidot.* Hebrew manuscript, 1298.

Horovitz, D. "Shas' Interior Minister Accused of Blackmailing Local Government." *Jerusalem Post,* Nov. 26, 1989.

Huberman, S. "The Costs of Religious Disunity." *Journal of Jewish Communal Service,* 1989, *65* (3), 190–196.

Jaffe, E. D. *Child Welfare in Israel.* New York: Praeger Science, 1982.

Jaffe, E. D., and others. *Gemilut Hasadim: Free Loan Funds in Jerusalem.* Jerusalem: Hebrew University of Jerusalem, 1989.

Jewish Community Federation of Cleveland. *The Central Fund for Traditional Institutions.* Cleveland, Ohio: Jewish Community Federation of Cleveland, 1985.

Jung, L. *Guardians of Our Heritage.* New York: Block, 1958.

Kahan, M. *The World of Yeshivot: Torah Institutions in the Holy City of Jerusalem.* Herzelia: Landface Publishers, 1988.

Katz, J. *Out of the Ghetto.* Cambridge, Mass.: Harvard University Press, 1973.

Krivine, D. "The Politics of Extortion." *Jerusalem Post,* Nov. 12, 1989.

Liebeman, C. S., and Don-Yehiya, S. *Religion and Politics in Israel,* Bloomington: Indiana University Press, 1984.

Petreanu, D. "Real Electoral Reform Is Still a Long Way Off." *Jerusalem Post,* Dec. 15, 1989.

Ravitzky, A. "Exile in the Holy Land: The Dilemma of Haredi Jewry." In P. Medding (ed.), *Israel State and Society, 1948–1988,* pp. 89–125. New York: Oxford University Press, 1989.

Talmud. Shabbat, 127a, Mishna Peah 1:1.

Vital, D. *The Origins of Zionism.* Tel Aviv: Tel Aviv University Press, 1978.

Part Three

Eastern Europe
and the Soviet Union

A number of current and former communist nations are currently in a state of transition. Moving away from an all-encompassing etatist ethos of pervasive government control, officials in many of these countries have begun to tolerate and even encourage the development of citizen-based nonprofit organizations. Part Three examines the legacy of communism.

Gábor Hegyesi provides a provocative analysis of these developments in Chapter Seventeen, "The Revival of the Non-profit Sector in Hungary." Both the role of Stalinism in crushing the region's voluntary association activities after 1948 and their subsequent reemergence beginning in the late 1970s are explored. As Hegyesi explains, Eastern Europe's nonprofit organizations are more politically oriented than their American

305

and Western European counterparts. Despite their recent reappearance, these fragile institutions are currently plagued by a variety of problems, from a dearth of public and private funds to the lack of a clear legal status, information, applicable models, and training procedures.

Andrzej Kapisewski examines the independent sector in Poland, both past and present, in Chapter Eighteen. As he points out, nonprofit organizations played an important role in Poland's quest for independence and national revival. Poland's situation is perhaps unique because of the continuing importance of the Catholic church, the country's ongoing opposition to communist domination, and the incomplete nationalization of its business. Although suppressed in 1981, Poland's nonprofit activities continued to grow, resulting in the passage of legislation legitimizing foundations (1984) and associations (1988). Like Gábor Hegyesi, Kapisewski concludes his chapter with a discussion of current problems and needs.

Stephan E. Nikolov reviews the emerging nonprofit sector in Bulgaria in Chapter Nineteen. As he explains, although the Bulgarian government failed in its promise to provide uniform welfare services, Bulgarian citizens have little surplus cash or time with which to initiate private nonprofit services on their own. Moreover, until recently, charitable activities were outlawed or discouraged, condemned as the vestiges of a discredited bourgeois past. When quasi-nongovernmental organizations were developed, they often served as fronts for bureaucratic chicanery. Current needs for promoting voluntary sector activities include legislative and tax reforms to regulate and stimulate institutional development.

In "The Independent Sector in the USSR: Formation, Purposes, and Effects," Chapter Twenty, Nina Belyaeva essentially agrees with Stephan Nikolov, noting that the government's near monopoly on production has left little in the way of discretionary funds for nonprofit development. Nevertheless, some organizations have emerged to challenge state monopolies in the economic, political, and ideological arenas. In the Soviet Union, as elsewhere in Eastern Europe, better training, legislation, and information are needed if the sector is to grow.

Deborah A. Brody and Elizabeth T. Boris paint a more optimistic picture in "Philanthropy and Charity in the Soviet Union," Chapter Twenty-One. Contrary to the other authors in this section, they argue that the recent growth of Soviet philanthropy stems from long-standing traditions of voluntarism and mutual aid. Grant-making foundations have begun to appear, despite the lack of a legal framework, as the result of the contributions of numerous small donors and the country's new openness to foreign models. As in other countries, these efforts in the Soviet Union have been hampered by such things as a tenuous legal status and the lack of adequate training.

Chapter 17

The Revival of the
Nonprofit Sector in Hungary

It is very important to review the beginnings of the revival and
rise of the nonprofit sector in Hungary over the past decade as
a prelude to much greater changes that will occur in the future.
The subject is large and complex as my distinguished colleagues
from Bulgaria and Poland detail in Chapters Eighteen and
Nineteen.

In Hungary we have a saying: "No tasks are impossible
to fulfill, but we have to wait a bit for miracles to happen." This
statement is apt because we learned in 1989 in Eastern Europe
that miracles do happen and that they are worth waiting for.
If we understand the outlines of the history of Central and Eastern Europe since World War II, we can come to appreciate what

the emergence and the rise of the nonprofit sector may come to mean in the future. Stalinism was the fundamental force in society during this period, and it was the sometimes covert, sometimes open struggle against Stalinism that led to the transformation of society that is occurring in Hungary today.

What Kind of a System Was Everyday Stalinism?

As the reader will recall, Ronald Reagan described the Stalinist USSR as the "evil empire." I think a more accurate way to describe Stalinism is that it was an ultraclever system of state control over every area of life. It was a system of governance that imposed the superiority of those in control of the state over all aspects of life: economics, culture, politics, social policy, morals, all areas of belief, and private life. This objective of total control was served by every institution, including the Communist party (in a party-state system), centralized institutions for economic planning, state-managed cultural and educational organizations, and continuous police control and observation. One consequence of this system of control was that every organization not managed by the state was banned, harassed, and dismantled. No organization aimed at advancing welfare, economic development, political action, religious expression, or cultural creativity was allowed to exist unless the state controlled it. This point is clear: we had no independent sector under Stalinism, although we did have points of resistance, some passive and some active. You might call them a hundred "points of light."

The Stalinist era in Eastern Europe began in 1948 and tended to follow a similar pattern of development throughout most Eastern European countries. I happened to have been born in that same year, and when I think of Stalinism, I think of my own life span, from infancy to adulthood. The social environment in which I came of age greatly affected my life and its possibilities, but it also now gives me the chance to plan my own future. The complex weave of society breaks, from time to time, to provide us insights into history. Just as a dream offers a window to the unconscious, our own lives, if properly analyzed, can contribute to the understanding of social forces that shape history. Permit me, then, to list some of the political events of 1948 (with some help from the useful work of Flomer Hankiss, 1989, pp. 27–72):

- The multiparty system was eliminated.
- The Communist party was amalgamated, by force, with the Social Democratic party.
- The noncommunist president of the Hungarian Republic resigned.
- The role of parliament was limited.
- A constitution was prepared that provided the Communist party a position superior to laws and institutions. (This constitution was adopted by this limited parliament in 1949.)
- The judicial system was brought under the control of state and party administration.
- Party control was established over the executive branch by two major methods: (1) almost everyone nominated (or quasi-elected) to leading positions was a party member, and (2) candidates could be nominated for leadership positions only with party approval.
- Civil rights were suspended by fiat: practically no one was allowed to speak up, to assemble with others, or to choose a place of work.
- Central control of information media — radio, newspapers, and later television — followed their nationalization.
- The situation was further exploited to indict and try individuals like Cardinal Jozsef Mindszenty in order to frighten citizens and impress them with the power of the party.

This era is illuminated by my own personal experience. As a small boy in the early 1950s, I was stopped on the street by a young man who claimed that he was Puskas, the famous football player. He promised to present me with a ball if I told him whether my parents listened to the broadcasts of Radio Free Europe. Luckily, I did not know, or else we would have had yet another trial in Hungary.

In 1948 the following major economic steps were also taken:

- Nationalization transferred all industrial organizations that employed more than 100 persons to state ownership, thereby controlling 83 percent of manufacturing. (The following year firms employing more than 10 workers were similarly nationalized.)
- Beginning steps were taken to nationalize commerce, banks, and mines.
- The stock exchange was dismantled. (It would resume operation in 1988.)
- People were forced into economic cooperatives. (Even growing flowers in one's own garden to sell in markets would result in the plot's being destroyed by a wandering truck.)
- Private retail trade and artisan shops were restricted. The number of small private artisans was reduced to one-seventh of its original number in a single year and later almost disappeared.
- The centralization of economic decision making was affected. (A central planning office opened in 1949. This office served as the main dispenser of investment funds, distribution of the labor force, commodities, products, wages and benefits.)

In that same fateful year, 1948, a process was initiated to eliminate the autonomy of churches (a process that took three years to complete). As a first step, some 4,000 Catholic associations and clubs were closed. The publication of school textbooks became a state monopoly, and most church-operated schools were nationalized; only 8 of the original 300 were permitted to remain in existence. Moreover most religious orders were dismantled (four out of fifty-nine were allowed to remain), and state approval was required to nominate individuals to leading church positions. Most church publishers of religious books, newspapers, educational materials, and pamphlets were closed down (two out of forty-eight remained). All twenty-one printing presses ceased operation, and most newspapers and periodicals were banned (four out of sixty-four remained). Finally, nine of the twenty-one theological academies were allowed to remain in operation.

In addition, trade unions were nationalized (the first independent trade union was established in 1988 under the name Democratic Trade Union of Scientific Workers). Courts where citizens could bring claims against any state authority or institution were eliminated; and local governments were replaced by Soviet-type councils, who saw their role as executing the central will.

In 1948, approximately 13,000 to 14,000 clubs and associations existed in Hungary, excluding sports clubs. All but 100 of these were dismantled, including all organizations engaged in social and welfare work (such as the League of Children), charitable institutions, organizations providing voluntary service, funding organizations — in essence, nearly the entire sector.

Three manifold actions reveal Stalinism in its classical, most virulent form, and the process was nearly identical in the other countries of Central and Eastern Europe. To be sure, there was no drastic collectivization in Poland, nor were preexisting political parties dismantled in the German Democratic Republic, but in essence the process served the same goal, to replace the autonomy of citizens with state control in all areas of their social, economic, political, and spiritual life by means of similar methods. In each case the nonprofit sector was the victim because its essence is to utilize the initiative of individuals and communities in the context of a supportive state government.

The drastic changes wrought by Stalinism were introduced with the conviction that the suppression of the other sectors (market, nonprofit, household) would lead to the emergence of a problem-free pioneer state. Cautions about unbridled power were not heeded, and the result was bloodshed, pain, and the devastation of the human spirit. I believe it is not accidental that it was in Eastern Europe that the state ideal became so popular: the Asian cultural background of most of these societies and the leading role of the state in modernization in previous centuries created a fertile soil for centralization.

In any case, the picture I have drawn of 1948 illustrates the nature of the classical Stalinist system. Once developed in its oppressive form, its main elements evolved differently in various countries. In Hungary, Poland, and Czechoslovakia, for instance, a refined version of "post-Stalinism" came into existence: In Hungary, a kind of consumers' socialism emerged. In Poland, the Catholic Church survived, as did the private ownership of land. In Czechoslovakia, at least before 1968, a "humanized socialism" emerged before its suppression by Soviet troops.

In the other countries, too (except Romania and the Soviet Union), the harshest tools of oppression — internment, the use of court trials, and denigration — fell into some disuse. Instead, efforts were made to gain the support of the people by making them fully dependent on the state, atomizing them from reliance on each other, bombing them with references to traditional values, forcing them into corrupting situations, and condemning group identities — in short, making them accomplices to the manipulation of the state leadership.

After 1948, the cited political and economic changes were further complicated by international trends toward industrialization, urbanization, modern life-styles, and the gainful employment of women. As a consequence of such forces, some specific population groups, such as pensioners, parents with large families, and some in the gypsy and youth populations, have become alienated. Furthermore, a number of groups with multiple social disadvantages and problems have become sources of social tension.

These emerging social tensions were not directly addressed by the state, whose ideology was premised on a new society free of social problems, and this left little room for services targeted specifically to groups in need. Rather, a state built on nationalization, full employment, low prices, and guaranteed wages was supposed to provide an acceptable standard of living for all. The unavoidable problems of life, such as sickness, retirement, and disability, were compensated for by social security programs, which provided free medical services and low-rental housing. And the welfare state did achieve some of its goals to provide universal assistance.

Something was lost in this search to meet common needs, however. Individual and group requirements for specialized social, cultural, health, and religious services were ignored.

Especially in Hungary and Poland, this desire for differentiation began to emerge. Hungary in the 1970s saw the development of a strong second, or "shadow," economy, which helped it become "the merriest barracks." Poland developed a second political system by 1980, with the emergence of the Solidarity trade union. In these two countries the search continued for parallel social reform, while elsewhere, the sense that something was missing remained strong. Everywhere, the absence of a third sector was felt, the absence of a civil society in which individuals could feel autonomous and could also join in association with others. By the end of the 1980s, however, this sector was rapidly developing. How, then, in a period of just a few years, like grass after the rain, did the nonprofit sphere revivify itself after years of repression?

Glowing Embers Beneath the Ashes

Karoly Polanyi, the Hungarian-born American economic historian, notes that three systems integrate all societies (Polanyi, 1957): the market, redistribution, and reciprocity (or mutual exchange). The role of these systems varies from one society to another. Stalinism, for example, attempted to rely primarily on the redistribution of power and money by the state, leaving almost no room for the other two integrative systems. Despite these efforts, however, the market and mutual exchange systems persisted in the "marketing" of plans within the government, in a "second economy" and in many voluntary activities that survived under cover in Hungary.

We know that many nuns in banned monasteries continued to adhere to their vows, visited each other, and helped and nursed one another and other people in need around them. We know of village cultural centers that operated as settlements serving members of the community instead of directing centrally imposed cultural events upon the population. Furthermore, we also know that members of the Hungarian Freemasonry, banned in 1950, gathered together every month until they were again authorized in 1989.

My own research (Hegyesi, 1987) and the investigations

of others (Sik-Kelen, 1989) also reveal that house-building systems based on the simple exchange of labor persisted, primarily in the countryside, together with neighborly relations based on the exchange of services. One survey discovered that only 3 percent of the population of a town of 10,000 availed themselves regularly of the social services provided by the sociopolitical institutional system (they were mainly poor people, the ill, and the elderly). Almost 90 percent of the residents never used this system, except to visit physicians, and relied upon their personal networks for the resolution of their problems. One person took care of the sick child of a neighbor; the other pruned the vines of the caretaker. That was how individual voluntary organizations developed, out of the links of everyday reciprocity between neighbors.

Independent voluntary and nonprofit organizations re-emerged in Central and Eastern Europe during the late 1970s and throughout the 1980s. At first it was not clear, but by now it is readily apparent that the struggle for the third sector contributed significantly to the success of the political reform movement; these efforts worked hand in hand to break state monopolies. It is because of this partnership in struggle that the voluntary sector in Central and Eastern Europe differs from much of the third sector in the United States and Western Europe. It is much more politically oriented, and it is likely to remain so until the political situation stabilizes.

Mapping the Nonprofit Sector

New Initiatives of the Late 1970s and 1980s

Many social movements began from voluntary bases in the late 1970s and 1980s: Charta 77 in Czechoslovakia, Solidarity in Poland, and Szeta in Hungary (the poor relief fund). Szeta, for example, was formed in 1979 by a group of intellectuals who sought to help people in need with financial grants and the distribution of clothing. At this time, poverty was officially declared to be nonexistent in Hungary, and many Szeta members lost their jobs as their activities became a matter of concern to the ruling party. At the end of the 1980s, the founders of Szeta were among the most active leaders of the Free Democratic party, one of the nation's leading political parties.

Another forerunner in Hungary's nonprofit sector was the LARES Cooperative for Human Services. The Enterprise Act of 1981 provided an opportunity for socially minded people to play a role, and LARES was founded in 1982. (The author of this chapter is a founding member of LARES, and serves as its volunteer vice president.) LARES sought to help families resolve daily problems, such as taking care of children, providing supplies to the elderly, and dealing with family crises. Before the establishment of small cooperatives became authorized, the founders, with the help of debates in the press, sought to convince government officials of the value of a mixed system — governmental and voluntary — for social services. This effort proved successful and was a step in the direction of the progressive reform of Hungarian social policy in the 1980s.

The Bloom of Nongovernmental Activities After 1988

The second half of the 1980s prepared Hungary for the miracle that was soon to follow. Just as Gorbachev realized that the Soviet Union was approaching the edge of an abyss, he also recognized that the post-Stalinist regimes of Eastern and Central Europe would have to change. What is not yet final in the Soviet Union is already historical fact in several of these countries.

In the context of rapid change, new organizations began to mushroom. Here are just a few examples from the Hungarian experience, as charted by Gyori (1988) and myself (Hegyesi, 1989). Voluntary associations and interest groups include the Association for Environmental Protection, the Association for Healthy Life, the Association for Large Families, the Association of Foundations, and the Association of Social Workers. These organizations broke through the political paradigm that claimed that social groups could not stand up to protect common interests and that only the omnipotent state could make decisions for them. Presently, associations, federations, and even parties are in the process of rapid formation, a process of significant importance for future social policy as well.

Voluntary services and organizations related to churches include the Reformed Mission for the Rescue of Alcoholics, the Baptist Section for Neglected Youth (helping drug addicts), the Mental Health Service of Roman Catholic Charity, the "meals on wheels" service of the Jewish community, and the Maltese Charitable Service. The situation of church-related services has changed tremendously. Following the previous policy of oppression and liquidation, these services are now promoted, especially in such areas as drug and alcohol problems and care for the elderly.

Self-help and problem-oriented groups include clubs of parents of autistic children, clubs of alcoholics, and clubs of cancer patients. The number of self-help and problem-oriented groups is growing rapidly, and the emergence of the self-help movement is a clear sign of the breakup of the overcentralized system.

Among the partly nonprofit enterprises are LARES, which offers baby-sitting and home care service; Tolerancia, which offers guidance services; and Minerva, which offers mediation services. These groups face the dilemma that they were established with the goal of providing needed services for the entire population on a nonprofit basis, but they enjoy neither institutional backing nor subsidies from the state. They face difficult conditions because they are still within the framework of the Enterprise Act, while they seek to overcome the unsolved problems of many low-income Hungarians.

Hungary now has over 500 foundations, including the Poor Relief Foundation, the Soros Foundation, and the LARES foundation, but most of them are poor.

Problems of the Newly Emerging Voluntary Sector in Hungary

It is obvious that the general economic crisis that is sweeping through the region will affect this new voluntary or independent sector. In Hungary, the state budget is in deficit, though some governmental funding is provided in the form of grants, contracts, and assistance. (However, at this time, access to this support is determined by informal connection rather than objective regulations.)

In the Stalinist era the state sought to control everything; now the opposite danger arises. The state appears eager to withdraw from responsibilities and to rid itself of every type of financial burden. Of course, this dismantling of government responsibility is one of the reasons why the indebted states of Central and Eastern Europe are supporting the development of the nonprofit sector. However, the central budget is not the only one in imbalance: household budgets are ravaged by inflation; corporations are in economic disarray; and funds for existing nonprofit organizations are slender. Most organizations do not receive sufficient subsidies to cover the cost of their operations.

The Absence of Adequate Regulations for the Nonprofit Sector. Hungary has yet to develop an administrative framework to determine the legal status of the nonprofit sector and its appropriate fiscal role. Only those associations and foundations that charge no fees for their services qualify for nonprofit status in Hungary. Associations that charge fees are considered to be "profit oriented," though often against their will. Moreover, public administrators seem to be more suspicious of nonprofit organizations than they are of profit-oriented enterprises. Nonprofits are often suspected of wishing to grow rich by avoiding taxation. Perhaps a residue of suspicion of the truly independent voluntary organization remains: the new nonprofits tend to be closely allied with the forces of moral and political change in society. Were they to receive tax-free standing, traditionalists within the state perceive a double loss, one in financial terms and the other in moral defeat.

Lack of Knowledge. It is evident that in Hungary we find a shortage of professionals familiar with the theory and practice of the nonprofit sector — whether as volunteers, administrators, staffers, or researchers. It seems apparent that development could be enhanced if we were not compelled to start everything almost from the beginning but could rather move to adapt knowledge and experience accumulated elsewhere in the world to the new conditions in Hungary.

Lack of Research. Directly contributing to the lack of knowledge about the third sector is the absence of research, which means that even those of us who work in and study this sector do not know enough about each other or the stage of development our work has achieved. Granted, studies have been initiated to survey the role of the nonprofit sector as employer and important steps have been taken to look comparatively at the development of the sector in international perspective.

Looking into the Future

Addressing the Economic Problems of the Sector. It seems appropriate to suggest the value provided by the establishment of specialized funds oriented to Eastern and Central Europe. Such a line was opened by the George Soros Fund, which has already attracted several major followers. Another example from Hungary is the Rubik Cube Fund, which provides a line of funds with mixed ownership. Foundations from the United States and Western Europe should establish centers in Eastern and Central Europe to get acquainted with the situation here. This would help them to determine what support would make the most difference. Such efforts by foundations in other nations to establish centers would be a very important step because at the present time there is no significant private capital or surplus that can support the nonprofit sector in Hungary or other Eastern and Central European nations.

Overcoming Problems Linked to the Lack of Knowledge and Research. Important links have been created to provide knowledge to nonprofit leaders in Hungary. Worthy of particular note are scholarships for the study of nonprofit organizations at Johns Hopkins University, Yale University, and the City University of New York. Among the other universities and institutions that are also taking a genuine interest in our area are Case Western

Reserve University, Rutgers University at Camden, the University of Pennsylvania, the United Way of America, the Salzburg Seminar, and INDEPENDENT SECTOR. Indeed, an effort at international collaboration is underway at Interphil and the Charities Aid Foundation (Great Britain), the European Center for Social Welfare, a consortium of Israeli organizations, and others. Study tours and conferences for practicing leaders of our emerging sector are important and useful.

However, we also need the benefit of training institutes in nonprofit organization leadership and management, access to a network of consulting services among the countries of Central and Eastern Europe, and the direct wisdom and experience of those who have studied the nonprofit sector in other nations.

Institutes of these sorts cannot be developed at this time from our own exhausted resources and limited bases of knowledge, but they could eventually come to be sustained by local organizations. Such institutes could also serve as clearinghouses for specialized literature that we could begin to include in our texts and training materials as the subject of nonprofit organization study and management begins to enter our curricula. A related need for the dissemination of knowledge could be met by the establishment of an international information network and the publication of periodicals and other materials in each country to propagate useful ideas and information.

The first steps are also being taken to develop national and international research that will guide and benefit the redevelopment of the third sector in Central and Eastern Europe. We need to continue this basic research, for there is much to learn and the situation is in rapid flux. However, it would also be reasonable to conduct international applied research on organization management so that experiences could be shared quickly. Furthermore, joint efforts could create even better nonprofit institutions.

The kinds of action research projects that have been described will not only be vital in sustaining our miracle, but they will also help us create new miracles as well.

References

Gyori, P. *Community Social Initiatives in Arat a magyar.* Budapest: Magar Tudomanyos Akademia, 1988, pp. 267–283.

Hankiss, F. *East-European Alternatives.* Budapest: Közgazuasagi ēs Jagi Känyukiads, 1989.

Hegyesi, G. "Social Policy of Veuzto." In *Szocialpolitikai Ertesito.* Budapest: Magyear Tudumanyos Akademia Szociologiai Kutato Intezet, 1987.

Hegyesi, G. "The Crisis of Statist (Stalinist) Social Policy: The Appearance of Nonprofit and Profit-Oriented Nongovernmental Social Services in the Eighties in Hungary." Paper presented at an international conference on nongovernmental organization and public policy, Jerusalem, May 22–24, 1989.

Polanyi, K. *The Great Transformation.* Boston: Beacon Press, 1957.

Sik-Kelen, E. A. *Kalaka Forever: The Sociology of Philanthropy.* Budapest: GUNDOLAT, 1989.

The Independent Sector
in Poland: Past and Present

Eastern Europe is in a stage of rapid transition, from a highly centralized Stalinist-type of totalitarian communism to a democracy. In Poland the changes started over a decade ago; in other countries, only in the last few years. All these countries still differ in the amount of democracy they have already achieved; in every one of them, however, the erosion of the Communist party's political and ideological monopoly seems to be irreversible.

One of the key elements of democracy is freedom of association. Along with this right, one of the most visible manifestations of the recent changes has been the explosive reemergence of independent, voluntary, nonprofit organizations: foundations, associations, clubs, professional societies, trade unions, and political parties. They have mushroomed because (1) the ever-present crisis of the inefficient and demoralized state generated a genuine interest in the reconstruction of long-oppressed civil society, (2) more and more people realized that this kind of activity was substantially enriching the democratic pluralistic systems being reintroduced, and (3) in the extremely difficult economic situation in most of the eastern European countries the civil society is forced to fill the growing gap being created by the withdrawal of the state's financial and organizational support in areas such as social services, education, and culture. Furthermore, one of the objectives of the democratization process going on in eastern European countries is more sovereignity, in both domestic and foreign affairs. This creates a revitalization of national identities. In this part of the world, national identities were never built on state structures but in opposition to them. For the people living there, "states" often meant only the persecution of the occupying powers. Contrary to the situation existing in the West, where modern nations were usually built in and through the state and its institutions, in eastern Europe they were formed to large extent through social groupings: family, religion, the intelligentsia, exiles, and so on. From this perspective, the reconstruction of the civil society with autonomous, nongovernmental associations is essential to national revival and an important element in the fight for full independence. "Solidarity" in Poland, "Popular fronts" in the Baltic republics, and the "Civic Forum" in Czechoslovakia all represent umbrella social movements serving this purpose.

Constraints to Voluntary Activity in a Communist Country

The independent sector and its role, taken for granted in Western societies, is something quite new in eastern Europe. This does not mean that voluntary, nonprofit organizations did not exist and operate under the communist regimes. They did, but they operated only within the strictly defined social space and under regulations that severely limited their potential. In every communist country major constraints to voluntary activity were the so-called "etatist" social policy of communist governments and the impact of the *nomenklatura* system of leadership in voluntary organizations.

The etatist social policy originated in the beginning of the Stalinist period. It means that the communist state, "the best possible formation of society," determines the norms of social services centrally, tries to fulfill all the needs for such services on the so-called "higher level" (cheap housing, cheap children's wear, full employment, and the like), and it alone establishes and operates the organizations to fulfill these needs.

Because of such an ideology, all voluntary organizations independent of the government were closed or taken over by state authorities. At the same time, some major statewide organizations were established by the authorities. Often called "associations of the higher public utility," they were, for example, the Red Cross, the youth organizations, or the committees to fight alcoholism. Such organizations, however, based primarily on the voluntary activity of their members, could carry out only official state policies, were 90 to 100 percent dependent on the state budget, and were not independent; their top executive officers had to be nominated or at least approved by the Communist party.

Along with the etatist social policy, one could not create additional institutions or organize voluntary activity in the areas where "associations of higher public utility" already existed. The idea of alternative organizations was perceived by the authorities to be a potential threat to the existing order. Voluntary organizations could not be established to help the poor, the homeless, or drug addicts because in communist countries there were supposedly no such people.

In these countries, however, authentic voluntary activity always existed. Even in the worst Stalinist times, local community groups organized themselves to build roads or water supply systems in the villages, to set up parks for children, or to organize cultural events in city housing developments, and so on. The voluntary organizations were rarely completely independent, however. Every full-time officer or member of the leadership body had to be a part of the nomenklatura system. *Nomenklatura* is a

Russian word meaning "to be named to a position." It was the party and its organs, not the members of the organization, that decided who should be nominated or "elected," and these should always be the people whose political credentials and loyalty were beyond question.

In every voluntary organization such people, almost always Communist party members, were ready to realize state policies and curb any independent activity of their members if necessary. Moreover, in the highest and most important body in the state, the Central Committee of the Communist party, there was always a special department to oversee all voluntary organizations in the country. Because of this lack of full autonomy, the legally operating voluntary organizations often did not have enough credibility to attract many people to their activities.

The Changing Political Situation in Communist Poland and Its Impact on Voluntary Organizations

Poland was always the least totalitarian country in the Communist bloc. Freedom of action was usually much greater there than in other states in eastern Europe. Really voluntary activity was possible, and its independence was always greater in Poland than it was in neighboring countries. Even under a communist system, the Catholic church remained an independent, powerful institution and played a very important role in the country. It was always a natural, legal, and well-organized opposition to the system in a society that is 95 percent Catholic. The agricultural sector was never fully nationalized, and most land remained in the hands of the Polish peasants. The huge Polish emigration abroad, mostly to the United States and western Europe, assured the maintenance of close ties between the Polish people and those of the West and thus limited the impact of communist propaganda and censorship. Moreover, private enterprise survived, albeit on a very small scale. Finally, opposition to the system was always very strong in Poland, marked by the workers' and intellectuals' revolts in 1956, 1968, 1970, 1976, and 1980–1981.

The political situation in the country heavily influenced the voluntary sector. Right after World War II, in the period when legal opposition to the newly introduced, Russian-backed, communist government still existed, that is, in the years 1945 through 1948, many authentic voluntary organizations were established, especially charitable ones, helping the victims of the war, orphans, the disabled, and the elderly. Many of them operated under the umbrella of the Catholic church, with the cooperation of foreign relief agencies. With the introduction of the rigid Stalinist type of system in 1948, those organizations were dissolved or taken over by the state. Only a limited number of church-related institutions (for example, a few private schools) remained. From 1956, when the workers' revolt brought substantial relaxation to the system, until the end of the 1970s, some grass-roots initiatives in politically neutral areas were allowed to develop and some truly voluntary activities were carried out by many organizations alongside the state-established "associations of the higher public utility." Moreover, again under the umbrella of the Catholic church, clubs for the Catholic Intelligentsia were registered in several cities and became centers of cultural, educational, and charitable activity independent from the state authorities.

The first completely autonomous, formally illegal, voluntary organization outside the Catholic church was organized in 1976. It was the Workers Defense Committee (Komitet Obrony Robotnikow), established by a group of intellectuals to mobilize public opinion in defense of persecuted workers. In spite of police harassment and arrests, it attracted hundreds of people of different ages and professional backgrounds who were willing to engage in the struggle. The Workers Defense Committee, later renamed the Social Self-Defense Committee, systematically collected documentary evidence about repressions and abuses of power in the country, developed a communication network among workers in a number of industrial cities, published underground journals, and organized financial, legal, and medical help for the victims of persecution. The scope of its activities gradually expanded to encourage civic initiatives in trade unions and in cultural and political areas in order to restore the centers of civil society. Largely as a result of the committee's efforts, a number of opposition groups were formed, some with

a pronounced political profile and others of a more general nature. For example, a large group of scholars and intellectuals
initiated the "flying university" to teach unofficial academic
courses in areas especially distorted by political taboos and ideological dogmas: current and recent history, political economy,
sociology, and political science.

The strikes that occurred in the summer of 1980 and led
to the creation of the Solidarity trade union were rooted in economic and social crises, but the Workers Defense Committee
was essential to the way the workers voiced their grievances and
articulated their demands.

During the Solidarity revolution of 1980–1981, voluntary
activism exploded. The independent Solidarity movement, only
formally organized as a trade union, became the major institution of its kind. At the same time, old organizations were trying to adapt to new situations by freely electing new independent leaders. Some new organizations were also established, even
as old laws made it difficult to receive the obligatory state approval of their constitutions. For example, students founded the
Independent Students Union and environmentalists established
several organizations to fight pollution.

When marshal law was proclaimed in Poland in December 1981, all autonomous organizations were suspended. Many
organizations really stopped operating, some went deeply underground, and a substantial number of their leaders were imprisoned. Slowly, in 1982 and 1983, voluntary activity started
to develop again, at first mainly around the only independent
structure that existed at the time, the Catholic church. Groups
organized themselves in the parishes to distribute foreign aid
to those in need. Underground journals, newspapers, and books
started to appear. Actors protesting against the suppression of
Solidarity by the state boycotted the official media and started
to play on church grounds. When marshal law was finally lifted,
the underground opposition, though still persecuted, began to
surface and expand its activities. Many new independent initiatives were introduced. As the power of civic society began
to grow again, the authorities were forced to accept or at least
not to disturb the operation of more and more autonomous

voluntary organizations. For example, Monar was established to help the growing number of drug addicts. This was the first time the people learned about this problem in Poland. Environmental associations began to fight against nuclear plants proposed for Poland; again, this was the first time public discussion was permitted. In 1984 the Polish parliament passed the Foundation Act, which enabled both Polish and foreign foundations to be established in Poland. In 1988, after short but very intensive work by two teams (from the Communist party and the Catholic church), the new, relatively democratic Association Act was introduced, and it became possible to establish autonomous, voluntary, nonprofit organizations. The etatist social policy and the *nomenklatura* system were limited, and alternative organizations were allowed to register. For example, "alternative" journalist and writer associations and an "alternative" committee to help renovate the city of Krakow began to operate. In each case, the old association was still connected to the state authorities and the new autonomous one was aligned with the relegalized Solidarity.

Finally, the introduction of the Solidarity government in August 1989 gave a special boost to autonomous activity and the reconstruction of civic society in Poland.

Autonomous Organizations in Contemporary Poland

By the end of 1989 almost 200 foundations were operating in Poland, together with thousands of autonomous voluntary organizations. The variety of these organizations and the scope of their activities greatly surpass the situation existing in other eastern European countries. All the actors who play an important role in contemporary Poland have been involved in this development: the old state apparatus, the Solidarity movement, the Catholic church, and many foreign institutions. It serves more than an illustrative purpose to mention some of them. It provides a closer look at the scope of activities of the emerging independent sector in Poland — at its uniqueness, on the one hand, and at its similarity to the Western sector on the other.

1. With the direct support of communist authorities still in power several foundations have been established. The Polish Cultural Foundation supports different cultural initiatives, such as the renovation of historical monuments in the old Polish territories belonging to the Soviet Union since World War II. The Foundation to Renovate the Historical Monuments in Krakow, under the aegis of the City Council, is helping to restore the medieval capitol of Poland; (so far it is the biggest foundation in Poland). The Peace Foundation supports various peace initiatives in the country.

2. Under the umbrella of the Roman Catholic church, foreign donations were used to establish a foundation to build water supply systems in villages.

3. Foreign individuals and organizations have established, for example, the Stefan Batory Trust, financed by George Soros, a Hungarian-American millionaire, to help increase Polish scholars' studies abroad and to finance purchases of foreign scientific equipment for Polish universities; the Nissenbaum Family Foundation: to renovate ruined Jewish cemeteries in Poland; and the Foundation for the Development of Polish Agriculture, under the supervision of the Rockefeller Brothers Fund, to help the private farming sector to recover.

4. Polish and foreign individuals and organizations working together have established foundations such as that to clear the polluted Baltic Sea (financed mostly by Scandinavian companies) and a foundation to sponsor contacts between Poland and 15 million members of the Polish diaspora (under the sponsorship of the Warsaw-based Society for Relations with Poles Abroad).

5. Some state institutions — for example, major universities — are trying to increase their independence from the state budget by establishing autonomous foundations to generate financial support for their activities.

6. Even individual Poles have established foundations, such as one financed by Andrzej Wajda, a well-known Polish movie director, who donated a substantial prize he received from the city of Kyoto to create in Krakow a museum for

a famous Polish collection of old Japanese prints and modern Japanese technology.
7. Finally, at the end of 1989, under the sponsorship of the Solidarity movement, a foundation was created to teach Poles democratic procedures and to prepare them for local elections to be held in mid-1990.

Among the thousands of voluntary associations that have recently been established thanks to grass-roots initiatives, some seem to be of special importance in the Polish situation:

• Human rights associations: to press for democratic, legal acts dealing with the rights of prisoners, to protect women's right to have an abortion, and so on
• Ecological associations: to fight pollution, to make people aware of environmental problems, to protest against building nuclear power plants, and the like
• Commemorative associations: to reestablish ties with old Polish cities now in the Soviet Union, to commemorate the lives of certain political figures, and so forth
• International friendship societies: to improve relations with the United States, Germany, and Israel, countries often characterized in the past by state propaganda as unfriendly
• Political clubs: to discuss political issues (by the end of 1989, some of these had transformed themselves into political parties)
• Minority group associations: to take care of the problems of Lithuanian, Ukrainian, Bellorussian, and German minorities in Poland who were deliberately ignored in the past
• Educational societies: to establish and govern private nonsectarian schools
• Business associations: to support the development of private business and a market-oriented economy (at the end of 1989, Rotary clubs were reinstituted after fifty years)
• Health associations: to help people with rare diseases who previously did not receive proper assistance from the state health care system

At the same time, many old voluntary associations are trying to become autonomous and to gain more credibility in society. One good example is the Polish Boy Scout organization.

Obviously, then, the independent sector in Poland is already doing fairly well. Some significant problems remain, however. First, for forty years philanthropy was rarely promoted as an important humanistic value. Two generations of Poles grew up and were educated and indoctrinated under socialism; now, of course, they expect to receive everything from the welfare state. Many Poles, therefore, are not psychologically ready "to give and share."

Second, the independent sector faces serious financial difficulties because tax incentives are not yet good enough to attract substantial corporate donations and no tax incentives exist at the personal level. (The majority of Poles do not pay any income taxes.) What may help eventually, however, is the fact that according to Polish law, many foundations and associations are allowed to maintain business activity to support their statutory activities.

The size and internal diversity of the emerging independent sector already require some umbrella organizations to promote its ideas, to lobby for new laws, and to be a clearing house for domestic as well as international information. Western expertise will be necessary to further the development of this sector.

Poland is a country in which, after many years, people are finally able to accept responsibility for themselves and for their future. Autonomous, nongovernmental organizations should help to make Poland a prosperous European nation.

Chapter 19

The Emerging
Nonprofit Sector in Bulgaria:
Its Historical Dimensions

Unpredicted events are continuing to spread in Eastern Europe.
Initiated under powerful pressure from and support by Gorba-
chev-launched *perestroika* in the USSR, rapid changes in the
Eastern European countries have far exceeded the frame and
scope within which the Soviet leader confined himself. Shaped
in their own pattern, varying from the relatively longtime record
of steady struggle in Poland and Hungary to the faster fall of
the Czechoslovak Stalinist regime imposed by the Soviet invasion of 1968 to the fascinating dismantling of the terrible Berlin Wall to the slow but steady evolution in Bulgaria after the
ousting of the thirty-five-year dictatorship of T. Zhivkov to the
bloody revolution in Romania, these events reveal the over-

whelming aspiration of the people to take their fate into their own hands. Ironically, this was proclaimed as a primary goal of the earlier communist revolutions, which over time became one of the most cynical lies in history because of the selfish seizure of power and the embezzlement of national wealth by a handful of self-proclaimed "servants of the people."

The changes are impressive, with yesterday's political prisoners and exiles occupying high official positions and taking an active part in the decision-making process, huge crowds stating in full voice what not very long ago they did not dare to whisper except to their closest friends, and children eating for the first time in their grim lives a banana or an orange. More important, these changes occurred not as a result of an internal, secret deal by the ruling clique, as used to happen in the typical style of the mafialike communist decision-making process but — especially in what was formerly East Germany and in Czechoslovakia and Romania — under the pressure of a tremendous mass popular upheaval. Moreover, these mass demonstrations have expressed the people's firm will to change the very nature of their societies, denying the Communists any reason to continue their domination and insisting on the investigation and trial of the previously glorified "leaders of the people" because of their fraud, corruption, and abuse of power. Actually, until the more peaceful transitions in East Germany, Czechoslovakia, and Bulgaria (which left their ex-rulers untouched, under house arrest, to await the results of a thorough investigation of their deeds), they were given the opportunity not only to witness the conversion of their numerous mansions and palaces into hospitals, rest houses, children's summer camps, orphanages, or — at least — museums of their greed but also to see the dead body of their "beloved comrade," the cruelest dictator among them — Ceauşescu.

With varying speed, but steady determination, the countries of Eastern Europe have moved or are moving toward a full rupture with the remaining totalitarian system. New political forces have emerged to compete with and to defeat the Communist parties' power monopoly through any fair elections. As for the economy, even the most orthodox dogmatists now avoid advocating central planning, strict state ownership of the means of production, and the legacy of Leninism—state monopoly of foreign trade. As a matter of fact, even the Bulgarian antireformist administration of Zhivkov appeared eager to introduce certain reforms in the economic system, abolishing the central planning authority, permitting relatively large opportunities for private initiative, and relaxing the legal requirements for foreign investments. All these bastions of Marxist economic dogma were quickly abandoned with only one main intention: to save the Communist party's political monopoly. However, the top party leaders and their advisers seemingly forgot one of the basic Marxist assumptions: the strict mutual interdependence between politics and the economy, which refutes any changes in the economic order without respective political shifts.

Originally, socialist society—the first stage before the utopian dream of the affluent workers' heaven of communism—had been projected as a genuinely nonprofit one, where the only and ultimate benefactors should be the working people. Under the state monopoly of almost every means of production, any economic unit, be it a huge metallurgical conglomerate or agricultural farm or even a barber shop, could not dispose of the financial profit from the products sold. It was the state, or actually its bureaucracy, that determined the quantity of items to be produced, as well as their price, and again the state absorbed almost all balances, both positive and negative, of the enterprises. It was presumed that this was the only way to avoid the shortages and evil elements inherent in market-oriented societies: periodical crises of overproduction, price speculation, and exploitation of the labor force. Through state control of resources and goods, it was expected that planned and steady growth could be attained, along with just distribution according to one's personal share in the common welfare. The socialist state succeeded in securing jobs for everybody, free and universally accessible medical care, and by means of budget donations, in maintaining relatively low prices for basic food commodities, utilities, public transportation, and housing. All this, without doubt, was an important historical achievement when compared with the past deprivation of large masses of the population in these mostly backward countries. However, it was far from sufficient to meet the growing expectations and needs of the people. A lack of market competition combined with chronic shortages led to a decrease in demand for quality goods by the state itself and by consumers, who were ready to accept mediocre and poor products rather than not to receive any products at all. Party-state dignitaries, who satisfied their own "bigger" needs (hidden from the public eye) for top-quality Western goods, managed to justify this dead-end situation by means of ideological indoctrination, citing either persistent "temporary difficulties" or the necessity of extending international assistance to "brother countries" such as Cuba, North Vietnam, Angola, Ethiopia, Mozambique, or Nicaragua.

As a result, the socialist state failed to carry out its own genuine premise: to promote the welfare of everybody and of the whole of society. Huge amounts of resources were directed toward a massive military buildup and maintenance of the ever-growing bureaucracy and repressive apparatus. Such an artificial system, deprived of virtually no checks and balances, left these resources in the hands of a small circle of dignitaries. This naturally led to excessive abuses — embezzlement, self-enrichment, and corruption — and the total breakdown of the entire system.

Any nonprofit, charitable, or philanthropic activity presupposes the existence of personalities and institutions capable of donating resources to benefit all the population of deprived members of the community. There are simply no such individuals, organizations, and institutions under socialism other than the state itself — the main, and in many cases the only, possessor and distributor of the national wealth — when all other members of the society are confined to a guaranteed but minimal share of it. Moreover, any such activity has been either outlawed (especially when performed by the church or when it is connected with interests abroad) or at least considered to be strongly suspicious and generally discouraged.

Can the recent and current changes overcome existing obstacles to the flourishing of nonprofit activity in socialist countries? Is such activity necessary for these societies? If so, in which

fields especially? Can a society with a developed nonprofit sector remain a socialist one, or must it first abandon that social
order? What is the role of Western countries and their respective organizations in assisting Bulgaria to work through these
major issues? These are the questions that I will attempt to answer in this chapter.

Especially in the case of Bulgaria, no specific research has
been conducted on nonprofit activity simply because such activity is unknown. (It is even difficult to find an exact term for
it in the Bulgarian language.) However, my effort to answer
these questions will be based on the large amount of data gathered through the all-national sociological inquiry *The Town and
the Village, '86* (Mikailov and others, 1988–1989). It was conducted in parallel with the census of the population of a representative sample of 18,000 persons sixteen years old and above and
covered a vast spectrum of social features, ways of life, and economic activity.

Philanthropy and Nonprofit Activity Under Socialism:
The Case of Bulgaria

The Bulgarian tradition of charity has its roots in the centuries
of Ottoman-Turkish domination (1396–1878), when the Christian faith as well as the Bulgarian language and identity were
preserved through the donations of individuals and communities. These donations enabled the building and maintenance of
churches, schools, and the so-called *chitalishta* (literally meaning "places for reading," or clubs where libraries were combined
with active cultural promotion, such as lectures, amateur theaters, and the like).

After the liberation, some wealthy Bulgarians and foreigners donated resources and land for the building of the new state's
capital, Sofia; the most prominent examples are the brothers
Evlogui and Christo Guerguievs, whose generous charity made
possible the establishment of the first university in independent
Bulgaria. Stipends were irregularly provided through philanthropic donations for talented young men and women to study
in the country and abroad.

These emerging positive traditions were entirely abandoned after the seizure of power by the Communist party (1944–1948), for according to Marxist ideology in its crudest Stalinist interpretation, the party-state was the sole manager of the whole spectrum of economic and social activity, which included not only the production of goods, but also all emergency and informal activities previously viewed as the functions of philanthropy and charities. As a matter of fact, philanthropy was officially condemned as a "bourgeois remnant," and Western foundations and endowments were portrayed as a "hidden arm of the CIA."

It is well known that the nonprofit sector in the United States and most other industrialized countries is a major economic sector with assets and transactions comparable to those of the largest multinational for-profit corporations and exceeding the GNP of a number of small countries. To distinguish it from big government and big business and also to recognize its strength and dimensions it is called the third sector.

However, it took several centuries for charitable activity to progress from a generous but unsystematic activity — vulnerable to suspicious and jealous governments and selfish, envious, and greedy people — to this third sector. This gradual evolution required great sacrifice from many benevolent men and women, and even now, this great enterprise of giving would collapse without the enormous efforts of an army of volunteers: fund raisers, local organizers and promoters, thousands of hands that build, piece by piece, the great system of support for those in need.

Volunteerism is the first precondition of any move toward reliable nonprofit activity. It is of special importance for societies such as that of Bulgaria that have not yet established a considerable network of nonprofit organizations and that have no elaborated legal system for dealing with such activity. To develop the foundations of the system, these societies must initially rely exclusively on the voluntary, apostolic drive of hundreds of nonpaid, goodwill promoters.

To find some variables that will help us formulate necessary conclusions about the grounds for further development of a genuine nonprofit sector in Bulgaria we must study the overall picture of public and social activity of the Bulgarian population.

Some important data in this field were accumulated during the earlier mentioned sociological inquiry known as *The Town and the Village, '86,* but the data deserve additional explanation and commentary.

Bringing the overall population into the ranks of the existing official mass sociopolitical organizations is one of the most important features of totalitarian society. Actually, only about 3.9 percent of the Bulgarian population sixteen years of age and older is not affiliated with at least one of the four basic political organizations: the Bulgarian Communist party (BCP), the Bulgarian Agrarian People's Union (BZNS), Communist Youth (DKMS), or Fatherland's Front (FF). The ruling Communist party members make up 13.87 percent of the older population. There are, indeed, special rules and requirements for joining the CP, primarily a working class background and an excellent work record, including active involvement, especially in the Communist Youth organization. Most discussions on who is to be invited to join the party occur behind closed doors, and even potential candidates are often not aware of the deliberations and the inquiries about their personal lives and relations. The CP, which seeks to maintain its proletarian character, insists on admitting primarily young laborers, but they are usually reluctant to join the party unless they are interested in a political career.

Members of the middle class and the intelligentsia are the most eager to become party members because of the advantages such membership provides for job promotion. Their growing share of the party membership is the very basis for internal changes in the party, including the abandonment of orthodoxy and a transition to more pragmatic policy, a process that has been taking place in Eastern Europe. A new generation of party leaders, who emerged in recent years in Poland, Hungary, former East Germany, and Czechoslovakia, is carrying out these social changes. They are professionals rather than pure *apparatchiks;* they are not so heavily influenced by emotional and other ties to the revolutionary struggle and Moscow; they are less manipulative and less obedient than their predecessors. As a result they are more broad-minded and interested in the real development of their own countries, not in utopian dreams. Although in some countries the CP may eventually disappear, in the near future it will more likely continue to exist but with a diminished role in the reformed versions of the party. And this will be its last chance to regain public confidence.

For about forty years BZNS, the oldest agrarian party in Europe, has been a puppet of the Communists, deprived of its own platform, and compelled to adopt the rules of the Bulgarian Communist party. The BCP interfered brutally in BZNS's internal matters, including its membership policy. Only 2.17 percent of the elderly population are members of the BZNS because of the restrictions imposed by the BCP. These restrictions were designed to prevent any additional power of the "allied party" (which originated from supporters of allied forces in World War II) that could endanger the CP's monopoly over existing power. However, some inquisitive intellectuals, often with little or no connection to farm life and agrarian problems but quietly opposed to the CP's dominance, managed to join the BZNS, and within weeks after the ousting of the Bulgarian dictator T. Zhivkov BZNS came to life. Once considered a fully destroyed faction of the opposition (led by Nikola Petkov, who was hanged by the Communists in 1948 as an "American agent") BZNS was restored, and there is every reason to expect that before the first democratic parliamentary elections, BZNS will transform itself into a real alternative force, seriously challenging the Communists' power.

The Communist Youth organization, or Kimitrovian Communist Union of Youth (DKMS), contains 20.11 percent of the total population but about 99 percent of the age-group from fourteen to thirty. Membership in the DKMS is not formally obligatory, but it is unavoidable, for without such affiliation young men and women are not eligible to enter the university or to hold nonmanual jobs. However, in spite of various measures by the BCP leadership, including police actions and punishment for allegedly "pro-Western" behavior (such as wearing long hair, beards, and blue jeans and listening and dancing to rock music), there has been a drastic increase in disobedience, apathy toward Communist-inspired undertakings, and the repeated rise in predominantly small, semi-illegal, nonformal groups ranging from the far left to the far right. Young people are the most militant participants in the struggle to restructure society. The courageous armed resistance of the students and graduates in neighboring Romania against the Ceauşescu loyalists deeply impressed Bulgarian youth. Their current development of and membership in a host of new organizations such as the Independent Student's (graduate's) Society, Agrarian Youth, Young Ecologists, and so on, together with the demise of the DKMS, not only marks the end of the CP's domination over the youth but makes young people a strong force to be reckoned with.

The saddest fate under "developing socialism" was reserved for the Fatherland's Front and the Bulgarian Trade Unions. The FF was an umbrella organization promoted by Communists in 1942 to unite the country's political parties and organizations located to the left of center in their common struggle against fascism and Nazi domination. However, after the Communist coup d'etat in September 1944, FF was transformed into a giant threshing machine, in which any noncommunist tendencies were doomed to conform or to vanish. Fatherland's Front is now a ridiculously phony body, including almost the entire elderly population (members of the BCP and BZNS are also affiliated with the FF). But this is a membership only on paper, and to retirees it is an important source of diversion in their old age. (Members organize local meetings, discussions, fairs, exhibitions, celebrations, and the like.) Curiously, but understandably, it was mainly the elderly, including longtime party veterans with nothing to lose, who were, during the years of rigid dictatorship, the only ones who dared to criticize abuses of power and deserved to be called by an irritated party official "our militant opposition"—a sort of socialist "Gray Panthers."

Trade (labor) union membership is reduced to a pure formality: all who are employed (and socialism is proud of maintaining full employment in spite of the heavy burden and tension for the economy) are members of the BTU. At one time, even one's membership fee was directly charged against one's monthly salary, much like an income tax. Contrary to some Western assumptions, it was the trade unions, together with the state-run Social Welfare Administration, that undertook some of the functions that typically belong to private and nongovernmental organizations in the United States and other Western countries, such as financial and other support for families and individuals in need. Professional associations, such as the Writers' Union, the Union of Artists, and the Union of Actors, established their own foundations to support financially their unemployed members and their families in need. Since the state established free education and medical care for all, the foundations provided some stipends for the best or financially troubled students, as well as some grants for medical treatment, especially for sophisticated surgical operations abroad. The trade unions were reduced to promoting and propagating the BCP's policies. Neither the BCP leadership nor that of the BTU was capable of learning a lesson from the rise of the Solidarity (*Solidarnosc*) trade union in Poland. In 1989, a small independent trade union, named Podkrepa (meaning "support") was formed in the town of Stara Zagora and, despite repression, grew rapidly, including in its membership not only intellectuals but also workers from various industries. As for the BTU, it is currently transforming itself into a truly independent organization to serve the interests of the working people.

Becoming aware of its inability to cover all necessary measures and expenses in the fields of social welfare and human development, especially those of education and medical care, in the 1970s the state began to urge individual enterprises and local authorities to provide resources for the education of students from their own budgets and profits under an agreement that those students who benefited would work for the respective enterprises after they completed their education. This was aimed at stopping or at least limiting the mass migration of young specialists from remote regions to the big cities. However, the plan failed, as increasing numbers of professionals flocked to the cities and were often employed as taxi drivers, waiters, and bartenders instead of the engineers, teachers, and physicians they were trained to be. Moreover, the plan also failed to relax the heavy burden on the state budget.

A relatively new and uncommon movement also began

in the 1970s: the creation of quasi-nongovernmental endowments based on the pattern of Western societies, especialy the United States. These endowments especially flourished as part of the celebration of 1300 years of Bulgarian statehood (1981) under the personal auspices of the then head of state Zhivkov and his ambitious daughter Liudmiela, who died at a young age. One of these endowments was named after her; another one, named "1300 years of Bulgaria," was assigned to gather and preserve gifts and donations from Bulgarian residents, Bulgarians living abroad, and foreigners on the occasion of the anniverary. A third endowment, "Banner of the Peace," had the task of promoting international activity and contacts among talented children. Characteristically, all three endowments were presided over by the ex-Bulgarian dictator's son, Vladimir, a playboy now under investigation for gambling with state funds and other crimes.

These new endowments did produce some positive results. The most spectacular among them provided financial support, for the first time since the establishment of Communist rule, to students selected through a national competition (observed by an independent commission and including foreign instructors) to attend colleges in the United States and other Western countries. Other endowments contributed to the development of the arts, cultural exchange with foreign countries, cultural education of the population at large, and the encouragement of talented children. These endowments worked actively with such Western counterparts as Armand Hammer, Robert Maxwell, the West German Krup Foundation, and many others. Yet these activities were mainly a facade intended to attract naive and emotional Western businessmen and philanthropists. Under a system that lacks even the basic means for public control and checks over such financially sensitive matters, even the most noble drives could easily be abused or misused as a front for prominent and low-level officials to enrich themselves.

Shortly after the ouster of Zhivkov, under the pressure of mass demonstrations, the National Assembly decided to launch an investigation to reveal how these funds had been mismanaged. The investigation commission, initially composed exclusively of leading members of the BCP, was taken under parliamentary control, and a number of respected independent representatives of the nonofficial groups were included. This heightened expectations for a fair inquiry open to the public. Simultaneously, some suggested that the positive beginnings and potentials of these endowments should not be destroyed in an emotional upheaval. In other words, "Do not throw out the baby with the bath water." Rather, they have argued that these endowments should be developed into independent, genuinely nonprofit institutions and renamed after ancient Bulgarian educators, such as Saints Cyril and Methodius, Saint Kliment Okhridski, and others (Boicheva, 1989).

The preceding description raises some arguments for the conclusion that socialism is contradictory, noncompatible, and even hostile to the very idea of nonprofit charitable activity. However, faced with insurmountable obstacles in fulfilling the officially proclaimed task of "satisfaction of the ever-increasing needs of the population," socialism reluctantly admitted a few forms of nonstate donations to recipients who could be carefully selected and controlled. At the same time, there was great room for embezzlement and hidden corruption because of a lack of public scrutiny of the size of the resources and how they were used.

Until recently, the development of nonofficial groups of any kind were insufficient and negligible in Bulgaria. There is a well-grounded argument that the church serves an important role as a major source of support for political movements of various types, providing them with both material and moral support, as well as organizational cadres and genuine experience (Dwyer, 1983). This is a far more necessary function for societies in which any unofficial group is exposed to excessive pressure from omnipotent official authorities. The church in Bulgaria, a semi-independent branch of the Eastern Orthodox church, has traditionally been dominated by secular rulers — unlike Catholicism, which managed to be a solid counterforce to the policy itself. As such, it submitted itself relatively easily to Communist authority. Moreover, unlike the Roman Catholic and Protestant churches, the Eastern Orthodox church has mainly been a recipient of donations rather than a donor or promoter of charity for other than its own purposes. Other churches have very limited and widely dispersed constituencies in Bulgaria. Some forms of underground self-help activities were developed by the communities of followers of Islam — erroneously generalized as one "Turkish" minority. As such, they have been persecuted by the security forces, and their promoters have been jailed, forced into internal exile, or expelled from the country.

A typical and widespread Bulgarian tradition is voluntary labor for the benefit of the community or neighborhood. This includes participation with labor, resources, and materials in the construction or repair of schools, churches, bridges, roads, and other facilities that have a public purpose. A remarkable decrease in such activities occurred after the Communists took over. People were taught to believe that in this state, they only had to take care of their own kitchen or bedroom. Volunteerism was still alive, but mainly among elderly people in the countryside and members of tourist and hunting societies. Generally however, people were discouraged even in this noble venture because of increasing personal welfare troubles and shortages of construction materials.

Time is also a major contributing factor in the development of philanthropic and charitable activities. Most contributors are unpaid volunteers, and the way of life in socialist society leaves very little time for voluntary activity. Overtime labor, the ordeal of getting daily supplies of food and basic commodities, and poor transportation to and from working places all curtail possibilities for contributions to the welfare and entertainment of others.

Another factor that needs to be seriously considered as a premise for the activities noted above is the prevailing attitude toward volunteerism. Fund raising, promotion, and the supplying of services are all unthinkable without the assistance of hundreds and thousands of men and women. Such volunteers must be ready to deliver their time and abilities and to share their resources and facilities with others, without any material benefit to themselves. A proven motivation for serving others is religious faith, especially Christian faith. Socialism destroys this important base for voluntary action. Moreover, socialism generally frustrates efforts toward voluntary action. Voluntary participation and affiliation with Communist organizations is by no means encouraged when the Communist party is in opposition or underground because mass support is necesary for its leaders to seize power. Communism has its saints and martyrs, men and women with clear intentions, missions, passions, and refusal of material goods or other compensation. Unfortunately, most of these heroes fall during struggles. With few exceptions, after the triumph of socialism, yesterday's fighters were quickly transformed into people greedy for power and wealth, who obeyed the will and guidelines of the Great Leader of the Communist Party, who strongly, sometimes violently, urged the masses to work hard and devote themselves to stubborn labor in order to reach "the brightest peaks" (or "the golden dream") of communism. Everything forced is considered to be voluntary in the language of the Communist argot, whether imposed, dictated, or enforced "enthusiasm" for the purposes of public show.

It is also worth noting that according to sociological inquiries in Bulgaria, the introduction of a five-day work week in the mid 1970s has not led to an increase in leisure time. On the contrary, people do not use their extra hours for recreational or public-purpose activities but rather for a kind of moonlighting to grow vegetables on available land, either to earn some additional income or to provide themselves with a basic food supply. Emerging fundamental changes in economic regulations, namely, the steady introduction of some market-economy principles (competition, the abolition of central planning, the promotion of individual and group initiative), cannot be expected to enlarge any activity that is not self-centered. Because individuals become far more concerned with their own welfare and social security, they pay less attention to causes that directly affect them. This will be the case until socioeconomic stability and prosperity occur, unlikely events in the near future.

What Is to Be Done?

The problem for Bulgaria is how to create a wholly new sociopolitical structure that was previously nonexistent or completely destroyed under socialism. The necessity of such a structure is more than clear: it will introduce a necessary order and systematization of fields vital to the society (especially human services, medical care, child care, and education). These areas of service are far from perfect and certainly will suffer the most during the initial stage in the transition to a market-oriented society. In order to avoid any drastic deterioration in these sensitive fields, it is necessary to establish the respective nonprofit organizations network as an alternative, counterforce, and counterpartner of the exhausted state and confused economy sector. Indeed, this is not an easy task. It means reshuffling and restructuring long-existing patterns, as well as drastically reducing the powerful bureaucracy of important functions, for example, firing a large number of administrative clerks, most of whom are unqualified for any job other than shuffling papers. But this is only the beginning. Two preconditions must be met in order to ensure a suitable environment for the successful development of nonprofit activity:

1. There must be laws regulating nonprofit activity; confirming its legal status, scope, objectives, and options; abolishing all artificial restraints that hamper it; and establishing an independent publicly controlled body to conduct audits.
2. The archaic taxation system that restricts rather than encourages fund raising and donations must be replaced and tax-exemption provisions for charities must be introduced.

It seems unlikely that these objectives can be attained under existing circumstances of instability, general unrest, and an overall lack of funds and basic experience. There is no way to improve the situation without assistance from those Western countries that are able and willing to invest both advice and money. Unlike most Eastern European countries, especially Poland, Bulgaria has a small and widely dispersed community abroad that is disinterested in the events within the "grandfather's fatherland" and therefore cannot be relied upon for substantial help. Moreover, due to historical circumstances, Bulgaria is a country without well-established relations with any of the highly industrialized countries, to whom it is a marginal rather than a strategically important partner. Some help may be possible from such countries as Germany, France, Italy, and Great Britain. Yet even these prospects are not sufficient and may be questionable. Inevitably, any such effort must involve support from the United States, especially from the American nonprofit sector. A confirmation of the existing interest in and openness to the dynamic developments of change in Eastern Europe was the visit of the president of the U.S. Council on Foundations, James Joseph, to the Soviet Union in the spring of 1989 (*Pravda,* 1989). However, American organizations should give more attention to the "dwarfs" of the former Soviet bloc, such as Bulgaria.

The creation of a third sector in the present socialist countries would have consequences far beyond the scope of the sector itself. It would allow a vital sphere of the society to be released from partisanship and depoliticized and to be concerned solely with the general public and its needs. Thus, it would provide a formidable victory on the road to true democracy and give us the right, after more than 150 years, to repeat for our societies what Alexis de Tocqueville (1966 [1835]) said of the American society: "Democracy does not provide a people with the most skillful of governments, but it does that which the most skillful government cannot do; it spreads throughout the body politic a restless activity, superabundant force and energy never found elsewhere, which, however little favored by circumstance, can do wonders. Those are its true advantages."

References

Boicheva, M. "Some Worked in Defense of the Endowment." *Anteni Weekly,* Dec. 27, 1989.

Dwyer, L. S. "Structure and Strategy in the Anti-Nuclear Movement." In J. Freeman (ed.), *Social Movements in 60s and 70s,* pp. 148–161. New York: Longman, 1983.

Mikailov, S., and others. *The Town and the Village, '86.* 6 vols. Sofia: Central Statistical Agency, 1988–1989.

Pravda. Interview with James Joseph. *Pravda,* Apr. 7, 1989.

Tocqueville, A. de. *Democracy in America.* New York: Harper-Collins, 1966, p. 225. (Originally published 1835.)

The Independent Sector in the USSR: Formation, Purposes, and Effects

In the Soviet Union, there was previously no urgent need to define the term *independent sector* since it hardly existed; while the sectors known as government and business were easily understood, the third sector logically comprised all that was left. However, a comparison of the independent sector in various countries is only possible if nations have the same or similar social and economic structures. Therefore, defining the independent sector in the Soviet Union has become a serious question for discussion because the phenomenon has spread so far beyond the borders of the so-called developed Western countries, where it has existed as a natural and significant part of the societal structure for centuries.

The inclusion of the Eastern bloc countries in the cross-cultural study of NGO activities gives an important perspective in defining the role of the independent sector in society. If we want to use the same term worldwide, we must realize, in addition, that the term *can be expanded* by the wider range of tasks that the third sector includes in socialist societies and by the great variety of factors that motivate citizens to become active in voluntary movements. Furthermore, we must consider as well the *various forms* that public activity may take and the criteria by which the independent sector can be defined.

The term *independent sector* came to the Soviet Union from the West, where the society itself and the way of life are believed to be much more independent than elsewhere. Why, then, is the sector we are studying also called independent? Although the term *independent* has been criticized by Western scholars, the reason for using this word is to emphasize the divergence of values and methods from the two other sectors, the political and commercial, as well as the difference in the priorities set on the one hand by government and on the other by business. The first of these is ruled by political parties, and the second by private interests. Both of these interests, though strong, are temporary in their content: they *depend* on the current situation following individual demands and decisions of the leaders fighting for survival and dominance under conditions of tough competition. That is why the role of the independent sector serves *to escape dependence* on these private interests and serves the basic needs of the society as a whole. This sector incorporates universal values of education, science, the environment, ethics, charity, and so on. If recognized as basic and universal, these goals can secure both public support and governmental protection. Or, according to British charity law that goes back to the British common law, fulfilling these goals will be understood as beneficial to the community and therefore respected and promoted.

If the Anglo-American system in the charitable sphere dates back to British common law, we in the Soviet Union did not retain our old legal traditions because the political structures were changed dramatically. That is why it is so important now to develop new criteria under which voluntary activism in the Soviet Union can be recognized as a specific sector of social life that is "beneficial to the community" as the Soviet Union moves from a totalitarian government to a more open and democratic society. Therefore, the main purpose of this chapter is to attempt to answer two basic questions: First, what does the term *independent sector* mean given the Soviet conditions of today? Second, what impact could this sector have on Soviet society if the sector were significantly widened and given the same recognition and privileges as exist in Western countries?

The main trend of developing nonprofit organizations in the West focuses on the unification of efforts to solve common goals of the citizens versus private interests. In socialist countries, the independent sector tends to support and develop private initiative and diversity versus a previously enforced "collectivization" of mind and action.

Under the prevailing conditions in the Soviet Union, for example, where people have been forcibly unified by a system of total control and decisions are made centrally from above and where independent ventures and activities have always caused trouble for the initiators, the most important task for the entire independent sector is, as it is understood by its initiators, to save and develop a small circle of "active strata" that has survived and is still working in every field of creative endeavor. The independent sector in such a social environment has the task of bringing together, supporting, and encouraging those who can work creatively on their own, who can face challenges independently, and who are able to take the risks as well as the responsibilities to further this special process for the benefit of the people. Thus one critical aspect of the independent sector's role is finding, educating, and training the new type of personality needed to organize innovative activities.

As the independent or third sector supplements what is lacking in the government and commercial sectors, it serves an important function in the social sphere of the Soviet Union. What is needed now is the ability of nonprofit organizations to work on their own — from setting goals to obtaining results — without control by political institutions enumerated in the Soviet constitution. In this sense, independence means independence from administrative monopoly, from party bureaucracy, from old thinking and old structures, and from being a part of the mechanism that somebody else operates from above. That is why this "sector" of independent activity is now being created in all the main spheres of Soviet life: economic, political, and ideological.

Another important characteristic that distinguishes Soviet society from the West is that the Soviet Union still does not have a business sector, which is taken for granted in most other nations. For a very long time, we had a planned state economy that is now frightened of losing its monopoly and is resistant to the creation of independent, self-sufficient, economic structures. That is why the business sector is in the same situation as the independent sector. Both sectors are very closely connected and are developing together under similar conditions; that is, both must fight for every step in their independence from the state. They are also closely connected through the people who participate in both sectors. These are the independent and creative people who did not fit the previous governing system and, therefore, were opposed or ignored. At present, whenever there is an opportunity, scientists, journalists, engineers, doctors, teachers, and nurses start their business ventures not only for the sake of money but in order to work independently, to develop their professional skills, and to realize their old dreams. That is why journalists started the information cooperative to publish their own newspaper. A musician opens a cafe so that his own tiny band has a place in which to perform. The business sector and the voluntary sector do not contradict each other very much in these early stages of development. They often involve the same or similar people, motivated by creativity and social work, but hoping, first of all, to be more successful in what they attempt to accomplish. The uncertain position of both business and voluntary activity and their mutual dependence on state decisions make the independent sector in the USSR very different from the typical nonprofit organization in the West. Although the model that is developing in the Soviet Union may simply represent a revolutionary model in the overall development of a nonprofit sector, we must recognize and study this process in order to strengthen it for the benefit of the community.

Regardless of the type of system — whether capitalism or socialism — the role of the independent sector depends on the relations between the state and society and, in particular, on the duties individuals take upon themselves to further their own self-sufficiency. When these individual responsibilities are limited or not noticeably developed, it means that individuals within the society *are not able to* take on these responsibilities or that they *are not allowed to*. In other words, government suppresses individual initiative. Five years ago in the Soviet Union we could blame the state system for preventing the development of civil society. Now, when this pressure is slowly being removed, we must pay more attention to whether or not the society itself is ready, developed, educated, and organized and, finally, whether or not it is *willing to* take upon itself these duties and responsibilities.

New voluntary efforts in all spheres of Soviet life are emerging. In each sphere, we can ask the following questions: How are the independent forces organized at the outset? What are the conditions under which they begin their activity, specifically in regard to the role of the state through legislation? What types of people participate in these activities? What is their social background? What are their motives? Finally, what level of development has been attained so far, and what are the results of these efforts to date?

The "Voluntary Sector" Within the Economy

It may seem unusual to describe economic structures as part of the independent sector, but there are at least two reasons for doing so: (1) there is an absence of concentrated independent funds for voluntary activity, and (2) material or commercial means must be developed to provide the resources for voluntary activism. First, there has been little possibility to accumulate serious and enduring sources of philanthropy in the Soviet Union because the majority of citizens are very poor. They are poor because of the exclusively governmental distribution of funds and because the organizations that hold these funds cannot operate freely. Second, voluntary activism needs concrete funding to get a start. It needs information networking and technology, an office (or at least, a tiny room with a telephone), office equipment, and publishing facilities. Organizations involved in cultural activities and sports need materials. There are no sources from which to obtain these materials unless they have been planned for, approved by, and distributed by official government agencies.

It is much quicker to earn, buy, or even create and manufacture materials because organizations in the independent sector need their own independent economic freedom in order to sponsor their own activities. In the economic sphere, relations between the state and society are strictly controlled by the state, the owner of all resources, and nothing can develop openly without the approval of the state. That is why new economic ventures are restricted to possibilities given them under current legislation. Therefore, these alternative structures cannot naturally grow by themselves to meet the economic needs or demands of society. They are still dependent on the "level of permission" available through government. Within this limited system, the following examples provide illustrations of new ventures and their levels of state supervision and control.

The first example is the establishment of the Program on Technology and Scientific Creativity of Youth, a "state and public structure" as it was called in founding documents. Set up by the Council of Ministers of the USSR in 1986, its official goal is to encourage the development of technology. It put state funds and resources into the hands of joint councils, constructed on the basis of the territorial Komsomol (Young Communist League) committees, and invited "specialists" and "directors of state enterprises" to take part. These councils distribute funds to individual investors or their groups in order to sponsor the development of pioneering ideas, mostly technical in nature. The councils then buy the results from the investors along with the right to market them to state enterprises, which receive from 40 to 60 percent of the profit for their aid. On the one hand, they are promoting the technical creativity of the youth, but on the other, all the property of these public technology councils is owned by the state and they operate under the same rules as the state enterprises (Young Communist League, Central Committee, 1986). The system for making and distributing contributions is under the auspices of the chairman of the State Committee for Science and Technology.

These public councils, however, serve as an illustration of one of the first partnerships between government and the private sector that are now widespread in the Soviet Union. They emerged out of a necessity to meet the demands of an awakening activity of a civil society, but they were formally created by governmental authorities at the state level, through the Communist party, or through an established "mass public organization," such as trade unions. The goal was to keep these activities under control. Nevertheless, these public councils have been allowed to include some young "new thinkers" who have convinced the councils to support financially some very sound ideas. The ideas may come from a purely informal voluntary group that would otherwise not have received any recognition or funding, or they may come from individual inventors whose ideas were not accepted at their regular place of employment.

The Youth Housing Complex is another example of this quasi-governmental and private structure. It illustrates a method used by government authorities to solve social problems in cases where the state was ineffective and tried to give more responsibility to citizens, that is, to allow the very people who sorely needed this service to develop it voluntarily. The idea of the state authorities was as follows: to have young people who were in urgent need of housing work on the construction of housing themselves. Thus, volunteers could join together and form a public organization to build a housing complex. Most of the young people who supported this idea already had their own families but very limited living space, were still living with their parents, or had been on a waiting list for years for new state housing. The materials for the construction of the complex represented the combined resources of the enterprises in which the team worked.

Initiators were supported because there was deep dissatisfaction with regular state housing (presently just a place to sleep) and a strong demand for at least a model of a suitable living space that provides everything important for a comfortable life in harmony with art, exercise, and nature. This idea came not only from those who were in a hopeless situation in terms of housing, but also from sociologists, philosophers, economists, architects, and teachers, who brought the Youth Housing Complex rather wide recognition.

As the youth teams planned numerous special facilities for art, culture, technology, and other forms of voluntary activity, especially experimental teaching and training for children, many volunteers rushed to join the teams, which provided a real "island" for various activities of the independent sector.

The housing complex movement immediately spread to 170 cities and now encompasses more than 200 cities. However, the legislative base, set up through decisions of the Council of Ministers between 1987 and 1988, failed to define the question of ownership of the physical facilities. Because of the vagueness of the legislation, only those who were able to register Youth Housing Complex teams as separate legal bodies—namely "voluntary societies" according to the only existing legislation at that time (the law of 1932)—have survived as independent islands of voluntary activism. About thirty of these existing complexes are strong enough to support voluntary action in their domain. At the last conference of the Youth Housing Complex, representatives proclaimed that the aim of the movement was to strengthen independent structures for civil society (Conference of the Youth Housing Complex, 1988).

Another example of the quasi-governmental, independent structure in the economic sphere is the Youth Centers Are Komsomol Enterprises. This program supports productive venture structures with a wide variety of business applications, ranging from the sponsorship of disco concerts and studios to the development of instruction videos on how to produce heavy machinery. Even though this program supports the creation of goods and services for profit, its activity is assumed to be "needed by youth." So far, its activities are totally tax exempt. The program became possible in 1988, through a special decision of the Council of Ministers, when the Komsomol gained the right to start its own business activities through specially created structures called youth center enterprises. These enterprises are tax exempt because the Komsomol is a mass public organization, according to the Soviet constitution, and everything it does is automatically assumed to be related to charity. Although youth centers do not receive or distribute state funds or planned material resources, they still represent an attempt to maintain ideological control. The authorities' intention is to bring young people closer to the Komsomol by providing them with a much easier opportunity, through tax-exempt enterprise, to try their hand at being entrepreneurs.

The youth centers enjoy full legal status, although the territorial Komsomol committee has to be one of their sponsors. They have the right to sell and buy, to create and produce, to have credit in banks and invest money in joint ventures, to participate directly in foreign relations, and to market their goods and services to state organizations and citizens.

Because of their exclusive status, youth center enterprises spread throughout the entire country within a year. In this short time, more than 4,000 centers were created, with a total economic activity of 3.5 billion rubles circulating in bank accounts; they provide 150 types of goods and services, ranging from sewing children's clothing to building hospitals and fishing on center-owned ships. However, the significance of the centers is not the amount of their profits but rather that they reinvest these profits back into the social programs. The main purposes of the centers are social, ecological, and educational in nature. They sponsor and supply equipment for cultural activities, sports, and the other voluntary and amateur activities. They also provide services for citizens more effectively than the state does and are much cheaper than cooperatives. The centers also make direct donations to charity. The Iskra Center in Moscow contributes 5 percent of its income (30,000 rubles) to charity. While this is not a very large sum, the aggregate donation of 4,000 centers is 120 million rubles. In terms of charity this is a significant amount indeed. The only problem is that the centers do not legally own what they produce. Everything belongs to the Komsomol, which can meddle at will and also change the legal status of the centers (Youth Housing Complex Department, 1989).

Another form of organization with less state control is the cooperative. This new productive structure is in fact, economically independent. Members of co-ops, according to the new law on cooperatives, *own* their property. They are allowed to earn money and divide the profits, and they are not subject to any governmental authority other than the financial inspector. Rather, co-ops are managed by their own council. However, fearing that these cooperatives may become too successful and thus compete with state enterprises, co-ops had their taxes increased by 60 percent in trade cooperation. Furthermore, the government charges co-ops three times as much as it charges state enterprises for equipment, transportation, and gasoline.

The official government press launched a campaign against cooperatives, blaming them for the shortages and corruption in the nation and succeeded in turning public opinion against them, in spite of the fact that this "corrupted" cooperative sector represents only about one percent of the national economy and could hardly be responsible for corrupting the whole society (personal interview with Alexander Gerasimneko, 1989). Many different kinds of people participate in cooperatives, but few of them initially joined the movement for the sole purpose of making a profit. Many of the first cooperatives used their money to avoid the endless bureaucracy of state-controlled charity to help those in need directly. For instance, the family of Antonina and Mikle Valfkovitch and their seven children — Catholics living in Moscow — founded a co-op, the House of Charity, which cares for lonely elderly people. This whole family works devotedly with the help of a team of volunteers. They currently are saving the money they make from creating and selling copies of folk art (Mikle is an artist) to reconstruct a building they own in the Dzerginsky district of Moscow to offer their "clients" better living conditions. In another example, Victor Lizunkov, who lost hope of receiving government aid, helped himself by making prostheses, for he was without both legs. Willing to share his experience, he founded the co-op Inva-Teknika ("invalid" or "disabled"), where only disabled persons are employed in making prostheses and providing other means of assistance for those who are completely paralyzed. Inva-Teknika takes in everyone who wants to return to an active life. A third example involves people who feel obligated to help those who have less, such as the members of the co-op Vasilok in the Sverdlovsky district in Moscow. This organization makes free lunches for 250 families in that district. The Moscow cooperatives Farhad and Slastena do the same type of thing, as do cooperatives in Leningrad, Irkutsk, Odessa, and other cities. There could be many more such co-ops providing programs like these if the state would recognize the importance of encouraging cooperatives to engage in charitable giving by offering them tax-exempt status. However, the state does not appreciate the growth of independent services, and co-ops must pay a 40 to 60 percent tax on their total income regardless of how they spend it (Ivanova, 1989).

This brief description shows the evolving process of the formation of voluntary organizations and charitable efforts in the economic sector. The main result of these seminal organizational efforts has been to build an independent economic resource base for the independent sector in the Soviet Union. Thus far these efforts have not been very significant because of legal limitations and financial disincentives. Activity to build independent resources in the entire economic sector represents no more than 5 percent of the national economy.

The Independent Sector and Political Action

The political sector is another exception to the usual Western model in which the independent sector is separate from politics and political issues. There are again, however, at least two reasons to include the political sector in this analysis. First, during the present period of major social change, political restructuring, and changes in political power and institutional relations, every form of organized voluntary activity becomes politically significant. For example, ecologists who advocate professional expertise on a construction project approved by the authorities are arrested as "political radicals" for violating existing laws against demonstrations. Even though such individuals did not intend to be even remotely political, they are often treated in this way by the authorities. These advocates become somewhat politically oriented after they experience a few arrests, although it was not their original intention to join together in such efforts.

Second, after state and party monopolies were broken and the enforced "Unity of Soviet People" was no longer imposed, different groups in society suddenly recognized their social and cultural differences as well as personalities — their different needs and interests. Since the traditional divisions of "working class," "peasants," and "intelligentsia" do not function any more, completely new social forces are now coming into existence through the independent sector's structures. Inevitably, they are participating in the political reshaping of the country.

What follows is a description of the kinds of groups that have been formed to advocate the interests of different groups and organizations within the society. The array of these various organizations provides a picture of the society's needs within this new sociopolitical movement.

Councils for territorial self-government and electors' clubs are a new group of voluntary organizations that represent a sociopolitical movement that came into being during the election campaign of 1989, when the citizens groups within various territories worked together to organize meetings to nominate and support their candidates. These neighborhood groups are concerned with solving practical issues of the urban environment and local self-government, which they intend to accomplish by getting public control of their neighborhood through local elections. During the 1989 elections, this movement involved approximately 300,000 participants in Moscow and 100,000 in Leningrad. During the election campaign for local and republican People's Councils (Soviets) in 1990, they became even more numerous. In December 1989, electors' clubs existed in every one of the thirty-three districts in Moscow; the Moscow Union of Electors, created in the summer of 1989, now has more than 1,000 members and even more supporters. Such unions, like the one in Moscow, are being created throughout the country. These unions are forming "blocks for democratic candidates" and involve participants and enjoy support from voluntary groups of all types, including cultural, environmental, artistic, and educational organizations. For example, the Democratic Russia block, formed during the 1990 elections, was joined by the Memorial Historical and Cultural Society, a writers' association known as April, and the Socio-Ecological Union, among other voluntary organizations. Political activity is not the main goal for self-government committees and electors' clubs. They usually do not nominate political candidates but instead support those candidates who are more oriented toward solving local neighborhood problems. Most of their efforts are directed to organizing citizens and politically educating them (Interlegal Research Center, 1990).

Another set of organizations — people's fronts — were the first really popular public movements that began in Estonia in 1987 and spread quickly throughout the Baltic states and other regions of the country. In the nationally united and better developed Baltic republics, the leaders of the people's fronts were elected to the highest legislative organs of the republics and to the Supreme Soviet of the USSR. The people's fronts managed to win elections through the efforts of support groups organized by volunteers in almost every enterprise and rural community. Together, they built a strong movement, united by the idea of democratization, building a national renaissance and fighting the state and party bureaucracy. This process transformed the people's fronts within a year from centers of political information and education to formal representatives of people's power. Controlling the situation within the republics, the people's fronts continued to support all sorts of creative activity. For example, in Estonia they helped to found Russian and Jewish cultural centers in Tallin, to organize a festival of national minorities in Estonia, to promote historical and cultural research, and to found a movement to reconstruct old villages and castles. In Lithuania these public movements are very much concerned with the environment, national culture, education, and the support of national artists' unions, including a photographic art voluntary society.

Organizations similar to the People's Front of the Popular Block of All Democratic Forces in the Baltic states are more or less visible now in nearly every town throughout the country, although they are not as strong, organized, or influential as those in the Baltic states. The largest of such movements are the Ukrainian movement RUKH, with 250,000 supporters, and the Birlick movement in Uzbekistan, which has approximately 400,000 members, including the affiliated youth organizations. The People's Front of Russia unites representatives of forty-five cities and the Far-East Association of Democratic Movements. In October 1989, there was an attempt to unite all existing organizations of this type into one structure at a meeting in Chelyabinsk (Siberia), but the participants preferred to exist as independent bodies, although they support each others' actions through networking (Interlegal Research Center, 1990).

The final type of public association on the list of voluntary bodies within the political sphere is the newly formed protoparty structure indirectly related to the independent sector as a form of voluntary action. The major roles of these quasi-organizations is to develop structures needed in a civil society, rather than encouraging in the direct political activity. This protoparty structure is at a preliminary stage preceding the formation of a real political party. Some organizing work has been completed and some political agendas have been prepared that are necessary if individuals are to understand their interests, articulate them, and join together with others who share similar political views. These associations are not formal structures with required membership or any other obligations to the participant but represent identification with certain ideas and goals as well as the necessary means of achieving them.

While Soviet society has started moving gradually toward a multiparty system, more than a dozen associations call themselves political parties, though they are far from being sufficiently organized or influential. Those associations that deserve mention are the Social-Democratic Association, the Christian-Democratic movement, the Democratic Platform block within the Communist party, and the Democratic party of Russia. It is clear that these organizations are very involved politically and therefore should not be included in the traditional context of an independent sector. However, with the exceptional revolutionary changes taking place in the Soviet Union, many organizations that would not normally be politically active are engaged in these new civic and proto-political movements.

Another reason for describing these organizations is to note the changing image of a political activist. No longer does the mention of political activists conjure up the image of small groups of "dissidents" living within their own circles and regarded by the public as being "dangerous" even to speak to. Nor are they considered part of an informal activist association, closer to the average citizenry and engaged in expressing their needs and working to gain some public support. Rather, current activists are regarded as part of the public itself. The person who goes to a local election club and supports the popular front is an ordinary Soviet citizen who cares about his family and his job. Thus, monitoring this emerging political process is important to the development of an independent sector: average citizens are beginning to feel responsibility for the future development of the country. The most important effects that such independent groups can have on the ability of society to engage in self-organization lie in teaching people how to organize, how to stop feeling fear, and how to work in coordination with other groups toward common goals.

Independence Versus Ideology: Free Press

In the Soviet Union, the government sector has responsibility for declaring what political, philosophical, and social ideologies are acceptable. While individuals have the right to choose ideology or a system of belief, that choice should be made on the basis of information about diverse views, beliefs, and facts. The goal of independent sector organizations is to dismantle the requirement of a centrally imposed ideology that pervades all areas of social and political thought through the establishment of a free press and the establishment of information services.

Over the past few years more than ten independent regional information agencies have been established in Lithuania, Estonia, Armenia, Georgia, and Siberia. These agencies have correspondents in more than thirty cities. They issue the press bulletin *Northern Telegraph* in Leningrad (IMA Press). The Moscow Bureau of Information Exchange issues the paper *Panorama,* and press releases are based on the local and capital information (*samizdat*) service of the *Daily News.* Other strong and influential agencies are *Glasnost,* which publishes daily news and even video materials, and *Express-Khronica,* which has its own correspondents in every region of the country and no fewer than thirty staff journalists. A more impressive example is the Post Factum information agency that has more than one hundred staff employees spreading a network of correspondents to sixty cities around the country and producing news releases three times a day. This agency is also famous for its serious analytical reviews, covering domestic, political, and economic affairs. There are also two religious information centers, the Christian Information Center and the Bulletin for Christian Public Activity. Among their more than 800 publications, 75 percent are politically oriented, 10 percent are religious and philosophic, and 15 percent concern themselves with literature and art. A special bulletin, "Independent Bibliograg," prepares an overview of press stories from voluntary groups on a regular basis.

Although a new law was passed in the Soviet Union providing for freedom of the press, this law is already under pressure by President Gorbachev himself, who is demanding more restrictions on the press to make it more "objective." Such pressure, however, does not prevent people from writing, producing, or selling papers created by voluntary groups. They are sold directly in the street or sent to the subscriber at his or her address. The sellers do indeed take risks, but such risks do not keep them from continuing their work.

Clearly, the authorities have very little power in this sphere. Once one has started thinking independently, one cannot stop until one is dead. It was Gorbachev who called for independent thinking and citizen participation. The results of this process are both wonderful and dramatic: people do not believe myths anymore even if a reporter produces them. They want to hear the arguments and the real facts so that they can make judgments for themselves. The effect of a free press is vital for an independent sector because independent thinking is what produces independent action.

Traditional Charities, Amateur Clubs, and Religious Organizations

There are three other institutions that must be mentioned in this chapter because they are the traditional parts of the independent sector in other countries: charities, amateur creative clubs, and religious organizations. Just as these organizations exist in some form in most societies, so also were they to be found in the Soviet Union before the onset of *perestroika*. However, since *perestroika* many changes and much restructuring have occurred among them.

In summary, after five years of rapid change, it is clear that not even the most stable and traditional organizations could escape the turmoil and change going on about them. *Perestroika* exposed all of the hidden contradictions in many organizations, making clear the differences that existed within them between the old and the new, between the real and the artificial, between being self-sufficient and being totally dependent, and between charitable means and selfish means. The following examples demonstrate this diversity.

Formal or registered charity is closely associated in the West with the word *foundation*. However, a foundation as a specific entity does not have any formal description in Soviet legislation, though in practice the word is used more and more widely for most officially established organizations such as the Foundation for the Survival and Development of Humanity, the Foundation for Social Innovations, and the Charity and Health Foundation, all of which came into being through individual decisions of the USSR Council of Ministers. As a synonym for *foundation,* the word *fund* is used even more frequently for both entities established by the Council of Ministers, such as the Peace Fund, the Children's Fund, and the Cultural Fund, and for voluntarily created bodies, such as the Andrei Sakharov Fund, the Deputies Initiatives Fund, the Democratic Russia Fund, and hundreds of local funds that work basically like community foundations or public charities in the West.

Since *perestroika* began, lawyers have been debating the new legislation concerning public associations in order to establish certain provisions that make distinctions among different types of associations, especially foundations, because of their special tax status. However, the law that was finally passed by the Supreme Soviet of the USSR on October 9, 1990, does not give any recognition to specific legal features or distinctions of foundations. In fact, the new law put foundations, voluntary groups, movements, and political parties under one provision. Thus, Article No. 1 — the concept of public associations (The Law of the Public Association) in Chapter 1 — General Provisions, states: "Public associations shall include political parties, mass movements, and trade unions; women's and veteran's organizations, organizations of the disabled, organizations set up by youth and children; scientific, technological, cultural, educational, sports, health, and other voluntary societies, artistic unions, fraternities, funds and other public associations." This is how funds are mentioned, assuming the foundations are included, in order to give them at least general legal recognition.

Article 11 states that the registration of the statutes of public associations shall be carried out by the USSR Ministry of Justice (and for those active only within one republic, by the organ, assigned by the Republican legislation).

Concerning the taxation of the association, Article 17 states: "Enterprises and organizations that set up public associations shall make payments to the budget in the amount and manner determined by Law." In other words, associations have some form of taxes to pay.

There is no exact norm in this new law, only a reference to the tax law that is also very vague. The tax law states that economic activity of charitable funds is tax free whatever they do, but again it gives no definition of what a charitable fund is. Rather, a few examples of what are deemed charitable funds are provided: the Children's Fund, the Cultural Fund, the Charity and Health Fund, and others.

In practice, though, many financial organizations will not

agree to give tax benefits to any foundations not directly named in the tax law. Charitable gifts are also taken into account for tax-deduction purposes only if they are given to the five foundations established directly through administrative edict. If financial officials decide each case "individually," a good deal of room is left for governing authorities to express their personal preferences or disregard certain charities they do not like. Such decisions without definitive legislation can lead to favoritism and corrupt practices.

Among those who give to the "official funds," very few know that besides the Charter, which delineates the purposes of the fund, is widely circulated and publicized, the Council of Ministers has made special decisions concerning the administration of some of these funds. For example, special council decisions can relate administrative hierarchy of a fund to the powers of the administrative head and staff. Such decisions are made individually but often include the right of the chairman and vice chairman of a fund to use the offices of government, such as the Kremlin and special privileges at grocery stores (given to government employees), for their private purposes, and the right of the staff of the foundation to travel abroad without having their baggage searched by customs officials. Such special privileges do not improve the image of the "official charity."

There are also informal charities that have no professionally copied color brochures about their activities. The group of Andrei Verbitsky is one example. Verbitsky is a scientist and doctor who has gathered a team of about twenty young people who care for the disabled and families with difficult home lives in which alcohol abuse plays a large role. The young workers put in their time at hospitals and children's homes. They do this every day in Moscow. Similar teams exist in almost every city, but these groups are not included in the official system of health and charity.

Amateur creative clubs are examples of the simplest type of associations. Here people come together to share hobbies or other mutual interests, such as nature exploration, bird watching, or cultural activities. These clubs have been in existence at the grass-roots level since the Soviet state was founded. They were not required to register until 1986, when they were allowed to gain the status of a legal body through the decision of their sponsor, who was then supposed to control their activity. However, according to the same act, they could also be given only limited status if the sponsor preferred to remain the owner of all the property or materials needed to perform their activities. Finally, most of the clubs were simply registered on behalf of their sponsors with no status at all, but many of their members were happy for any kind of official recognition. Although their sponsors were industrial enterprises or factories, after registration, the clubs were included within the statistics of the trade unions. In 1986 there were an estimated 30,000 clubs. However, when it became possible to engage in independent business and own property, many of these clubs were no longer satisfied with their status. Those clubs that were creative and energetic wanted to be freed of the control of their sponsors and began demanding more economic rights. After two years of bargaining with the Ministry of Culture, under whose auspices this system was regulated, a new structure was created. The All-Union Methodological Center for People's Creativity and Culturally Enlightening Work of the Ministry of the USSR organized thirteen all-union associations of special-interest clubs, such as those dealing with cats, fish, birds, flowers, and so on. The methodological center opened several bank accounts for these united associations and helped them to organize. These thirteen associations contain 500 voluntary clubs, with 35,000 members. The total membership in all voluntary clubs is estimated at ten million (Trade Union Cultural Commission, 1987).

There are also property-holding, self-sufficient, and productive artists' associations that may combine in one organization the creation, production, performance, marketing, and even teaching and studying of art. One example is the artistic studio Sokoloniky, which began as an ordinarry literature club but now has wonderful facilities for additional workshops on theater, music, literature, poetry, ceramics, and precious stones. Within the Sokoloniky structure, there is space for those who want to study literature, poetry, and music and a club for professional writers. While the studio does not produce consumer goods, it makes an annual profit of about 300,000 rubles. The same types of cultural, self-sufficient enterprises now exist in Tallin, Naberezhnye, Chelny, Odessa, Tbilisi, and many other cities (personal interview with Anatoly Ribakov, 1989).

Research is needed on the growth and change in religious movements in the Soviet Union, particularly as they relate to the changing leadership in the ruling hierarchies in the various church structures. For example, it should be interesting to study whether new democratic movements influence the dogma and practices of the Russian Orthodox church. One trend that is discernible in the religious community is that the structure of the Russian Orthodox church is divided into those who are members of upper circles in the presidium — who hold property, have the power, and make the decisions — and followers who must obey, even if they have no trust in their official leaders. Though the belief in one God is supposed to bring people together, recent democratization and the movement toward pluralism have clearly exposed the political differences within the Russian Orthodox church.

For example, the recently formed voluntary religious movement "Believers in Perestroika," headed by Gleb Yakunin, accuses the official leaders of the Russian Orthodox church of corruption and close contacts with the KGB, especially during the period of stagnation, when the appointment of priests to the churches was heavily controlled by government authorities. Although it is difficult to produce real evidence now, it is difficult to explain why these Russian Orthodox leaders did not support Yakunin when he was pursued and imprisoned by authorities for the open expression of his Christian beliefs. These same leaders informed neighborhood groups who had nominated Christian People's monks as candidates to various levels of government that monks are now allowed to accept a nomination directly from their neighborhood or voluntary movement without the blessing of church authorities. Furthermore, the appeals printed and distributed by religious activists for the citizens and deputies in support of the right of religious people to return to their churches were signed by deputies of the Supreme Soviet, independent religous agencies, scientists, artists, and journalists but not by any of the official Russian Orthodox church leaders. These incidents reveal a serious split within the Russian Orthodox religious community and the emergence of new democratic forces within this community that also seek to be an independent sector within their own sphere.

Conclusions

The independent sector in the USSR is forming not as a separate, third sector apart from government and business but as a functional part of the economic, political, and ideological spheres of societal life to oppose the monopoly of the administrative system. The emergence of this sector calls for and gives new opportunities to the formerly suppressed forces of creativity and activism that are so important in the restructuring of society.

In the political, ideological, and cultural spheres, the significance of innovative ideas and their influence on public opinion is very strong; this is not the case in the economic sector, however, where the state-planned and still state-controlled monopoly continues to hold more than 95 percent of funds and resources. This means that initiatives have very limited possibilities for independent funding.

In no sector of Soviet life do the legal conditions concerning the "independent zone" meet the needs of society. In many cases the new legislation is so contradictory that it limits or even prevents the natural development of voluntary activism. On the other hand, society itself is not always ready to accept the responsibility for self-sufficiency, since most people have had no experience in individual freedom. There is also a great lack of trained leaders and qualified organizations.

Therefore, the most important step that needs to be taken to improve this situation is the drafting and introduction of new legislation to provide for and regulate an independent or nonprofit sector. This legislation should draw upon the experience of other countries with well-developed sectors. Second, direct contact among volunteer organizations, movements, researchers, and sponsors of independent activities in other nations needs to be established and expanded for the exchange of experiences and improved education and training. Only through such continued and concentrated cooperation with the independent sectors of other countries can real improvement be made in this sphere in the Soviet Union.

References

Interlegal Research Center. Information estimated through monitoring the electoral campaign, Moscow, 1990.

Ivanova, O. Information about charitable activities of the cooperatives collected and analyzed, 1989.

Sverdlosk. Unpublished materials from the Conference of Youth Housing Complex Organizations, 1988.

Trade Union Cultural Commission. *Report to the Central Committee Plenary Meeting.* 1987.

Young Communist League, Central Committee. *The Statute of the Councils for the Scientific and Technical Creativity of Youth.* 1986.

Young Communist League, Central Committee. *The Economic Report of the Youth Housing Complex Department to its Central Committee Plenary Meeting.* 1989.

Deborah A. Brody
Elizabeth T. Boris

Chapter 21

Philanthropy and Charity
in the Soviet Union

In the United States, we often differentiate charity from philanthropy. Charity denotes administering aid to the needy, treating a symptom rather than a cause; a synonym for charity is mercy. Philanthropy is different. It denotes a general "love of humankind" coupled with the desire and means to improve systematically the condition of humanity by treating causes, sometimes at the expense of symptoms.

In the Soviet Union, this distinction between the two concepts is just beginning to be understood. In fact, through the first three decades of the Soviet Union's existence, the word *charity* was not included in any Soviet dictionaries or encyclopedias, yet *charity* was listed as a synonym for *philanthropy*. Beginning in 1950, a definition for charity was derived: "Aid hypocritically rendered by representatives of the ruling class in an exploiter society to a part of the poor population in order to deceive the workers and divert them from the class struggle" (Tretyakov, 1989). Even as recently as 1987 Soviet officials asserted that the concept of charity was alien to the socialist system and did not exist. Yet visitors to the Soviet Union testify to the generous nature of the people and their strong sense of community and altruism. We know that a multitude of voluntary organizations exist and are flourishing in the Soviet Union, but these groups have not been counted and categorized in any systematic way. How, then, can the Soviet state come to terms with the widespread giving traditions and tenacious philanthropic organizations that have existed throughout the Soviet Union's history and those that are currently proliferating?

Part of the answer lies in the forms of these organizations and traditions and in the interpretation of their function in society. The modern "Western" notion of philanthropy that has made inroads into Soviet society in recent years has surely helped with this process as has the fact that human need defies ideology. And while bettering humankind seems infinitely more acceptable than giving alms, the helping traditions that have existed throughout Russian (and Soviet) history, be they almsgiving, charity, philanthropy, or generosity, have existed as much under socialism as they did under tsarism.

A long-standing Russian tradition of distrust toward government and a compassion for the less fortunate is most evident in Russian peasant society, where a strong tradition of mutual aid developed and has endured. Importantly, this is not help administered by a landowner to a laborer but among people of equal status, where one person's situation has dropped below that of the others (often due to illness or natural disaster). Here the community's goal is to help restore the unfortunates to their original condition. Known as *pomoch*, this aid is based on shared labor. "Pomoch is a tradition which is complex in structure. It involved peasants working together for no charge in order to complete a particular stage of urgent work for an individual household" (Tretyakov, 1989). This mutual aid assumes that those in need are willing to work but are temporarily unable.

By the same token, there seems to be a traditional abhorrence toward the indigent. For example, Peter the Great fined anyone giving money to beggars and ordered the indigents to reside in stark hospitals and almshouses. Beggars were an embarrassment to be cleared from the streets (Massie, 1980). This is much the same today. Mendicants are not evident in Soviet cities, but rumors of mental institutions and hospitals for the indigent abound.

The socialist revolution brought to fruition the idea that every person — regardless of abilities or contributions to society — is entitled to a minimum standard of living. In a just society, there are no beggars. While beggars may have been eradicated in the Soviet Union, clearly there is inequality as well as needs that are not met by the state. Thus, throughout the twentieth century, philanthropy has been practiced as well as preached in the USSR. Even Vladimir Lenin advocated mutual aid. In a letter dated 1921 he wrote, "It is absolutely essential to promote 'mutual aid' both among the members of the same class and among the toilers of other classes" (Tretyakov, 1989).

Although there is little documentation about the unmet needs of Soviet citizens and subsequent philanthropic activities, Vitali Tretyakov, the deputy editor of the *Moscow News,* has written the only comprehensive document available on this topic. In *Philanthropy in Soviet Society,* Tretyakov estimates that 7 or 8 percent of the Soviet Union's population of 285 million are in "risk groups." These groups include the following:

- People who receive wages that are too low to ensure them the basic necessities
- Large families
- Young couples (especially students) whose parents do not support them
- People who have lived in hostels (except students) or shared flats for a long time
- Large families that occupy small apartments
- Single or low-income old-age pensioners

- Elderly people who live in villages whose inhabitants leave to seek jobs and residences in towns and cities
- Elderly people who are lonely and sick and incapable of looking after themselves
- Single mothers whose former husbands (or the unregistered fathers of their children) do not earn enough to support their children
- People with handicaps
- Young orphans
- Certain categories of migrant workers and their families
- Students from low-income families who are attending college far away from home
- Alcoholics and drug addicts
- Vagabonds and bums who tend to live in one specific region and survive by doing odd jobs
- Ex-convicts who have not become habitual offenders but are not ready to return to a normal life

Tretyakov also mentioned one new group, bureaucrats, who as a result of the massive restructuring of the Soviet government no longer have work.

Just as there have always been needy in the Soviet Union and elsewhere, there has always been philanthropy, often in the form of donated labor. Philanthropic activities and organizations have existed throughout the history of the Soviet state and have blossomed under *perestroika*. As Tretyakov states, "human altruism is indestructible and will always manifest itself."

Postrevolution forms of socialist charity reflected the earlier philanthropic traditions of prerevolutionary Russia, particularly pomoch. For example, communist *subbotniks* — people who worked for no pay on Saturdays or Sundays to help the young Soviet state revive its industry — were first initiated in 1919. Workers worked for no pay on Saturdays or Sundays to help the young Soviet state revive its industry. A month after the first subbotnik, a mass subbotnik was held on the Moscow railway. Over time, subbotniks have become a popular way to perform community service. Since 1919, they have been held both locally and nationally in the Soviet Union. The money that the workers would have earned is applied to meeting social needs such as support for orphanages and nursing homes.

Another significant example of voluntarism in the Soviet Union is the literacy campaign of the 1920s and 1930s. The majority of the literate Soviet population donated its time and energies to teaching illiterate Soviets to read. The volunteers formed a society called Away with Illiteracy to raise funds to help the state finance this campaign. And, indeed, this literacy movement is one of the remarkable accomplishments of the Soviet regime. In fewer than fifty years, an 80 percent illiterate population reversed these figures and is estimated now to be 80 percent literate.

Thus, throughout the early years of the Soviet Union, numerous voluntary efforts to combat economic and social problems were mounted. This was compatible with the new socialist system as efforts were aimed at eradicating the unjust residue of the former capitalist state (Tretyakov, 1989).

After World War II, the Soviet Peace Fund was established to collect money from the public for national defense. The Peace Fund has succeeded in raising huge amounts of rubles that have been used in part for Soviet defense and in part to bolster the image and cause of Soviet communism throughout the world.

Tretyakov divides socialist philanthropy into four categories: (1) state and social philanthropy, a system of state and social programs financed from the national budget but carried out by public organizations, such as trade associations; (2) public philanthropy, programs backed by the state and carried out by foundations, associations, and societies set up by the state; (3) a combination of public and private charity, voluntary organizations set up by the people to meet a need that the government is not adequately meeting and that later earn approval and accolades from the state; and (4) private philanthropy, activities totally initiated and funded by private citizens.

Tretyakov lists and describes several official Soviet philanthropies (or what we would call traditional charities) that were formed well before the advent of *perestroika*. These include the Alliance of the Red Cross and Red Crescent Societies of the

USSR, the Soviet Peace Fund, the All-Russia Society for Protection of Historical and Cultural Sites, the Soviet Cultural Foundation, the All-Russia Society of the Deaf, and the All-Russia Society of the Blind.

Moreover, throughout the history of the Soviet regime, especially during the darkest days of Stalinist repression, a whole cadre of underground voluntary organizations developed. These organizations existed for a variety of purposes: to circulate and discuss forbidden literature, perpetuate religious practices, protect fugitives, or even to funnel foreign currency and goods through the black market.

The *perestroika* breed of philanthropy includes organizations of all shapes, sizes, and forms. Philanthropies once considered renegade by the system are now officially sanctioned as a result of *perestroika*. These include the Lenin Soviet Children's Fund, the All-Russia Society of the Handicapped, and the Foundation for Social Innovations. Although many use the word *foundation,* they bear very little resemblance to private foundations in the United States. U.S. private foundations rely on accumulated wealth and are designed to exist in perpetuity, spending only the income earned from investing their capital. They are generally endowed by an individual, a family, or a corporation.

In contrast, Soviet foundations are started with many small contributions from different Soviet citizens. With an estimated 400 billion rubles earning very low interest (about 2 percent) in Soviet banks, fund raising is the least of the problems faced by these organizations. Similar to "public" foundations, which are defined by the Council on Foundations as those that raise the funds they distribute from a variety of sources rather than exclusively from one, they spend with one hand what they raise with the other. Some money is also beginning to flow from the new "cooperatives" (comparable to employee-owned companies in the United States) that can realize significant tax advantages by contributing to charities under newly developed laws. Like many U.S. corporations, they are also finding it in their self-interest to be involved with their communities.

Most Soviet foundations are small and devoted to a specific purpose; however, a few, with millions of rubles, fund a wide array of projects. No clear regulatory framework governs these organizations yet, but efforts are underway to provide guidance in this arena. Most notably, in 1989 an international seminar on foundations was held in Moscow to discuss the role of foundations in the development of a civil society. Convened by the Foundation for Social Innovations and cosponsored by the Rockefeller Brothers Fund, this conference brought together experts from Australia, Canada, the Netherlands, the United States, and the Soviet Union.

The group developed "principles and core concepts" that should govern foundations in a civil society. This work could be the beginning of a legal framework for Soviet philanthropies. For now, however, each foundation is established by a special decree from the Central Committee or the Council of Ministers. According to one Soviet foundation officer, this is equivalent to our requiring an act of Congress for each foundation formed in the United States (Kidder, 1989).

No standard spending or public reporting requirements exist, and organizational forms vary greatly among philanthropies in the Soviet Union. Most importantly, there are no clear distinctions in two critical areas: (1) there is no delineation between the funding of social causes versus political ones, and (2) there are no restrictions on how money can be raised and dispensed. An example of the blurring between charitable and profit-making activities is evident in the plans of a group called Chelovek (meaning "man"). Based in Leningrad, this group plans to build and operate a hotel, an ice-cream factory, a limousine service, and numerous other ventures to raise money to provide food, medicine, and machinery to invalids. In the United States this type of arrangement could violate the fine line between business and philanthropic interests (for example, competition with business and private benefits to the organizers of the charity). Finally, it is common for grass-roots organizations in the republics (such as Sajudis in Lithuania) to fund the very political causes that are undermining the stability of the USSR.

Rushworth Kidder, in a *Christian Science Monitor* article, asserts that most Soviet foundation officials believe that a few important developments have allowed their organizations to flourish: the economic crises, which caused the government to look toward private solutions to public problems, the new openness to foreign (particularly American) models of organization and capitalism; growing official interest in individual initiative; and willingness to discuss and reassess the past. Moreover, he likens the philanthropic situation in the Soviet Union to "primordial soup" in which foundations, informal social-action groups, new political movements, private enterprises, and government entities are swirling about in relatively undifferentiated states (Kidder, 1989).

Three of the largest foundations in the Soviet Union are the International Foundation for the Survival and Development of Humanity, the Foundation for Social Innovations, and the Soros Foundation–Soviet Union (also called the Cultural Initiative). Of these three, the Soros Foundation is most similar to a U.S. grant-making organization and is considered a private organization by both U.S. and Soviet standards. Founded in 1987 by Hungarian-born American millionaire George Soros, the foundation has offices and staff in New York, Budapest, Moscow, and until recently, China. Its grant making focuses on legal studies, social sciences, ecology, libraries, museums, and archives, among other things. In 1988 the Soros Foundation received 4,000 proposals, 100 of which were funded. Soros Foundation staff members said in interviews that they are committed to fostering creativity and economic opportunity in the USSR and that both the American and Soviet staff compare their work to that of surgeons, "replanting social tissue from the West."

The International Foundation for the Survival and Development of Humanity was formed and operates internationally, with offices in Moscow, San Francisco, Washington, D.C., and Sweden. Its board is made up of prestigious international leaders such as Yevgenii Velikov, Abus Salaam (Pakistani Nobel Prize winner in physics), Apple Computer chairman John Sculley, Metropolitan Petirim of the Russian Orthodox church, and UNESCO director general Frederico Mayor. The late Andrei Sakharov was also a member of the board. The foundation was initiated with a $1 million contribution from American industrialist Armand Hammer and several million rubles donated by the Soviet Peace Fund. The foundation raises funds in both dollars and rubles as one of its ongoing responsibilities. The money raised supports a variety of causes from environmental matters to arms control to health and education throughout the world. This foundation is also considered completely private, or "nongovernmental."

The Foundation for Social Innovations, founded in 1986 by Russian geophysicist Gennady Alferenko, in contrast, clearly has strong ties with the Communist party. The foundation operates under the auspices of *Komsomolskaya Pravda,* the youth version of the Communist party newspaper. Funds are raised in a highly creative way. Each week, Alferenko writes a column about a pressing social need and specifies a bank account number into which donations will be accepted for this cause. Donations pour in from interested people, and the foundation collects and then disburses these funds to applicants with innovative solutions to the problem. According to Lou Knowles, director of international programs at the Council on Foundations, the purpose of the Foundation for Social Innovations is to stimulate new directions, organizations, and institutions to deal with contemporary social problems (it is similar to the Soros Foundation in this regard).

Each of these foundations faces organizational difficulties. Each must make hard choices about what to fund. Although this is true for U.S. foundations as well, in the United States we have some guidelines and standards for funding and proposal writing. Even so, it is often still difficult to decide which endeavors to fund. In the Soviet Union, proposal writing and the notion of private funding are still new and developing concepts. As one foundation staff person said, "Every applicant wants a personal computer or a trip to the United States." Indeed, reminiscent of Peter the Great, there seems to be much emphasis on "looking to the West" for guidance and information. In Moscow and other parts of the Soviet Union, the members of the September 1989 Council on Foundations delegation met Soviets who were undeniably interested in adopting the ways of the West and in receiving American assistance on all fronts. Nonetheless, offers of assistance and advice were rejected by philanthropic leaders in the Republic of Armenia, who preferred to organize in their own way.

Added difficulties for Soviet foundations and other organizations stem from the lack of basic equipment such as computers and photocopy machines. Several visitors to the Soviet Union have noted the lack of basic management and meeting skills as well. However, in time-honored tradition, forming and participating in voluntary groups have proved excellent ways for Soviets to develop organizational skills. In fact, many of the Soviets most active in voluntary organizations are the same ones who are developing and managing cooperative businesses.

Some groups, particularly grass-roots groups in the republics, fund social as well as political causes. For example, a group called Charity in Armenia was formed by leaders of the Nagorno-Karabakh movement to regain control of the Nagorno-Karabakh region, historically a cultural center of Armenia but currently a part of neighboring republic Azerbaijan. The founders of this group engaged in a hunger fast to obtain registration by the central Soviet government. Once registered, the leaders of Charity were able to open a bank account and establish payroll deduction fund raising throughout Armenia. The group, while funding a variety of social causes ranging from suicide prevention to earthquake disaster relief, also funds Armenian political causes.

Thus, the deep roots of charity and philanthropy are quite evident in the Soviet Union today. While the religious traditions and the charity of noblesse oblige were systematically stamped out with the communist revolution, voluntarism and obligated giving were encouraged and required for such activities as the massive literacy campaign and establishment of the Peace Fund. The Red Cross and Red Crescent have operated undisturbed through this century, with official sanction and encouragement. The socialist regime has stressed the giving of labor rather than money (which is usually in short supply). Outside the system there exists a venerable tradition of dissent, both religious and political. Underground newspapers and well-developed informal networks have served to link activists and have become the dominant means for acquiring goods and services outside the official economy.

Given Russian history, the uncertainty of *perestroika* and *glasnost,* the unrest and ethnic passions of the various republics, and the deterioration of the economy, what are the prospects for the philanthropies that have arisen? They are undoubtedly useful to the regime as well as the society. Like U.S. foundations, they are working on issues too important to be ignored but too peripheral in an era of crisis for the government to address adequately. They are vehicles for cooperation nationally and internationally and bring expertise into the country. The foundations also serve to harness the energy and initiative of some of the most active citizens, who have the potential for making trouble in other arenas. Moreover, they put to good use idle rubles while attracting coveted foreign currency.

Despite its importance, organized philanthropy in the USSR rests on a fragile base. Some segments of the society are openly hostile toward this movement. These include bureaucrats who feel threatened by the movement's activities as well as some representatives from the official government charities who view groups in the movement as upstarts and rivals.

The legal status of the new institutions is tenuous; moreover, the potential for their undermining the interests of the state or succumbing to individual greed is omnipresent. In reality, they exist at the pleasure of the state, subject to the script of the unfolding political drama. Although the aims are philanthropic, everything in this rapidly changing social context is at the core deeply political. Encouraging citizens to undertake organized initiatives to improve their lot and that of their neighbors — outside of the context of the party and state — is no less than revolutionary for this society.

Another danger is high expectations, the hope that the voluntary sector can accomplish what the government could not. With all of the goodwill that has been generated, there is still a limited amount that these groups can do to alleviate the pressing problems of Soviet society. Most would agree that the government — albeit much more decentralized — must still meet the majority of social needs in the Soviet Union. It is not just a matter of resources but also of know-how. Observers have noted the lack of organizational skills and the need for technical assistance among the emerging philanthropic organizers. It will take time to develop the expertise and resources necessary to achieve a significant impact.

The success of the voluntary sector in the Soviet Union will depend on the ability of those involved to build on the traditions and idealism of the people, while providing some sense of progress and popular control. Although many are disillusioned with the socialist state, the Soviets remain idealistic and communitarian in many respects. They value literacy, educational opportunities for all, and extensive public transportation systems so that young, old, and poor are mobile. Most striking to Americans is the care and attention Soviets give to their children and the very low rate of violent crime, even in large cities.

The new Soviet philanthropic organizations are drawing upon the values and strengths of this society in their efforts to combat social ills. Whether they will have the opportunity to take root and the time to develop effective operations in the face of current social, political, and economic unrest remains to be seen.

A Partial List of Philanthropies in the USSR

Alliance of the Red Cross and Red Crescent Societies of the USSR

All-Russia Society for Protection of Historical and Cultural Sites

Bell Programme (a Soviet-British group to coordinate the efforts of charitable foundations)

Charity — Armenia

Charity and Health Foundation

Chelovek ("Man")

Children's Foundation

Foundation for Social Inventions

International Foundation for the Survival and Development of Humanity

Society of Charity

Soros Foundation–Soviet Union (Cultural Initiative)

Soviet Peace Fund

U.S.-Canada Institute (quasi-governmental; enlists scholars to study the United States and Canada)

Lithuania:　Greens (environmental)
Caritas
Lithuanian Women's Charitable Fund
Committee for Investigations of Crimes of
Stalinism
Sajudis (communist opposition group)

References

Kidder, R. "USSR Builds on New Foundations." *Christian Science Monitor,* Aug. 24, 1989.

Massie, R. K. *Peter the Great: His Life and His Works.* New York: Ballantine Books, 1980.

Tretyakov, V. *Philanthropy in Soviet Society.* Moscow: Novosti Press Agency, 1989.

Part Four

Developing Countries
Worldwide

Questions about giving, voluntarism, and the scope of nonprofit development thread their way through the chapters on the developing world in Part Four. Unlike the situations described in Western Europe, where discussions centered on the role of nonprofits as service providers as an extension of the state, many nonprofits in developing areas are heavily dependent on foreign funds. Moreover, organizations working in volatile areas such as human rights are often cast in an adversarial role with their host governments. Rather than providing public services in tandem with the state, many of these organizations are seeking to promote far-reaching social and economic reforms.

385

In Chapter Twenty-Two, Andrés A. Thompson examines the underlying reasons for the growth of Latin American voluntary sector activities in "Democracy and Development: The Role of Nongovernmental Organizations in Chile, Argentina, and Uruguay." Church groups, popular opposition to authoritarian regimes, and the contraction of state services all contributed to the growth of the region's nonprofits. Thompson suggests that there have been three "generations" of nonprofit development in the Southern Cone: traditional charities, many of which date from the first half of the twentieth century; opposition groups that arose under authoritarian rule; and an upsurge of social activist and development organizations with the return to democracy in the 1980s.

In Chapter Twenty-Three, "Indigenous Philanthropy in the Arab World: Contrasting Cases from Egypt and Palestine," Barbara Lethem Ibrahim discusses the fact that while Ottoman and English rule encouraged the development of nonprofit organizations in both areas, excessive governmental regulation discouraged the growth of Egyptian philanthropy after 1952. Conversely, political conflicts in the West Bank gave rise to new types of voluntary organizations and donors. Ibrahim explores these trends, as well as recent governmental efforts to encourage giving in Egypt and to discourage nonprofit activity on the West Bank.

In Chapter Twenty-Four, "Voluntarism in Rural Development in India: Initiative, Innovation, and Institutions," Anil K. Gupta explains that the roots of voluntarism are quite different in Eastern, especially Indian, societies, from those in Western societies. In addition to discussing a number of recent catalysts for volunteer activity in India, he critically examines the heavy dependence of many Indian nongovernmental organizations on foreign donors, their low accountability to the poor they seek to serve, and the need to draw the poor more fully into the development process.

Onny S. Prijono examines the nature of voluntarism and voluntary organizations in Indonesia in Chapter Twenty-Five, emphasizing some of the implications inherent in the shift from village-based mutual aid to more formal nongovernmental organizations (NGOs) over the past twenty years. As she points out, until recently, the Indonesian government has focused on top-down development schemes, with little input from grass-roots organizations. After surveying the range of activities carried out by the country's religious, social welfare, social, and community development organizations, she concludes that there is a need for better communication between government policy-makers and these groups.

Paul P. L. Cheung's discussion of the development of private philanthropy in Singapore in Chapter Twenty-Six shifts the focus from the state to private-sector initiatives. Unlike the governments in Australia and Western Europe, Singapore's government has adopted a limited role in service provision. While religious and ethnic pluralism historically gave rise to an array of nonprofit services, the country's rapid economic growth encouraged private giving. In addition to several foundations, a Community Chest was founded in 1983. Cheung questions whether the advent of the Community Chest has discouraged other types of fund-raising and philanthropic efforts, such as corporate giving.

Junhai Zhang examines the voluntary sector in the People's Republic of China in Chapter Twenty-Seven, attributing the reemergence of China's nonprofit sector to the government's decentralization policies and its efforts to stimulate business growth since the late 1970s. Here, as elsewhere, the growth of these institutions has been hampered by citizens' lack of surplus cash and time, as well as the dearth of positive tax incentives.

Finally, in Chapter Twenty-Eight, Virginia A. Hodgkinson and Russy D. Sumariwalla lay out the issues and challenges that face nonprofit organizations and propose the kinds of new programs that are needed for international collaboration among nonprofit organizations in the areas of research and practice.

Andrés A. Thompson   Chapter 22

Democracy and Development: The Role of Nongovernmental Organizations in Argentina, Chile, and Uruguay

Over the past decade, nongovernmental organizations (NGOs) have grown considerably in every country of Latin America, drawing the attention of governments, academics and researchers, churches, and the international private and public donor community. This new institutional phenomenon is playing a relevant role in the current process of democratization and in the struggle against poverty and underdevelopment.

   In the 1970s the Southern Cone, particularly Chile, Argentina, and Uruguay, witnessed the establishment of military regimes that curtailed the rights of labor unions and political organizations, violated human rights, closed the political system, and engaged in market-oriented economic policies. The

389

change in the role of the state and the resulting deterioration
of the living conditions of millions of people led to the emergence of numerous civil associations, both formal and informal,
that attempted to serve as alternative institutional channels of
participation and as service providers for the low-income sectors. This new generation of nongovernmental organizations,
most of which were under the umbrella of the churches and supported by international agencies from the north, was born under
adverse political and economic conditions. The question of their
survival was therefore a central one.

The return to democratic rule in the 1980s implied many
challenges to the NGO community. The opening of the political system and the restoration of public liberties provided a new
scenario for the activities of nonprofit organizations. Within that
context, the competition for international funds, the increase
in the demand for their services, and the need to approach public
institutions on different terms became the principal signs of the
multiple pressures on their traditional activities. Therefore, the
current dilemmas turn on the need for professionalization, for
shaping public opinion, and for securing funds to strengthen
their institutional development.

This chapter deals with the main processes that nongovernmental organizations in the Southern Cone have undergone.
The first section following this introduction presents a global
picture of the NGOs in Chile, Argentina, and Uruguay. It
stresses the variety of institutions in each country and the different legal forms they adopt. The second section enumerates the
main stages in their development, focusing on changes in the
political regimes and the reorientation of the economies. The
third section deals with the current constraints and prospects
of nonprofit organizations under the process of democratization.
Finally, some conclusions are presented.

An Overview of NGOs in the Southern Cone

It has been often pointed out that the term *nongovernmental organization* is commonly used to refer to a wide variety of organizations with very different institutional forms, styles of work,

and purposes. The term *voluntary, nonprofit,* or *private* is frequently added to it to specify the nature of these organizations more precisely. None of these terms, however, have the same meaning in different geographical and socioeconomic contexts. While the scope of the nonprofit sector in Latin America is very broad, in the case of the Southern Cone, the common reference to NGOs is to those concerned with the broad issue of development. Their rapid growth, their links with grass-roots organizations and international donors, and the impact of their action make them relevant in various senses for the design of social policies for the urban and rural poor and as agents of the democratization process. In this section I will describe broadly the NGOs involved in development in three countries: Chile, Argentina, and Uruguay.

Chile

Chile's NGO sector is the most developed of those of the three countries. Chileans have traditionally been active organizers and group participants, both at the intermediary level and at the base. Chile has one of Latin America's highest ratios of development-related NGOs per capita. Although precise statistics are elusive, one survey claims that at least 500 grass-roots support organizations (GSOs) exist (Abalos Konig, 1988b). Two-thirds of the 500 are involved in social development. The number of GSOs changes constantly because it is very easy to establish and to disband GSOs. Schematically, various groups of NGOs can be identified.

Independent development associations typically adhere to the legal title of *Sociedad de Profesionales*. These groups represent a new organizational phenomenon not to be confused with sectorial professional organizations such as bar and medical associations. The largest single sector numerically speaking, these are interdisciplinary groupings of socially committed professionals, usually ranging from five to twenty individuals. These groups have proliferated under the Pinochet regime as other, more traditional forms such as foundations and university groups have been subject to oppressive political control. They exist throughout the country, usually based in an urban center, and they assist both the rural and urban populations. Many of the key participants are intellectuals and former program leaders of university and government-sponsored development programs of the 1960s and early 1970s.

Catholic church institutions have been both the backbone and the heart of grass-roots development since 1973 (the year of Pinochet's military coup). They have been by far the most significant single institutional voluntary actor in Chile in the last fifteen years. In many ways they have served to replace missing social and economic services since the government's withdrawal in 1973. One study identified seventy-five Catholic church organizations involved in development and poverty programs, excluding parish-level programs (Abalos Konig, 1988a).

Four different subcategories of Catholic church organizations can be identified: foundations, research and action centers, institutes, and diocesan organizations of the church hierarchy. The last category includes church social action agencies, usually called DASs (*Departamentos de Acción Social*) or DARs (*Departamentos de Acción Rural*), which operate under the jurisdiction of Chile's twenty-four bishoprics.

Membership organizations (MOs), closely linked with much of Chile's large NGO sector, represent an even larger group of grass-roots membership organizations. Although many are informal, especially in the urban sector, a surprisingly high proportion have legal status. Many are part of second- and third-level membership organizations. According to various sources, the total number of Chilean MOs exceeds 25,000. However, almost half of them are not organizations of the poor but rather associations of middle- and upper-class Chileans. Among the MOs, the prevalence of housing and savings and loan cooperatives is very high. In Santiago alone, there exist at least 968 neighborhood mutual support groups involved in community betterment endeavors such as public health, low-cost housing, and cooperative food purchasing and distribution. The participants in these groups are predominantly female slum dwellers.

Apart from the foregoing groups, one can find development-oriented universities (eighteen), independent research/

action centers (thirty), non-Catholic church agencies (ten to fifteen), Chilean affiliates of international organizations (Rotary and Lions clubs and local chapters of the YMCA and Boy Scouts and Girl Scouts), and private foundations (predominantly conservative and family based). A very few but interesting coordinating bodies, such as the Task Force on Development Cooperation (*Taller de Cooperación al Desarrollo*) and the Task Force on Local Development (*Taller de Desarrollo Local*) have emerged more recently.

Argentina

Argentina's NGO sector is proportionally smaller than the Chilean one, but it has expanded considerably since the country's return to democracy in 1983. Despite a long associative tradition that dates from the beginning of the century, the mid 1940s emergence of a strong welfare state based on a pervasive union organization limited its growth. Nevertheless, long periods of military administration gave rise to human rights organizations; free market policies and the unequal distribution of income generated single-issue groups; the decentralization of the state spurred increased activity of various voluntary groups at the local level; and poverty led to the creation of social development organizations. In addition to trade unions and grass-roots membership organizations, Argentine NGOs can be classified as foundations, cooperatives, single-issue organizations, private research centers, or nongovernmental development organizations.

Foundations are the oldest and most traditional voluntary organizations in Argentina. The latest survey (taken by the Fundación Aragón) counted 811 foundations. The majority are concentrated in Buenos Aires, and their main areas of activity are education, health, the arts and culture, and social work. Only a few of these are grant-making foundations, and the largest proportion of these are operating foundations. However, given the lack of local resources, only a few of these foundations really operate in practice. The last few years have shown an important increase in the number of foundations, most of them formed in order to raise funds for political parties and groups and to channel funding for public institutions (for example, theaters and departments of social action). Foundations have also played a key role in the rise of the environmentalist movement and the movement against the abuse of drugs.

Cooperatives of various kinds have a similarly long history in Argentina. Although they are considered to be nongovernmental organizations, not all of them fall into the nonprofit sector. According to 1976 figures (Carracedo, 1980), the total number of cooperatives in the country (rural and urban) was 4,841, with almost seven million members. (Argentina's total population is thirty million). Since 1983, this sector has grown considerably because of favorable legislation as well as public and private promotion. Particularly interesting are the labor cooperatives formed within the urban informal sector as a result of increasing unemployment.

Single-issue organizations, the third important group of voluntary NGOs, include organizations that are aimed at promoting specific rights. They constitute a heterogeneous and varied group, whose total number is unknown. Many of these organizations were established during the last military regime in part because of the disappearance of the traditional participatory institutions such as political parties and trade unions. Similarly, this development was closely related to the elimination of all kinds of popular organizations promoted by the state authoritarianism. In a sense, these groups represent the institutional form adopted by the so-called new social movements (human rights, women's issues, youth movements, environmentalism, popular housing, and so on).

Private research centers constitute one of the most important NGO groups in Argentina in terms of international links. The financial and academic decay of the universities and the persecution of intellectuals favored the emergence of these centers, which sought international support in order to develop their activities. Since 1983 they have grown considerably in all fields of research (social sciences, political science, and economics). The total number of private research centers is estimated to be seventy.

Nongovernmental development organizations (NGDOs) are also a particular type of NGO. Oriented toward servicing, training, and assisting low-income groups, communities, and social organizations, they operate mainly within the informal sector. Though their subsidiary groups, organizational structures, and operative contexts may vary, NGDOs are the only associations that explicitly emphasize the issue of social development. According to a 1989 directory (Group of Analysis for Social and Institutional Development [GADIS], 1988), there are 115 NGDOs in Argentina, including five consortia. Their greatest growth took place in the 1980s, particularly after 1983. Most of them are located in Buenos Aires and in the provincial capitals. Their main areas of activity are community and human resource development (twenty-five), popular housing (twenty-five), nonformal education (fourteen), and research (eleven).

Uruguay

Uruguay's NGO sector is the smallest one in comparative terms but has a dynamic that was unknown in the country until recent years. According to one study (Barreiro and Cruz, 1988), the voluntary sector in Uruguay has four different categories: (1) a variety of social, cultural, and sports groups concerned with free time and leisure; (2) cooperative units of different types that combine economic activities with values such as participation, solidarity, and mutual help; (3) grass-roots organizations at the local level that are concerned with strategies of survival and basic social demands; and (4) formal nongovernmental organizations that are concerned with development issues. As in Argentina and Chile, this last group seems to be the most interesting one, and its pattern of development has also been a result of authoritarianism, increasing poverty, and the withdrawal of the state from the provision of social services.

   According to the same study (Barreiro and Cruz, 1988), development NGOs in Uruguay are mainly concerned with study and research, social promotion, the condition of women and youth, human rights, education, communications, and quality of life. The approximately 130 NGOs in Uruguay employ about 1,850 people, execute 270 projects, and publish about forty periodicals.

Summary

The nonprofit sector in the Southern Cone countries includes a wide variety of organizations concerned with almost every aspect of social, cultural, and economic life. They are a vivid expression of the pluralism of their civil societies. Because of the increasing problems caused by poverty, backwardness, and state inefficiency, development-oriented NGOs represent the most dynamic group within the voluntary sector. During the years of authoritarianism, they also played a significant political role. They served as alternative channels of expression and participation for different social groups when the activities of parties and other social organizations were prohibited.

Until recent years NGOs were not considered to be a separate sector. However, the emergence of networks and co-ordinating bodies and a stronger presence vis-à-vis the state and private business have assured their international recognition as agents of development. The growing amount and quality of research being done on their activities are clear indicators that nongovernmental organizations will be privileged political and social actors during the 1990s.

Development and Roles of NGOs

Most NGOs play various roles simultaneously. From the donors' point of view, NGOs are means for external funding and for promoting a set of humanitarian and democratic causes. This view is based on the notion of identity of interests between indigenous leaders and external donors, as well as donor disappointment with public bureaucracies in Latin America.

Others see NGOs as an expression of an expanding civil society that is acquiring a density of decentralized organizations and a nongovernmental sector that can capture significant resources for poorer groups, represent their interests, and articulate their demands. Still others see NGOs mainly in political terms, as alternative organizations that emerge during periods of authoritarianism and as providers of employment opportunities and arenas of action for socially committed professionals of the middle class. According to this view, NGOs should disappear once democracy is reinstalled and traditional organizations of action and work (political parties, universities) start to function normally. More pragmatically, others see NGOs as useful entities in mitigating repressive regimes or as gap fillers for public services when the states are in bankruptcy.

In fact, NGOs in the Southern Cone combine elements of all of the different viewpoints mentioned above. However, the central argument to explain the different combination of roles and their enormous growth lies in the imposition of authoritarian military rule during the 1970s and in its consequences in the political, social, and economic systems. Chile and Uruguay suffered military interventions in 1973 and Argentina in 1976. These were the result of the failure of political parties and social organizations (mainly the trade unions) to achieve a kind of compromise or agreement capable of sustaining democratic processes and maintaining economic stability. Although the military occupied the states by force, this happened because the civil societies were weak and no strong pluralistic and democratic alternative was available. (This kind of explanation is by no means a justification of the military coups; on the contrary, it is an attempt to look at the militarization of the political processes from the point of view of the weaknesses of the civil societies.)

The military takeovers (often supported openly by the United States government on the grounds of a supposed previous threat to democracy) resulted in the violation of human rights; the persecution of social, political, and union leaders; the control and disarticulation of grass-roots organizations and trade unions; and interventions in the universities. In the principal cities, unemployment rose rapidly. The governments adopted radical free market policies that resulted in a flood of imported goods and accelerated the collapse of the manufacturing sector. New labor legislation virtually eliminated the bargaining power of unions, and real wages declined.

That moment of emergency led to the formation of isolated groups of Catholic and other church leaders (particularly in Chile) and socially committed professionals and intellectuals, who joined forces to protect lives, defend human rights, and help preserve some minimum degree of social organization. Although historically different in their origins and forms, a second generation of NGOs was born in the Southern Cone; these were distinct from the traditional, more conservative ones (foundations, charities). As one Chilean researcher (Vargas, 1988) has argued, these were not nongovernmental organizations but rather contragovernmental organizations, and thus their emphasis on their political role as agents of democratization and their self-perception as transitory organizations that should disappear with a return to democratic rule. Commitment to the poor and oppressed, social justice, and participation are strongly rooted values in the NGOs that emerged during that period. For the same reason, effectiveness, skills, and professionalization were of secondary importance.

Soon after the emergency period, NGOs came to realize that in developing countries relief was not enough. Along with violations of human rights and the dismantling of social organizations there arose health, employment, land tenure, and housing problems. Public social policies during the authoritarian period followed a pattern of exclusion of large social sectors of the population, which were also in an unfavorable condition to improve their standards of living in the new free market economies. The new informal sector turned out to be the main object of the NGOs' move toward broader "development" goals. The new NGOs were "established by groups of activists who support a certain cause and who create their organization with the explicit goal of helping people other than their own membership. These later NGOs are sometimes called professional NGOs, in the sense that working in such activist organizations becomes a full-time professional commitment and specialized activity for their animators" (Cernea, 1988, p. 8).

That was the second stage in the development of the current NGO fabric. It was a period of growth, specialization, and diversification. Grass-roots support organizations (in Chile) and nongovernmental development organizations (in Argentina and Uruguay) are now a spreading phenomenon in the Southern Cone. They are often portrayed as alternatives to public services, although their goals differ widely. Some pursue inward-oriented strategies aimed at survival, protection, or self-sufficiency in the economic, cultural, or environmental realm. Others concentrate their strategies on income and employment objectives. A third category supply the basic social necessities, while a fourth might be termed an empowerment category.

Under similar contexts, NGOs in Chile grew more rapidly than those in Argentina or Uruguay. The important role played by the Catholic church, the international consideration of the Chilean dictatorship as a cause célèbre, and the role played by exiled intellectuals and professionals in calling attention to the Chilean situation were all factors that contributed to this growth. In all three countries, however, learning from past experience, networking, and organization building became the landmarks of the second stage.

What could be called a third stage in the development of NGOs in the Southern Cone came with the return of political democracy. As a result of changes in the domestic and international context, free elections were held in Argentina (1983), Uruguay (1985), and Chile (1989). The revival of democratic values as the axis of the reconstruction of civil society implied new challenges for the NGOs. Nongovernmental, professionalized action was revitalized and extended their linkages with initiatives undertaken at the bottom of society and with different levels of the governmental sector. The creation of new NGOs resulted in a growing competition for funds. Efforts were made to develop joint ventures with the state. Social research on nonprofit, nongovernmental action also became more relevant. Broadly speaking, NGOs became less political as result of the revival of traditional political parties while they realized that they were there to stay.

Under the new democratic circumstances, one of the main contributions of NGOs has been to show to a wider public that there are alternative development strategies to those originated by the state or the for-profit sector. When *privatization* and *reduction of the state* become fashionable terms in political and economic discourse, it is important to show that it is possible to be private and in favor of decentralization while having a nonprofit vision. Yet these alternative development strategies are still confined to a micro level and cannot cope with all the social consequences derived from the economic structural adjustment plans typical of the period. Many NGOs are also aware that the democratization processes that are taking place in Eastern Europe will certainly increase the competition for funds and reduce the interest of Western European development cooperation agencies in Latin America. Therefore, issues such as the coordination of actions and international networking, the replication of microprojects on a larger scale, and the development of a more political vision again become relevant in the NGOs agenda for the 1990s. (This vision, for example, was put into practice in Argentina in May 1989. As the result of hyperinflation and a lack of food in the popular neighborhoods and shantytowns, a group of thirty-five NGOs joined in an "emergency campaign of social solidarity" to channel funds to grass-roots organizations, exchange information, and advocate an urgent, nonrepressive solution. In Brazil, some NGOs are in the process of establishing direct links with NGOs in Eastern Europe.)

Current Constraints and Prospects

The legitimacy of NGOs in the Southern Cone is still weak when compared with the state or the for-profit sector. For the vast majority in the NGO community, the state in Latin America continues to be seen as the engine of development, as the actor who can set the guidelines for the behavior of all the social, political, and economic organizations. Paradoxically, the general trend is of a weakening of the functions of the state in order to make more room for the private initiative. Therefore, the hegemonic ideological approach of the Southern Cone governments is that the state should only deal with macro economic and political issues (including the control of inflation and the reduction of the fiscal deficit) combined with charitable social policies to compensate for the social impact of the economic adjustment plans, while the for-profit sector should command the economy. According to this view, the democratic functioning of the political system should limit the responsibility of the state, while the growth of the economy should be left in the hands of private business and the market. This will result in the increase of investments, rising employment, better conditions of living, and political democratic stability. The Latin American experience, particularly in the Southern Cone, however, provides evidence that strongly refutes these arguments. During recent years, policies that have led to the "marketization" of the Southern Cone economies have resulted in increasing poverty of those social groups that cannot compete in the market.

Although NGOs are not yet an alternative to the market or the state, they have appeared as a challenge to traditional development thinking in Southern Cone societies. A small but growing body of literature explains the ways in which the nongovernmental organizations combine the design of innovative social and economic development projects with the democratic participation of the target populations. Particularly at the local level, where the linkages and interactions with state bureaucracies and other social organizations are easier, NGOs are showing their greatest potential. "People-centered development" or "development at a human scale" are phrases usually employed to describe the kind of approach of NGOs to the problems of poverty and underdevelopment. According to this view, "development" is not only measurable in economic terms but mainly in its social and human dimensions. Democracy and development therefore go together with social justice and participation.

If the values and methodologies of the NGOs are going to have any influence on the path of development in the Southern Cone societies, there is an urgent need to link the provision of social services and the empowerment of grass-root organizations at the micro level with stronger and more efficient advocacy policies at the level of the political system (government and political parties). To effectively convince people that there are feasible alternative development strategies within a democratic context, NGOs have to influence public opinion through new and original communication policies, increase their managerial capacities, articulate efforts among themselves and with the state, and explore new ways of funding by promoting domestic philanthropy. Research on the work of the NGOs can be a central instrument to that end.

We need to know more about the real dimensions of

voluntary organizations in the three countries and, more particularly, about the real impact of their projects in terms of effectively contributing to the amelioration of the living conditions
of the urban and rural poor. As far as the fact that most NGOs
receive funds from international donors is concerned, the research questions raised by Smith (1986) are still of great importance: How much of this assistance actually reaches the grass-
roots level, and what impact does it have on the quality of life
of the poor? Does it promote self-reliance among the poor, or
is it so small that it is uneffective? How do the poor themselves
relate to these new NGOs, and are the NGOs sensitive to their
input in decision making?

More serious research is also needed on the different forms
of relations of the NGOs with the state. Although there have been
very interesting experiences regarding such relationships in Argentina and Uruguay, the inefficiency of public bureaucracies
and the instability of many officials led to the failure of various
joint ventures between NGOs and the state. Which are the ways
in which voluntary organizations can cooperate equally with
governments remains an issue that needs further exploration.
On the other hand, the true dimension of state support of the
overall NGO sector needs to be more seriously addressed. For
instance, there is increasing evidence that the size of government
donations and subsidies for nonprofit activities directed toward
people with handicaps and toward child care is great in Argentina.

A better understanding of these issues could strengthen
the position of voluntary organizations within each country's
institutional framework and provide a more equitable and cooperative relationship with the state and the for-profit sector. Furthermore, the need to blend public policy-making with efforts
at the bottom level of society — in other words, to arrive at a
minimum consensus about possible solutions to the most ac-
cute social and economic problems — is one of the key challenges
facing the new democracies of the Southern Cone.

Conclusions

The new nongovernmental organizations in South America were
born within a context of authoritarianism and the transforma-

tion of economic systems. Compared with the older, more traditional NGOs, these second-generation nonprofit organizations have a strong belief in social participation and democracy. In that sense, their distinctive character was to break with the charitable tradition by which benevolent organizations relieve the suffering of poor people without altering the status quo.

For a long time, NGOs played a strong political role. They supported grass-roots initiatives to organize themselves independently from parties and government, both to satisfy their basic needs and to put pressure on governments. The strong belief that self-organization should lead to improvement in the living conditions of the poor was at the heart of the work of nongovernmental organizations. During the period of darkness and repression, the need to defend human rights was a stimulus for the engagement of technicians and professionals in self-help and the promotion of the low-income sector. The democratic spirit that guided the reconstruction of a pluralistic voluntary sector was, at the time, enough to justify international help.

The return to democracy brought many changes in the social and political life of South American societies. The opening of the political systems, the return of the exiled, and the new opportunity to act freely contributed both to the expansion of the scope of NGO activities and to the increase in the demand for their services. Within that context, the weaknesses of NGOs emerged: their inability to gain legitimacy within their own societies and to raise funds locally, the secondary role given to management issues and institutional development, and their isolation from other social institutions. Particularly striking were the difficulties in establishing a permanent relationship with state agencies, which had also undergone a process of restructuring.

Confronted with the challenges of political democratization and the social impact of economic adjustment, NGOs suddenly found themselves in the middle of a storm. The new winds posed many dilemmas for nonprofits, which in turn provoked complex tensions. While NGOs focus their activities on specific issues, they desire global changes; they defend cultural traditions and identities but have close relations with the Western culture; they defend their autonomy but depend upon foreign funds; they have less rigid structures than public agencies but need to be efficient; they have a strong voluntary component but are involved in a process of professionalization. The complexity of the political and economic environment pushes them to reconsider their own history, methodologies, and aims. Nongovernmental organizations have proved that they are not a transitory phenomenon. They are here to stay.

The dilemmas and their possible outcomes are becoming a matter of discussion. The central question underlying that discussion refers ultimately to the degree of strength of the civil societies of South America to produce reform and change toward a better life for their populations.

References

Abalos Konig, J. "Instituciones de apoyo y centros académicos privados en Chile: Antecedentes, realidades y desafíos." Santiago: Latin American Council of Social Sciences (ILET), 1988a.

Abalos Konig, J. *Organizaciones no-gubernamentales post 73*. Santiago: ILET, Documentos de Trabajo, 1988b.

Agurto, I., and Piva, C. "Las ONGs de promoción y desarrollo urbano en Chile. Una propuesta de investigación." Santiago: Latin American Institute of Transnational Studies (FLACSO), 1988.

Barreiro, F., and Cruz, A. *La dificultad de ser: ONGs en el Uruguay de hoy: El desafío de la democracia*. Montevideo: Instituto de Comunicación y Desarrollo, Fundación de Cultera Universitaria, 1988.

Carracedo, O. "Inventario y evaluación de la economía cooperativa en la República Argentina." *Cuadernos de Economía Social*, 1980, 2, 5.

Cernea, M. *Nongovernmental Organizations and Local Development.* Washington, D.C.: World Bank, 1988.

González Meyer, R. *Instituciones de apoyo: Subjetividades y tendencias*. Santiago: CIPMA, October 1988.

Group of Analysis for Social and Institutional Development. (GADIS). *Primer directorio de organizaciones no-gubernamentales argentinas de promoción y desarrollo*. Buenos Aires: GADIS, 1988.

Inter-American Foundation, Various documents.

Martinez Nogueira, R. "Ciclo de vida y aprendizaje en las organizaciones no-gubernamentales de promoción." Buenos Aires: Group of Analysis for Social and Institutional Development (GADIS), 1988.

Smith, B. "The Church, Voluntary Organizations, and Development in South America." Paper presented at the INDEPENDENT SECTOR Spring Research Forum, New York, 1986.

Thompson, A. "The Voluntary Sector in Transition: The Case of Argentina." Working paper. New York: Center for the Study of Philanthropy, 1989.

Vargas, D. "Organismos no-gubernamentales y desarrollo local." *El Canelo,* 1988, *3* (11).

Indigenous Philanthropy
in the Arab World:
Contrasting Cases
from Egypt and Palestine

Societies of the Arab Middle East have rich cultural traditions of philanthropy, rooted in Islam and Eastern Christianity. For much of the early part of this century, however, the region was emerging from a long period of economic, political, and social decline during which philanthropic institutions, like most others, were weak and ineffectual. The collapse of the Ottoman Empire at the end of World War I ushered in an era of independent state building in the Arab world. This was a period of consolidating central authority, often accompanied by a socialist vision of national welfare. Newly formed governments were optimistic that public institutions could satisfy the rising demands for services and thus did little to encourage private initiative. It is only recently that a generation of new philanthropists has emerged, stimulated in some instances by persistent problems of poverty and underdevelopment and in others by opportunities for largess arising out of the unprecedented oil wealth accumulated since 1975.

Unlike the West, where research on philanthropy is well-established and theoretical models to explain cross-national variations are emerging, the philanthropic experience of the contemporary Arab world remains largely undocumented. A few survey articles have appeared recently in Arabic, but comparative field studies have yet to be undertaken. As a result, little is known about the overall impact of modern philanthropy, and most organizations in the field operate in isolation from one another. This chapter is an initial effort to trace the history and current profile of philanthropic institutions in Egypt and Palestine, two important but politically divergent societies in the region. Though necessarily incomplete, it may encourage other researchers to expand and deepen scholarship in this area in the future.

The following account is largely descriptive. Theoretical formulations developed to explain patterns of philanthropic activity in Europe and North America are for the most part inappropriate for understanding Third World settings. They tend to assume the presence of electoral political systems or free market economies and ignore the potential role of external factors such as international aid or foreign political hegemony. While many developing societies appear to be moving toward greater democratic practices and/or open capital markets, these trends coexist with the reassertion of other traditional values and institutions. Moreover, external influence of one sort or another is a fact of life for developing countries. Thus, we must continue the search for conceptual frames and theories that can accommodate the experience of less-developed societies, as well as those of the Eastern bloc countries, Japan, and others outside the North American—West European axis.

Both history and politics have played a central role in defining the parameters of Arab philanthropy. Current institutional forms were to a large extent forged in the contact between indigenous and European institutions over the past one hundred years. As elsewhere in the Third World, the Arab region has variously emulated, modified, and rejected Western cultural influence. The newly independent states tended to choose selectively from the offerings of the West, accepting science, technology, and universal education, but often as not rejecting other institutions, such as decentralized government, civic associations, and the separation of church and state. In particular, Arab regimes have maintained uneasy relations with local voluntary societies, whether religious or secular. As these regimes struggled in their early years to consolidate power, voluntary associations, especially those that drew their leadership from well-educated professional and business classes, were seen as a potential threat. Some regimes banned all associations not affiliated with the ruling political party. Others passed a succession of laws giving governmental agencies close control over the programs and finance of all voluntary or nonprofit organizations. Yet within these strictures, an impressive range of survival responses emerged in the nonprofit sector.

In order to highlight some of the diversity and continuity in philanthropy in the Arab region, two cases are presented in greater detail below—those of Egypt and the Palestinian territories of Gaza and the West Bank. These are geographically contiguous societies with a common cultural heritage and many parallels in their history as outposts of the Ottoman Empire. Yet because of strikingly different historical experiences since the interwar period, Egypt now represents an example of the overregulated philanthropic sector, while Palestinian institutions have developed in the absence of a recognized government and, for the past twenty-two years, under the constraints of external military occupation. Voluntary associations have proliferated under both conditions, albeit with very different rationales. Endowed foundations, however, are rare in Egypt, whereas they have been a prominent part of recent Palestinian development. Reasons for these and other patterns are explored in the sections that follow.

Traditions of Philanthropy in the Arab World

The Middle East provides an interesting locus for comparisons with Western societies because both areas inherited the cultural traditions of Judaism, Greco-Roman civilization, and early Christianity. With the advent of Islam, however, the two regions embarked on divergent paths of cultural development, punctuated by political and economic confrontations that often exacerbated the cultural differences. Today most countries of the Arab Middle East are steadily integrating themselves into global systems of trade and technological advances while maintaining strong attachments to Islamic cultural traditions. Similarly, in patterns of philanthropic giving and voluntarism, Arab countries display a mix of deeply rooted traditions alongside modern, secular innovations.

In common with Judaism, Islam is a religion that combines monotheistic beliefs with extensive prescriptions regarding the conduct of everyday human affairs. Central to the ideal of a Muslim social order is individual charity and collective responsibility for the material welfare of others. Thus, one of the five pillars of the faith is a regular tithe of personal and corporate income, the *zakat*. In the past, wealthier households would distribute *zakat* in the form of clothing and food during religious feasts, following the traditional formula of giving first to less advantaged relatives, then to extended clan members, and finally to the broader community (Abdel Rahman, 1988). Today, mosques have taken over much of the responsibility for determining need and distributing *zakat*, especially in urban communities. The trend in recent years has been toward increasing contributions to these *zakat* funds, both in terms of numbers of people contributing and, while this is hard to document, in terms of the proportion of income devoted to *zakat*.

Unfortunately, in most Arab countries definitions of worthy applications for *zakat* remain limited to fairly standard charitable activities—donations to support orphans, widows, people with disabilities, the homeless, and the poor. Religious leaders in Jordan, however, recently issued a pronouncement that *zakat* funds could also be applied to some development projects aimed at increasing the self-reliance of the poor. Similar changes are under discussion in other Arab countries.

Another noteworthy trend is the growth of modern business ventures based on Islamic commercial practices. These companies are proliferating in many fields, including banking, investment, publishing, and industry. Their strict adherence to the principle of devoting a share of profits (usually 2½ or 3 percent) to *zakat* means that sizeable new philanthropic funds are being amassed throughout the region (Abdel Rahman, 1988).

Historically, another important source of Islamic philanthropy was the system of property bequests called *waqf*. *Waqf* property was traditionally real estate—date groves, agricultural land, or buildings. Literally translated as "stopping," this form of bequest takes property out of circulation in perpetuity, so that its income can be devoted to a specified beneficiary. Schools, hospitals, orphanages, and similar institutions were often supported in this way. In a number of Arab countries, administration of *waqf* properties was taken over by the state, and in Egypt, for example, new *waqf* bequests ended abruptly once the system was nationalized in the 1950s.

Islam generated a number of other philanthropic forms during the centuries of its flowering in the Middle East, including scholarly research centers (*dar el hikma*), endowed hospitals (*bimarstan*), and public fountains (*sabil*). By the beginning of this century, however, most of these conventions had fallen into disuse, and the remaining examples of earlier endowments were poorly maintained.

Side by side with Islamic philanthropy, a smaller number of Christian philanthropies have existed for centuries, designed to provide services for their communities. In every Arab country with a Christian (or Jewish) minority, political traditions permitted that community to maintain its own churches, legal courts, fund-raising bodies, and system of social services. It was only after the emergence of modern states in the region that legal systems were unified and the state took control of some formerly private services. Social service institutions remain strong in the Christian community, however, and as a result of close partnerships with European donors, some of these institutions have established progressive programs in the fields of health care, community development, and education (Latowski, 1986). In Egypt, for example, a number of the largest private organizations addressing rural development needs are affiliated with Coptic or Protestant churches.

Against this backdrop of the religious sources for early philanthropy, we now turn to a closer examination of the Egyptian case as it has developed in this century. Egypt is important as the Arab world's most populous country and because of its long-established political and cultural influence in the region. Egypt also has the region's longest history of modern state institutions and an equally long experience with a secular nonprofit sector. By studying the problems and prospects of philanthropy in Egypt, several lessons can be drawn with respect to the region generally.

Egypt: Blurring the Lines
Between Public and Private Initiative

Egypt entered the twentieth century under occupation by British troops, its economy administered to recover huge debts and to protect British interests in the Suez Canal. From this close contact, Egyptians gained an appreciation for modern education and other social welfare institutions at a time when indigenous systems were in decline. As part of an awakening nationalist movement, wealthy patrons established schools, hospitals, and other social services and formed societies to manage them. Egypt's Red Crescent Society (an affiliate of the International Red Cross), the Islamic Benevolent Society, and a number of other important associations date from the period 1900 to 1915.

In the interwar years, Egypt gained independence from Britain and began building public institutions to administer basic services. Because of earlier momentum in the private voluntary sector, however, it expanded rapidly as well. Urban centers were by then a rich mix of ethnic and religious minorities, and these formed the bases for most philanthropic activities. Lebanese, Greeks, Armenians, Copts, Jews, Nubians, and others maintained active membership associations to provide education, health care, leisure activities, and burial facilities for their respective communities. In this period, trade unions, professional associations, and feminist organizations also flourished in Egypt. Their agendas typically mixed explicitly political and nationalist goals with social service provision for their membership.

Thus, on the eve of its revolution in 1952, Egypt was a highly mobilized society. The middle and upper classes were still small relative to the total population, but their rates of civic participation were extremely high, and the bulk of social services were funded and administered by private nonprofit institutions. This created a dilemma for the young officers who seized power, since their sweeping reforms of the economic and political landscape would require centralized authority. They opted for the creation of a pervasive single-party system, and soon trade unions, political parties, and other interest groups were subsumed under the single-party Arab Socialist Union (ASU).

Private voluntary organizations (PVOs) faced a similar fate, all placed under the direct supervision of the Ministry of Social Affairs, which approved programs, controlled fund raising, and often seconded ministry staff to run these organizations. Law 32 for 1964, which is still in effect today, regulates the activities of PVOs, but in reality the lines between public and private are often blurred. In recent years, the ministry has established hundreds of local "voluntary associations" funded solely by government in order to carry out its programs for child care, vocational training, family planning, and so forth.

Voluntarism was slowly undermined during this period, as can be seen in the profile of leadership in the PVO sector today. Ministry employees and former employees make up the bulk of the active leadership, with voluntary participation greatest among those above the age of sixty, who would have entered the sector prior to the reforms of the 1950s and 1960s. Subsequent generations channeled their activism elsewhere — the ASU or local organizations affiliated with mosques and churches.

Perhaps the most significant impact was felt on philanthropic giving. While figures are not available for the nonprofit sector as a whole, studies of local community associations indicate that over the past twenty-five years, real budgets have remained fairly static or declined, with government providing a steadily increasing proportion of funding (the exception being PVOs supported by foreign donor contributions). The relative decline in private contributions can be attributed partially to restrictive legislation governing allowable fund raising for PVOs. In addition, tax incentives for individual or corporate donations to PVOs are minimal and poorly understood by the population at large (Salem, 1990).

Poor motivation seems not to be the primary factor, however, since levels of voluntary giving to religious organizations have remained high. One must conclude that as PVOs have become identified with the public sector, Egyptians are less likely to extend to them private support and have consequently shifted their giving to other channels. Evidence of this can be seen in the phenomenal growth of certain benevolent programs sponsored by respected newspaper editors. These rely on published newspaper appeals for funds to ameliorate the problems of poor or sick individuals. Other evidence of Egyptians' willingness to contribute for charitable purposes can be seen in the impressive growth of *zakat* giving for local services organized around the neighborhood mosque. The latter operate in rich and poor, rural and urban neighborhoods alike, often engaging in much the same areas of activity as PVOs but outside the regulatory framework of Law 32.

Despite problems associated with government regulation, the PVO sector, by virtue of its size and tenacity, remains a significant component of nonprofit activity in Egypt. Recent estimates of the number of registered PVOs in Egypt exceed 10,000, far more than the total for all other Arab countries combined (Abdel Rahman, 1988). While a large but unknown number of those PVOs are inactive, ministry records indicate that over one million Egyptians are annual dues-paying members of PVOs, and approximately 300 PVOs have memberships in excess of 100 individuals. New PVOs face formidable red tape in order to register, security investigations, and requirements for elaborate record keeping. As a result, an increasing number of new nonprofit organizations seek registration as companies, their founders believing that by avoiding PVO legal status they can operate more effectively. This trend contributes to a further distortion of the definition of nonprofit activity in Egypt and makes accurate statistical profiles of the sector difficult to compile.

Corporate philanthropy is a relatively recent phenomenon in Egypt, emerging along with a reinvigorated private business sector in the 1970s. Large companies such as Arab Contractors have set a model for others by endowing hospitals and vocational training programs for the disadvantaged. In cooperation with the governor of Cairo, a number of companies, organized by sector, have pooled contributions to help beautify the city by restoring broken fountains, planting trees, renovating statuary, and maintaining public gardens. The potential exists for much greater participation of this kind as the private sector expands.

Conspicuously absent from the philanthropic scene in Egypt are funding institutions that resemble the private foundation. As discussed above, the traditional equivalent was the *waqf* system, which once flourished in Egypt but was effectively ended by nationalization. Alternatively, inheritance laws in Islam allow for up to one-third of an estate to be willed to beneficiaries other than stipulated family members; however, this mechanism for bequeathing assets is also generally avoided in Egypt. An important factor in discouraging major endowments was the experience of the 1950s and 1960s, when the government undertook a widespread program of property confiscation in the name of land reform. Even though property rights are now protected under the law, distrust lingers in the minds of potential benefactors.

In principle, a section of Law 32 includes provisions for the establishment of *moasasat* (endowed foundations) to operate in the fields of education, health, and social welfare. As with PVOs, however, the law specifies that all financial transactions of a foundation must be approved by the Ministry of Social Affairs. The law for charitable foundations, like that for PVOs, gives the Ministry of Social Affairs the right to place its representatives on boards of directors, dissolve elected boards and reappoint new members, merge exiting foundations, or dissolve a foundation altogether (Salem, 1990). Not surprisingly, from 1964 to 1988, only one organization registered under the terms of this law. Individuals and corporate entities preferred to maintain autonomy in their giving, with the consequence that philanthropy in Egypt is poorly developed, remains ad hoc in nature, and loses the benefits of professionalism and continuity that in-situtionalization can provide.

Currently, a number of legal challenges are pending against Law 32, including one to test its constitutionality. In the meantime, the Ministry of Social Affairs introduced a ministerial decree in 1989 to soften the impact of the existing law in order to encourage new foundations. Nine foundations are now registered in Egypt, and the ministry plans several new initiatives to further promote this sector. Given the postwar history of restrictive control, however, Egypt may need to institute much stronger incentives, such as generous tax benefits, in order to reestablish vigorous philanthropic giving.

In summary, Egypt today benefits from robust traditions of voluntarism and philanthropy, grounded in religious custom but now including secular institutions for both charitable and development activities as well. Since 1952, systematic state policies to regulate the nonprofit sector made most voluntary associations counterparts of government in providing social services. At the same time, close supervision of the sector restricted its development, especially with regard to private foundations and autonomous voluntary associations. While the private business sector has enjoyed liberalized state policies since the mid 1970s, a similar relaxation of controls on the nonprofit sector has yet to be legislated. One result is that nonprofit activities are increasingly organized under for-profit legal statutes such as limited liability firms. In addition, a large volume of social service activity in urban areas is conducted informally to unregistered neighborhood groups.

Philanthropy in the Palestinian Territories

Until the creation of the state of Israel in 1948, philanthropy in Palestine and Egypt followed similar historical paths. Liberal policies of the Ottomans toward religious and ethnic affairs allowed philanthropy to develop within each community relatively undisturbed. Because of Jerusalem's importance as a holy city, Moslems, Jews, and a multitude of Christian sects maintained institutions there for worship, scholarship, and welfare of the poor.

The British Mandate period from 1920 to 1948 brought increased contact with Western forms of philanthropy. Wealthy Palestinians responded to the lack of universal education and health care in their society by establishing a number of schools and hospitals. As in Egypt, philanthropic activists came predominantly from an urban, upper-class elite, who were motivated by a mix of religious commitment, noblesse oblige, and nationalist aspirations. Large private endowments during this period created the Makassad Hospital in Jerusalem and the Arab Development Society near Jericho. Birzeit and al Najah colleges were founded by local donations as well, forming the nucleus for a future university system.

The partition of Mandate Palestine to create a Jewish state in 1948 was a crushing blow to Arab nationalist hopes, and in the ensuing war Palestinians lost even the limited statehood proposed under the United Nations partition plan. The territories remaining to them were physically separated by Israel, with the Gaza strip under Egyptian administration and the West Bank under Jordanian control. Sixty percent of the Palestinian population were left homeless, nearly one million people became refugees, and commerce, agriculture, and services were severely disrupted.

In the relief efforts that followed, existing local societies expanded rapidly and at least six new relief organizations were founded; but they were unable to respond adequately to the magnitude of the tasks. Local institutions were unprepared to cope simultaneously with an ambiguous political status and massive humanitarian needs. Believing that a political settlement would soon restore their homeland, Palestinians deferred issues such as resettling refugees and welcomed UN and other foreign assistance as a temporary measure.

The aftermath of the 1948 war ushered in a period of major international aid to the territories. UN, bilateral, and private foreign donors quickly became the dominant philanthropic presence in the West Bank and Gaza. As hopes for a peace settlement receded, the programs of these agencies took on a more permanent character. External aid continued to dominate philanthropy in the territories until the 1980s, when heated debates arose over issues of dependency versus local self-reliance. In the interim period, however, sweeping changes had occurred in the nature and composition of voluntary activism in the territories.

As in most agrarian societies, women's roles were circumscribed in prepartition Palestine. Relocated in refugee camps, however, they soon developed important household and community positions as adult males emigrated in search of employment. Education for girls took on new importance so that they could qualify for jobs as teachers or community workers. The growing philanthropic sector thus became a source of much-needed employment as well as voluntarism. By 1967, sixty-eight local charitable societies were active in the territories, concentrated primarily in Gaza town, Jerusalem, Hebron, Ramallah, and Nablus (League of Arab States, 1984).

During this period students, workers, and professionals also organized unions that were registered either with Jordanian or Egyptian authorities. More overtly political and less service oriented than the charitable associations and women's unions, these groups represented a small but growing activist segment of the society. The 1967 War was a watershed for popular mobilization, for with Israeli military occupation of the West Bank and Gaza, Palestinian hopes for an early peace settlement evaporated.

The period from 1967 to 1987 witnessed a growing struggle against both the occupying authorities and reliance on external support, whether from Arab governments or the international aid community. In the process, several new generations of grass-roots organizations emerged to fill previous voids in public services. Over 400 local organizations and work committees were established in fields such as community management, agricultural development, primary health care, and small-scale enterprise. Together with an enlarged student movement, women's unions, and trade associations, these new organizations represented unprecedented mobilization of an Arab society in the absence of a recognized government (Abed, 1988).

While many grass-roots organizations operated on shoestring budgets and local in-kind contributions, major shifts were underway in the sources of funding for indigenous philanthropy.

As Palestinians in the diaspora established themselves in business and the professions, their remittances to the territories began to equal and then exceed contributions from Jordan, Egypt, and elsewhere in the region. In the beginning, most remittances were channeled to family members or a specific project in the home community. After 1967, however, a number of Palestinian organizations were established to administer contributions for higher education, housing, health, and so on. Some of the funding agencies were affiliated with a political wing of the national movement, but others were established as independent private foundations. Palestinian foundations include both corporate models, individual endowments, and groups of donors each pledging annual contributions.

In surveying the field of Arab foundations, it is striking to note that Palestinians are disproportionately represented relative to both population and wealth in the number of private foundations established over the past twenty years. They have also shown leadership in both management and quality of programming for social development.

That this should be the case is not surprising given previous observations about the context of Egyptian philanthropy. There, excessive regulation discourages donors from institutionalizing their giving. Moreover, the high profile of government in traditionally nongovernmental areas of social welfare has deflected private philanthropy toward other outlets.

In the Palestinian case, the situation is reversed: given the virtual absence of governmental infrastructure inside the territories, Palestinians are highly motivated to contribute toward filling the vacuum with institutions and programs of their own. For Palestinians in the diaspora, contributing to the building of institutions and, through these institutions, alleviating hardships of life under occupation, are seen as a national responsibility. Furthermore, contributing through foundation channels became increasingly attractive for potential donors as disposable income expanded in the 1970s and early 1980s; this was especially true of the sizeable group of Palestinians who worked in oil-producing countries.

Individual donors who wish to make major contributions have been encouraged by foundation models such as that of the

Welfare Association based in Geneva. While its grant and loan programs are concentrated in the Occupied Territories and Israel, registration in a European country gives the Welfare Association the advantages of operating under a liberal regulatory framework. Other foundations are incorporated in Holland, the United States, and Panama.

Palestinian foundations have contributed to a lively debate within the territories about the appropriate roles of grants, external aid, and charitable activities in promoting self-reliant development. Twenty-two years of occupation sharpened the contradictions between localized service projects, no matter how well-conceived, and obstructed development at the national level. In this regard, charitable associations and aid agencies, both local and international, are increasingly challenged to show how their activities promote true development. A growing number of Palestinian nonprofits, for example, are rejecting grant assistance for economic development activities where they believe loans or equity investments are more appropriate. Similarly, donor funds are unwelcome from sources that simultaneously support continued occupation by Israel.

In late 1987 a popular uprising against the occupation began inside the territories and has continued until the present time. As one consequence, Jordan ended its formal ties to and administration of the West Bank. Observers note that the widespread presence of local voluntary organizations and funding channels made it possible for communities to rapidly establish networks of alternative services that have sustained the uprising. In addition to day-to-day services in areas such as health care, police protection, and garbage collection, voluntary organizations are also addressing long-term needs for education policy, agricultural development, financial institutions, and other requirements of an independent society.

Conclusions

Voluntary activism in Egypt and the Palestinian territories has been motivated by the desire to provide local communities with basic human services. Of equal importance, it has provided channels for the creation of participatory structures in the absence of open, democratic institutions at a national level. In Egypt, the government's extensive involvement in voluntary activities has discouraged some forms of private initiative. Conversely, the absence of a recognized government in the Palestinian territories has led to widespread voluntary activism and more recently to the attempt to build institutions that can substitute for the role of government.

Experiences under occupation have sharpened the debates over appropriate roles for PVOs, donor agencies, and the for-profit sector in promoting Palestinian development. Those debates are beginning in Egypt as well and include a thorough review of the role of government regulation of the nonprofit sector. Regulations that inhibit the establishment of private foundations were revised in 1989, leading to several new foundation applications for registration in the ensuing years. Likewise, a committee within the Egyptian Ministry of Social Affairs has been reviewing the laws that govern private voluntary associations.

The short-term outlook for philanthropy in the Palestinian territories is less promising, with a number of prominent voluntary associations now closed down by the military authorities, and local voluntary leaders facing arrest and deportation. Nonetheless, commitment to expanding the scope and quality of service activities in this sector remains strong. Voluntary participation in local organizations and the building of new structures for planning and coordination of services are important because they represent nonviolent alternatives for the expression of national aspirations. As these organizations move into areas of activity more traditionally executed by government, their leadership will face the challenge of learning new skills in such areas as economic planning and policy formulation.

Finally, an encouraging trend within the past few years can be seen in increased communication and cooperation among Arab nongovernmental organizations throughout the region. A number of regional meetings have been held to address common issues among NGOs and to provide for ongoing coordination. Repeatedly, participants in those meetings have noted the pressing need for reform of the existing laws, as well as for more research and documentation. Thus, the last decade of the twentieth century, with its stirrings toward democracy and self-determination in so many areas of the world, may prove to be a turning point in the efforts to revitalize Arab philanthropy.

References

Abdel Rahman, I. H. "Some Current Trends in Philanthropy in Islamic and Arab Countries." Paper presented at the World Congress on Philanthropy, Toronto, May 1988.

Abed, G. *The Economic Viability and Development Options of a Palestinian State.* Geneva: The Welfare Association, 1988.

Latowski, R. "The Financing of Community Development Associations." A report of the Tanta Integrated Social Services Center (ISSC), Egypt, 1986.

League of Arab States. *Women's Associations and Committees in the West Bank and Gaza Strip.* Tunis: League of Arab States, 1984.

Salem, A. *Law 32 for 1964 on Associations — A Deterrent Against Participation.* Giza, Egypt: Arab Human Rights Organization, 1990.

Voluntarism in Rural Development in India: Initiative, Innovation, and Institutions

The individual urge to extend one's responsibility for social change beyond mandated or formal duties is far more pervasive than is generally assumed. However, not each individual with such an urge takes voluntary initiatives. In still fewer cases are initiatives transformed into innovations. Only rarely are innovations institutionalized in society.

This chapter is based primarily on a review of literature and my personal experience of more than fifteen years in the field of rural development and my involvement in extensive interactions with voluntary organizations and volunteers working in public and private commercial organizations. My contention is that the literature on voluntary organizations or NGOs has neglected the scope of voluntarism that exists among professionals working in mainstream organizations. Thus, I distinguish the phenomenon of voluntarism from the actions of voluntary organization. Given the fact that problems of rural development in India are complex and widespread, isolated initiatives of voluntary organizations (*volags*) may not be able to bring about large-scale social change. There is a need for linking the organizational space that *volags* provide with the urge for change among developmental volunteers (DVs). The DVs work in various organizations but find only limited opportunity for the creative expression of their urge to relate to socially disadvantaged groups. Donor agencies have also given lesser attention to developmental voluntarism than they have to NGOs in developing countries. Public and private organizations cannot sustain support to voluntary organizations in the long run without nurturing voluntarism among a minority of employees within.

The first section of this chapter traces the roots of voluntarism in the context of Indian culture. The second section reviews the trends in the growth of voluntary organizations vis-à-vis voluntarism in rural development and social change, and the third section draws some implications for research and action at both the global and national levels.

Voluntarism in Eastern Societies

It has not been widely appreciated that the roots of voluntarism are quite different in Eastern societies, in particular in Indian society, from those of Western societies. The result has been the implanting of an alien culture in most NGOs, no matter what their ideology is.

Aparigrah, a Sanskrit word, implies the value of nonaccumulation or of not keeping anything more than is necessary for one's minimal needs. The concepts of sacrifice and charity are also differently rooted in the Indian mind. When one gives away one's dearest object to a needy person, the sacrifice could be considered charity. If giving away something is only for one's own self-purity and not aimed at someone else's well-being, it is *tyag* (sacrifice) but not charity. Contrast this with the Western notion of giving away something that one can do without, or that one needs less, or that one has much more of than one needs.

I am not implying that the motivations of voluntarism in India are in any significant way related to the notion of *aparigrah*. What I do suggest is that for strengthening voluntarism in Indian society, support systems and organizations cannot ignore the cultural anchors of the spirit of voluntarism. Even if few people believe in *aparigrah* in urban and middle-class society, there remains a large mass of rural people who do respect a volunteer who follows the principle of *aparigrah*.

Voluntarism based on *agarigrah* has another dimension, and this is the willingness to receive knowledge from whoever is knowledgeable. Thus, giving something away (*pradan*) is accompanied by the inculcation or assimilation of humility and duty toward others (*grahan*). Voluntary organizations that emphasize giving as the basis of a relationship with poor people are either seen as paternalistic by the people or seen as a source of external resources and skills. Hardly any voluntary organizations try to tap the historical reserve of knowledge (technical, institutional, and social) of the poor. The term *resource poor* masks the "richness" of economically poor people. The *grahan* or "assimilation" of knowledge from the poor does not constitute "richness" to many NGOs. Lest this richness of the poor become a paradox, let me explain it in cultural terms.

In Western society, there are only a few words, say, *aunt* or *uncle*, *nephew* or *niece*, for characterizing a whole range of relationships from the mother's or father's side of the family. In Indian languages, each class of relationship has a specific word. People thus have a web of relationships, many of which operate on different planes. Richness in the ability to maintain subtle differences in protocol and mutuality provides a "safety net" of kinship linkages.

In developmental paradigms the neglect of the role of cultural roots, religious identities, and the philosophical basis of social responsibility has led to a crisis among many voluntary organizations. At a recent meeting of voluntary organizations, mostly with Marxist-Leninist leanings, organized by the Institute of Development Studies, Jaipur, it was admitted that despite one and a half decades of mobilization of the people around social and economic causes, there was still a wall of silence between the people and volunteers on the issues of cultural, religious, and caste/ethnic identities. The question "Where do you come from?" or "To which village or region do you belong?" was considered unacceptable in developmental dialogues as a basis of relationship (Aruna Roy, personal communication with the author, 1990). Any effort to build on spatial or other ethnic identities was considered reinforcement of parochialism.

Another cultural element of voluntarism is reciprocity. This includes both *giving* and *receiving* but not in the form of exchange. As Ellis (1989, p. 1) puts it, "It is the giving and not the gift that is important." Eastern as well as African societies have evolved ways of keeping track of reciprocities. Ellis adds that reciprocities are characterized further by (a) wealth being equated with one's esteem or prestige in society based on giving behavior, and (b) the assurance of good return because many people owe it to the giver.

Moreover, the poor use a longer time frame to settle reciprocities than the rich, and in high-risk environments, such as drought-prone areas, generalized reciprocities dominate specific ones (Gupta, 1981, 1984). Studies on voluntarism have not exploited the potential of reciprocal economics versus exchange economics for fostering collective action.

The extent to which *initiatives* calling for deviance from accepted norms, even for social good, are sanctioned by different societies also differs in the West and the East. Cultures that provide the concepts of *aparigrah* and *tyag* also contain codes of sanction against deviance from a certain social order. The exploitation of the poor may thus become possible not merely through the "selfishness" of dominant social classes but also through "learned helplessness" (the opposite of voluntarism) on the part of the poor people.

To illustrate how cultural codification of compliant and conformist behavior takes place, a story from *Mahabharat,* an Indian epic, may help. Droncharya was a renowned teacher who had an *ashram* (a type of school based in a forest) to which royal families considered it a privilege to send their children.

He had taken a vow to make one of the five royal brothers (Pandavas), namely, Arjun, the best archer in the world. One day a tribal boy named Eklavya hesitantly approached Droncharya to seek admission into the school. Droncharya refused admission saying that only the children of royal families could be admitted to his school. Eklavya returned home dejected, built an idol of Droncharya (whom he had accepted as his teacher in his mind), and started practicing archery.

One day Droncharya was moving in the forest accompanied by the Pandavas. A dog started barking and disturbing their conversation. Eklavya, practicing nearby, heard it. He filled the mouth of the dog with arrows. Droncharya could not believe it. He told the Pandavas that if somebody was such a good archer then he surely needed to be met. They soon found Eklavya and asked him how he had learned to be such a good archer. Eklavya, recognizing Droncharya, attributed the excellence of his skill to Droncharya himself. Droncharya was flabbergasted because he had never taught Eklavya. However, on hearing the story of how Eklavya worshipped Droncharya's idol and practiced archery, Droncharya asked for *dakshina,* a sort of fee for providing that knowledge. Eklavya immediately agreed. Droncharya asked for the thumb of Eklavya's right hand, which Eklavya immediately cut and gave away, becoming unable forever after to practice archery. Almost everyone in India has heard this story, which is essentially intended to ingrain two virtues: obedience and deference toward a teacher and perseverance.

Whenever I asked students or professionals from developmental organizations to speculate on the dilemma of Droncharya and Eklavya, they admitted that their parents had never told them about these matters. With some effort, they could speculate upon Droncharya's dilemma, for example, fear of (1) not being able to make Arjun the best archer; (2) not getting the children of royal families as students in the future because he might not be treated as the best teacher; and (3) the possibility of the tribal boy Eklavya passing on his skill to other tribal individuals, who might challenge the established social order, dominated by the "higher" castes and royal families. Yet nobody ever thought that Eklavya also might have had some dilemmas.

Almost everybody argued that it was "natural" for Eklavya to accept the order because thus he is remembered; or he proved his excellence because cutting off his thumb was a sort of certificate of excellence given by the best teacher. He achieved his life's objective. But did he?

Whether Eklavya had any loyalty toward his kith and kin, who fed him and spared him from the normal chores of hunting and food gathering, did not occur to any student or professional. The aspirations of other tribal members to have their children trained by Eklavya never seemed to matter. In other words, the professionals from voluntary agencies and commercial organizations and students from different disciplines completely failed to identify the dilemma in the mind of the dalits (downtrodden), for whom compliance and conformity to a given social order seemed virtually the only choice. Furthermore, deference toward a teacher was so ingrained that even unethical behavior on the part of the teacher was not to be questioned.

The enculturation of compliance and conformity through such powerful metaphors gets in the way of people taking initiatives and questioning the given social order. Those whose social conditions need to be changed the most are the least likely to take initiative. This does not imply that the poor have no concrete alternatives for change. It simply means that innovations needed for survival are quite different from innovations needed for accumulation.

Just emphasizing the "giving" without "acknowledging" or "assimilating" the knowledge of the people often weakens people's self-help potential and curbs the growth of voluntarism among the people themselves. The institution-building process in society suffers when outside volunteers do not plan for their redundancy by developing local leadership. In another meeting of voluntary organizations held at the Institute of Rural Meeting in Anand, it was acknowledged that building people's own organizations so that eventually they would not need outside professional help was a distant dream (Jain, 1989).

My contention is that there are thousands of Eklavyas dispersed in different mainstream organizations. They have a strong sense of taking the initiative and achieving excellence in skills that may be needed in society. However, middle-class conservatism prevents them from becoming entrepreneurs. Voluntary organizations do not consider fostering or nurturing such initiative as part of their major role. The tremendous reserve of human energy that remains untapped by mainstream organizations generates frustration on both sides — the NGOs find bureaucracy stifling and generally unhelpful, and the "compliant" or "conformist" Eklavyas find no organizational or societal space for merging the pursuit of excellence with the search for socially useful innovations. If a linkage between volunteers in public/private commercial organizations and the enabling voluntary organizations can be forged, perhaps society's institutional capacity for self-renewal can be increased considerably.

Trends in Voluntarism in Rural Development in India

My emphasis is much more on voluntarism than on voluntary organizations as instruments of social change. I do not disregard the niches that market forces and state and public agencies leave unfilled, but I argue that these niches can be filled not only by the third sector or voluntary organizations but by the "developmental deviants" or "entrepreneurs" or "volunteers." These volunteers, while remaining in the mainstream public or market organizations, can create new alignments between social needs and institutional support. The excessive attention on voluntary organizations by aid agencies seems misplaced insofar as these agencies almost completely neglect the DVs.

By supporting only NGOs, agencies reduce pressure on public and market agencies for reform and self-renewal. NGOs led by managers or leaders who are often from an urban context, by their own creativity, suppress or fail to nurture the creativity of the local disadvantaged. Social change thus becomes more and more dependent on external leaders.

Rural development as part of social change is defined here as a process of expanding the decision-making horizon and extending the time frame for appraising investment and consumption choices by rural disadvantaged people collectively, and not necessarily at the village level but at even higher levels of aggregation.

Sustainable processes will require correspondence between people's *access* to resources, *ability* to convert access into investments (that is, skills for using resources), and *assurance* of future returns from present investments (vertical assurance) and about others' behavior vis-à-vis one's own (horizontal assurance or collective rationality). The changes in the network of access, ability, and assurance for DVs and the people have to be achieved simultaneously.

Voluntarism may affect any one or more subsets of the developmental triangle of access, assurance, and ability of the people and thus may remain restricted in its impact. The propositions that follow deal with the way that voluntarism has been related to the process of social change in India. Given the range of experiences, it is indeed a synoptic account.

Process of Voluntarism

1. *Voluntarism triggered by a natural crisis such as flood, drought, or cyclone may legitimize the entry of outsiders in a given region, but depending upon the mobilization process, NGOs that emerge in response to such crises often diversify into other areas of social development and remain community oriented rather than class oriented.*

Several church-based NGOs came into existence when international aid agencies offered relief at the time of the Bihar famine in the 1960s. Most of the relief was in the form of consumables such as foodstuffs, clothes, and medicine. The organizational structure for the distribution of this aid was different from the structure for managing durable assets such as rigs for drilling wells, transportation, and buildings. The move from relief to reconstruction attracted many young people. Instead of going back to pursue their professional careers, they remained behind to organize people, manage food for work programs, drill wells, or provide health and educational facilities.

Many aid agencies sought legitimacy through relief but subsequently indulged in other interventions. The reaction of state agencies was to incorporate such volunteers or voluntary organizations as appendages of public relief and development programs. Such incorporation also took place in many NGOs, which came into the picture much later. An interesting feature of these organizations was that having begun with a community approach (relief was needed by all), they continued to use an eclectic approach to development.

Social conflicts were merely noted by some and participated in by others. The institutionalization of voluntarism in intermediary support or funding organizations or grass-roots organizations gave a technomanagerial start to the intervention strategies. A negative feature of such aid was that in regions prone to frequent natural calamities, people started losing their self-help initiative. State relief in the form of employment or food was not linked with a mobilization of voluntarism among the people. Dependency so created made the task of many radical NGOs even more difficult. People could not understand why mobilization around a radical ideology should be a reason for forging immediate material benefits.

2. *Voluntarism triggered by man-made disasters such as the Bhopal tragedy can get caught in the dilemma of legitimizing the state's indifference by becoming part of urgent relief and rehabilitation vis-à-vis questioning the basis of the tragedy and the complicity of the state in its consequences.*

Ravi Rajan (1988), while analyzing rehabilitation and voluntarism, observed four distinct styles: (1) intervening organization took on the provision of relief and rehabilitation as its primary task, became dependent on the government, and with the diminution in the governments' own commitment to the cause, soon collapsed; (2) volunteers served as "conscience keepers," pursuing change through systematic research reports; (3) trade union activists demanded charge of the industrial plant to provide employment through alternative use of plant and machinery; and (4) perhaps the most significant strategy by volunteers was to reject the idea of voluntarism as propounded by the state. Rather, voluntarism was redefined to include sustained mobilization, the struggle for better relief, access to medical data, questioning the secretiveness of the part of the government, legal activism, and questioning the right of the government to give such a low priority to the life of the poor. Voluntarism of this nature is difficult to mobilize in backward rural areas given the dispersed nature of settlements and weak social articulation, low media attention, and poor networking among interventionists.

3. *Voluntarism as manifested in the 1960s by a protest against agrarian disparities (in the form of a violent leftist movement, known as the naxalite movement) and by social reconstruction (initiatives by students, professionals in the mainstream organizations, and voluntary organizations) has undergone a sea of change in the wake of recent economic liberalization.*

Radical groups using violent means of social change have sought support essentially from Maoist philosophy. After the Chinese aggression in 1962, covert support to these groups increased, and income disparities intensified after the first phase of the green revolution. Technological change had provided the spur for a large number of young people, particularly from West Bengal and Andhra Pradesh, to plunge into the field of violent social change. The attempt was to annihilate rich farmers and other symbols of perceived oppressive classes or those considered class enemies.

Another stream of volunteers who entered the field of rural development came with innovative ideas for providing relief during the 1964–1966 drought in different parts of the country. These volunteers became crucial instruments of social dynamics. The war in 1965 with a neighboring country led to a slowing down of U.S. aid to India. The search for indigenous alternatives became intense, and the legitimacy of voluntarism increased.

The period between 1966 and 1972 was full of economic crises. The economic environment in the preceding decade had been aimed at the closure of the Indian economy through import substitution. Droughts, wars (1965, 1971), devaluation of currency, and inflationary pressure created an environment of social unrest in the organized and unorganized sectors. Death from starvation was supposed to have been eliminated (almost) after the drought of 1965–1967. Maharashtra started an employment guarantee scheme during the drought of 1972. In the wake of large-scale violence in 1966 and 1967 by left-wing radical groups, the report of a confidential inquiry committee by a committed civil servant (Appu) set up by the Home Ministry argued for an immediate thrust toward target group oriented programs of rural development suited to location or ecology and class-specific needs.

The Small and Marginal Farmer and Agricultural Labourer Development agencies, the Drought-Prone Area Programme, and the Tribal Development and Hill Area Development plans followed. Decentralized development in the policy was accompanied by greater political centralization from 1970 to 1977. A movement based on Gandhian values that called for total social revolution was spearheaded by Jaya Prakash Narayan in 1973 and 1974. It attracted a large number of young people, particularly in Gujarat, Bihar, and Maharashtra, and many of these young people continued with voluntary work.

The government declared a state of emergency from 1975 until 1977, after a prolonged railway strike, and even urban people realized for the first time the implications of a nondemocratic coercive state. Voluntarism was also sought out as a sign of despicable deviance. People had the option of being incorporated into the repressive state structure or being jailed or victimized. The post-1977 phase of change in political continuity through the single-party rule brought many Gandhians committed to decentralized development into the mainstream. Tax concessions for voluntary initiatives by commercial companies were introduced for the first time by the Janata government in 1978, and many innovative organizations came into being. A number of developmental volunteers who worked in commercial organizations found this an opportunity for exploring new organizational space. Some misused this option but many did not.

For the first time, professionals and young activists were offered competitive salaries in addition to autonomy for work unheard of in mainstream organization by and large. These events were also accompanied by a change in the policy of international aid agencies, which started shifting from funding better implementation of government programs bureaucratically to better implementation by NGOs. It was unfortunate that creative avenues in the NGOs got generally fossilized because of their proximity to the state and their participation in implementing standardized programs.

A change of government in 1980 and the restoration of rule by the Congress party led to the expected withdrawal of tax concessions; the centralization of voluntarism (companies could contribute to the Prime Minister's fund for rural development and seek fresh grants from it for action programmes); the halting of the direct transfer of funds from a commercial balance sheet to the social (less easy to account) balance sheet; the standardization of developmental programs such as the Integrated Rural Development Programme (IRDP); the withdrawal of higher allocations to the IRDP for backward areas and putting them on par with other areas; and the merger of earlier adaptive or responsive programs into a standardized IRDP, with credit-linked subsidy as the dominant mode of relationship.

Another interesting development was the return of naxalite (radical Maoist leftists) underground workers to the mainstream as nonviolent but articulate strategists of social change. For the first time, several ex-naxalites sought election in 1977 and some were elected.

The social space for alternative development was filled by volunteers with varying backgrounds: ex-radicals; liberal or social democrats who were dissatisfied with the workings of the state and wanted to influence the distribution of resources; enthusiastic urban activists who after looking for a career, failed to get one and returned to a mainstream profession rather quickly; young professionals with technical or other disciplinary backgrounds who launched action-research projects or supported other professional groups; retired civil servants, ex-Gandhians, lawyers, and so on, who formed independently or with the support of aid agencies large NGOs; and quasi-state organizations promoted to provide technical, financial, marketing, or other support to NGOs, artisans, and other beneficiaries of state-sponsored developmental programs.

At the time when social space for volunteers was widening, opportunities for career growth in mainstream organizations also began to increase. The first phase involved the growth of the banking sector after nationalization in 1969. A large number of bright young men and women with backgrounds in science, the humanities, or engineering joined banks, insurance corporations, and other such systems. "Brain drift" as opposed to "brain drain" took a heavy toll by depriving academic disciplines of bright students and luring some professionals on the margin away from other direct social development systems.

The post-1980 boom in the consumer goods industry and the continued growth of banking and other public and private ventures further increased the flow of young people toward such careers. The opportunity cost of those who chose to work in NGOs did indeed increase.

The question we want to address next is "What are the processes by which voluntarism in mainstream organizations can complement the efforts of NGOs not merely in bringing about social change on the microlevel but also in influencing public policy in favor of the disadvantaged?"

Implications for Action and Research

Generating extra-organizational space for developmental volunteers within mainstream organizations is a necessary condition for sustainable social development. One study on bank and NGO cooperation for poverty alleviation in backward regions noted that there was no NGO working in the fifty most backward subregions of Gujarat. State organizations like the National Bank could not gain credibility in supporting NGOs if they did not provide the opportunity for exploration and experimentation to volunteers within their system. NGOs often did not recover even the operating costs of many services from people. In the process, such NGOs remained perpetually dependent upon aid agencies. Moreover, accountability of the NGOs in regard to the poor was so low that most NGOs did not aim at inducting poor people into their own management structures.

One nationalized bank invited its clerks to volunteer for two years in a village development program in an area of their choice without any loss of seniority upon their return. This triggered numerous innovative experiments by DVs.

The hands of DVs in technology generation, adaptation, and diffusion system working on unpopular problems of larger social concern needed just as much attention. How can professionals who disregard professional rewards and devote attention to such problems but cannot put pressure for reform on their own organizations be sustained? Empowering them will require recognition of their voluntarism by a body of concerned scholars and activists. No national award has been given to date to any bank officer for initiating innovative schemes. So much so that about ten million rupees for new innovative schemes for rural development provided at the national level remained unspent because no system existed for identifying and recognizing DVs within the mainstream system.

Can the capacity of urban people to manage their own affairs be provided by urban volunteers who come from very different cultures? The poor do not cooperate with developmental organizations because they are not recognized as possessing any *richness* in terms of their cultural and moral fiber. The findings of our research are seldom shared with those from whom we collect data (Gupta, 1987a, 1987b). Involving the rural poor as co-researchers of social phenomena, building upon cultural roots of voluntarism, and showing respect for common property institutions can change this situation. Acknowledging local initiatives can spur their transformation into innovations. Documenting people's knowledge and identifying the scientific merit of some sustainable resource management alternatives can rekindle people's experimental ethic.

Institution building requires the dispensability of external leadership, the recognition of an inverse relationship between status and skills, and the discrediting of values that generate helplessness. "Lateral learning" among developmental volunteers and NGOs can be triggered to provide empirical basis for building a "theory in and of" action.

Concepts of voluntarism such as *zakat* among Muslims, *gupt dan* (anonymous charity) among Hindus, *Kar Seva* (voluntary labor for the common good) among Sikhs, and so on, are examples of the positive bases on which different religions build organic institutions. Different languages have words like *andi* (Haryanavi) and *dhuni* (Hindi), implying a person obsessed with ideas generally for the social good. Why has appreciation for this trait vanished? Anonymous voluntarism, a unique and long-standing tradition of the east, has been absorbed by voluntary organizations that believe that voluntarism can only exist in their types of organizations. This vision is limited, because it denies the possibility of institutionalizing culture throughout a full range of institutions, not just voluntary organizations.

Finally, neither NGOs nor the developmental volunteers can succeed unless those long-ingrained values that inhibit change among rural poor people are brought into question.

Voluntarism in rural development in India has not been accompanied by pressure for policy change except in regard to environmental issues. Often action at the local level has not been linked with lobbying at the macro level. Recognizing that the state and markets perform better if kept under constant check, developmental volunteers within the organizations will have to serve a sort of "insurgent" function so as to align, anonymously, with grass-root activists, NGOs, and professionals. International agencies can strengthen local social change by broadening local ideas and innovations into global thinking and by providing global space for developmental volunteers to validate their hypotheses. Right Livelihood awards constitute one such source of international recognition. If the rural poor of India could communicate with the homeless in America, surely the cultures of deprivation would provide the basis for collective action. Social innovators and DVs around the world are struggling for similar space in a society where one does not have to go through a phase of unbridled accumulation followed by guilt, charity, and benevolence for the have-nots.

Sustainability in nature and society requires players, whistle blowers, spectator rules, and creative chaos. DVs are arguing that the losers in a game should not lose the right to play on the same field again. Asking them to play only on separate fields (in the form of volags) will eventually rob the game of the chaotic waves of sorrow and joy. Should we let it convert the spectators into warriors?

References

Ellis, W. N. "Reciprocity Economics vs. Exchange Economics." *Community Service Newsletter,* 1989, *37* (6), 1–3.

Gupta, A. K. "Viable Projects for Unviable Farmers: An Action Research Enquiry into the Structures and Processes of Rural Poverty in Arid Regions." Paper presented at the symposium on rural development in South Asia, IUAES Inter Congress, Amsterdam, 1981.

Gupta, A. K. "Small Farmers Household Economy in Semi-Arid Regions: Socio-Ecological Perspective." CMA project report based on field survey in 1979–80 and 1982–83, IIM, Ahmedabad, 1984. (Mimeographed.)

Gupta, A. K. "Bank-NGO-Poor Interface in Backward Region: Alternatives for Action." *Indian Journal of Public Administration,* 1987a, *33* (3), 662–679.

Gupta, A. K. "Why Poor Don't Cooperate: Lessons from Traditional Organizations with Implications for Modern Organizations." In C. G. Wanger (ed.), *Research Relationship: Politics and Practice of Social Research.* London: George Allen and Unwin, 1987b.

Jain, P. (ed.). *Perspectives on Voluntary Organization.* Anand, India: Institute of Rural Management, 1989.

Rajan, R. S. "Rehabilitation and Voluntarism in Bhopal." *Lokayan Bulletin,* 1988, 6(½), 3–31.

Voluntarism and Voluntary Organizations in Indonesia

This chapter presents an overview of voluntarism and voluntary organizations in Indonesia. It begins with a brief review of voluntarism as practiced in traditional agrarian village communities. The spirit of *gotong royong,* or mutual help, can be regarded as the basis of Indonesian voluntarism. In recent years, rapid social and economic change, especially in urban areas, has dampened this spirit, such that in modern Indonesia it is often carried out by private voluntary nonprofit organizations. These organizations will be discussed in this chapter under four headings: religious institutions, social welfare organizations, social associations, and self-reliant community development institutes. As the reader will see, differences in size, scope, motive, and mission make this a difficult task.

The chapter continues with a discussion of the legal status or regulatory context of private voluntary nonprofit organizations in Indonesia. As yet no legal framework governs foundations here, and thus there is no provision for government oversight.

Both government programs and NGOs have their strengths and weaknesses. Therefore, the relationship between the government and NGOs needs to involve increased understanding and new mechanisms for the effective collaboration and flow of information between the two sectors.

Many sectors of the government still do not know much about self-reliant community development institutes (*lembaga pengembangan swadaya masyarakat,* or LPSMs) and what these organizations can do. This lack of knowledge leads to misunderstandings, which in turn hamper cooperative efforts and efficiency. One LPSM, Bina Swadaya, which is based in Jakarta but supports community-based projects in many rural areas, provides an example of how nongovernment agencies and the government can work together and by sharing information build trust that can lead to joint initiatives.

The chapter concludes with some observations regarding the implications of the findings for further policy and research.

Gotong Royong, or Traditional Mutual Help Activities

In Indonesia, 73 percent of the population lives in rural areas, and in such areas the agricultural workload is often still carried by the community in a traditional way, based on the spirit of *gotong royong,* or mutual help. This spirit is actually a universal phenomenon of traditional agrarian village communities.

The spirit of *gotong royong* applies not only to agricultural work but also to other aspects of social life. Its basis is a feeling of mutual need among community members (Koentjaraningrat, 1977). As a result, in an agrarian village community, various mutual aid activities are carried out willingly and spontaneously. For example, in the event of death, sickness, an accident, or other disaster, neighbors and villagers contribute money, goods, and services without expecting any reward. In preparing a celebration, such as a circumcision or a wedding, not only relatives but also neighbors participate. If someone needs assistance in repairing a house or replacing or digging a well, the owner will ask his nearest neighbors for assistance, and in return he will provide them with meals. In implementing public works projects, such as roads, bridges, and irrigation systems, the community will execute the work on a voluntary basis with the guidance of the village headman. The activation of *gotong royong* would not be possible without the help of the *rukun kampung* (RK) and *rukun tetangga* (RT). The *Rukun Kampung* are neighborhood associations comprised of *Rukun Tetangga*, or neighborhood associations, each of which is usually made up of about twenty households.

The spirit of *gotong royong* appears to be eroding as a result of social and economic change. The sense of sharing the workload on a voluntary and reciprocal basis is fading away. People increasingly prefer to employ workers on a wage basis because of the availability of low-cost labor. Moreover, providing meals for voluntary workers could become expensive and complicated, depending on the employer's socioeconomic status.

Since the introduction of the green revolution in Java, the *gotong royong* system related to rice harvesting is also changing in certain areas. The intimate relationship between harvesters and landowners is being replaced by a more formal one. As a consequence, voluntary associations have become necessary to deal specifically with issues of economic growth and poverty reduction.

Private Voluntary Nonprofit Organizations in Indonesia

Many private voluntary nonprofit organizations have come into being in Indonesia during the past twenty years. It is not an easy task to classify such organizations because of their number and diversity. The classification scheme I have chosen is one of type: religious institutions, social welfare organizations, social associations, and institutes for community development. However, this scheme is imperfect, involving some unavoidable overlapping.

Religious Institutions

Among Indonesia's religions, Islam and Christianity are particularly noteworthy for the volume and variety of private voluntary nonprofit organizations and institutions they have generated.

Muhammadiyah, one of the nation's largest Islamic organizations, was a pioneer in the establishment of orphanages, hospitals, and clinics. Nowadays, the main mosques in big cities are generally associated with health clinics (Dien and others, 1980).

Muhammadiyah and Nahdatul Ulama, the other major Islamic organizations in Indonesia, have also founded educational institutions throughout the archipelago. The number of Islamic student organizations and youth organizations has increased markedly since 1970. Islamic university student organizations include the Islamic Student Association, the Indonesian Islamic Student Movement, and the Muhammadiyah Student Union. These student organizations are treated as social associations, which are discussed below.

Catholic and Protestant churches in Indonesia also have a long tradition of community service activity. Catholic missionaries from the Franciscan, Jesuit, and Dominican orders have had a particularly strong influence in the eastern part of Indonesia. Their most pronounced activity has been in the field of education (Dien and others, 1980). Catholic schools are often considered the best in many communities.

Domestic financial resources in support of these various religious voluntary organization activities — Islamic and Christian — come mainly from individual donations. Foreign financial sources are an additional important source of funding. In regard to this matter, in 1978 the Ministry of Religious Affairs issued Decree No. 77, "Foreign Aid to Religious Institutions in Indonesia"; a sequel, the joint Decree No. 1 was issued the following year by the Ministry of Religious Affairs and the Ministry of Home Affairs to regulate, guide, and direct foreign aid to religious institutions in Indonesia.

Social Welfare Organizations

Social welfare organizations (*organisasi sosial*) are registered with the Ministry of Social Affairs and are extremely widespread in Indonesia. At the local level, in Jakarta alone the Social Welfare

Activity Coordinating Board (BKKKS) coordinates twelve organizations for the welfare of infants, forty organizations for the care of orphans, nineteen for family welfare, ten for care of the aged, twenty-four organizations for home care, seventy-six schools for the handicapped, and 103 other social welfare organizations.

At the national level, the Indonesian National Council for Social Welfare (DNIKS) assists the Ministry of Social Affairs in the coordination and development of social welfare activities and community development.

According to two regulations (Decree No. 77 of 1983 and Decree No. 54 of 1984) of the Ministry of Social Affairs, social welfare organizations must have written permission from the minister to receive foreign aid. An organization that receives foreign aid is required to provide quarterly reports of how funds are spent. The minister is empowered to evaluate the activities financed with foreign aid.

In 1980, prior to the issuance of the Law on Social Organizations, the Ministry of Social Affairs issued Regulation No. 40, by which each social welfare organization is obliged to acknowledge *Pancasila,* Indonesia's official state ideology, and the Indonesian constitution as the two bases of the organization; to agree to function as a partner of the government, coordinating its activities with the government; to report on its activities to the minister; to have the organization legalized and formally registered at the ministry; and finally, to submit to the supervision of different government agencies. Any organization that fails to comply with these regulations can be dissolved by the minister (Witjes, 1986).

Social Associations

Social associations (*organisasi kemasyarakatan*) are to be distinguished from two other forms of organizations, social welfare organizations (*organisasi sosial*) and self-reliant community development institutes (*lembaga pengembangan swadaya masyarakat*).

The law on social associations (Law No. 8 of 1985) states that social associations are "organizations established voluntarily by citizens of the Republic of Indonesia, on the basis of shared activities, professions, functions, religion, and the belief in one and almighty God, for the purpose of participating in national development with the aim of achieving the national goal, within the framework of the Unitary State of the Republic of Indonesia" (Article 1). Organizations established by the government, such as the boy and girl scouts and also the civil servants' association (KORPRI) do not fall under this law. Profit-making and profit-seeking associations that operate in the economic field, such as cooperatives and limited companies (PTs), are also excluded.

The functions of social associations, according to the 1985 law, are to organize activities according to the interests of the members and to develop the capabilities of the members in the realization of the association's objectives. Broadly defined, these associations are seen as a means to channel the aspirations of their members and as an opportunity for members to meet people and to establish contact with other social organizations, sociopolitical organizations, the People's Consultative Assembly, the House of Representatives, and the government.

The law stipulates that social associations, including religious institutions, adopt the state philosophy of *Pancasila* as their "sole principle," which includes five parts: (1) belief in the one and Almighty God, (2) a just and civilized humanity, (3) national unity, (4) democracy, guided by consultation and representation, and (5) social justice for all Indonesians. Aside from this "sole principle," it is recognized that the objectives of each social association will differ according to their specific nature. The Ministry of Home Affairs recently reported the existence of 449 registered social associations. These associations are marked by considerable variety in their membership and purpose.

One group of associations includes those created for the purpose of carrying out common, not-for-profit activities. At the time of the 1985 law, there were 112 such organizations, of which the best known is probably the Indonesian Family Planning Association, the nation's pioneer family planning organization.

A second group of social associations represents various professions. Probably the best known of the 122 associations in this group is the Institute for Economic and Social Research, Education, and Information (LP3ES), Indonesia's prominent think tank for younger Islamic intellectuals. Yet a third group of associations is functionally oriented. The ministry reported 127 associations of this type, a prominent example of which is the Union of All-Purpose Mutual Aid Organization (KOSGORO), a federation of veterans' organizations that continued to be a political force into the 1970s. Finally, a fourth group of associations is based on religious affinity. There are eighty-eight of them, of which Muhammadiyah and Nahdatul Ulama (NU), previously mentioned, are the most prominent.

It is evident that many associations could be placed in more than one of the official categories according to the language of the law. It is not easy to devise a strict classification of social associations. It is even more complicated to determine whether an organization is a social association or a self-reliant community development institute.

The financing of social associations may come from membership fees, donations, and other lawful means. Financing may also come from foreign sources provided that governmental approval is obtained.

Self-Reliant Community Development Institutes

Organizations involved in community development and related work are known primarily as self-reliant community institutes (*lembaga swadaya masyarakat,* or LSMs), or self-reliant community development institutes (*lembaga pengembangan swadaya masyarakat,* or LPSMs). LSMs focus their activities on grass-roots projects that are aimed at making self-reliance a reality at the community level and at helping the powerless in society by promoting broader social change. Groups and organizations involved in such activities include philanthropic foundations, special-interest associations, cooperatives, research and training institutes, credit unions and village savings and loan unions, women's organizations, work brigades, and other citizens' groups (Betts, 1986).

These institutes play a significant role as a liaison between the government and the communities, with their diverse needs and particular aspirations. The government has also become increasingly aware of the institutes' ability and willingness to experiment with new ideas that government agencies would not attempt to try. In addition, these private groups attempt to demonstrate a strong orientation toward the true needs and concerns of the people and a full understanding of local situations. As a consequence, foreign donor organizations or grant-making institutions seem to be increasing their funding to LSMs and LPSMs. One danger is that the LSMs may become overly dependent on foreign funding, but most report that foreign aid tends to be for general support, and funds are not restricted to fulfill a donor's goals.

Taking into account their important role, LPSMs have been involved in a wide range of activities, including education and training programs, community development work, the promotion of cooperatives, publications, research and development, captial formation, appropriate technology, legal aid, protection of the environment, family planning, health and nutrition programs, consumer affairs, transmigration, and income-generating projects.

The Regulatory Context of
Private Voluntary Nonprofit Organizations

The Indonesian civil code evolved from the Dutch civil code that was in force in 1945, when Indonesia declared its independence. Only later, on May 31, 1956, did the Netherlands promulgate a law on foundations. Thus, there were no laws or regulations governing the establishment or operation of foundations in Indonesia. Even so, it has been assumed that a foundation (or *yayasan*) is a legal entity in which certain wealth is set apart to be used for specific goals as established by a board of organizers or governors.

The only regulation in the civil code that refers to such legal entities is found in Chapter IX of the Third Civil Code, Article 1653, which defines *zedelijke lichamen*. This article lays down general rules for the three kinds of legal entities, namely, those that are (1) organized, (2) recognized, and (3) permitted by law. The article is interpreted by jurists to cover both public and private legal entities. Institutions or organizations that are denoted as legal entities are organizations (*perkumpulan*), limited corporations (*perseroan terbatas*), cooperatives (*koperasi*), and foundations (*yayasan/stichting*). A number of articles in the civil code describe the nature and characteristics of these legal entities (Rido, 1986).

Although the foundation is neither described nor mentioned explicitly in the civil code, institutions called foundations have been present since Indonesia's independence in 1945. Hundreds of foundations have been established as a result of the ease with which they can be created. A foundation can be established with a notarial document that describes its status, name, and domicile; its assets; the form and structure of the board or organizers; the procedures for replacement and discontinuance of board members; and the procedures for the disposition of assets in the event of dissolution (Soerodibroto, 1989).

A foundation can be established by one or more persons. A minimal amount of capital is required, for example, Rp.5000.00 (US $3.00). A foundation can be used for various purposes: social, political, and even commercial. No institution has the right to interfere in a foundation's internal affairs, and the board of directors possesses unlimited authority. In addition, foundations are not accountable to the public. The board of directors is not even obliged to make public the establishment of the foundation, nor is it necessary to have the foundation legalized by the Ministry of Justice, as is the case with the establishment of a corporation. From the government's point of view, it is quite difficult to control the operation of foundations, especially in relation to the management of their assets. A foundation is not allowed to change its status to that of an association or corporation, however; once established, it must pursue some idealistic goal.

Currently, there are different views on the legal status of foundations. One view is that they are legal entities as per the Supreme Court decision of June 27, 1973 (No. 124/K/Sip/1973).

On the basis of that decision, it can be concluded that foundations have a board of directors to represent them in and outside the court and that they may possess their own wealth and property. Another view holds that foundations must become legal entities based on and regulated by law before they have the right to use the court and collect wealth (Soerodibroto, 1989). As a consequence of these differences of opinion, some people believe that a law regulating the establishment and operation of foundations is necessary or, at the least, highly desirable.

According to the Tax Law of 1984, foundations are exempt from payment of taxes if their income was used for philanthropic purposes that meet the following requirements: (a) activities limited to the fields of religion, education, health, and culture; (b) activities that increase social welfare; and (c) activities that are neither profit seeking nor profit oriented.

A foundation's profit is the surplus that results from an excess of income over operation costs and as such it is not taxable. In the event that the surplus is invested in other fields that are not defined as social activities, such as in bank accounts or corporate shares, then the income derived from these activities — if it is used for financing social activities — is also not taxable. The 1984 tax law does not provide tax deductions to donors for their charitable contributions.

Relations Between the
Government and the LPSMs and LSMs

Philip Eldridge (1988), an Australian researcher, has studied the activities of major NGOs in Indonesia. He identified three kinds of approaches that guide LPSMs and LSMs in shaping their relations with the Indonesian government. NGOs that are purely charity oriented were not included in this study. The first approach is described as "high-level partnership: Grass-roots development," which involves cooperation in official development programs with an orientation that emphasizes grass-roots development rather than mobilization. Examples of this model include Yayasan Indonesia Sejahtera (YIS), which operates in the field of health and community development, and Bina Swadaya.

which promotes small savings groups, credit unions, and joint efforts. The second approach is described as "high-level politics: grass-roots mobilization." Unlike groups with the first approach, organizations with this approach do not cooperate in official development programs but maintain close relations with decision makers and therefore may influence them when seeking protection and space for local mobilization. In carrying out these politically oriented activities, these organizations tend to have contacts with military, bureaucratic, and social networks. The Lembaga Studi Pembangunan (LSP), which operates primarily in the urban informal sector, represents this model, as does the program to develop social awareness in traditional Islamic schools run by the Institute for Economic and Social Research, Education and Information. The third approach focuses more on the local level than on the national level; Eldridge refers to it as "empowerment at the grass roots." Like those with the second approach, groups with this approach also emphasize consciousness-raising and helping their members understand their rights, but they have less contact with state organizations. The Legal Aid Study Group (KSBH), based in Yogyakarta, is an example of this sort of organization. Other examples are smaller and more diffuse groups, which are found in many fields of activity pursued by the second model, particularly those related to ecology, legal and human rights, and women's issues. The network associated with the Indonesian Environmental Forum contains elements of both the second and third models. This is also true of the groups associated with the Indonesian Legal Aid Foundation, which is concerned with legal and human rights.

Thus far, the Indonesian government has tended to focus on central planning that involves a top-down approach to development, giving higher priority to overall national programs, such as food, nutrition, production, family planning, and infrastructure improvement (Tjondronegoro, 1984). Many of the development programs formulated to date have not involved deliberations with grass-roots organizations or reflected their priorities. Consequently, in certain instances they have failed to respond to local needs.

Bina Swadaya: A Successful Example?

Bina Swadaya, an agency for the development of community self-reliance, is an example of successful cooperation between the government and LPSMs in Indonesia. Members of Bina Swadaya consider this cooperation essential if their ideas are to have an impact. Their strategy in working with the government has been to apply an *usaha bersama* (UB) approach to family planning, transmigration, and small holders' programs. *Usaha bersama*, meaning "joint efforts," are informally structured cooperative enterprises.

A *usaha bersama* venture, on the other hand, would typically arise from the efforts of a promoter or catalyst to stimulate a community to reflect on its common problems and needs. It often begins by organizing existing groups in communities, such as rotating credit associations, for funding purposes. One of its projects for developing self-reliance among transmigrant communities is located in Rasau Jaya, West Kalimantan, funded by the Konrad Adenauer Foundation. According to Indonesian government policy, the concept of transmigration is considered to be a nation-building program targeted to increase national unity and security and is no longer seen only as a resettlement program to move people from high- to low-population density areas. The program is also geared to the more effective use of human and natural resources, the creation of job opportunities, and balanced regional development. In the long term, these measures are expected to improve the income and welfare of everyone (Office of the Minister of State for Population and the Environment, 1985).

Although the government, via the Department of Transmigration and collaborating sectoral departments such as Health, Public Works, Agriculture, and Education, provided technical and material support, the settlers also needed assistance in developing integrated and self-reliant communities. Before the Bina Swadaya project for developing self-reliance was implemented in Rasau Jaya, the transmigrants faced a number of problems, such as poor agricultural conditions, lack of appropriate skills, poor community adaptation, and absence of local institutions. The transmigrants lost more than 30 percent of their population when these people left the resettlement site. Those who stayed remained dependent on government subsidies and other private relief services.

The Bina Swadaya challenge was to help the transmigration communities make better use of their human and natural resources in order to become economically independent in the new environment. As a consequence in Rasau Jaya, Bina Swadaya, through its Institute for Guidance and Development of People's Cooperatives set up loan programs, opened up land for collective farming projects, established a marketing committee to handle produce prices, and submitted plans for the development of small-scale businesses. As a consequence of those efforts, the government was able to develop a working village cooperative unit, which had previously not progressed beyond the organizational stage. The approaches and methods used in Rasau Jaya have subsequently been applied to other transmigration areas.

The UB training provided by Bina Swadaya motivated villagers to form their own UB unit. It began with the community expressing its interests, knowledge, skills, and needs. The program stressed self-motivation and learning-by-doing, allowing villagers to set their own pace and creating opportunities for them to learn through direct, hands-on experience. By the end of the pilot project period Rasau Jaya had become a model for transmigration and was referred to as the "information center for self-reliant transmigration development" because of its success in developing strategies for the introduction of appropriate technology, development of effective cooperatives, and improvement of the economic situation in a difficult rural area (Office of the Minister of State for Population and the Environment, 1985).

Conclusions

The primary aim of LPSMs and LSMs is to serve people more directly, especially at the grass-roots level; to assist them in the process of development; and to strengthen their capability for self-reliance. In theory at least, they operate on the basis of development by the people and for the people, in response to expressed community needs. Planning is executed from the bottom up, starting by identifying problems and the mechanisms for solving them.

In this context LPSMs and LSMs need to work in close cooperation with the government. LPSMs are expected to be agents for catalytic change by bridging the gap between the people and government.

In order to improve relations between the government and the LPSMs and LSMs, a greater sharing of information, greater trust, and expanded opportunities for joint participation are recommended. By giving LPSMs and LSMs the opportunity to experiment, skills and expertise can be improved. Therefore, the government should encourage this process and foster a climate of independence for these organizations. Mutual understanding has become a necessity.

In summary, LPSMs and LSMs should be welcomed because they can provide valuable input to planners and others assigned to the implementation of Indonesia's development programs. These organizations can also play a useful intermediary role in program design, in identifying and mobilizing appropriate community groups, and in channeling funds to them. Their active participation can also enhance the quality of Indonesia's development programs by gradually reducing red tape and by widening popular participation in the development process. As LPSMs and LSMs have grown larger and are increasingly seen as having a significant and legitimate role to play in the national development process, some of them are having to face a new dilemma. On one hand, they are expected to cooperate with the government in order to obtain greater access to resources. On the other hand, there is a fear among some LPSMs and LSMs of losing their identity and links with the grass-roots communities.

In an effort to prevent unnecessary social tension between the LPSMs and LSMs and the government in implementing development projects, a forum should be set up so that periodically, LPSMs, LSMs, and other private voluntary organizations can present their views, based on their field observation and experience. At present, mistakes and poor communication caused by incompetence and faulty planning sometimes occur in the implementation of programs. In this respect, increased exchange of information between the state agencies and organization representatives would be extremely useful in helping to solve problems and should be promoted not only in Jakarta but also in the provinces.

References

Betts, R. "Institutional Mechanisms to Raise Funds for Indonesian Private Voluntary Organizations." Development Alternatives, Inc. (DAI), Feb. 1986.

Dien, U., and others. *The Development of Islam in Indonesia*. Jakarta: Office of Islamic Information Service, Ministry of Religious Affairs of the Republic of Indonesia, 1980.

Eldridge, P. "NGOs and the State of Indonesia." *Prisma*, 1988, *47*, 41–44.

Koentjaraningrat. "The System and Spirit of *Gotong Royong*." *Prisma*, June 1977, p. 20.

Koentjaraningrat. *Masalah-masalah Pembangunan, Bunga Rampai Antropologi Terapan*. Jakarta: Institute for Economic and Social Research, Education, and Information, 1982.

Office of the Minister of State for Population and the Environment, Government of Indonesia, in cooperation with the World Bank and the Ford Foundation. *Participation of Non-Governmental Organizations (NGOs) in the National Development Process in Indonesia*. A seminar report, Jakarta, Feb. 13–16, 1985.

Rido, A. *Badan Hukum dan kedudukan Badan Hukum Perseroan, Perkumpulan, Koperasi, Yayasan, Wakaf*. Bandung: Penerbit Alumni, 1986.

Soerodibroto, S. "Menyongsong Lahirnya Undang-Undang tentang Yayasan." *Suara Pembaruan*, Jan. 12, 1989.

Suparlan, P. *Kemiskinan di Perkotaan*. Jakarta: Penerbit Sinar Harapan dan Yayasan Obor Indonesia, 1984.

Tjondronegoro, S. M. P. *Social Organization and Planned Development in Rural Java.* Singapore: Oxford University Press, 1984.

Witjes, B. "The Indonesian Law on Social Organizations: A Study of the Socio-Political Context and the Consequences for Indonesian Foreign NGOs." *Nijmegen,* Oct.–Nov., 1986.

Chapter 26

The Development of
Private Philanthropy
in Singapore

Founded in 1819 as a British trading station, Singapore has since been transformed into a modern, industrialized city-state and a major economic center in Asia. Nation-building and economic modernization efforts began in earnest after full independence was achieved in 1965. Taking advantage of her strategic location and human resources, Singapore's economy expanded rapidly. By 1988, Singapore's per capita GNP, at $17,673, was the third highest in Asia, after Japan and Brunei. In slightly over two decades of independence, a firm economic base has now been established, with manufacturing, services, and commerce as the major economic sectors. With a land area of only 623 square kilometers and a population of 2.6 million, Singapore is compact and cosmopolitan, and it enjoys a well-developed physical infrastructure.

In the early years of nationhood, the need to achieve the nation's economic and social aspirations was translated into a number of major social policies. Among them is the policy concerning the allocation of resources for philanthropic or charitable activities. To reduce the welfare burden on the state and to preserve funds for developmental purposes, the Singapore government has adopted, since independence, a welfare policy that emphasizes the principles of individual responsibility, hard work, and family care. Welfare assistance from the state is provided only as a last resort. Instead, state provisions have been concentrated in the area of basic services: housing, health, and education. The guiding principle on welfare is best summarized by the following statement from the government: "The programs and policies which the Government will pursue in the fields of finance and economics, social and medical services, education and defence are all based on the inexorable premise, that rewards must be correlated to the contribution one makes to the total national well-being. We believe . . . that more and more pay for less and less work must lead to greater and greater borrowing and eventual bankruptcy. . . . The needy should never be allowed to become a permanent burden on the rest of the community" (*Mirror*, 1977, p. 8).

The reluctance of the state to become directly involved in the philanthropic sector means that voluntary or private organizations end up with the lion's share of the work. This indeed has been the case, and the importance of the voluntary sector remains unchanged as Singapore develops and prospers. Although it has been able to put away budgetary surpluses each year, the government has given no indication that its welfare policy will be revised. The reluctance of the government to provide direct welfare assistance, except to meet extreme needs, is regularly reiterated. With an increasingly affluent population, the resources available for private transfer from the well-off to the needy are not in short supply. Over time, the nature in which such resources are channeled into charitable activities and the manner in which philanthropic organizations are governed have undergone fundamental transformation. The emerging welfare or philanthropic sector is now well organized, secular, professionally managed, well funded, and centrally coordinated; this is a far cry from the chaotic days of many individual- or group-based philanthropies with cross-cutting causes and objectives.

Each society organizes its philanthropic or welfare activities differently, depending on its socioeconomic and political circumstances (Baron, 1989). As a case in point, this chapter traces the development of private philanthropy in Singapore and seeks to explain the emerging pattern. It has three parts. The first presents the legal framework for charitable organizations in Singapore. Part two traces the historical development leading to the present pattern, especially the changing relationship between the government and voluntary organizations. Finally, the chapter examines the emerging characteristics of Singapore's philanthropic sector.

Legal Provisions

The law governing charitable organizations and private philanthropies in Singapore is fairly straightforward. It provides an unambiguous definition of charity and aims to sanction any misuse of charitable funds. The legal provisions are contained in the Charities Act, 1982, which follows closely the English Charities Act of 1960 (Ricquier, 1982). The legal definition of charity in Singapore is therefore derived from the English Statute of Charitable Uses, 1601, as well as the subsequent interpretations as contained in English common law.

The 1982 act, drawing on Lord Macnaghten's 1891 classification in the Pemsel case, divides charity in four broad divisions: trusts for the relief of poverty, trusts for the advancement of religion, trusts for the advancement of education, and trusts for other purposes beneficial to the community.

The categories are not meant to be exhaustive, and the scope of each is to be reviewed as new social needs arise. However, no attempt has yet been made in Singapore to modify these categories (Lim, 1984). To be deemed legally charitable, a trust or organization must be established for exclusive charitable purposes. If it has as its objective a noncharitable purpose, then the trust or organization cannot be deemed charitable. It will, however, not fail to be charitable because of incidental benefits to the rich or other people who are not recipients of the charity in its operation.

The commissioner of charities is responsible for administering the Charities Act and has the authority to do the following:

Establish and maintain a register of all charities

Institute inquiries into the administration of charities

Take steps to protect property that belongs to a charity because of misconduct or mismanagement

Order the removal of a charity trustee for reasons such as fraud, mental disorder, bankruptcy, and the like

Statutorily modify Cy pres doctrine (which allows for distribution of assets or bequests to other organizations if the original charitable purpose becomes impossible or no longer exists)

Sanction an administrative action by a charity trustee if the action is in the interest of the charity, even if the action was not within the powers exercisable by the trustees

Under the Charities Act, fiscal privileges are granted to charitable trusts and institutions and gifts made to them (Ter, 1985). As long as a trust or institution remains on the Register of Charities, it qualifies for income tax exemption. There are three additional requirements. First, income from trade or business undertaken by the charity is tax exempt only if it is used solely for charitable purposes. Second, at least 80 percent of the income of the year preceding the year of assessment must have been spent on charities or charitable objects in Singapore. Finally, the income must be used for charitable purposes in accordance to the objects of the institution. Tax will be levied for income used otherwise.

Charities are also exempt from entertainment duty if the whole of the takings of the entertainment are devoted to charitable purposes in Singapore or elsewhere. In addition, buildings used exclusively for charitable purposes are exempt from property tax. Finally, a gift made between living persons for public or charitable purposes (bona fide) twelve months before the death of the donor is exempt from estate duty.

The number of registered charities in Singapore in 1988 is shown below, according to category:

Category	Number
Religion	414
Community	105
Education	57
Mixed	75
Poverty	5
	Total: 656

It is the view of income tax officials that the finances of philanthropic organizations are fairly well supervised in Singapore. Because of the ruling that 80 percent of annual income must be spent on charitable activities and that annual returns must be submitted for scrutiny, few are likely to be tax shelters in disguise. The preclusion of setting up charities as a form of tax shelter is not surprising. Singapore is well known for her clean government and above-board financial dealings. To have pseudocharity organizations established by large businesses or leading families for tax evasion would run against the ethos of the government.

Changing Pattern of Philanthropy

Singapore has a long tradition of private philanthropy, going back to the founding of Singapore as a trading post. When the East India Company acquired Singapore in 1819, its intention was to expand its commercial empire, not to establish a permanent settlement. Faced with a lack of concern and a shortage of officials, the administration was light and lax. This laissez-faire policy led to deficiencies in the provision of essential social services. In direct response, private philanthropic activities sprang up to meet the need.

Charities established by Western religious orders were

among the early ones. In 1852, for example, the Institute of the Sisters of the Infant Jesus opened a home for children. In 1874, the Canossian Daughters of Charity established a service center, providing food and educational services. The YMCA has been in operation since 1902. Many of the services, such as homes and family service centers, are still in existence today and are coordinated by the Catholic Welfare Service, which was established in 1959. Similar services were also developed by the Salvation Army, the Anglicans, the Presbyterians, and the Methodists, though they were much smaller in scale.

When Chinese immigrants came to Singapore in volume as migrant labor in the late nineteenth and early twentieth centuries, they also brought along their clan, district, and dialect associations (Cheng, 1985). Many of these associations built schools, medical facilities, temples, and even transit centers for the new immigrants. They also provided food and helped the new arrivals find jobs. At a time when the colonial government limited its role to commerce and security matters, these clan associations helped manage their own welfare quite effectively. Membership in a clan association represented the link to a well-established support network. Resources and funds were raised from successful businessmen, who were often the leaders of the associations as well. In return, the community accorded respect and legitimacy to the donors' social status. Many of the donors, being former immigrants themselves, were sentimentally inclined to help the newcomers.

These associations were tolerated by the colonial government as long as they did not constitute a threat to the established order. It was in fact preferred to have the various ethnic and dialect groups cater to their own needs. Alongside the Chinese clan associations, there were Indian temples and Muslim mosques that served as service centers to the needs of their respective groups. In 1928, the Ramakrishna Mission began operating homes for Indian migrants. For the Malays, the Muslim Trust Fund Society (Darul Ihsan) came into existence in 1904 to offer services to Muslim Malays.

The English-educated upper and middle classes played a somewhat minor role in direct involvement in philanthropic activities. Many, however, could have helped through church-based programs. An example of private philanthropy of this nature is the Chinese Ladies Association, which was established in 1916 under the patronage of the wife of the Anglican bishop. The association aimed to encourage Chinese women to participate in community services, to give assistance to welfare agencies, and to develop interests in hobbies.

As Singapore became more of a settled community, the colonial government began to introduce administrative apparatus for planning and delivering education, health, and welfare services. Though very rudimentary, a civil administrative foundation was laid for the emergence of the various organs of the state. After the war, in 1946, the Department of Social Welfare was formed, marking the beginning of government organized welfare services in Singapore. Because of the immense problems confronting the postwar society, the government, apart from its own efforts in offering relief, continued to rely on the services provided by the various philanthropic organizations. From 1950 onward, a host of social service agencies were being established by interested civic groups, providing specialized, professional services to the needy.

When the People's Action party (PAP) took office in 1959, there was much concern among Western-style organizations managed by people with a middle-class background. The radical statements the political party made during the election induced fear of a general takeover by the state of all such organizations. That, however, did not occur, as the PAP shed its far-left image and faction to become pragmatic and middle-of-the-road. In effect, the government continued to rely on voluntary organizations to deliver needed services. These secular organizations eventually replaced the clan associations as the dominant group of service providers.

As nation-building efforts began in earnest, the government left an indelible impact on philanthropic organizations formed across ethnic lines. Because their organizations were primarily tied to religious establishments, the Malay and the Indian organizations were not as affected. They were, however, monitored for any extreme religious sentiments. In the case of the Chinese, associations affiliated with the temples were also spared. It was the Chinese clan and dialect associations that were dealt a heavy blow by the government because their very existence was anachronistic to the government's national integration efforts. Suspicions regarding these clan associations were raised on two counts: they were perceived as the hotbed of communism and as ethnocentric symbols at odds with nation building. Clan leaders were investigated for their political inclinations, and some were eventually detained during the tumultuous years of the 1960s. The social status accorded to the clan leaders eventually eroded as the clan associations sought to reestablish their identity and loyalty. Many kept a very low profile to avoid confrontation with or investigation by the government.

Because the clan associations were under close scrutiny by the government, their level of activity was greatly reduced. Prior to independence, many associations were active in the field of education. The first Chinese secondary school was established as early as 1919, under the leadership of the Hokkien Huay Kuan. In 1956, the first Chinese university, Nanyang University, was established by a group of clan associations. To avoid challenging the new government's control in education and other social services, the clan associations slowly phased out their involvement where competition might arise. As a result, most clan associations concentrated on the administration of mutual aid schemes and the provision of scholarships. The mutual aid schemes operated on the basis of a small contribution from each member per month, usually about $1 per month. When death occurred, the members' beneficiaries would be provided with a sum of money and loan of funeral requisites.

The reduced role of clan associations continues today. Although there has been a revival of sorts, the associations have not been able to attract younger, English-educated members. Moreover, most young Singaporeans no longer harbor strong identity with their lineage or place of origin. Interest in preserving valuable Chinese traditions among the increasingly Westernized Chinese has led the government to reexamine the role of these associations. There has been a concerted effort to revitalize such associations to promote what is intrinsically "Chinese."

On their part, in 1986 the associations formed an umbrella body, the Singapore Federation of Chinese Clan Associations, to promote Chinese heritage through sports and cultural events.

At present, the majority of philanthropic organizations are the professionally managed social service agencies such as associations for the blind and the deaf. All of them are members of the Singapore Council of Social Service, which was formed in 1958 to coordinate the nongovernment welfare sector. In 1988, about 175 organizations were affiliated with the council. Some are also members of the Community Chest of Singapore, which was established in 1983 to mobilize funds from the public for charitable causes. In 1988, some $14 million was raised by the Community Chest and allocated to thirty-three organizations. All provide direct services to the public, particularly disadvantaged groups.

A minority of the charitable organizations fall into the category of foundations, whose funds are privately raised and allocated with total discretion. The well-known ones are the Shaw Foundation and the Lee Foundation, with a combined annual income of over $30 million. Similar to the Community Chest, these large foundations provide supplemental funding to direct service organizations. They also donate large sums for educational research and institutional support. Aside from the foundations, there are also wills and trusts, with dedicated purposes.

In recent years, foundations sponsored by the government or the ruling political party have also emerged. The PAP Community Foundation, set up in 1987, carries out both direct and indirect services. It is currently launching child-care services and offering tuition assistance and other welfare asistance programs. Many view the foundation as being politically motivated because it was established at a time when the party was losing ground. Nonetheless, it is an important instrument to rally resources for the needy. Another important foundation sponsored by the government is the Yayasan Mendaki, which promotes the education of Muslims and provides aid and assistance to help raise their educational level. This is in recognition of the fact that the Malays as a group have not done as well as others in education, although they are granted free education under the constitution.

Charity in an Organized, Affluent Society

The future of Singapore's philanthropic sector is likely to be shaped by several developments. The first is the growing momentum toward the formalization of resource flows, largely because of the emergence of the Community Chest of Singapore as the dominant fund-raising body. Given Singapore's small size, the aggressive selling of the Community Chest (CC) has created a centralization of private philanthropic funds, and a centripetal force leading to greater concentration. Since the inception of the CC, other philanthropies have reported significant declines in the returns of fund-raising activities. The social legitimacy for other philanthropies to raise funds from the public seems to have eroded, and the CC has somehow become the only legitimate fund raiser. The growth in the dominance of the CC in private philanthropy has indeed been phenomenal.

Since the Community Chest provides 100 percent financing to its member agencies, its financial control over the agencies is enormous. It is therefore able to exert pressure on the nature and the quality of services of the agencies to meet its expectations. The stated goal of the CC is to extend its membership to all social welfare agencies in Singapore. At present, it has included almost all of the major agencies. If the goal is indeed achieved, the CC's middleman role between the donors and the agencies will be of utmost importance. This would also force other resource providers, such as the existing foundations, to reconsider their roles. Theoretically, they could channel funds to the CC and let it be in charge of the eventual allocations. Otherwise, the agencies would have to explore other funding opportunities not covered by the Community Chest. The dominance of the CC clearly has adversely affected the establishment of new philanthropic foundations for welfare activities. Corporations, for example, have donated large sums to the Community Chest. Without it, these corporations might have created their own foundations to manage their donations.

One distinct advantage of the dominance of the Community Chest in fund raising and allocation is perhaps the emergence of a more rational basis for resource distribution and greater efficiency in service delivery. The CC is subject to public scrutiny, and a system of reviews has been established to ensure fair and equitable distribution. This is in stark contrast to the style of all private foundations, in which funds are allocated primarily on the basis of the chairman's whim and fancy. The professionalization of fund raising and allocation could mean a more efficient use of philanthropic resources. The Community Chest could also ensure that the services provided are cost-efficient through budgetary controls.

The second development that will probably shape the philanthropic sector concerns the changing social needs. As Singapore becomes more affluent, the nature of social problems changes. The traditional philanthropic activities such as feeding programs, free medical care, and even tuition grants are no longer in demand. The new types of social problems cannot be readily solved by direct assistance; many of them require professional expertise. One cannot, for example, solve the problem of youth alienation by, say, a cash donation. There is, therefore, a natural limit to the usefulness of traditional philanthropic activities. Channeling resources into professional service agencies may become an acceptable form of philanthropy.

The affluence of Singapore has enabled the Community Chest to raise adequate funds for its agencies. In fact, the CC has been able to add the unallocated surplus to its reserves in all the years of its existence. It is eager to dispense the unallocated funds as the accumulated savings could damage its public image as an efficient fund manager. As a result, the Community Chest has to induce the existing agencies to expand their current services and to move into new services.

In the long run, there will continue to be private philanthropies in the forms of scholarship funds, wills, or trusts. Their impact, nonetheless, will be very minor. The larger foundations will continue to exist, but they will have to contend with the Community Chest as firsthand fund provider. It is likely that they will move into areas not covered by the CC, such as the promotion of arts or other national causes. The managers of these foundations are not unhappy because they can remain sheltered from public scrutiny of their funding policies. The pressure on these foundations to be accountable to the public is much reduced as they fade into the background.

It is clear that the Community Chest and its member agencies are likely to be the key players in the private philanthropic sector of the future. This will become even more the case because the government hopes to transfer direct services under its charge to the private sector. When this eventually occurs, the role of private philanthropy will be enlarged, with a greater demand on private charitable funds. Whether the public is prepared to shoulder the additional financial burden as the government enjoys budgetary surpluses is not clear. The continued reliance on private transfer in resource allocation has its limits. The backlash on private donations of any tax increase could be severe. The public may perceive that they are being taxed twice, once for government expenses and surpluses and again for welfare activities. The government eventually may have to reconsider the proper balance between private and public resource transfer.

References

Baron, B. "Philanthropy and the Dynamics of Change in East and Southeast Asia." Background paper for the International Symposium on Organized Private Philanthropy in East and Southeast Asia, Bangkok, Aug. 7–9, 1989.

Cheng, L.-K. *Social Change and the Chinese in Singapore.* Singapore: Singapore University Press, 1985.

Lim, K.-T. "Clearing the Charity Muddle — A Statutory Proposal: The Charities Act, 1982." *Malayan Law Review,* 1984, *26,* 133–150.

The Mirror. Singapore: Ministry of Culture, 1977.

Ricquier, W.J.M. "Charity Begins . . . At Home?" *Malayan Law Review,* 1982, *24,* 323–326.

Ter, K. L. *Law of Singapore — Cases and Materials.* Singapore: Butterworth, 1985.

The Voluntary Sector
in the People's Republic
of China

Many people in the United States have asked whether there are voluntary organizations in China. Up to now, it seems that few researchers have attempted to answer that question.

Many people know that China has a 4,500-year history and has inherited a rich cultural tradition. It also has the largest population in the world, 4.5 times that of the United States. Moreover, China has gone through great social upheavals in the twentieth century, from feudalism and republicanism to socialism. Abrupt changes in social structures greatly influence the roles of the public, private, and voluntary sectors and thus affect every aspect of social and personal life. More importantly, China is still undergoing dynamic changes in many areas, particularly in its economic and social structures. Few people know, however, what impact such fundamental changes have on the voluntary sector. Little Chinese research has been found so far in this field. Although the boundary between the public and private sectors in China is very clear, the concept of the voluntary sector is not well understood and seldom discussed. Furthermore, it is impossible to base this discussion on the concept of tax exemption as it is used in the United States because there is no special provision for voluntary or charitable organizations in the Chinese tax laws.

An Overview of the History of Philanthropy and Voluntary Organizations

As early as the fifth century B.C., Confucius, the famous Chinese educator, defined philanthropy as loving all men. Chinese philanthropy is a product of Chinese civilization. The ancient old-age pension system was initiated in 2255 B.C. During the Han dynasty, 206 B.C. to 24 B.C., the Imperial Edict of Emperor's Cane stipulated that all elderly people over the age of seventy could receive a cane from the imperial court as a symbol of respect. They enjoyed special treatment, including pensions from the emperor (Wang, 1987). The earliest almshouses for sheltering the poor were built in 1271 (Chen, 1974 [1911]). Foundling hospitals were built under the order of Emperor Kang Hsi in 1711 to take care of castaway children throughout his empire. In earlier years, clans and later guilds mainly embodied the private initiative in dealing with poverty and other social problems (Tsu, 1912). The first private charity society was formed in Shanghai in 1805, under the name of the Hall of United Benevolence (Tsu, 1912).

At the beginning of the twentieth century, every big city had both a large philanthropic institute, serving as a coordinator, and a number of smaller-size voluntary organizations. Their goals could be classified into three categories: charity to the poor, mutual benefit through relief and protection by reciprocal efforts, and civic betterment by means of the promotion of public welfare through voluntary cooperation (Tsu, 1912).

Poor Laws, which defined the "worthy poor," existed in the Qing dynasty of 1644 and 1911. These laws recognized such individuals' right to relief and stipulated that sufficient relief be provided and any negligent magistrate be punished (Ta Tsing Leu Lee, 1966). Yet these laws were never effectively implemented.

Private Charities Before the Revolution

Throughout the nineteenth and first half of the twentieth centuries, the economy of China was barely able to meet the basic needs of the population. The size of the voluntary sector fluctuated with changing needs because of wars. By the end of World War II, 1,200 civic voluntary organizations and foundations were recorded. Private and semiprivate charitable organizations supported one-third of the educational institutions. Community and commissary hospitals outnumbered public hospitals by 25 percent because the government could not provide adequate services. Special acknowledgment should be made of the contributions by churches, which joined other charities in providing relief, medical care, and education (Tong, 1947). Charitable organizations provided, in comparison with the earlier stage, more institutionalized services.

Adaptation and Revival of the Voluntary Movement

With the introduction of socialism in China in the 1950s, the role of private voluntary organizations was found inappropriate because of the ideological conflict between public ownership and private charity. Government took from the private charitable organizations the responsibility of poverty and emergency relief, education, and social welfare services. Few private voluntary organizations survived; the Red Cross was an exception because it was historically recognized as a neutral organization. The majority gradually ceased operation during the collectivization and nationalization of all private forms of organizations in the 1950s. This left room for the creation of new forms of voluntary organizations, such as youth groups, residents' and villagers' committees, professional associations, and political organizations.

This was a period of transition and reposition of services in response to the growing public sector. The social revolution dramatically changed the established pattern of the voluntary sector. The Great Culture Revolution (1967–1976) again forced the charitable organizations to cease functioning, even though this was a time when people were free to form voluntary associations and most of them were maneuvred for political purposes.

A revival of charitable organizations took place during the late 1970s, with the policy of decentralization and the increasing utilization of private forms of business in the 1980s. The government began to encourage new approaches and partnerships with other sectors to deal with problems. Hence, voluntary organizations emerged in many fields where the basic needs had not been met and where the demand for public goods was increasing because of the government's inability to handle them alone. The concept of philanthropy, criticized earlier as a bourgeois idea, is gradually becoming officially accepted.

Dimensions of the Voluntary Sector Today

There exists, so far, no legal definition of voluntary organization in China. According to the latest data from the China Social Organization Research Society, there were more than 101,100 "social organizations," in 1989, which included political organizations, scientific and professional associations, social clubs, unions, foundations, and other mass associations. National organizations account for one percent, and more than 600 foundations have been reported (Whiting, 1990, p. 14). These organizations fit into the first three groups of Salamon's classification of nonprofit organizations in the United States (Salamon and Abramson, 1982, pp. 9–10): (1) fund-raising intermediaries, (2) member-serving organizations, (3) public-serving organizations, and (4) churches. In addition, there is a much larger subsector of more than 1,139,000 informal organizations. At the community level, 81,000 residents' committees, 950,000 villagers' committees, and 21,300 rural mutual help funds were reported in 1986. More than 37,360 social welfare homes and 24,710 welfare enterprises and service agencies offer their services (Xu,

1988). Approximately 3,100 private primary and high schools and 1,200 private universities and colleges were reported (Whiting, 1990). In 1987, 1,250,000 paid staff members were estimated to be working in all voluntary associations, accounting for 0.26 percent of the labor force (Xu, 1988; Worden, 1987). Since such little information is available, it is difficult to give a more complete picture of the sector.

In addition, there are few statistics on the funding patterns for the sector. The majority of voluntary associations receive government subsidies and grants. While relying on government funding, they are trying to diversify their funding sources to include the corporate sector and individuals. Between 1985 and 1990, over RMB 400 million Yuan ($108 million) was raised to support welfare work (Chen, 1990).

Many national organizations and foundations actively seek funds from foreign sources. For-profit services and enterprises that were established with funds from voluntary organizations, make contributions to their sponsors. This has become a popular method of pooling funds to develop more community services at the local level (Red Cross Society of China, 1987). Service fees can help maintain the nonprofit agencies in the fields of education and medical care, but many social service organizations offer free services.

The Relationship Between
Government and the Voluntary Sector

The attitude of the government and the Communist party toward voluntary organizations is to "bring, into full play, the autonomy of mass associations and grass-root mass organizations and allow them to function independently in accordance with their own objectives. . . . so that the masses will gradually take care of their own business according to the law" (Zhao, 1988). However, when a voluntary organization is formed, an application must be filed to and approved by a relevant governmental agency, one closely related to the organization's activities. Final approval for setting up a foundation is further controlled by the People's Bank of China, which is empowered to monitor all the financial transactions in the public, private, and voluntary sectors. No government agency had been empowered to register voluntary organizations until 1988, when the Department of Associations and Organizations was set up within the Ministry of Civil Affairs to register new foundations and social organizations.

The "Regulation of the Management of Foundations" was adopted by the government in 1988; it forbids a foundation's direct involvement in managing for-profit business and limits the stock purchase of a particular enterprise to 20 percent. A new law on social organizations is being drafted. For the benefit of better cooperation, many voluntary organizations invite state leaders, congressmen, or key public figures to sit on their boards or offer them honorary positions. The same practices were used earlier by some American nonprofits (Salamon and Abramson, 1987). Government officials, however, are not allowed to hold positions in the governing body of a foundation to preclude the abuse of power.

Confrontation and tension with the government are not common for most voluntary associations since relevant government agencies closely monitor these organizations. In certain areas, voluntary organizations accomplish certain functions that are beyond the government's capacity, such as the repatriation of criminals across the Taiwan Straits through the Red Cross.

Supplementation of the Public Sector

The voluntary sector in every country develops in response to its unique and special historical circumstances. "Public failure" and "market failure" theories could explain why the U.S. nonprofit sector developed alongside the public sector. In China, starvation and malnutrition are virtually nonexistent, and literacy of the young urban population is nearly 100 percent (Pegels, 1986). Homeless people are few. The strong public sector relegates the voluntary sector to a supplementary role. The government still tries to provide directly as much in the way of public goods as possible by expanding the public sector. This is in contrast to the U.S. government, which contracts out services whenever possible. In China, the government had, for a long time, deemed it a duty to handle all social problems. However, because of the low level of economic development, limited financial resources, and the gap between demand and supply of public goods, in terms of both quantity and quality, the government has accepted contracting policies, decollectivization, and reprivatization of certain services. Enterprises, voluntary organizations, and private individuals are all encouraged to pool funds to "help" the development of education, community services, and other public services. Some researchers advocate the establishment of social security committees in local communities, based on "mass organizations," to coordinate the development of mutual help services and turn them into professional services (Wei, 1988).

The Voluntary Sector

Some Characteristics of the Voluntary Sector

The concept of pluralism is not widely advocated in China even though there are many mass organizations. The distinction between services provided by the voluntary sector and the public sector is less evident here than it is in the United States. People vaguely know that charitable organizations are doing something good but have no clear idea what benefits they provide. This is because their lives are not strongly connected with these organizations through programs or choices of services. Instead, personal life in China is always closely connected with the workplace, which acts as the steward of public wealth. People expect all kinds of benefits, ranging from housing, free medical care, insurance, and subsidies for day-care centers to poverty relief. The workplace also intrudes in and controls people's private lives, as in granting one permission to marry, to divorce, or even to have a baby. The government's social welfare policies are actually implemented through the workplace. Therefore, people have not yet turned to the voluntary sector as an alternative.

Most major national charitable organizations and foundations were created within the past ten years. Private foundations with single endowments are few, and the majority of foundations set up to raise funds might be classified as "public foundations," with multiple sources of contributions from individuals, public agencies, corporations, and international organizations.

Associations and foundations usually have a board, while informal organizations seldom have one. Some organizations like the Red Cross have grass-roots units in schools, hospitals, and workplaces. Since China is one of the few six-day work-week countries, it is difficult and uncommon for one to volunteer outside working hours. This leads many grass-roots units to organize charitable activities during working hours. Students and retirees are another important source of volunteers. Interestingly, many public officials volunteer, or are invited to volunteer, and are placed in leadership positions.

Fields of Voluntary Activity and Organizations

In order to analyze the voluntary sector in China, I will examine four fields of endeavor: education, health, culture and art, and relief. Then I will briefly discuss the roles of religious organizations and advocacy groups in China.

Public education plays a predominant role in China, with private education accounting for only 0.2 percent of the total (Xu, 1988). A growing demand for adult higher education has boosted the growth of private colleges and night schools because only high school graduates are eligible to enter public colleges in the same year in which they graduate from high school. There are nonprofit colleges for elderly people, the first of which was set up by the Red Cross in 1983 in Shandong. The China Fund for the Handicapped and the China Social Welfare Lottery Committee provide funds to public schools and nonprofit institutions for the special education of the disabled because more than 50 percent of illiterates or semi-illiterates are people with handicaps. Farmers and overseas Chinese play an important role in setting up private educational institutions.

As is the case in education, 80 percent of all health institutions are public. About 29,320 health institutions, in the form of co-ops, receive subsidies from government health agencies and depend on service fees and contributions from communities and corporations. Red Cross health dispensaries cover 35 percent of the urban areas with the cooperation of residents' committees. Some of the 133,000 registered health practitioners also work in the Red Cross dispensaries. A five-year refresher training program for village doctors has been organized through Red Cross channels in Tibet.

In terms of culture and art, almost all urban museums, large libraries, and radio and television stations are run by government agencies. Increasing public interest, however, has been aroused to help preserve the Chinese cultural tradition. Voluntary organizations such as the China Art Festival Foundation and the Beijing Symphony Fund were set up to raise funds in support of arts development. Private giving was generous when it was solicited in 1984 for the reconstruction of the Great Wall, and RMB 2 million Yuan ($540,000) poured in during the first three months from over 20,000 donors ranging from kindergarten children to farmers to private business owners to overseas Chinese (Xu, 1985). A number of foundations have provided grants to charitable projects such as Soong Ching Ling Children's Science and Technology Center and the Children's World in Tianjin. It has been reported that the cultural and art institutes are trying to form joint ventures with corporations and organizations. In the rural areas, however, there are 170,000 private culture facilities, either for-profit or nonprofit, to fill the gap between demand and supply of cultural facilities.

As a welfare state, the government has been trying to cover public needs as much as possible. However, only 9.09 percent of the population is covered by the social security insurance provided by the government. Only employees working in state-owned or large collectively owned enterprises, government agencies, and some nongovernmental organizations are covered (China Statistics Bureau, 1988). In comparison, only three million people or 0.3 percent of the rural population, mainly the childless elderly, people with handicaps, and orphans, who are unable to work and have no income, were covered in 1985 with funds pooled from township government, individuals, and enterprises. Few pension funds exist for farmers, and only 600,000 farmers had pensions in 1984.

Voluntary organizations are more prevalent in the social welfare field in terms of activities, voluntary spirit, and number of organizations. Because of financial restraints, government funds in 1987 covered only 66.2 percent of the needs in this field, and the rest were contributed by individuals, enterprises, and voluntary organizations. There exist over 146,000 social security funds (Chen, 1990). Of the 37,368 social welfare institutes for the aged, children, and the mentally handicapped, 95.2 percent were collectively owned and sponsored by township and state-owned enterprises, neighborhood committees, and other voluntary organizations. The number of private nursing homes is also increasing. Voluntary organizations such as the Red Cross are working with residents' committees to set up a social welfare network in local communities that includes health clinics; clubs; free regular delivery services to aged widows and widowers, the sick and those with handicaps; rehabilitation centers for those who are disabled; day-care centers for children with mental handicaps; health counseling; and so on. Volunteers from hospitals, shops, grocery stores, police stations, and schools have been organized into this grand goodwill network. Volunteer Associations, a mutual help group, appears in the cities, and in Tianjin, the third largest city, there are 120,000 members, who do voluntary work twice a month at 7,940 facilities (Tianjin Xinhua News Agency, 1990).

The Red Cross is very active in relief operations; it provides medical care, raises funds, and channels contributions from other sources to victims. Private contributions to relief operations are generous in comparison to responses to other types of solicitations. The government, however, still undertakes the major responsibility for relief. As an example, the relief operation in Tangshan, following the worst earthquake in the world, mobilized 100,000 soldiers, 283 medical teams, and 130,000 employees. Obviously, handling this disaster was beyond the capacity of private relief organizations. As to poverty relief, the government civil affairs agencies shoulder this heavy burden.

Religious organizations play a very limited role in terms of both contributions received and services provided. Only 2.73 percent of the population are religious followers. Still, more than 2,000 religious organizations cooperate with 40,000 temples, mosques, and churches (Li, 1990), and there are thirty-five religious schools in China. Religious institutions such as the YWCA also run training courses for nursery school teachers and courses in children's art. Such institutions have also set up day-care centers and nurseries because of the shortage of public nurseries.

Advocacy groups, which are not yet well developed in China, are limited to those concerned with women's rights, problems of people with handicaps, and humanitarianism. Voluntary organizations and foundations are also operating in the areas of environmental protection, nature preservation, and research.

There are many needs still to be met in China, such as shelters for temporarily homeless people in the cities. Moreover, no voluntary organizations have considered offering professional services to dropouts, abused children, or families in crisis.

Private Philanthropy in China

Private voluntary organizations prevail in many countries. In China, private foundations operate primarily in the field of education. In the 1980s, RMB 700 million Yuan ($196 million) was contributed to the State Teachers Award Foundation (Cai, 1990). The Soong Ching Ling Foundation collected RMB 1,410,000 Yuan ($307,800) and in-kind contributions worth RMB 280,000 Yuan ($75,600) in 1989 and 1990 for children's education projects (Li, 1991). Some privately sponsored ambulance centers also exist in the rural areas since the number of ambulances is far from adequate (Zhang, 1988). Yet this is not a typical trend. Given the current economic and political environment in China, private philanthropy is not expected to play a major role in the near future. Perhaps an analysis of the donations to the China Fund for the Handicapped, one of the largest foundations in China, will give a better picture of the situation.

In 1988, only thirty-one residents gave donations of more than RMB 100 Yuan, an equivalent of $26.95, which is almost two-thirds of the average monthly salary. Individual contributions accounted for less than 0.57 percent of the total contributions of RMB 9,076,630.88 ($2,450,690), which equaled only 0.40 percent of that received by Johns Hopkins University, a private U.S. university, in 1989. Only eight organizations and companies gave more than RMB 10,000 Yuan ($2,695.41), and another twenty-eight enterprises, government agencies, schools, research institutes, shops, voluntary organizations, and armed forces made some donations, which constituted 86.70 percent of the total giving. ("Final Operating Statement of China Fund for the Handicapped," 1989). Individual donations in the United States, on the other hand, amounted to 83.1 percent of total philanthropic giving in 1988 (American Association of Fund-Raising Counsel, 1989). The factors outlined below may account for this difference. These factors are (1) the lack of a tradition of giving, (2) a low standard of living, and (3) the absence of charitable incentives in government policies.

Researchers in many countries agree that one of the roots of philanthropic giving is a tradition of participating in and regularly donating to religious institutions. The relatively short history of Christianity and its limited religious influence in China have not cultivated philanthropic giving on a regular basis. Similarly, the intergenerational continuity of philanthropy through endowments and foundations, which fosters a spirit of philanthropic giving among succeeding generations in the United States, has not yet been developed in China because of the low accumulation of wealth and the absence of inheritance taxes. This does not mean that people do not respond to solicitations for good causes or for special occasions. National fund-raising campaigns, though few, have been very successful in China. In 1985, the Red Cross raised $3,504,000 for the relief of famine victims in Africa and $3,234,500 in the worldwide "Sport Aid 88" event for the benefit of children in China. Donations from students in primary and middle schools similarly embody the philanthropic spirit. However, fund raising is still undeveloped and regular giving is uncommon in China, whereas in the United States, fund raising has become a profession and a prosperous industry. It will be a hard struggle to instill a spirit of regular giving in China because the government continues to emphasize the people's dependence on the government.

The average annual income in China in 1987 was RMB 496 Yuan ($133.69), and about 11 percent of the total population lived below the poverty line. In the United States, per capita income was $12,772 even though 13.5 percent of the population lived below the poverty line. There are relatively few wealthy people in China as compared to the United States, where there were reportedly 350,000 to 500,000 millionaires in 1981. Only 2 percent of the total population of China paid income adjustment taxes in 1987. The low income and little accumulated wealth leave little room for the majority of people to make large charitable gifts.

All incorporated foundations and associations in China benefit from income tax exemption. Some social welfare enterprises that employ more than a certain percentage of people with handicaps also benefit from tax exemptions because most such enterprises are a form of mutual help and rehabilitation for people with handicaps. Tax deductions for charitable giving, considered to be an important incentive by many researchers and labeled as one of the two cornerstones of U.S. tax policy toward charitable activities (Clotfelter, 1985), are not a part of the tax system in China. Some corporations, however, are allowed to deduct, as production costs, contributions to "public purposes" (Whiting, 1990). It is not clear whether the charitable gift deduction will make its way into the Chinese tax laws in the near future. Since the importance of charitable giving has never been discussed before, charitable giving is not very common in China and, as noted earlier, few people in China pay income tax. On the other hand, rapid growth in the private business sector and large contributions from state-owned corporations may prophesy a future of private philanthropy if tax incentives can be provided. At this point, however, the government seems reluctant to reduce tax revenue by allowing funds to flow to voluntary organizations.

The Future of the Voluntary Sector in China

Increasing Demands for Services

China's one child per couple policy will inevitably increase social problems because of the disproportionate growth of the elderly in the coming twenty-five to fifty years. The present family-oriented models for the care of the aged will be inappropriate, if not obsolete. It will be necessary to experiment with, increase, and diversify services to this segment of the population.

Presently, 99 percent of rural inhabitants, accounting for 80 percent of the total population, are not covered by a government social security system. With the introduction of the responsibility-contract system, farmers have retreated to a family-centered form of production. Those covered by the cooperative medical care program dropped from 90 percent in 1979 to only 40 to 50 percent in 1987. Some voluntary health insurance programs established by farmers face difficult managerial problems. The government has projected a long-term plan to set up a rural social security insurance network on a voluntary basis, which may possibly further the development of voluntary organizations (Xu, 1987).

New Challenges in the Voluntary Sector

Two fundamental factors will challenge the existence and development of the voluntary sector in China: self-reliance and customer orientation.

To reduce budget deficits, the government has been reviewing the possibility of reforming its current funding policies to mass organizations and may force them to rely entirely on their own resources. This may be an indication of inefficiency in these organizations, reflected in the competition for scarce public resources. However, the efficiency issue of resorting to voluntary organizations in China is a separate issue and will not be discussed in this chapter. Limited private donations and few foundation grants to support various services and programs may force voluntary organizations to reduce their services or to seek revenues by increasing their fees for services and setting up their own foundations such as the existing social welfare funds or social welfare development funds. Since most corporations do not make donations, even though they have the greatest potential for giving, corporate philanthropy should be advocated, pursued, and strongly encouraged. This will involve cultivating managers and employers and convincing the government to offer tax incentives for charitable giving. At this critical moment, the voluntary sector should also encourage research on other alternatives, such as sale taxes on cigarettes and alcohol, for the benefit of the voluntary sector and needy people to replace the loss of direct government grants.

Many charitable associations in China, being used to the mass-organizer role, are reluctant to become direct service providers. However, people place more value on services in a highly organized society than they do on recommendations about how to get services from other agencies or government. In recent years, customer orientation has received increasing attention among American nonprofit organizations. Various programs and services have gradually become institutionalized to satisfy customer needs by means of professional services. These services, rather than the original advocacy purpose of the organization, attract financial support, volunteer participation, and patronage. This concept of customer orientation has revolutionized the relationship between charitable organizations and their constituencies. Voluntary organizations in China should move in the same direction. Traditional goodwill services such as helping the homebound elderly, though still needed, fail to distinguish and promote the image of a charitable organization since many governmental and nongovernmental organizations, schools, and political organizations have done the same thing for years and years, and the problem of image confusion among the general public reduces the enthusiasm of direct financial support. Considering the accelerating differentiation and specialization in industrialized societies, a reorientation and professionalization of services might help each organization firmly establish a position on a value base in the service market and in the communities.

The same problem is also true of the (administration-driven) organizational structure. The bottleneck in the organizational structure of voluntary associations occurs at the grass-roots level, within schools and workplaces that are already overcommitted to different missions. Though it might be easy to organize volunteers through the same administrative structure, it would not be very effective in differentiating their activities from other organized activities being carried out by the same institutions. Rather than paid administrators performing various voluntary tasks within a single institution, it would be better to have separate voluntary organizations that can attract people from various institutions outside of particular workplaces. Commitment outside the workplace and across organizational boundaries can offer volunteers opportunities for self-actualization if properly organized. The best organizational structure should be framed according to the need for services. Programs and services developed and run by individuals may attract financial support and volunteers and give volunteers greater satisfaction. Otherwise, alienation will remain between the organization and its constituencies because the latter will find it difficult to identify themselves with these semigovernmental organizations.

Future Development

The prevailing discussion among many organizations is centered on cooperation between voluntary organizations and the government. It is doubtful whether the voluntary sector will play a prominent role in the near future since many people are not even aware of the potential importance of self-reliance through such organizations. Politically, a strong private sector may be viewed as a threat to government power. The government's sharing of responsibility is limited mostly to the economical field. There is no clear indication from tax or other policies to infer that the government is going to further enhance the use of voluntary organizations to solve social problems.

If the voluntary sector is satisfied with a complementary role, a weak voluntary sector will be inevitable; if there is no distinction between services and functions, the public sector could replace or completely integrate the voluntary sector. If the service-delivery system is strengthened, commercialization of the voluntary sector will be necessary; and if more attention is paid to monitoring the government's performance and experimenting with pioneering ideas to introduce social changes, the sector can grow to a point where it is independent of government. Currently there is no evidence that a trend toward independence will take place, since such a movement would lead to a confrontation with government. But these issues should be addressed by every voluntary organization to determine the future of the voluntary sector in China.

Obviously, then, the future of the voluntary sector in China is still unclear. The degree to which changes can be made is hard to predict. On the one hand, the demand for services will increase, especially in the rural areas; on the other hand, the tightening of funds from government agencies as well as limited resources available from private philanthropy will undercut the operations of voluntary organizations. Reorientation and professionalization of services; expansion of direct participation by private nonofficial individuals in decision making; and stronger advocacy by voluntary organizations, researchers, and law makers will all be needed to bring this now invisible sector into the center of people's lives in China.

References

American Association of Fund-Raising Counsel. *Giving USA: The Annual Report on Philanthropy for the Year 1988.* New York: American Association of Fund-Raising Counsel, 1989.

Cai. "The Prevailing Contributions to Assist Education Amounted to RMB 700 Million Yuan in the Last 10 Years." *People's Daily,* Overseas Edition, Nov. 23, 1990, p. 4.

Chen, H. C. *Economic Principles of Confucius and His School.* Vol. 2. New York: Gorden Press, 1974. (Originally published 1911.)

Chen, Y. "Social Welfare Cause Made Remarkable Progress." *People's Daily,* Overseas Edition, Dec. 15, 1990.

China Handbook Editorial Board. *China Handbook 1951.* Taipei: China Publishing Company, 1952.

China Statistics Bureau. *China Statistics Yearbook 1987.* Beijing: China Statistics Bureau, 1988.

Clotfelter, C. T. *Federal Tax Policy and Charitable Giving.* Chicago: University of Chicago Press, 1985.

"Final Operating Statement of China Fund for the Handicapped." *Social Security News,* Mar. 17, 1989, p. 4.

Li, D. "Soong Ching Ling Foundation Sponsored Child Welfare Projects with Contributions." *People's Daily,* Overseas Edition, Jan. 7, 1991.

Li, X. "Patriotic Religious Organizations Grew to over 2,000." *People's Daily,* Overseas Edition, Dec. 24, 1990.

Ministry of Civil Affairs of the People's Republic of China. *Civil Affairs Work in China.* Beijing: Ministry of Civil Affairs of the People's Republic of China, 1987.

Pegels, C. C. (ed.). *Management and Industry in China.* New York: Praeger, 1986.

Red Cross Society of China. *Selected Thesis on Social Welfare Work.* 1987.

Salamon, L. A., and Abramson, A. J. *The Federal Budget and the Nonprofit Sector.* Washington, D.C.: Urban Institute Press, 1982.

Salamon, L. A., and Abramson, A. J. "Of Market Failure, Voluntary Failure, and Third-Party Government: Toward a Theory of Government-Nonprofit Relations in the Modern Welfare States." *Journal of Voluntary Action Research,* 1987, *16,* 31–32.

Ta Tsing Leu Lee. *Being the Fundamental Law and a Selection from Supplementary Statutes of the Penal Code of China.* Translated by G. T. Staunton. Taipei: Ch'eng-wen Publishing, 1966.

Tianjin Xinhua News Agency. "Voluntary Association's Services Warm the Heart of People." *People's Daily,* Overseas Edition, Nov. 30, 1990, p. 4.

Tong, H. *China Handbook 1937–1945.* New York: Macmillan, 1947.

Tsu, Y. Y. *The Spirit of Chinese Philanthropy: A Study in Mutual Aid.* New York: Columbia University Press, 1912.

Wang, K. J. "A Review of the Ways for Caring for the Elderly and Handicapped." *Social Security News,* Dec. 5, 1987, p. 4.

Wei, D. F. "Developing Community Services Through Welfare Enterprises." *Social Security News,* Feb. 2, 1988, p. 4.

Whiting, S. "The Non-Governmental Sector in China: A Preliminary Report." *Voluntas,* 1990, pp. 14, 16, 45.

Worden, R. A. *China, A Country Study.* Washington, D.C.: U.S. Government Printing Office, July 1987.

Xu, L. (ed.). *China Yearbook, 1984.* Beijing: Xinhua Publishing Company, 1985.

Xu, L. *China Yearbook, 1986.* Beijing: Xinhua Publishing Company, 1987, pp. 639–645.

Xu, L. *China Yearbook, 1987.* Beijing: Xinhua Publishing Company, 1988.

Zhang, J. P. "A Dead End Found an Outlet." *Red Cross News,* Apr. 3, 1988, p. 3.

Zhao, Z. Y. "Advance Along the Path to Distinctive Socialist Features." In *Document of the Thirteenth National Congress of the Communist Party of China.* Beijing: Foreign Languages Press, 1988.

Virginia A. Hodgkinson　　　　　　　　*Chapter 28*
Russy D. Sumariwalla

The Nonprofit Sector and
the New Global Community:
Issues and Challenges

Our global tour has ended; it has been a long journey. In the
preceding pages, we traveled across every continent except Ant-
arctica, visiting a large array of nation-states and learning how
human societies organize themselves to give expression to individual and group hopes, aspirations, and creativity and to produce public goods and social benefits for their members. In some
instances, the view was only an impressionistic one; in others,
the reader gained deeper knowledge. The landscape was not
always picturesque or heartwarming, but it provided nourish-
ment for reflection on the future shape of the nonprofit sector
among nations of the world. The purpose of this concluding
chapter is to focus on significant issues and emerging trends

detected by this volume; to discuss some common challenges that face leaders and practitioners, both volunteers and paid professionals, in the decade ahead; and to propose the kind of organization that could accelerate cooperation and collaboration among nonprofit sectors, philanthropy, and voluntary service around the world.

Common Purposes, Diverse Structures

The Nonprofit Sector in the Global Community provides us with some common ground for understanding how this nonprofit or voluntary sector functions across nations and in many different cultures. While the size, scope, and importance of nonprofit organizations vary among nations and in different cultures, these organizations have several similar functions. They provide vehicles for voluntary association. They are advocates for the poor, the neglected, and the disenfranchised. They are also advocates for social change. They provide social services, particularly to underserved groups, and in some nations serve as the major vehicle for the provision of social welfare. They provide innovation, are flexible, and can deliver more personalized services to specific groups or in local situations. Between the bureaucracy of the state and, in many cases, big business, these groups provide organization and services on a human scale. With their value orientation, they serve in many nations as moral associations, as de Tocqueville called them. In nations that are trying to reestablish voluntary sectors that were systematically stamped out as in Hungary and Bulgaria, the populations have developed values and practices that keep them isolated from the community at large for their own protection. In these societies, reestablishing public trust and public participation presents a formidable challenge. In these societies there need to be created institutions where citizens can learn to work, play, and worship together and where they can learn to become part of a civil society, as Nina Belyaeva states in Chapter Twenty.

Thus the first fundamental characteristic of the nonprofit sector is that it is based upon voluntary association and is ultimately very personal in character. It starts with neighbors helping neighbors, with individuals engaged in mutual aid or self-help. It starts with free association. It may be the civic association in Japan or the group of villagers in Africa who come together to work on common issues or challenges and in the process forge new alliances and new goals. The common issue that brings them together may be to help the elderly or those with handicaps, to increase the rights of aliens, to extend education or health care or social insurance, or to engage in community economic development. Where people are allowed to engage in such association, public power and public choice are increased, and so too are public responsibility and public trust.

Voluntary participation and the size of the nonprofit sector in a nation are somewhat indicative of the ability of citizens to associate freely, the size and power of central government, and the degree of heterogeneity in the society. In those nations that are emerging from communism or one-sector economies, it is not surprising that the voluntary sector had to be suppressed or totally eradicated. Thus the nations of Eastern Europe and the Soviet Union are challenged by how to structure and expand their voluntary sectors, how to expand public participation and responsibility, and how to build public trust. In the developing nations of the Third World, an uneasy tension arises between people engaging in their own development and central government authorities, for voluntary association empowers people, and empowering people threatens authoritarian governments.

In the more advanced developed democracies, voluntary association is built into the system of government in homogeneous societies, such as Sweden, where Boli (Chapter Thirteen) suggests that such association may have been co-opted by government. In the Netherlands, voluntary associations provide a balance of power among groups that hold different political ideologies and religious beliefs. In a group-oriented culture, voluntary associations in Japan have provided public space for women, leading to more empowerment.

While younger than many of these cultures, the United States, through its constitution, was built on the premise of freedom of association, starting with freedom of religion. While religion receives government support in many nations, because it is voluntary in the United States, there is no governmental support for religion. As such, freedom of religion provides the cornerstone for voluntary association among the highly heterogeneous population of the United States.

The importance of voluntary association and individual responsibility varies among nations. In mixed economies such as those of the United States and to some extent Great Britain, nonprofit organizations are dependent on private resources as well as government support. For this reason, the issue of independence of nonprofit organizations is partially defined by the level of support government gives these organizations. In the more capitalistic economies of the United States and Singapore, private support in the form of donations, voluntary time, and fees for service are more significant than in the advanced social welfare democracies of Western Europe and Scandinavia, where government support for the provision of social services by nonprofit organizations is accepted practice. While privatization in the United States has meant a decline in government support for social services, privatization in Western Europe has meant the increased use of nonprofit organizations to deliver social services without an increased expectation of private philanthropy. Instead, voluntary associations in these countries focus on areas in which increased public attention is needed — assistance for the very poor in France, particularly for some immigrants; care for people with handicaps; the empowerment of women; the remediation of environmental problems; and attention to international issues. In most of these nations, health care, social insurance, education, unemployment assistance, and housing are provided as rights. In nations such as the United States and Singapore, many social welfare services are not guaranteed; therefore, a substantial proportion of social welfare provision is provided by government and by private nonprofit and for-profit organizations. While the provision of voluntary service and individual, corporate, and foundation philanthropy are important to mixed economies, they are regarded for the most part as charity in social welfare democracies. In these nations, freedom of association is not as closely connected to individual responsibility for the community welfare as it is in capitalist nations.

Philanthropy and voluntarism seem to take on more importance in nations where government resources are limited, such as in developing nations or Eastern European nations and the Soviet Union, which are trying to establish or reestablish citizen participation and individual responsibility as they move beyond authoritarian governments. In these nations there are formidable obstacles to rebuilding the concept of voluntary association and public trust among populations where voluntary association was previously not permitted and where individual survival meant not trusting one's neighbor or the government. Reversing a half-century of social behavior and ways of thinking, even with a high level of motivation, is no easy task. Both Hegyesi (Chapter Seventeen) and Nikolov (Chapter Nineteen) are concerned about building community responsibility while not neglecting the responsibilities of government in the transition from communism to democracy. They look more to the European models of social welfare and worry about moving toward total capitalism in which social welfare services would be more reliant on individual philanthropy. They hope that their nations will seek a balance among the roles and responsibilities of the nonprofit sector and government.

Voluntary Associations May
Change Government, but They Cannot Govern

The second fundamental characteristic of voluntary organizations is that they are not a substitute for government. People who freely associate and form organizations can expand government responsibility, can create the public agenda, and in extreme cases, can overturn governments, but they cannot govern. These associations can expand individual freedom as they are doing in Eastern Europe. They can place issues on the public agenda, such as support for people with handicaps or assistance for the poor, the elderly, women, children, or the mentally ill — as they have done in most nations — but they cannot replace government. While they can preserve or expand individual freedom, increase public attention to issues, serve as the conscience of the public, and provide a variety of services, nonprofit organizations cannot perform the functions of government under law. Brian O'Connell (1989, p. 486) reminds us that philanthropy and voluntary action provide citizens with an extra dimension "through which Americans address their needs, pursue their hopes, and help keep government responsive and effective, but it does not take the place of government in serving as the basic agent of civic interdependence." While free association and citizen participation and responsibility enhance and preserve freedoms, they cannot substitute for a government that institutionalizes and protects those freedoms under law. "It is important to remember the basic values of American society: freedom, worth, and dignity of the individual; equal opportunity; justice; and mutual responsibility. Fundamental vehicles for preserving and enhancing those basic values are representative government, starting with one person, one vote; the freedoms of religion, speech, and assembly; a free press; a system of justice beginning with due process and presumption of innocence; and universal public education. Philanthropy and voluntary action help to preserve and enhance those values, but they do not transcend them" (O'Connell, 1989, p. 488).

Many of the authors in this volume demonstrate that citizens through free association can change the public agenda, but their ability to provide these contributions and other services is limited by the law. Thus, in China, where there is almost absolute government control in all areas of life, including voluntary organizations, Zhang (Chapter Twenty-Seven) questions whether there can be a strong voluntary sector in a nation where most activities, including those of voluntary associations, are subject to government approval and involvement. In Eastern Europe and the Soviet Union, where until recently there was little individual freedom, voluntary associations provide an opportunity for individuals to learn together, to engage in public discussion, and to build civic leadership. As such, these associations can begin to build a sense of public trust, cooperation, collaboration, and responsibility where little existed before. Thus Nina Belyaeva (Chapter Twenty) describes the growing number of people's fronts or civic associations that are beginning to meet to discuss common needs. In the Third World, the World Bank is increasingly working with nongovernmental organizations and including them in their grants to governments (Williams, 1990). The World Bank acknowledges that the contributions made by NGOs are their abilities to work at the grass-roots level, to raise the awareness of governments and other organizations to the needs of the poor, to advocate environmental impact studies of major industrial projects, to lobby for social programs, and to focus on humanitarian issues.

The strength of voluntary organizations is that they monitor government programs, make governments more responsive, get new issues on the public agenda, and provide innovative services with adequate financing. In a recent study of the role and functions of the nonprofit sector among the nations in the European Economic Community, it was suggested that although it was difficult to find adequate facts about the size and functions of the sector or the percentage of each population that volunteered, in all of these countries, voluntary organizations are leading efforts "to combat disadvantage and poverty. They are not just what is *left* once the statutory and private sectors have been considered. They often represent the conscience of a country, provide a laboratory for innovation, a voice for protest, and a stimulus to change, working at the very core of the social state and providing services which may be central to the effective implementation of public policy" (Robbins, 1990, p. 101). The author of this study further commented that one way to consider the contributions of voluntary organizations is to consider a nation without them: "Observers would perhaps miss their commitment, flexibility, lack of bureaucratic systems, their empathy with disadvantaged people, their closeness to the community, and their capacity to campaign, innovate, and communicate" (Robbins, 1990, p. 103).

Significant Challenges, Significant Needs

Understanding both the strengths and limitations of voluntary or nonprofit organizations provides a starting point to enumerate some of the significant challenges and needs in voluntary organization and voluntary action around the globe and to propose some ways in which these needs can be met within and across nations.

The first major challenge is the worldwide growth in individual participation and voluntary service. Preserving and increasing the tradition of volunteering and public service is an issue on the public agendas in the United States, Canada, Australia, Great Britain, and the nations of Western Europe. In the Third World, voluntary participation is supported in some countries to help stimulate economic development and to press for more services to people in poverty.

The concept of volunteering is a cause of concern in some countries because individuals are worried that governments want people to volunteer as a substitute for paid staff to provide social services. However, voluntary service in most nations is not limited simply to providing assistance to people in need. In the United States and to some extent in Canada, Great Britain, Australia, and some countries in Europe such as Italy (Robbins, 1990), volunteering covers a whole range of activities — from serving people in need to helping in the schools to helping in recreational activities. In other words, championing the rights of underserved populations by providing human services to underserved citizens is only one of many legitimate ways of volunteering one's time.

In a recent national survey of giving and volunteering in the United States, such human service volunteering represented only a small portion of the activities of volunteers. Approximately 54 percent of American adults reported volunteering an average of four hours a week. They served in a wide variety of organizations from religious organizations to those in health, human services, recreation, community development, education, youth development, civil rights and social justice, the arts and culture, and so on. The jobs they performed ranged from serving as a Sunday school teacher or church choir member, as a driver for nonprofit organizations, as a fund raiser, a committee member, a campaign worker, a volunteer at a blood bank, an official at elections, a community coordinator, and so forth. In other words, individuals were volunteering across the broad span of societal activities. Only 9 percent of total volunteer work was in human services and 7 percent in health. A substantial proportion of the time spent in both these areas was in fund raising to support the relevant organizations (Hodgkinson and Weitzman, 1990b).

Furthermore, a recent study conducted in Denmark at the request of Danish labor union leaders who were concerned about what support of voluntary service would mean to jobs found, as is true in the United States, that volunteers do not replace paid professionals but rather supplement the work of professionals, serve as advocates or as innovators, or identify areas in which public support is lacking (Robbins, 1990). In terms of the broader based definition of volunteering that includes giving time for a variety of community or organizational activities, very little information across nations is available. In Great Britain, about 30 percent of the British reported volunteering about 1.1 hours a week (Charities Aid Foundation, 1990); in Canada, 27 percent of citizens fifteen years of age and older reported volunteering about 3.7 hours per week (Ross and Shillington, 1989). In Italy, one survey showed that 1.4 million Italians volunteered an average of 7 hours per week (Robbins, 1990).

There is a definite need for the regular collection of information about the level and range of volunteer activities across nations. Second, there is a major need for an international organization of nonprofits where they can share their experiences and work toward building citizen participation, developing nonprofit activity, and engaging in public education about democratic practices. It is not enough to assume that simply overturning authoritarian forms of government will produce informed citizens who will know what to do under a new system of government. The authors from Eastern Europe and the Soviet Union as well as those representing Third World countries realize that training and developing an educated citizenry takes trained individuals at all levels of society. To accomplish such a transformation, far more collaborative efforts and investment in people need to be made. The solution, however, is not to replicate models from other countries but rather to share expertise and skills that can be adapted in various cultural situations. While *The Nonprofit Sector in the Global Community* demonstrates that various cultures will create different structures for the use of nonprofit organizations, it also demonstrates the striking similarity among the common roles and functions of nonprofit organizations and voluntary association across nations, particularly in those nations where freedom of association is guaranteed under law. Thus, sharing information and expertise can inform and strengthen nonprofit leadership in many nations.

A second major challenge is that of freedom of association, which is the foundation for voluntary organizations and citizen participation. This freedom must be guaranteed under law and protected as a fundamental right. Voluntary service is encouraged and made legitimate by governmental protection. Without such legal guarantees, organizations will be hampered by a lack of legitimacy and an inability to institutionalize activities and services as a vital part of society. As several of the authors of this volume note, without laws establishing the right to form and operate nonprofit organizations, it is difficult to raise the necessary resources to sustain operations, whether those resources are raised from within the country or abroad. Over the next few years, these nations will be rewriting or developing new laws to allow for multisector economies. Efforts are already underway in Eastern Europe and the Soviet Union to rewrite constitutions, but the challenges and obstacles remain formidable (Irish, 1990). Far more opportunity for exchange among the leaders of voluntary organizations around the world is needed to build the kind of knowledge and understanding necessary to structure the nonprofit sector within various nations and cultures. The euphoria of achieving free choice in some nations is also leading to the realization that the legal changes in government that citizens may want to make are just beginning. Thus another major need among nonprofit organizations is to share legal information and research that provides information on the kinds of laws and regulations that impede or support nonprofit activity.

Not only are laws necessary to preserve and protect nonprofit organizations and voluntary associations but laws and/or regulations are also necessary to establish the criteria that distinguish between charitable organizations and other types of tax-exempt organizations, such as political parties or lobbying organizations. It is clear that in many countries with emerging private sectors, little distinction is made between charitable organizations that advocate change for the general public and those organizations that solely support particular political parties. Nor are distinctions made about the differences between foundations and other nonprofit organizations. There is little regulation relating to the raising and use of funds. In other words, the other side of the legal establishment of private nonprofit organizations is the requirement of accountability. Such a requirement varies from nation to nation, depending on the level of support provided to such organizations by government or private donations. In the Netherlands, nonprofit organizations participate at all levels in the planning of services and report to government on the use of funds. In other countries where individual giving is more substantial, such as the United States, Canada, and Great Britain, tax policies encourage individuals to give and regulations monitor both the gifts given and the appropriate use of those gifts by recipient organizations. Brody and Boris (Chapter Twenty-One) mention this issue as a major stumbling block, especially in the legal formation of foundations, although efforts are underway to study how foundation law can be written in the Soviet Union. Another major stumbling block is the lack of standard reporting requirements.

Another major obstacle that nations with emerging nonprofit sectors face is the lack of distinction made between private business and nonprofit organizations. One example, provided by Brody and Boris, is that grass-roots organizations in the Soviet republics are funding political causes rather than social causes. Little distinction is made between private business and private nonprofit organizations. Although people open businesses and use some of the money to support nonprofit activities, as described by Belyaeva, the distinction between the functions of both types of organizations are blurred. In the United States and many other nations, there are laws for such hybrids and regulations concerning unrelated business income for nonprofits. In many countries in Western Europe, clear distinctions are made between private business organizations and nonprofit organizations. Less clear distinctions are made about cooperatives, which can be treated as nonprofits or for-profit ventures or both. In the United States and many other nations, cooperatives are tax exempt and are treated as membership organizations, but donations to them are not tax deductible. While it is not surprising that the for-profit and nonprofit sectors are emerging together from former one-sector governmentally controlled economies, distinctions must be made between their roles and functions under law. Otherwise, a lack of legal distinction between for-profit and nonprofit organizations could lead to fraud and abuse. Furthermore, these nations may find it difficult to attract external aid from foundations or individuals in other nations who must comply with their own laws regulating the use of donated funds.

A third major challenge is the issue of independence of nonprofit organizations. In nations where governments provide almost total support for the activities of nonprofit organizations and regulate their services many authors worry about how voluntary or how independent these organizations truly are. Events are such in Great Britain that the move to transfer government services to voluntary organizations, with its attendant funding and regulation, could threaten the ability of nonprofit organizations to question government policy, to adhere to their organizational missions, or to be flexible and innovative. Such a move could also lead to the stifling of voluntarism for fear of loss of government support under certain types of political leadership (Wolch, 1990). Rather than defining nonprofit organizations on the basis of the nondistribution constraint and an independent charter or statute, Knapp and Kendall (1990) suggest that nonprofit organizations need to be categorized by their distinctive qualities. They propose that nonprofit organizations that are providing services that are wholly or partially controlled by government should be characterized as governmental and quasi-governmental nonprofit organizations. On the other hand, those nonprofit organizations that are independent and whose primary financing comes from fees, charges, and/or donations could be characterized as wholly voluntary organizations on the basis of their accessibility and affordability to clients. The varying levels of independence and uses of nonprofit organizations among nations clearly demonstrate that much work and study are needed to compare the structure and practice of voluntary organizations across nations and to determine whether differences in characteristics affect their levels of independence. In other words, are there differences between nonprofit organizations that governments use as instruments to provide services and those voluntary organizations that have diversified forms of income, including volunteer service, to carry out their programs?

Among the questions that must be addressed in examining these distinctions are the effects of various types of finance and support upon the ability of voluntary organizations to advocate certain issues, to generate public support, and to recruit and retain volunteers. *The Nonprofit Sector in the Global Community* illustrates the fact that support of the voluntary sector takes many forms, from almost total government support in Sweden to almost total private support in Singapore. On the one hand, Boli wonders whether the freedom of voluntary organization has been co-opted by government, and on the other hand, Cheung worries about the private philanthropic sector carrying almost the whole burden of social welfare activities in Singapore. In Japan, Yamamoto sees the need to build a tradition of corporate philanthropy and to encourage giving that is not solely orchestrated by government. Prijono and Fisher speak out for the need of governments to recognize the importance and value of empowering citizens at the local level to organize and to engage in development efforts rather than simply focusing on centrally organized development projects at the national level. They argue for more decentralization and recognition of diversity, while Jaffe is concerned that one small minority religious group can control the lion's share of government support and limit the majority of citizens' public policy options.

The tapestry of nonprofit forms, with their limitations as well as excessive power, points to a need to explore what models work in providing for diverse needs, more tailored service delivery, protection of individual freedom of association, and a balance between governmental programs and control, voluntary association and governmental regulation, and for-profit business. By studying various cultures and systems, we can all gain knowledge about what mix among the sectors works best, the role of governments and the voluntary sectors at various stages of national development, and the kind of laws and regulations that encourage or stifle voluntary initiative. While all of the authors in this volume would agree that there is a vital role for the nonprofit sector and voluntary initiative, they are not certain about what the balance should be between the relative roles and responsibilities of voluntary or nonprofit organizations and government. These issues about the roles of nonprofit organizations, philanthropy, and voluntary service as contrasted with those of business and government have been reflected in public debate in the United States and in many European nations for more than a decade.

Nonprofit Organizations and Voluntary Associations May Not Be Interchangeable

The Nonprofit Sector in the Global Community demonstrates that institutional forms and voluntary association are not necessarily drawn from the same principles. Voluntary association, the bedrock of a civil society, deals with the freedom of citizens to associate and form groups. Such association allows for citizen participation and citizen responsibility in societies where citizens are allowed to vote. While such association can lead to the formation of nonprofit organizations engaged in providing services, public education, the advocacy of particular issues, such association is more likely to lead to mutual benefit associations, unions, political parties, and other advocacy groups. In the United States and several other nations, these last groups may have a tax-exempt status but are not considered charitable organizations working in the public interest.

They are important, however, to the preservation of democratic government, and while nonprofit organizations may be voluntary in nature, they may also may be created or co-opted as the institutional form through which governments deliver social services. Voluntary associations and organizations were found in communist countries, but they were controlled by government, and citizens were not free to form their own associations. While it can and has been argued that nonprofit organizations and foundations emerge from voluntary association, the more fundamental freedom is the right of citizens to associate in informal or formal voluntary associations. Hegyesi and Nikolov describe how such associations had to be stamped out and made illegal in order for a Stalinist regime to maintain control, and Kapiszewski (Chapter Eighteen) states: "One of the key elements of democracy is freedom of association. Along with this right, one of the most visible manifestations of the recent changes has been the explosive reemergence of independent, voluntary, nonprofit organizations: foundations, associations, clubs, professional societies, trade unions, and political parties." One of the major reasons he gives for this explosion is that the failure of government stimulated an interest in the "reconstruction of long-oppressed civil society." However, even in Poland, which had the strongest institution for the support of freedom in the Eastern European countries—the Roman Catholic church—and a massive initial growth in voluntary associations, the habit of individual giving, oppressed by government for more than two generations, is difficult to reestablish. The authors from Eastern Europe and the Soviet Union discuss the need for associations and for foundation funds to help citizens understand their rights and responsibilities in a democracy, to understand the procedures of democracy, or simply to understand the structures and processes that are part of a civil society. While such needs are central to establishing democratic government, the number and functions of nonprofit organizations providing social welfare services are a determination by citizens about how they will conduct their public business. In Sweden and Japan these services are primarily carried out by government agencies, while in the Netherlands and Germany, they are primarily provided by nonprofit organizations. Most countries that have both democratic governments and nonprofit sectors fall somewhere in between. However, Hegyesi is concerned about an opposite danger in some Eastern European countries—that the state will totally withdraw from responsibilities for social welfare at a time when citizens of these countries are in difficult economic straits and expect nonprofit organizations, which are small and poorly funded, to provide the bulk of social services.

Building the capacity of citizens to participate in and develop the structures of a civil society may be quite different from deciding the relative roles and responsibilities of nonprofit organizations in the provision of social welfare. Furthermore, voluntary association is different from deciding which types of institutions — governmental, private, nonprofit or for-profit — either alone or in some combination, will carry out the public business. It is also different from deciding how these services will be paid for, whether totally by government through taxation or through a combination of individual giving, government support, and fees for service, although voluntary associations may influence such decisions.

Finally, voluntary participation and voluntary service are different. While voluntary participation and voluntary association are fundamental to democratic government, voluntary service, if limited only to the provision of social services, may not be an essential ingredient, depending upon how a nation organizes the delivery of social welfare.

Voluntary service to human services is but one of many ways to contribute in the United States; more important is the contribution of time, lay leadership, and participation in activities across a broad spectrum of organizations ranging from religious institutions to civic associations. Sweden is a nation of associations, Boli reminds us, and participation is greater there than in the United States, but associations serve different functions. In Sweden, citizens participate in a variety of associations and interest groups to keep government services responsive. In the United States, the nonprofit sector incorporates advocacy organizations, mutual benefit associations, and the philanthropic organizations that provide health and education. These same services represent a substantial proportion of social welfare services supported exclusively by government in Sweden. Yet both nations would argue that voluntary association is important for preserving democracy in a socialist, a capitalist, or a mixed economy.

In the United States, voluntary service is regarded as important not only to preserve democratic traditions but also as an antidote to rampant individualism. In Sweden, voluntary association is important to assure that government remains attuned to people's needs at the local level. Special-interest groups make government aware of new issues, such as the rights of people with handicaps or the rights of immigrants. While most of these associations in Sweden are currently supported by government, Boli indicates that there is a movement in Sweden to found more autonomous organizations. The establishment of a nonprofit sector under law can also unleash ethnic rivalries which can destroy national unions. After guaranteeing freedom of religion and voluntary association, the Soviet Union is experiencing the rapid expansion of ethnic groups and associations throughout its various republics. While such movements can lead to recognition of minority groups, it can also lead to ethnic rivalries and hatreds, as has happened in the Baltic States. Recent events in the Soviet Union reveal how difficult it is to restructure a one-sector economy into a three-sector economy.

Several of the authors mention the needs for management development and training and for learning about how to develop a civil society, including how to build citizen participation, responsibility, and public trust. In each of these nations with emerging nonprofit sectors, the need for leadership, training, organizational development, and effective legislation to ensure civil liberties seems an insuperable challenge when whole nations are overthrowing systems of government, changing entire economic systems, and trying to build new traditions. Whether in a developing nation where development is centrally controlled and there are efforts to empower citizens at the local level or in nations that are transforming themselves from one-sector to three-sector economies or in industrialized nations ranging from purely capitalist economies to social democracies, the balance, the burden, and sometimes the very extent of individual freedom are determined by the strength of the nonprofit sector. In many countries, if resources are not forthcoming, either internally or externally, or if a cadre of trained leaders is not developed to form and lead organizations from the local to the national levels, this movement toward voluntary association and citizen participation could be short-lived or at least not very effective. Cooperative relationships must be fostered among government, business, and the nonprofit sector. Having said that, this volume provides many models that work in various nations as well as examples of models that inhibit such collaborative efforts.

The Need for a New International Organization

We cannot think of any time in recent history when the social, the political, or perhaps even the economic environment has been more propitious for the nonprofit sector across nations to make substantial contributions to the affairs of humankind than it is today. As the 1980s witnessed, and as many of the authors in this volume testify, the unprecedented and unanticipated political and social turmoil in different regions of the world has resulted in dramatic and fundamental changes on the global scene. Political systems and ideologies of the past have been discredited, and a new breeze of freedom, democracy, and self-determination is sweeping the globe. The future will determine whether this movement can be encouraged to grow and provide a "new world order," in the words of President Bush. We acknowledge that regardless of geography, culture, and socioeconomic and political systems, human needs, aspirations, and social problems abound. And regardless of the political system, nations of the world community are beginning to appreciate that government alone cannot respond to all of these needs, aspirations, and problems. The three major sectors of a polity — government, business, and nonprofit — are invariably intertwined and interdependent. More recognition of the value of each of these sectors and more cooperation among them are necessary for building stable societies and a global community. The authors of this volume bear testimony to such a mixed system to meet human needs and aspirations and to increase the quality of life for citizens. It was in the absence of such sectors that the human spirit was crushed and, as Gábor Hegyesi states so eloquently, rose as "burning embers beneath the ashes." Thus, we believe that the decade of the 1990s can serve as a powerful training and preparatory period for nonprofit sector organizations around the world to begin the development of a global community for the twenty-first century.

In the concluding section of this chapter, we propose the creation of a new global network of nonprofit sectors to support and promote solidarity among nonprofit institutions internationally and to link them into a powerful new force for the benefit of humanity.

Toward a New Social Order

What we propose here is a *new social order,* a redistribution or a better balance in the distribution of social responsibility among three sectors of society: business, government, and nonprofit. This redistribution should result in a larger share of social responsibility for the nonprofit sector in many nations, but most of all, as demonstrated by the authors in this volume, this redistribution will enhance public responsibility and increase the use of human talent, empowerment, and self-help activities in a number of nations where these talents are underutilized or not used at all. Whether in the rural areas of Indonesia or Africa or in the newly emerging democracies in Eastern Europe or in the highly developed nations of Japan, the United States, or Western Europe, greater participation and citizen responsibility lead to more innovative solutions to local and national problems. Increasingly, nonprofit organizations are providing leadership of problems, such as environmental issues, that require international collaboration. For many years, such organizations have been among the first to help solve the problems of famine and international disaster, to promote economic development, and to support human rights and displaced peoples.

Why are nonprofit institutions so important to human well-being? What is so special about them? In commenting on the role of nonprofit institutions, Salamon (1987) observes that these agencies have traditionally acted as mechanisms for promoting important social values, such as individual and group freedom, diversity, a sense of community, civic activism, and charity. He then lists more practical advantages of these institutions with respect to the delivery of human services, as compared with large bureaucratic government agencies: (1) nonprofit organizations offer flexibility in their ability to be formed or disbanded, and the leadership of these organizations is closer to the action; (2) in most cases voluntary agencies are working on a problem before government recognizes or can act on the problem; (3) voluntary agencies are generally smaller in size and can tailor services to particular client groups; (4) voluntary organizations are more diverse in structure and in the kind of services they provide; and (5) since they have all of the attributes listed above, they are more likely to treat a fuller range of individual needs rather than providing fragmented services over several governmental agencies. Brian O'Connell would add that these organizations empower people and help them to engage in activities for their mutual benefit (O'Connell, 1989). They foster human commitment and enhance the human spirit. They increase resources by stimulating human generosity in the form of individual donations and foundation and corporate philanthropy.

Since the founding of the United Nations almost a half-century ago, multinational governmental institutions have struggled to address and reduce the scourges of war, disease, poverty, crime, injustice, and illiteracy. Progress has been slow and painful on the political front until recently. More salutary progress has been achieved on the economic and social development fronts. Multinational institutions like the World Bank and the International Monetary Fund and specialized agencies of the United Nations like WHO, UNICEF, and UNESCO have made significant contributions to improving economic and social conditions in many nations. What we propose is a global organization that represents the nonprofit sectors of all nations and parallels the United Nations as a global organization. While we do not envision that this organization would have such a grand scale, we do see its function as building cooperation and sharing expertise throughout the world.

How would such an organization do? How would it be organized and financed? Suggested answers to these questions follow.

This global organization or center for nonprofit organizations focusing on voluntary action, nonprofit organizations, and philanthropy would be governed by a lay board of trustees representative of its international membership and managed by a small globally diverse staff in about five regional centers located in different parts of the world. The three major functions of this center would be to arrange conferences to provide a meeting ground for leaders of nonprofit organizations around the world, to engage in training and technical assistance, and to promote and encourage research and the dissemination of information.

A world conference might be organized every two or three years, and regional conferences could be organized annually. Conferences would serve as the major vehicle for nonprofit leaders from around the world to exchange ideas, to learn innovative approaches to problem solving, and to develop solidarity and community through mutual understanding. Collaborative projects could also be discussed to solve problems that cross national boundaries.

Training opportunities for nonprofit sector managers, professionals, and volunteers have been cited as a critical need. Furthermore, there is a need to provide technical assistance and training in the development of grass-roots organizations and citizen education and participation. Finally, the authors in this volume describe the need for assistance in crafting legislation and regulations relating to nonprofit organizations, foundations, and voluntary association. Regional offices of this global center could develop and conduct core training programs directly. Where available, they could contract with local academic and other institutions to provide the needed training. Staff members of regional offices could also compile directories of organizations capable of providing different types of training and consulting services in various regions and where necessary provide consulting and technical assistance to national and regional nonprofit institutions in different countries.

As already noted, the third major function of this global center would be to promote and encourage research and the dissemination of information. One key task would be to collect systematically information on nonprofit sectors in various nations as well as on multinational efforts and to disseminate such information to interested parties as well as to the general public. The National Center for Charitable Statistics of INDEPENDENT SECTOR provides a good model. This center does not undertake major research projects but rather works with scholars to promote and encourage research and with government to improve on its collection and reporting of information on the nonprofit sector. It also serves as a national repository of information for scholars, nonprofit organizations, and government. A world center could also sponsor a series of publications designed for various types of readers, such as scholarly journals, newsletters, and magazines.

The center also could foster and encourage comparative nonprofit sector studies, such as the one launched under the direction of Lester Salamon, director of the Institute for Policy Studies at Johns Hopkins University, and the development of an international clearinghouse on nonprofit sector activities, such as the current project being directed by Kathleen D. McCarthy at the Center for the Study of Philanthropy at the City University of New York. It could also support the establishment of regional foundation centers similar to the new Foundation Center established in Brussels to serve the European Economic Community nations. The global center could further serve as a catalyst to develop an international taxonomy of nonprofit organizations with a common language and common definitions of types of nonprofits in order to stimulate comparative research similar to the taxonomy project developed by the National Center for Charitable Statistics. It would foster research on the possibility of creating cross-national accounting systems for the purposes of uniform reporting and cross-national financial analysis, and finally, it would provide encouragement for the development of common definitions and frameworks for nonprofit organizations across nations.

The authors estimate that such an organization would need an endowment of several million dollars. This endowment could be contributed by individuals, foundations, and governments from around the world, and it would support core operations as well as establish and preserve essential independence.

Additional revenues could be derived from institutional membership fees based on an "ability to pay" formula. Project support could be raised from a combination of sources, including individual donations; support from corporations, foundations, other nonprofit organizations, and governments; and from fees and charges for services provided.

One may characterize our proposal as overly ambitious. We believe it is an idea whose time has come. We also know that people have had similar visions over the years, if not as ambitious in scope. It is our conviction that the value of nonprofit sectors and voluntary action is growing in importance in many nations. It is our conviction that in many nations the sector can play a far larger role both within and across nations. Nonprofit organizations can contribute to peaceful relations among different nations and diverse cultures, help improve the human condition, and expand human and financial resources. Such efforts need to be nurtured and supported so that new opportunities can be created, new ideas explored, and new freedoms preserved.

References

Charities Aid Foundation. *Charity Trends* (19th ed.). Tonbridge, Kent, England: Charities Aid Foundation, 1990.

Hodgkinson, V. A., and Weitzman, M. S. *Dimensions of the Independent Sector* (3rd ed.). Washington, D.C.: INDEPENDENT SECTOR, 1990a.

Hodgkinson, V. A., and Weitzman, M. S. "Giving and Volunteering in the United States." A national survey conducted by the Gallup Organization. Washington, D.C.: INDEPENDENT SECTOR, 1990b.

Irish, L. "Proceedings, Suggestions, and Principles from the International Seminar on Foundations." *1990 Working Papers.* Washington, D.C.: INDEPENDENT SECTOR and United Way Institute, 1990.

Knapp, M., and Kendall, J. "Defining the British Voluntary Sector." In *Working Papers.* Washington, D.C.: INDEPENDENT SECTOR and United Way Strategic Institute, 1990, pp. 23–24.

O'Connell, B. "What Voluntary Organizations Can and Cannot Do for America." *Public Administration Review,* Sept./Oct. 1989, 486–491.

Robbins, D. "Voluntary Organizations in the European Community." *Voluntas,* 1990, *1* (2), 98–128.

Ross, D. P., and Shillington, E. R. *A Profile of the Canadian Volunteers: A Guide to the 1987 Survey of Volunteer Activity in Canada.* Ottawa, Ontario: National Voluntary Organizations, 1989.

Salamon, L. M. "Of Market Failure and Third-Party Government: Toward a Theory of Government-Nonprofit Relations." In S. A. Ostrander and others (eds.), *Shifting the Debate: Public/Private Sector Relations in the Modern Welfare State.* New Brunswick, N.J.: Transaction Press, 1987.

Williams, A. "A Growing Role for NGOs in Development." *Finance and Development,* Dec. 1990, 31–33.

Wolch, J. R. *The Shadow State: Government and Voluntary Sector in Transition.* New York: Foundation Center, 1990.

Name Index

Subject Index

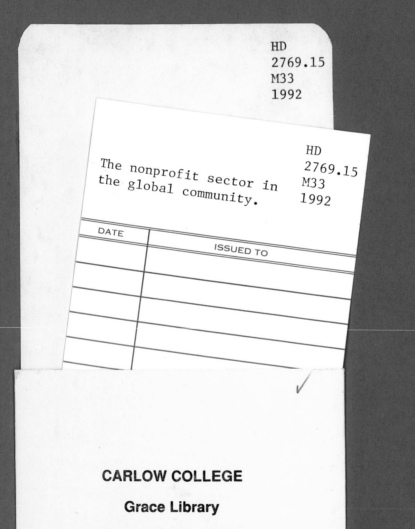